Day hikes around Napa
Valley : 88 great hikes
33305234275422
San   03/03/16

AROUND

Napa Valley

88 GREAT HIKES

Robert Stone

Day Hike Books, Inc.
RED LODGE, MONTANA

Published by Day Hike Books, Inc.
P.O. Box 865
Red Lodge, Montana 59068

Distributed by The Globe Pequot Press
246 Goose Lane
P.O. Box 480
Guilford, CT 06437-0480
800-243-0495 (direct order) · 800-820-2329 (fax order)
www.globe-pequot.com

Front cover photo by Bruce Fleming
Back cover photo by Robert Stone
Design by Paula Doherty

The author has made every attempt to provide accurate information in this book. However, trail routes and features may change—please use common sense and forethought, and be mindful of your own capabilities. Let this book guide you, but be aware that each hiker assumes responsibility for their own safety. The author and publisher do not assume any responsibility for loss, damage, or injury caused through the use of this book.

Copyright © 2008 by Day Hike Books, Inc.
1st Edition
Printed in the United States of America
ISBN: 978-1-57342-057-0
Library of Congress Control Number: 2007907349

Cover photo:
The Palisades formation along one of the premier hikes in Napa County, Hike 13.

Back cover photo:
Lake Berryessa, Hike 35

ALSO BY ROBERT STONE

Day Hikes On the California Central Coast

Day Hikes On the California Southern Coast

Day Hikes Around Sonoma County

Day Hikes Around Big Sur

Day Hikes Around Monterey and Carmel

Day Hikes In San Luis Obispo County, California

Day Hikes Around Santa Barbara

Day Hikes Around Ventura County

Day Hikes Around Los Angeles

Day Hikes Around Orange County

Day Hikes In Sedona, Arizona

Day Hikes In Yosemite National Park

Day Hikes In Sequoia & Kings Canyon Nat'l. Parks

Day Hikes In Yellowstone National Park

Day Hikes In Grand Teton National Park

Day Hikes In the Beartooth Mountains

Day Hikes Around Bozeman, Montana

Day Hikes Around Missoula, Montana

Day Hikes On Oahu

Day Hikes On Maui

Day Hikes On Kauai

Day Hikes In Hawaii

LINDA STONE

hiking partner, Kofax Stone

Acknowledgments

*I wish to thank the following people
for all their help, assistance, insights, and enthusiasm.
It made my time hiking these trails
a great experience.*

George and Andi Carl

Judy, Doug and Frankie Cook

Susan & Dave DeVries

Joan Finkle

Richard Flynn

Jim Fresquez

Nina Laramore · Laramore Communications

Lucy Lewand

Susan Meyer

Tyffani Peters · Wolf Communications

Ken Stanton for his valuable book
on Robert Louis Stevenson State Park

Kimberly Scargle · Napa Valley Conference & Visitor Bureau

Kurt Stevens

Kofax Stone

Linda Stone

Gary Venturi

6 - Day Hikes Around Napa Valley

Table of Contents

THE HIKES

Clear Lake Area
Lake County: North of Napa Valley

North Napa Valley:
Calistoga • St. Helena • Angwin

Central Napa Valley and the Eastern Mountains:
Rutherford • Yountville • Lake Berryessa

Sonoma Valley:
including Annadel State Park • Hood Mountain
Regional Park • Sugarloaf Ridge State Park • Jack London
State Historic Park • City of Sonoma

South of Napa Valley
Napa—Sonoma Marshes to Suisun Bay

Napa Valley and the Hikes

Napa Valley is recognized as one of the premier wine growing regions in the world and a prime tourist destination 50 miles from San Francisco. The broad valley spreads alongside the lush Napa River oasis between two mountain ranges. Agricultural lands blend smoothly with a myriad of regional parks and thousands of acres of public greenspace.

The Napa River flows 30 miles through the center of the valley and empties into San Pablo Bay. En route, the river creates a lush riparian corridor under a canopy of cottonwoods, bay laurels, oaks, and willows. The small, verdant valley is an agricultural paradise containing a wide variety of microclimates, more than 140 different soil types, and around 240 wineries. The south end of the lush, fertile valley is open to the cool breezes and summer fog off of San Pablo Bay. The north end of the valley is hot and dry with extinct volcanoes and naturally occurring mineral hot springs, geothermal vents, and steaming mud pots.

The first residents of Napa Valley were the Patwin and Wappo Indians. Around 1830, American settlers arrived to farm along the Napa River. California became a state in 1850 and Napa grew considerably because of the gold rush. By 1870, after the first wine grapes had been planted, nearly six-thousand Native Americans who freely roamed the valley were wiped out by smallpox, disease, and displacement.

Napa Valley has two main parallel thoroughfares—Highway 29 and Silverado Trail. Highway 29, from south to north, passes through the small towns of American City, Napa, Yountville, Oakville, Rutherford, St. Helena, and Calistoga, each with its own distinct personality. Silverado Trail skirts the east edge of the valley along the mountains. These principal highways are connected by numerous cross roads.

HIKES 1—9 lie in the vicinity of the Clear Lake area in Lake County, north of Calistoga and Napa Valley. The Mayacamas Range, along the west side of Napa Valley, extends northerly through the area. Hikes are found along Clear Lake, within the Mayacamas, and in the expansive Cache Creek Natural Area.

HIKES 10—26 are at the north end of Napa Valley around the towns of Calistoga, Saint Helena, and Angwin. Two large state parks are located here—Robert Louis Stevenson State Park and Bothe-Napa Valley State Park—as well as the highest peak in Sonoma County, Mount Saint Helena. These hikes travel along mountainous corridors through forests and across open slopes with spectacular views and interesting rock formations. Other highlights include several historic sites, a massive forest of petrified trees, and many biking trails.

HIKES 27—38 are dispersed along the hills and mountains that frame the eastern side of Napa Valley. Heading eastward out of the valley leads to this rugged and remote area of the county. Lake Berryessa (where Napa, Solano, and Yolo Counties converge) is a popular destination in the area. The lake stretches 26 miles long and is among the largest lakes in California. It was created in 1957 by damming Putah Creek at the southern end of the Monticello Valley. The public land around the lake is restricted from development, offering ample recreational activities and wildlife viewing.

HIKES 39—68 are located throughout Sonoma Valley between the cities of Santa Rosa and Sonoma. Several impressive state parks are found in the area, as well as wonderful hikes in the town of Sonoma itself. Public land includes Annadel, Hood Mountain, Sugarloaf Ridge, and Jack London parks. They are characterized by mountainous terrain, far-reaching vistas, and beautiful trails, which feel remote despite their proximity to urban areas.

HIKES 69—77 are located in the parklands of Napa. The city has preserved hundreds of acres of green space that remain largely undeveloped. Many miles of multi-use trails wind through the land. Landscape features include open grasslands, wooded hills, riparian canyons, and several excellent overlooks of Napa.

Napa Valley diverges at its south end into the massive marshes and tidal wetlands around San Pablo Bay, where several major watersheds drain into the bay. HIKES 78—88 offer excellent opportunities for bird and wildlife observation along the wetlands, sloughs, wildlife corridors, and rolling grasslands. Foothills and mountain ranges lie on the far-off horizons.

A quick glance at the hikes' summaries will allow you to choose a hike that is appropriate to your ability and desire. An overall map on the next page identifies the general locations of the hikes and major roads. Several other regional maps (underlined in the table of contents), as well as maps for each hike, provide the essential details. Relevant maps are listed under the hikes' statistics if you wish to explore more of the area.

A few basic necessities will make your hike more pleasurable. Wear supportive, comfortable hiking shoes and layered clothing. Take along hats, sunscreen, sunglasses, drinking water, snacks, and appropriate outerwear. Use good judgement about your capabilities—reference the hiking statistics for an approximation of difficulty, and allow extra time for exploration.

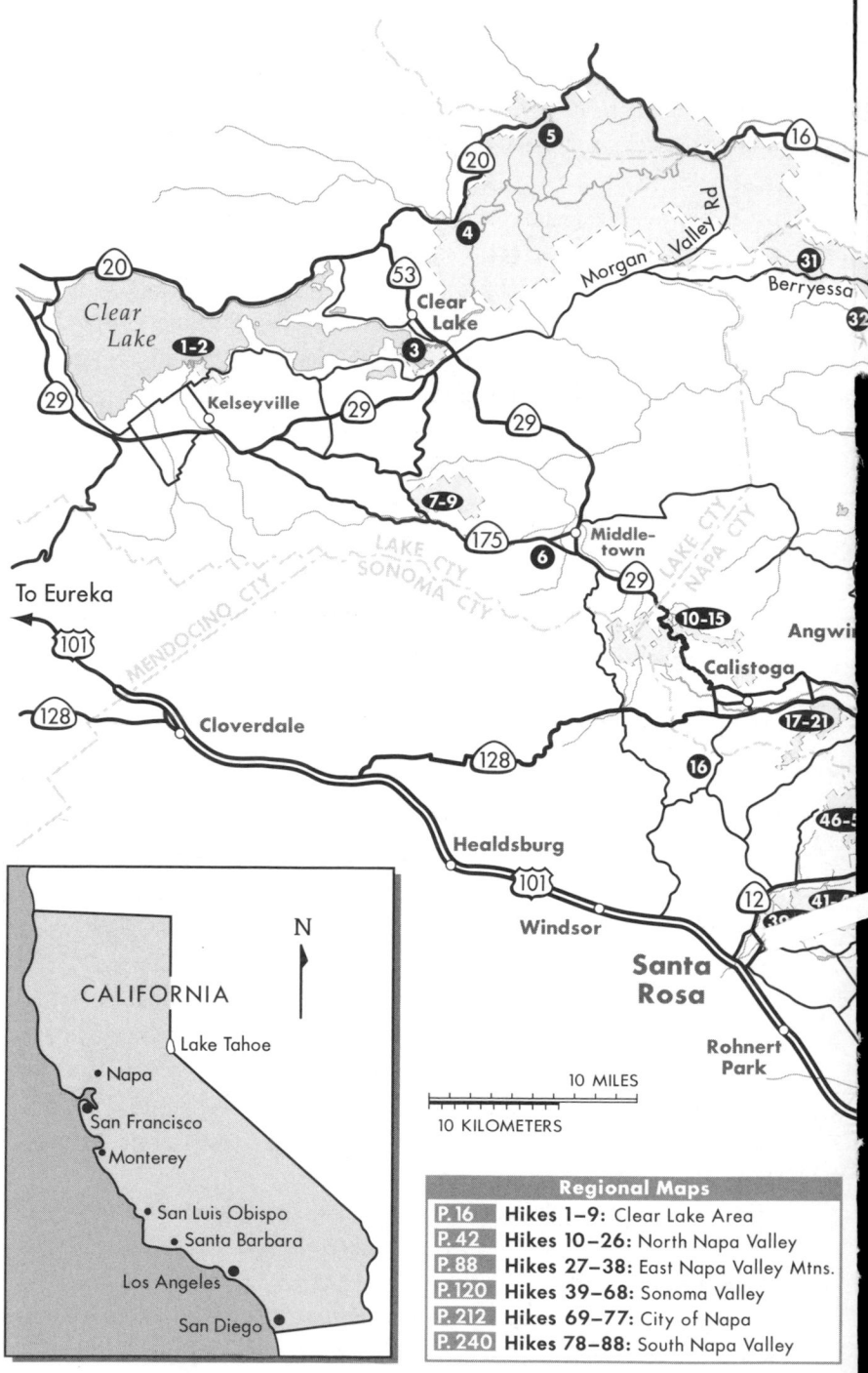

Regional Maps

P.16	**Hikes 1–9:**	Clear Lake Area
P.42	**Hikes 10–26:**	North Napa Valley
P.88	**Hikes 27–38:**	East Napa Valley Mtns.
P.120	**Hikes 39–68:**	Sonoma Valley
P.212	**Hikes 69–77:**	City of Napa
P.240	**Hikes 78–88:**	South Napa Valley

MAP of the HIKES

NAPA VALLEY and VICINITY

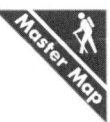

Master Map

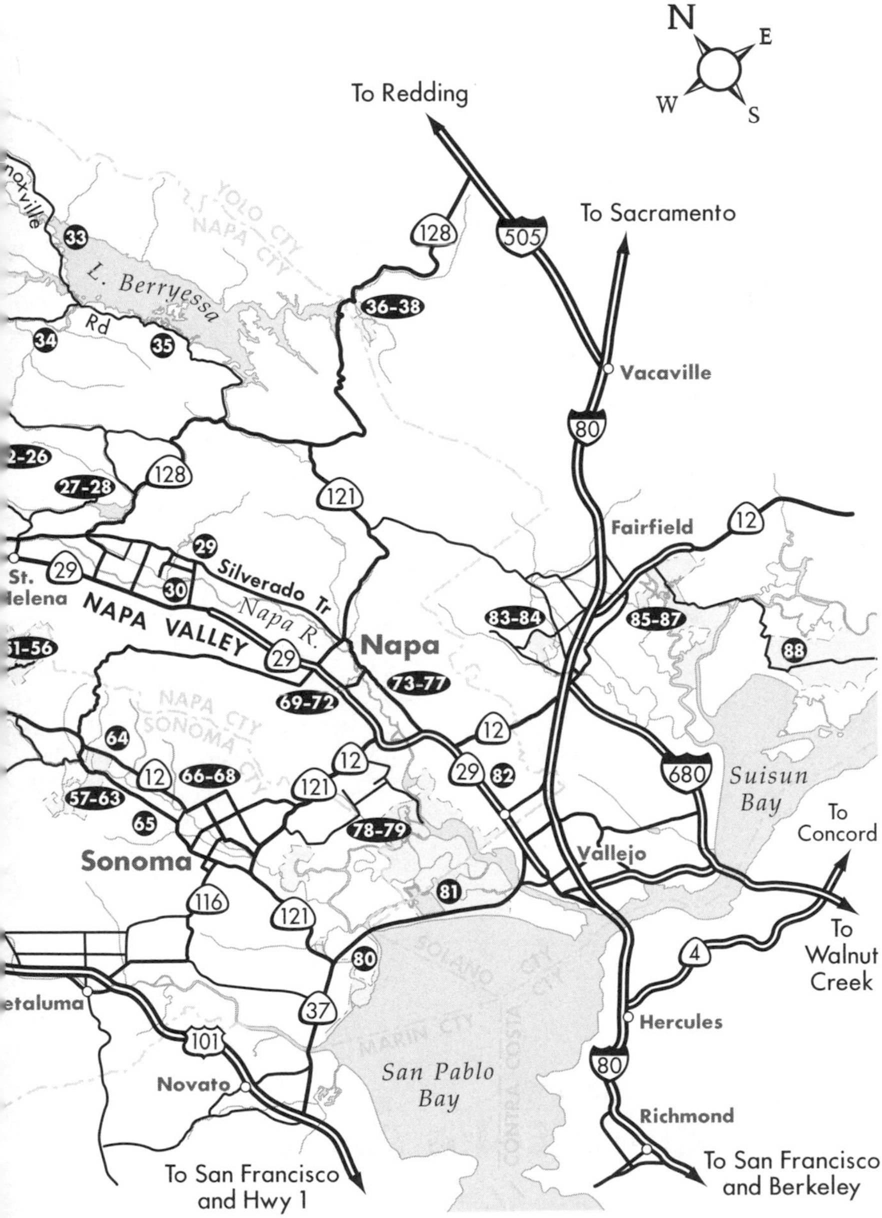

N
E
W
S
To Redding
To Sacramento
128
505
33
L. Berryessa
Rd
36-38
34
35
Vacaville
80
2-26
27-28
128
121
Fairfield
12
29
Silverado Tr
St. Helena
29
30
NAPA VALLEY
Napa R.
83-84
85-87
88
1-56
Napa
73-77
29
69-72
NAPA CTY
SONOMA CTY
64
12
12
66-68
121
29
82
680
Suisun Bay
57-63
65
78-79
To Concord
Sonoma
Vallejo
81
116
121
To Walnut Creek
SOLANO CTY
4
80
etaluma
37
Hercules
MARIN CTY
CONTRA COSTA CTY
101
San Pablo Bay
80
Novato
Richmond
To San Francisco and Hwy 1
To San Francisco and Berkeley

HIKES 1–9
Clear Lake Area
LAKE COUNTY

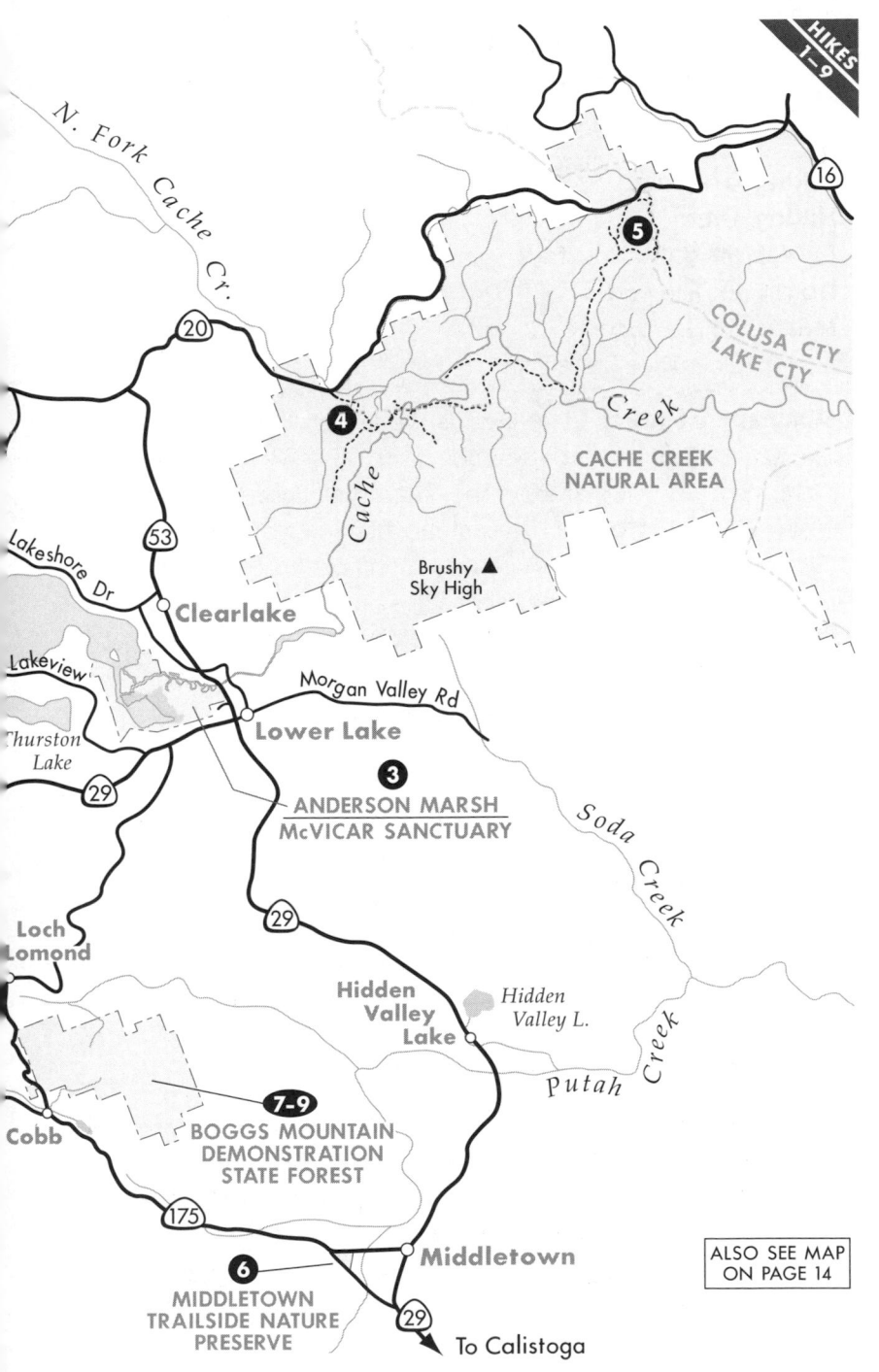

HIKES 1–9

16

N. Fork Cache Cr.

5

COLUSA CTY
LAKE CTY

20

Creek

4

CACHE CREEK
NATURAL AREA

Cache

Brushy ▲
Sky High

Lakeshore Dr

53

Clearlake

Lakeview

Morgan Valley Rd

Thurston Lake

Lower Lake

29

3
ANDERSON MARSH
McVICAR SANCTUARY

Soda Creek

Loch Lomond

29

Hidden
Valley
Lake

Hidden
Valley L.

Creek

7–9
BOGGS MOUNTAIN
DEMONSTRATION
STATE FOREST

Putah

Cobb

175

6

Middletown

MIDDLETOWN
TRAILSIDE NATURE
PRESERVE

29

To Calistoga

ALSO SEE MAP
ON PAGE 14

1. Dorn Nature Trail
CLEAR LAKE STATE PARK
5300 Soda Bay Road · Kelseyville

Hiking distance: 1.5-mile loop
Hiking time: 1 hour
Elevation gain: 200 feet
Dogs: not allowed
Maps: U.S.G.S. Lucerne
     Clear Lake State Park

Summary of hike: Clear Lake is the largest natural freshwater lake within California. It stretches over 68 square miles and has more than 100 miles of shoreline. The scenic lake sits in a broad basin surrounded by the coastal mountain ranges and is one of the oldest lakes in North America, dating back 2.5 million years.

Clear Lake State Park, established in the 1940s, is located on the southwestern shore of the lake along Soda Bay. The 565-acre park sits at the northern base of prominent Mount Konocti, a 4,300-foot volcanic cone. The park is a refuge and nesting place for waterfowl, attracting over 150 bird species. Within the park are two miles of shoreline with boat ramps, docking facilities, a sandy beach for swimming, picnic sites, two creeks, and four developed campgrounds. A visitor center houses interpretive displays about the lake, geology, history, and wildlife of the area.

The Dorn Nature Trail is a loop trail with access points from the visitor center, the Bayview Campgrounds, and the beach. This hike begins from the visitor center and winds through the hilly terrain above the lake through mixed woodlands. The footpath leads to overlooks of the lake and vistas of the surrounding mountains.

Driving directions: From Highway 29 and Lincoln Avenue in Calistoga, drive 30 miles north on Highway 29 (which is Lincoln Avenue through town) up and over the winding mountain road to the town of Lower Lake. Turn left, staying on Highway 29, and continue 14 miles to the town of Kelseyville. Weave 3 miles through town, following the signs to Clear Lake State Park on

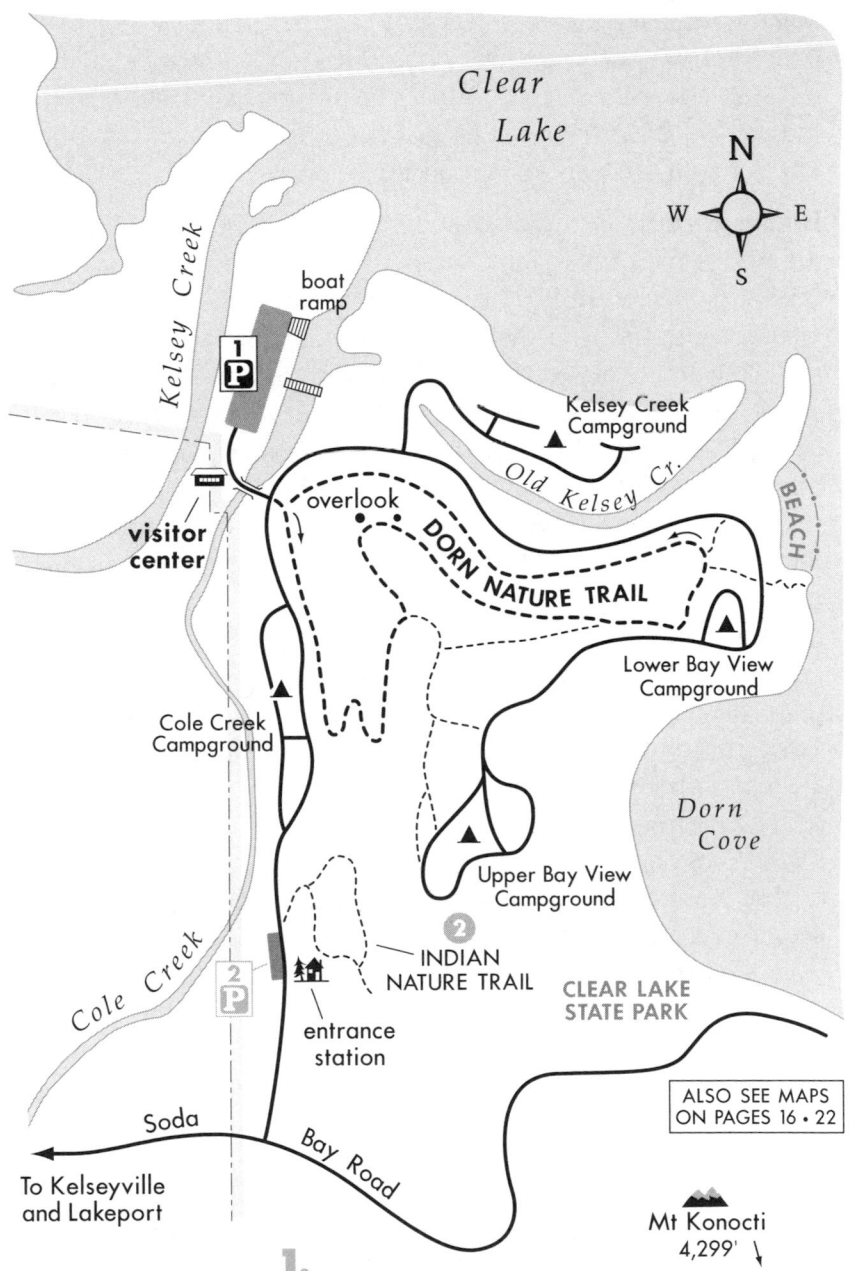

Clear Lake

N
W E
S

Kelsey Creek

boat ramp

1 P

Kelsey Creek Campground

Old Kelsey Cr.

BEACH

visitor center

overlook

DORN NATURE TRAIL

Cole Creek Campground

Lower Bay View Campground

Dorn Cove

Upper Bay View Campground

2 INDIAN NATURE TRAIL

CLEAR LAKE STATE PARK

Cole Creek

2 P

entrance station

ALSO SEE MAPS ON PAGES 16 • 22

Soda

Bay Road

To Kelseyville and Lakeport

Mt Konocti 4,299'

1.

Dorn Nature Trail
CLEAR LAKE STATE PARK

Main Street, State Street, and Gaddy Lane to Soda Bay Road. Turn right and drive one mile to the posted state park entrance on the left. Turn left and proceed 0.2 miles to the entrance station. From the station, drive 0.4 miles to the visitor center turnoff on the left. Turn left and park in the parking lot on the right.

Hiking directions: Walk back to the main park road, crossing the bridge over Cole Creek. Cross the park road to the posted Dorn Trail. Veer right 30 yards to a fork. Begin the loop on the right fork, and ascend the oak-covered hillside. Steadily climb the hill, with the aid of three switchbacks, to a minor ridge and Y-fork. The right fork leads to the Upper Bayview Campground. Bear left, staying on the Dorn Nature Trail. Continue up a knoll to the Lake Overlook, with a spectacular vista of Clear Lake, some vineyards, and the Mendocino Coast Range. Gradually descend through a forest of California buckeye, valley oaks, manzanita, toyon, chamise, and moss-covered rocks to a bench at another overlook of Clear Lake and Mount Konocti. Continue to a junction, in which the right fork returns to the Lake Overlook and Upper Bayview Campground. Stay left towards Lower Bayview Campground to a junction by the park road on the right. Bear left a couple hundred yards to another junction. The right fork leads to the beach and swimming area just north of Dorn Cove. Go to the left, staying on the Dorn Nature Trail. Traverse the forested hillside above Old Kelsey Creek. Pass gardens of mossy rocks and natural rock steps on the shady, fern-covered slope. Curve westward around the north end of the hillside, completing the loop. ▪

2. Indian Nature Trail
CLEAR LAKE STATE PARK
5300 Soda Bay Road · Kelseyville

Hiking distance: 0.5-mile loop
Hiking time: 30 minutes
Elevation gain: 100 feet
Dogs: not allowed
Maps: U.S.G.S. Lucerne
Clear Lake State Park

**map
page 22**

Summary of hike: Clear Lake stretches 19 miles along Big Valley and is eight miles wide. The enormous lake reached its present size from a massive landslide thousands of years ago, blocking the valley's natural westward drainage to the Russian River. As the lake rose, Cache Creek began draining the lake eastward into the Sacramento River. The productive lake has large populations of fish, and the broad basin is abundant with wildlife, which first attracted human habitation over 12,000 years ago.

The Indian Nature Trail, located near the park entrance, loops across a slope covered with trees and chaparral. The path passes an ancient village site; a mortar hole used to crush seeds and nuts; and an overlook of the broad, verdant valley. A park brochure describes the plant varieties within the park and how the Pomo Indians used the plants for food, shelter, clothing, boats, tools, weapons, musical instruments, baskets, medicine, and ceremonies. The self-guided loop has twenty numbered posts which correspond with brochure descriptions. The brochure is available at the entrance station and visitor center.

Driving directions: Follow the driving directions for Hike 1 to the Clear Lake State Park entrance on Soda Bay Road. Turn left (north) and proceed 0.2 miles to the entrance station. At the station, turn left and park in the lot.

Hiking directions: Walk 50 yards up the park road to the posted Indian Nature Trail on the right. Head up the hillside, passing the numbered posts which correspond with the brochure. Just beyond signpost 8 is a junction. Begin the loop to the right, hiking counter-clockwise. Pass a beautiful jumble of rocks in a mixed forest of elderberry, valley oak, blue oak, foothill pine, mountain mahogany, California buckeye, toyon, and manzanita. Traverse the hillside, gaining elevation to another junction. Detour on the right fork to the Meadow Overlook at the end of the footpath. From the bench atop the overlook are vistas of Big Valley. Return to the junction and continue north. Gradually descend and complete the loop.■

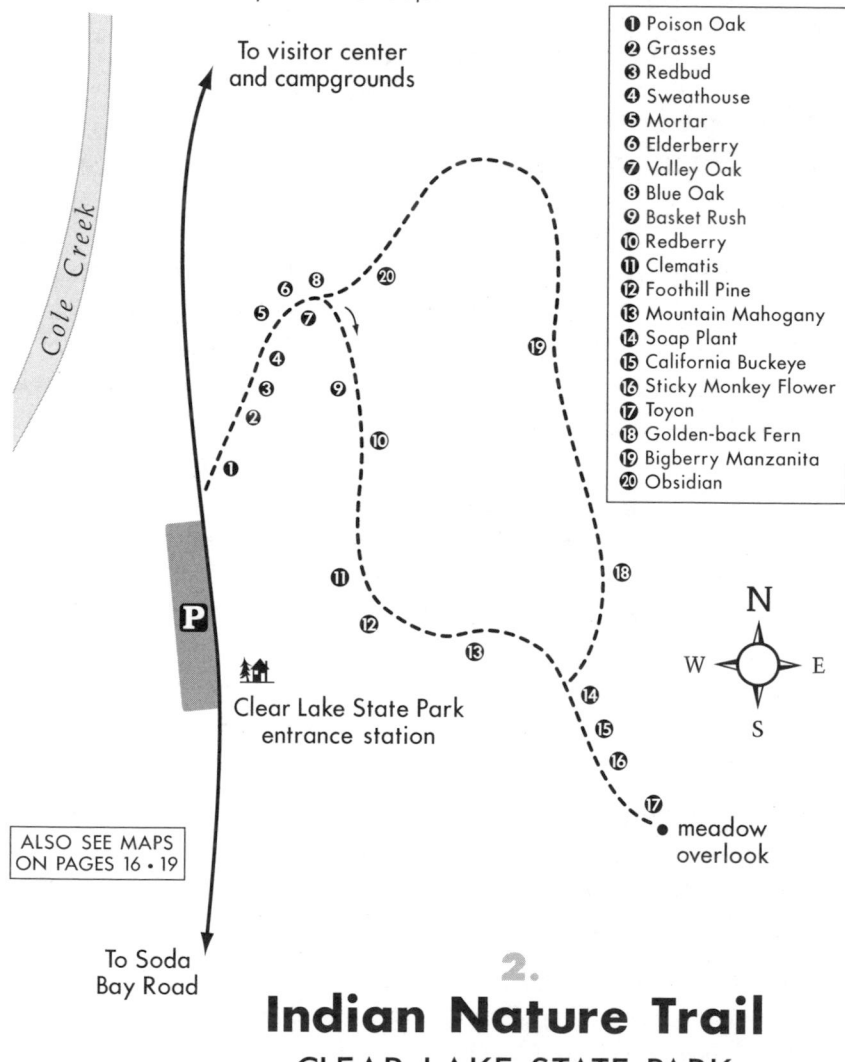

❶ Poison Oak
❷ Grasses
❸ Redbud
❹ Sweathouse
❺ Mortar
❻ Elderberry
❼ Valley Oak
❽ Blue Oak
❾ Basket Rush
❿ Redberry
⓫ Clematis
⓬ Foothill Pine
⓭ Mountain Mahogany
⓮ Soap Plant
⓯ California Buckeye
⓰ Sticky Monkey Flower
⓱ Toyon
⓲ Golden-back Fern
⓳ Bigberry Manzanita
⓴ Obsidian

To visitor center
and campgrounds

Cole Creek

P

Clear Lake State Park
entrance station

ALSO SEE MAPS
ON PAGES 16 • 19

To Soda
Bay Road

N
W · E
S

meadow
overlook

2.
Indian Nature Trail
CLEAR LAKE STATE PARK

3. Cache Creek—Marsh—McVicar Loop

ANDERSON MARSH STATE HISTORIC PARK
McVICAR WILDLIFE SANCTUARY

8825 Highway 53 · Lower Lake

Hiking distance: 5.8-mile loop
Hiking time: 2.5 hours
Elevation gain: 80 feet
Dogs: not allowed
Maps: U.S.G.S. Lower Lake and Clearlake Highlands
Anderson Marsh State Historic Park

map
page 25

Summary of hike: Anderson Marsh State Historic Park is a 1,000-acre protected nature preserve on the southeast corner of Clear Lake. It lies between the towns of Clearlake and Lower Lake. The fragile tule marsh habitat is a vital part of the Clear Lake ecosystem. The protected habitat includes freshwater marsh, oak woodland, riparian vegetation, and grasslands, providing protection, food, and breeding areas for a variety of wildlife.

The southeastern Pomo Indians lived in the area. The marsh's archaeological sites, among the oldest in California, date back more than 10,000 years. The Pomo Indians were expert basket weavers and tule boat builders. They made bows and arrows with tools made from local stone and obsidian.

The Grigsby brothers, settlers from Tennessee, built the existing ranch house and barns in the 1850s. Scottish immigrant John Anderson purchased the land in 1885 and started a cattle ranch. He and his family operated the ranch for 81 years. His descendants lived in the home and worked the ranch until the late 1960s.

This loop hike begins at the historic Anderson ranch house and visitor center, then explores the park's diverse habitats. The loop runs along the main outlet of Clear Lake through a lush riparian corridor along Cache Creek that is dominated by cottonwoods and willows. The trail leads through marshland habitat and an elevated woodland area with majestic blue oak, continuing through the forested wetlands into the McVicar Wildlife Sanctuary.

Driving directions: From Highway 29 and Lincoln Avenue in Calistoga, drive 30 miles north on Highway 29 (which is Lincoln Avenue through town) up and over the winding mountain road to the town of Lower Lake. From the junction of Highway 53 and Highway 29, continue 0.5 miles straight ahead (north) on Highway 53 to the posted state park entrance on the left. Turn left on Anderson Marsh Parkway, then immediately turn right. Go 0.2 miles to the parking lot.

From the town of Clearlake, Anderson Marsh Parkway (the park entrance road) is located 2.3 miles south of town.

Hiking directions: Head north past the historic ranch buildings and the park headquarters to the posted Cache Creek Nature Trail by the weather vane. Walk across the flat, open grassland to the south edge of a channel of Cache Creek. Curve left and follow the waterway, with grasslands on the left and riparian vegetation on the right. Cross a long, winding footbridge over a finger of the creek through a grove of cottonwoods and willows. Meander along the wide creek, passing private boat docks on the opposite shore. Curve away from Cache Creek, and stroll through the grasslands toward the oak-covered rise, reaching a posted T-junction with the Ridge Trail at one mile. Take the right fork. Loop around the north end of the ridge to Ridge Point, an overlook on the right side of the trail. Descend from the minor ridge, and continue on the Marsh Trail. Skirt the east edge of Anderson Marsh, parallel to the oak-lined ridge. Continue south, with panoramic views of the marsh, to a T-junction and interpretive panel at 1.6 miles. For a shorter 2.6-mile loop, bear left and follow the directions below from this junction. To continue the hike, take the McVicar Trail to the right. Descend and cross the south edge of Anderson Marsh along the park boundary. Enter the McVicar Wildlife Sanctuary in a lush oak woodland. Weave through the natural aviary to the far west end of Anderson Marsh and a picnic table at trail's end, adjacent to a vineyard.

Return to the Marsh—McVicar trail junction. Continue straight ahead 70 yards to the ridge and Ridge Trail. Bear right on the Ridge Trail, and follow the ridge through oak and manzanita groves. Weave gently uphill and slowly descend along the ridge. Return to the open grasslands, and follow the park boundary back to the trailhead on the Anderson Flats Trail. ■

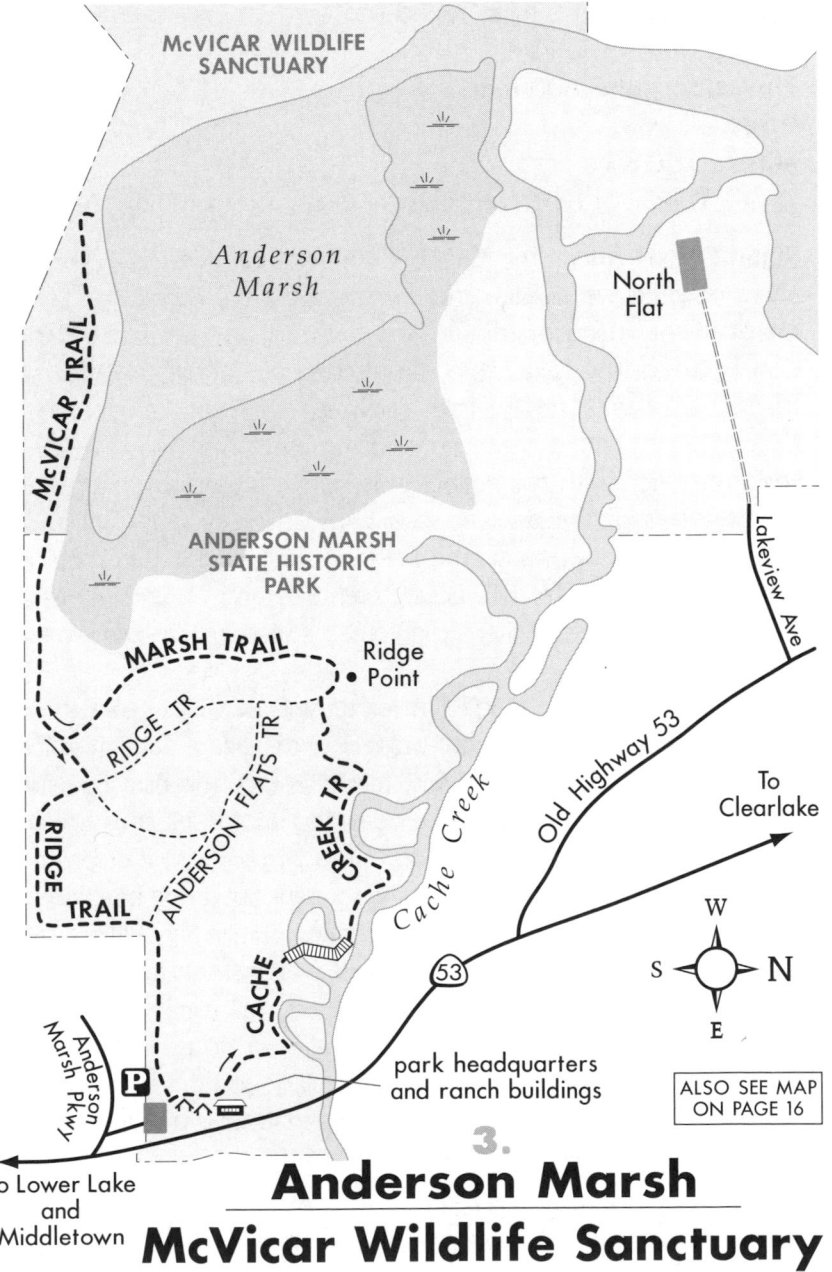

McVICAR WILDLIFE SANCTUARY

Anderson Marsh

North Flat

Mc VICAR TRAIL

Lakeview Ave

ANDERSON MARSH STATE HISTORIC PARK

MARSH TRAIL

Ridge • Point

RIDGE TR

ANDERSON FLATS TR

CREEK TR

Cache Creek

Old Highway 53

To Clearlake

RIDGE TRAIL

CACHE

53

W
S ✦ N
E

ALSO SEE MAP ON PAGE 16

Anderson Marsh Pkwy

P

park headquarters and ranch buildings

To Lower Lake and Middletown

3.

Anderson Marsh
McVicar Wildlife Sanctuary

4. Redbud Trail to Baton Flat
CACHE CREEK NATURAL AREA

Hiking distance: 5 miles round trip
Hiking time: 3 hours
Elevation gain: 600 feet
Dogs: allowed
Maps: U.S.G.S. Lower Lake
Bureau of Land Management Cache Creek Natural Area

Summary of hike: The Cache Creek Natural Area is 70,000-acres of primitive public land managed by the Bureau of Land Management. The isolated area is located just north of Napa County, straddling Lake, Yolo, and Colusa Counties. The diverse terrain includes steep-walled canyons, 30 miles of perennial Cache Creek, numerous feeder streams, and large grassy valleys. The land is rich with oak woodlands, native grasslands, chaparral shrublands, and riparian wetlands with cottonwoods, willows, and alders. Access through the seldom-used natural area is mainly limited to foot traffic, equestrian use, and mountain bikes. There are no developed camping areas, but primitive camping is permitted.

The Redbud Trail extends 7 miles to Wilson Valley, an expansive two-mile-long grassland dotted with valley oaks. It is an important range for the resident tule elk herd. This hike takes in the first 2.5 miles of the trail—beginning at the North Fork of Cache Creek and ending at Baton Flat, a large grassy flat on the banks of Cache Creek. The meadow contains towering black walnut trees planted in the late 1800s by Englishman Billy Baton. The Peninsula formation—weather-carved vertical cliffs—borders the east edge of Baton Flat. En route, the trail climbs 600 feet through pine habitat and oak woodland to a ridge with scenic vistas of Cache Creek Canyon, Wilson Valley, and the surrounding mountains. During the winter months it is a popular trail for viewing the migrating bald eagles.

Driving directions: From downtown Calistoga, drive 32 miles north on Highway 29 (which is Lincoln Avenue through town)

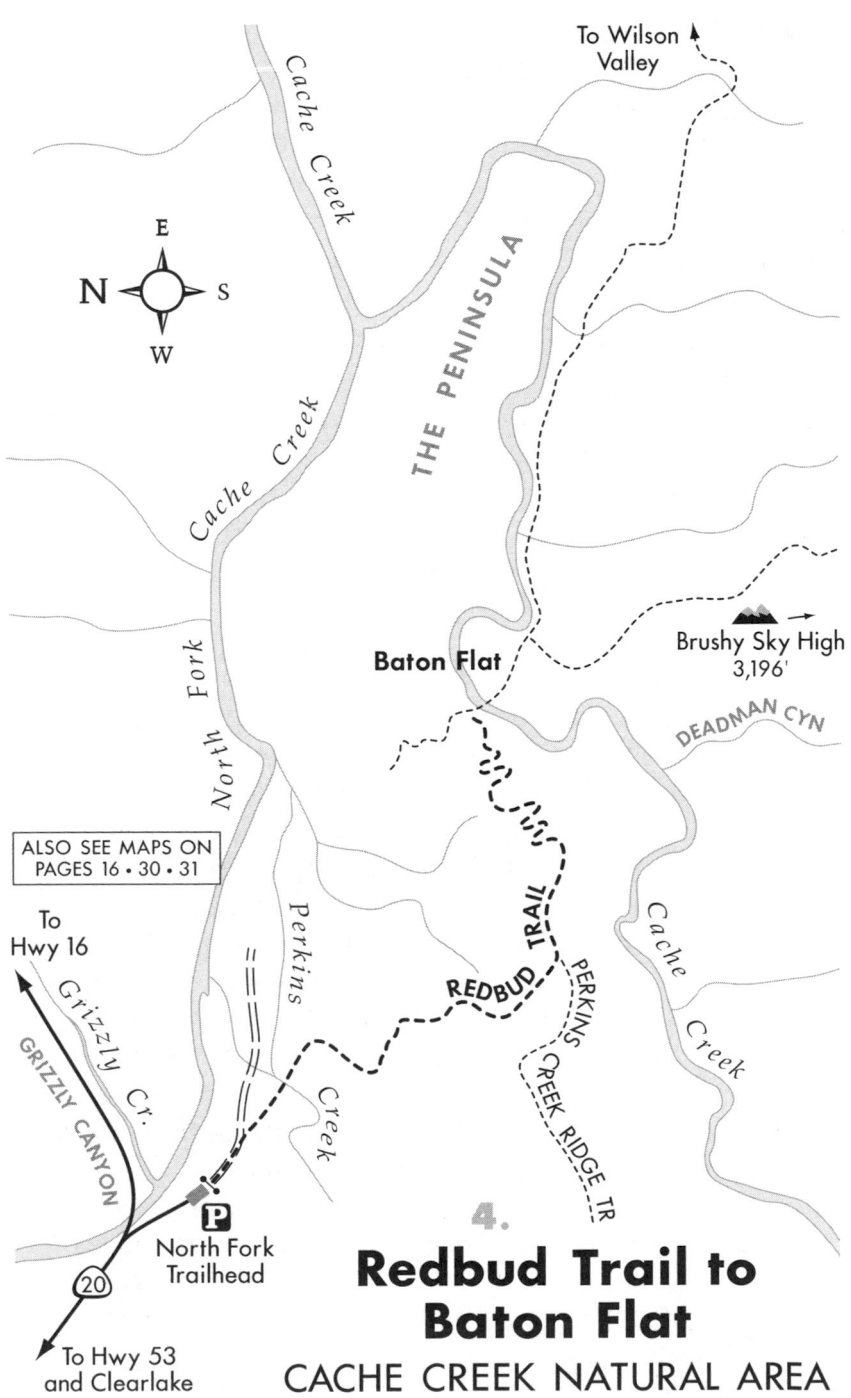

Cache Creek

To Wilson Valley

E
N — S
W

Cache Creek

THE PENINSULA

Cache Creek

North Fork

Baton Flat

Brushy Sky High
3,196'

DEADMAN CYN

ALSO SEE MAPS ON
PAGES 16 • 30 • 31

To
Hwy 16

Grizzly Cr.

GRIZZLY CANYON

Perkins Creek

REDBUD TRAIL

PERKINS CREEK RIDGE TR

Cache Creek

P
North Fork
Trailhead

20

To Hwy 53
and Clearlake

4.

Redbud Trail to Baton Flat

CACHE CREEK NATURAL AREA

over the winding mountain road to the town of Lower Lake. Continue 7.5 miles straight ahead on Highway 53 to a T-junction with Highway 20. Turn right and go 5.4 miles to the posted Cache Creek Management Area sign on the right. It is located just before crossing the bridge over Cache Creek. Turn right and drive 0.2 miles to the trailhead parking lot at the end of the road.

Hiking directions: Pass the trailhead gate and head southeast through the open meadow. Follow the gravel road, with views of the surrounding mountains, to a trail sign at 200 yards. Leave the road and veer right on the Redbud Trail. Cross Perkins Creek, a seasonal tributary of Cache Creek. Enter a forest of oaks, manzanita, and gray pines. Traverse the hillside above the meadow. At a half mile, begin climbing the hillside. Curve right and follow a ridge, parallel to a side canyon on the right. Steadily climb and top a ridge at one mile that overlooks Cache Creek Canyon. The Peninsula, the eroded 400-foot vertical mountain wall to the east, rises upward from the canyon floor. Continue up to the 1,400-foot grassy ridge that is dotted with majestic white oaks to a trail junction at 1.3 miles. To the right, Perkins Creek Ridge Trail follows the rolling ridge 5 miles, with spectacular views of the Cache Creek drainage and the Perkins Creek drainage. For this hike bear left, staying on the Redbud Trail. Follow the ridge east, enjoying the views of serpentine Cache Creek and 3,196-foot Brushy Sky High, the highest peak in the Cache Creek Natural Area. At 1.75 miles, begin the descent toward Baton Flat on the banks of Cache Creek. With the aid of eight switchbacks, descend 400 feet over the next 0.7 miles to Baton Flat. Cross the flat among mature black walnut trees to a junction. The left fork heads north and climbs a grassy slope to posted private land. The Redbud Trail goes right to the edge of Cache Creek beneath the precipitous face of The Peninsula, our turn-around spot.

In high water, Cache Creek is dangerous to cross and not advised. To extend the hike in low water conditions, wade across the creek. The trail continues 4.5 miles through gently rolling terrain to Wilson Valley and connects with the Judge Davis Trail (see Hike 5).■

5. Cache Creek Ridge
JUDGE DAVIS TRAILHEAD
CACHE CREEK NATURAL AREA

Hiking distance: 4.5-mile loop
Hiking time: 2.5 hours
Elevation gain: 600 feet
Dogs: allowed
Maps: U.S.G.S. Wilbur Springs and Wilson Valley
Bureau of Land Management Cache Creek Natural Area

map page 31

Summary of hike: The Cache Creek Natural Area is a secluded hilly expanse east of Clear Lake. Elevations range from 3,196 feet atop Brushy Sky High down to 600 feet at the eastern end of Cache Creek along Route 16. The primitive area offers recreational opportunities that include river running, hunting, fishing, wildlife observation, equestrian use, bird watching, and hiking. More than 154 species of birds have been spotted in the Cache Creek area, including bald eagle during the winter, great blue herons, belted kingfishers, and wild turkeys. Free-roaming tule elk and blacktail deer may be spotted grazing in the open grasslands and on hillsides near brushy cover.

Archaeological evidence of native occupation dates back 12,000 years. The Hill Patwin Indians flourished for centuries in this area. They then used it as a refuge after Euro-American contact disrupted their way of life.

This loop hike begins at the Judge Davis Trailhead near the Lake—Colusa county line. The trail climbs through an oak woodland and ventures along rolling green hills to the top of Cache Creek Ridge above Judge Davis Canyon. Atop the ridge are expansive vistas of the coastal mountains in the west to the snow-capped peaks of the Sierra Nevada Mountains in the east.

Driving directions: From downtown Calistoga, drive 32 miles north on Highway 29 (which is Lincoln Avenue through town) over the winding mountain road to the town of Lower Lake. Continue 7.5 miles straight ahead on Highway 53 to a T-junction with Highway 20. Turn right and go 14.5 miles to the posted

Cache Creek Management Area sign on the right by mile marker 46.06. Turn right into the trailhead parking lot.

Hiking directions: Walk past the brown gate by the restrooms, and head up the east side of the canyon. Follow the grassy path through a blue oak, gray pine, and manzanita woodland. Curve right and cross the head of the canyon to the ridge and a southward view of Blue Ridge, named for the dominant blue oak. Cross the ridge to a view into Judge Davis Canyon. Slowly descend on the open, grass-covered slopes scattered with oaks. Return to the ridge and weave through the gorgeous countryside to a posted "trail" junction at 1.5 miles. Veer to the right, staying on the Cache Creek Ridge Trail, and parallel an old barbed wire fence on the left. Follow the fence 0.2 miles and curve right. Wind up to the top of the sloping meadow with 360-degree vistas. The path levels out and leads through fields of chamise and scrub vegetation. Climb a short but steep hill, and descend to a metal gate. Westward is a view of Mount Konocti, a dormant volcano rising above Clear Lake. Pass through the gate

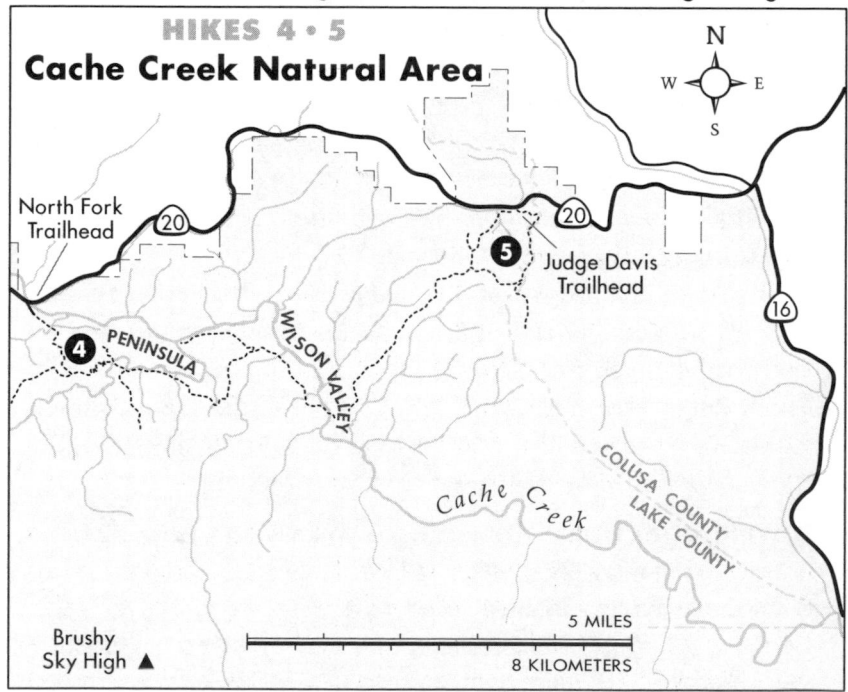

HIKES 4 • 5
Cache Creek Natural Area

North Fork Trailhead

Judge Davis Trailhead

PENINSULA

WILSON VALLEY

Cache Creek

COLUSA COUNTY
LAKE COUNTY

5 MILES

8 KILOMETERS

Brushy Sky High ▲

and continue downhill, passing endless vistas. At 3.5 miles is a knoll and a posted junction. The left fork descends into Judge Davis Canyon on the Judge Davis Trail. It continues 4 miles to the expansive Wilson Valley and connects with the Redbud Trail (Hike 4). For this hike, continue on the right branch to a Y-fork. Take the narrower path to the right, and traverse the south-facing slope. Descend into the canyon through a blue oak and gray pine woodland, continuing downward to the canyon floor. Cross a seasonal creek, and curve round the hill to Highway 20. Parallel the highway on the hillside path 0.2 miles to the trailhead parking lot.■

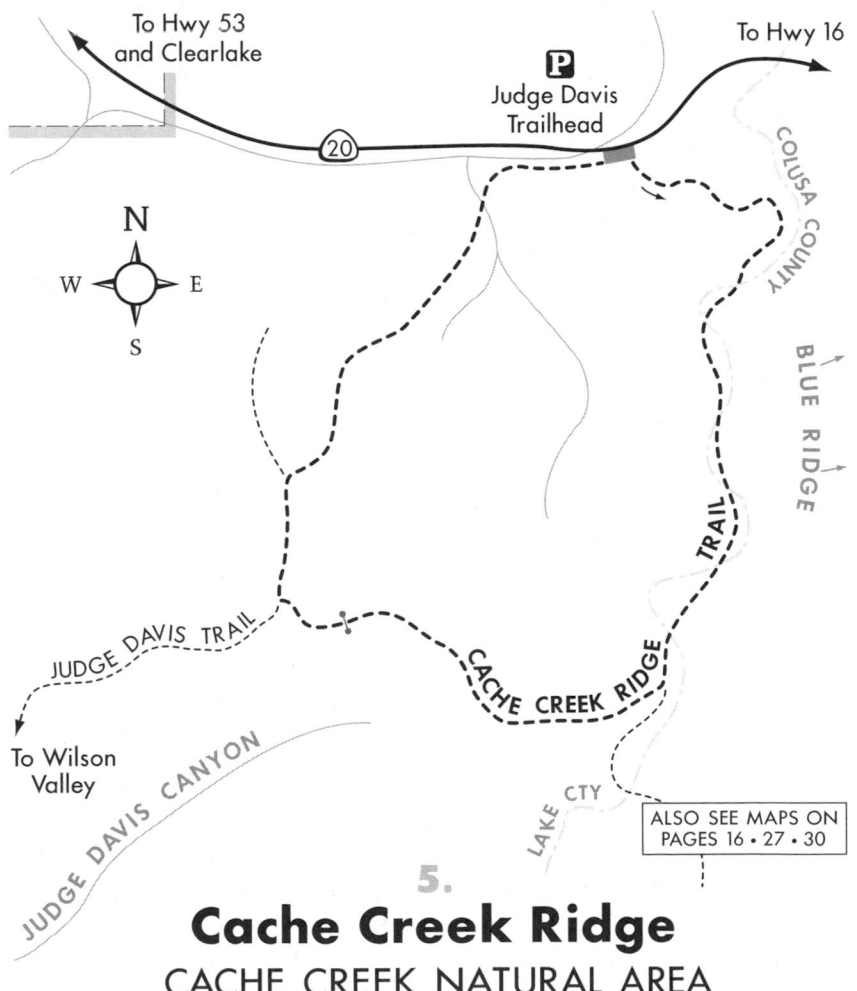

5.
Cache Creek Ridge
CACHE CREEK NATURAL AREA

6. Middletown Trailside Nature Preserve

21435 Dry Creek Cutoff Road · Middleton

Hiking distance: 1.5-mile loop
Hiking time: 45 minutes
Elevation gain: Level
Dogs: allowed
Maps: U.S.G.S. Whispering Pines
  AAA Clear Lake Communities

Summary of hike: Middletown Trailside Nature Preserve is a 107-acre parkland on the west end of Middletown. The town sits in the Collayomi Valley and is so named because it is midway between Calistoga and Lower Lake. The triangular-shaped park sits at the base of 2,351-foot Sugarloaf Peak. The area has diverse habitats that range from forested woodlands to seasonal wetlands with vernal pools and grasslands. The park is a popular hiking, jogging, bird watching, and picnic area. This hike loops around the perimeter of the park and explores all of the varied environments.

Driving directions: From downtown Calistoga, drive 17 miles north on Highway 29 (which is Lincoln Avenue in town) over the winding mountain road to Highway 175 in the town of Middletown. Turn left on Highway 175, and continue 1.5 miles to Dry Creek Cutoff Road. Turn left and go 0.35 miles to the posted park on the left. Turn left into the trailhead parking lot.

Hiking directions: Facing the trailhead map kiosk, take the trail on the left and head north. Pass two metal gates and stroll through the grasslands. Enter a mixed forest with digger pines, ponderosa pines, and Douglas fir, then curve left. Parallel Dry Creek Cutoff Road through the forest and bend to the right. Head east on the serpentine path, crossing a small stream. Parallel Highway 175 and a stream on the right. Emerge from the forest to a tree-dotted grassy wetland and vernal pools. The pools are natural depressions that hold water for a short time during rainy periods, then seep into the ground and evaporate. Follow the north edge of the meadow. Curve right by an access gate off of

Highway 175 to a picnic area on the left. Continue past another pond to a trail fork. The right fork returns to the trailhead for a shorter loop. Bear left through pockets of manzanita to the east end of the park, adjacent to the vineyards. Curve right and meander alongside a stream on the left. Veer right and complete the loop at the south end of the parking lot. ■

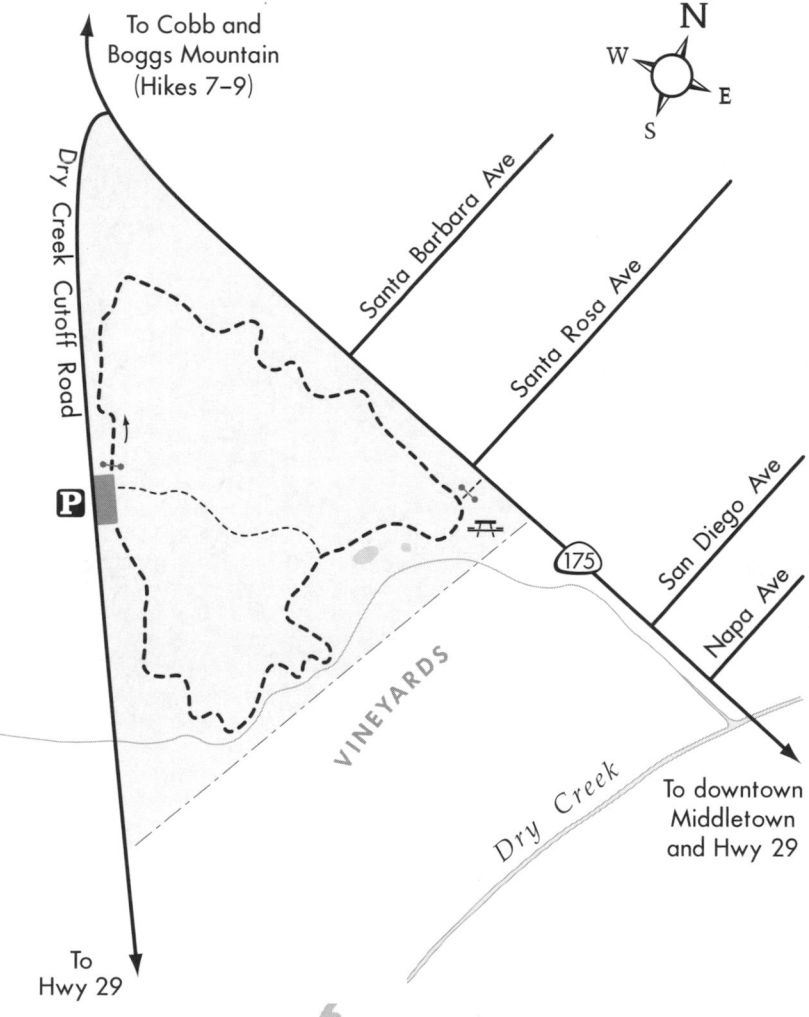

6.
Middletown Trailside Nature Preserve

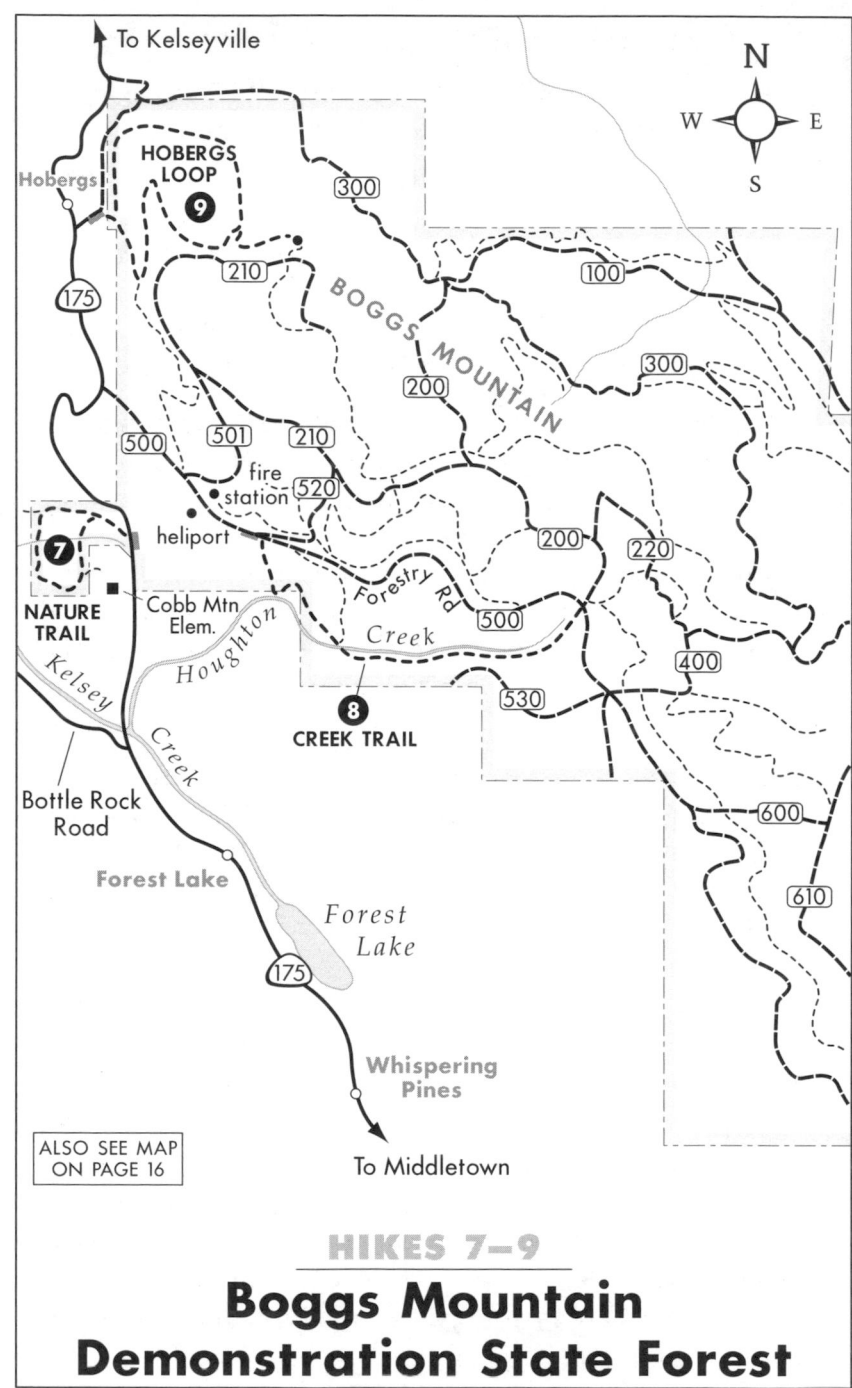

HIKES 7–9

Boggs Mountain
Demonstration State Forest

7. Boggs Ridge Nature Trail
BOGGS MOUNTAIN DEMONSTRATION STATE FOREST

Hiking distance: 0.7-mile loop
Hiking time: 30 minutes
Elevation gain: 50 feet
Dogs: allowed
Maps: U.S.G.S. Whispering Pines
Boggs Mountain Demonstration State Forest map
AAA Clear Lake Communities

map
page 37

Summary of hike: Boggs Mountain Demonstration State Forest encompasses 3,493 acres in the Mayacamas Mountains by the town of Cobb. Wappo Indians traveled through this area annually en route to their fishing and obsidian quarries at Clear Lake. In the late 1800s, Henry Boggs owned the land and used it for grazing livestock and timber operations with steam-powered sawmill sites. Boggs sold it to the Calso Company, who used the land for timber harvesting before selling it to the state of California. The state forest was established in 1949. It uses the land as a demonstration forest to grow and harvest trees; for wildlife habitation; as a watershed; and for recreation, including deer hunting, camping, picnicking, hiking, biking, and horseback riding. In 1986, John Zeigler and Eagle Scout Troop 43 constructed the Boggs Ridge Nature Trail on the only section of the state forest west of Highway 175. This easy hike loops through the small parcel of land at an elevation of 2,450 feet, adjacent to Cobb Mountain Elementary School.

Driving directions: From downtown Calistoga, drive 17 miles north on Highway 29 (which is Lincoln Avenue in town) over the winding mountain road to Highway 175 in the town of Middletown. Turn left on Highway 175, and continue 9 miles to a gated dirt road on the left. The gate is located a half mile past downtown Cobb at mile marker 19.00, just beyond Cobb Mountain Elementary School. Park in the pullout on the right, across from the trailhead gate.

Hiking directions: Cross the road to the wooden gate. Walk past the gate into a forest of ponderosa pine and manzanita. Skirt the edge of the grassy school fields to a clearing and an unsigned junction. Begin the loop on the right fork, straight ahead. Cross a small stream and slowly descend to an unmarked junction on the left. The trail straight ahead follows the north slope of the small canyon and exits by homes off of Rainbow Drive. Bear left and descend to the stream on the canyon floor. Cross the stream and climb east through madrones, firs, and pines. Bear left and meander to another unsigned trail junction. The main trail continues straight to Cobb Mountain Elementary School. Take the left fork and drop back down to the stream. Cross the stream and complete the loop in the clearing. Return 200 yards to the right. ∎

8. Creek Trail along Houghton Creek
BOGGS MOUNTAIN DEMONSTRATION STATE FOREST

Hiking distance: 2.5 miles round trip
Hiking time: 1.5 hours
Elevation gain: 350 feet
Dogs: allowed
Maps: U.S.G.S. Whispering Pines
        Boggs Mountain Demonstration State Forest map
        AAA Clear Lake Communities

**map
page 39**

Summary of hike: Houghton Creek, a tributary of Kelsey Creek, forms along the hillside in Boggs Mountain Demonstration State Forest. The Creek Trail parallels Houghton Creek through a narrow canyon amid shady fern gardens, trillium, and wild grapes. A woodland of sugar pines, Douglas firs, dogwoods, and alders envelops the trail. The hike begins on Forestry Road just past the fire station and leads to Calso Campground. Trail maps are located at the kiosk across from the fire station.

Driving directions: From downtown Calistoga, drive 17 miles north on Highway 29 (which is Lincoln Avenue in town) over the winding mountain road to Highway 175 in the town of

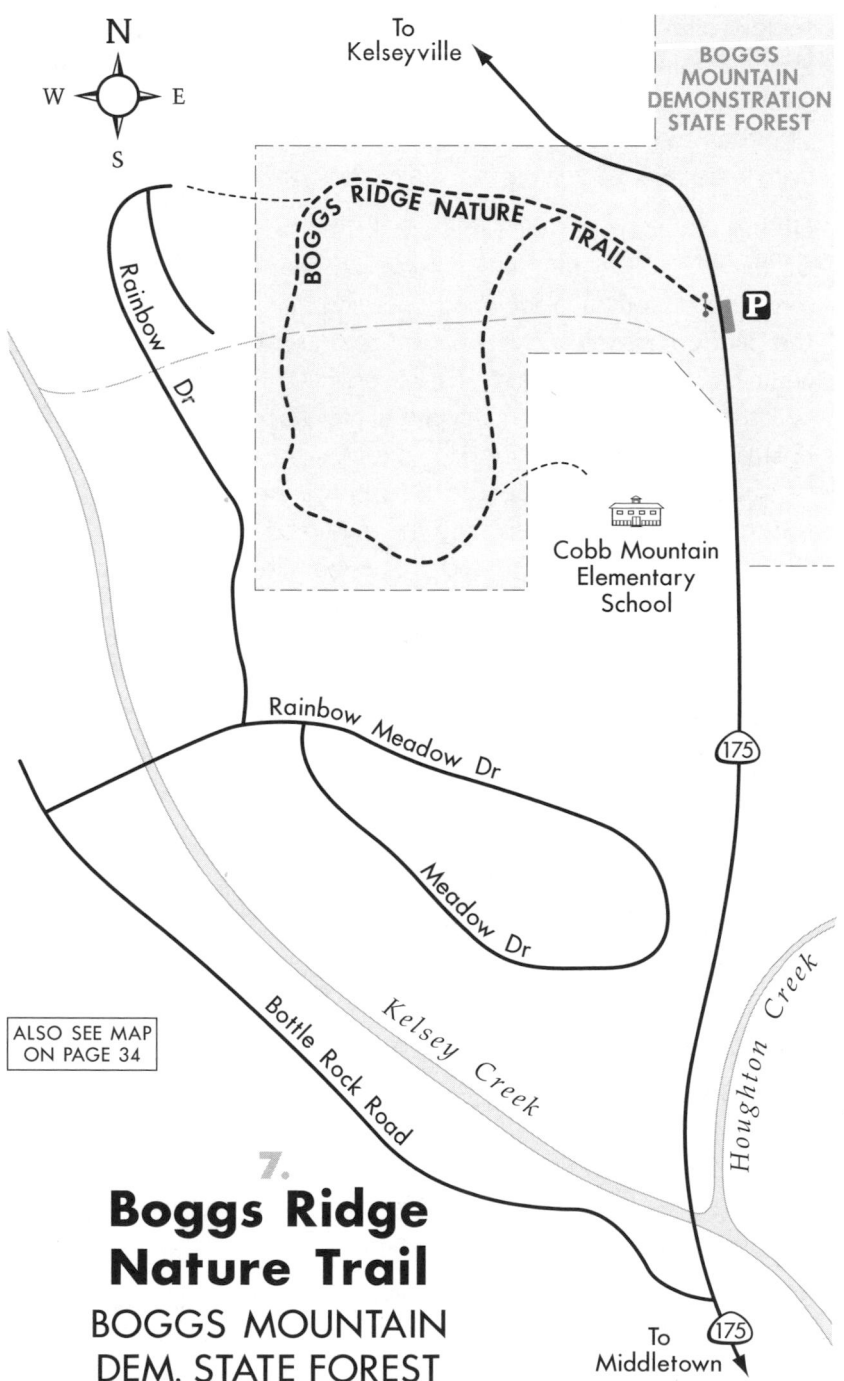

N
W ─ E
S

To
Kelseyville

BOGGS
MOUNTAIN
DEMONSTRATION
STATE FOREST

BOGGS RIDGE NATURE TRAIL

P

Rainbow Dr

Cobb Mountain
Elementary
School

Rainbow Meadow Dr

Meadow Dr

175

Houghton Creek

ALSO SEE MAP
ON PAGE 34

Bottle Rock Road

Kelsey Creek

7.
Boggs Ridge
Nature Trail
BOGGS MOUNTAIN
DEM. STATE FOREST

To
Middletown

175

Middletown. Turn left on Highway 175, and continue 9.8 miles to Forestry Road. The signed turnoff is located 1.4 miles past the town of Cobb. Turn right on Forestry Road (Road 500), and drive 0.6 miles to the posted Creek Trail on the right at a Y-junction with Road 520. Park in a pullout alongside the road.

Hiking directions: Pass the Creek Trail sign on the south side of the road. Traverse the hillside on the forested footpath through ponderosa pines, madrone, and manzanita. Descend on the padded, needle-covered path to a lush flat area with ferns and mossy boulders. Just before crossing over Houghton Creek, switchback left on an unmarked trail high above the creek. Head upstream, slowly descending through the dense forest to Houghton Creek and a posted Y-fork. The left fork switchbacks left, climbs the hillside, and returns to Forestry Road (Road 500) 125 yards east of the trailhead (for a shorter hike). For this hike, cross Houghton Creek, and head uphill on the south side of the creek. Traverse the slope through ferns, moss, and poison oak. Steadily gain elevation, passing the headwaters of the creek, to the east end of the trail. Emerge on Forestry Road by Calso Campground, tucked into a ponderosa pine forest. Return by retracing your steps, or follow the forested dirt road 1.1 miles back to the trailhead.■

9. Hobergs Loop to Vista Point
BOGGS MOUNTAIN DEMONSTRATION STATE FOREST

Hiking distance: 2-mile loop
Hiking time: 1 hour
Elevation gain: 350 feet
Dogs: allowed
Maps: U.S.G.S. Whispering Pines
      Boggs Mountain Demonstration State Forest map
      AAA Clear Lake Communities

map
page 41

Summary of hike: Boggs Mountain Demonstration State Forest has a complex trail network of interconnecting dirt roads and single track footpaths that stretch over the forest's 3,493 acres.

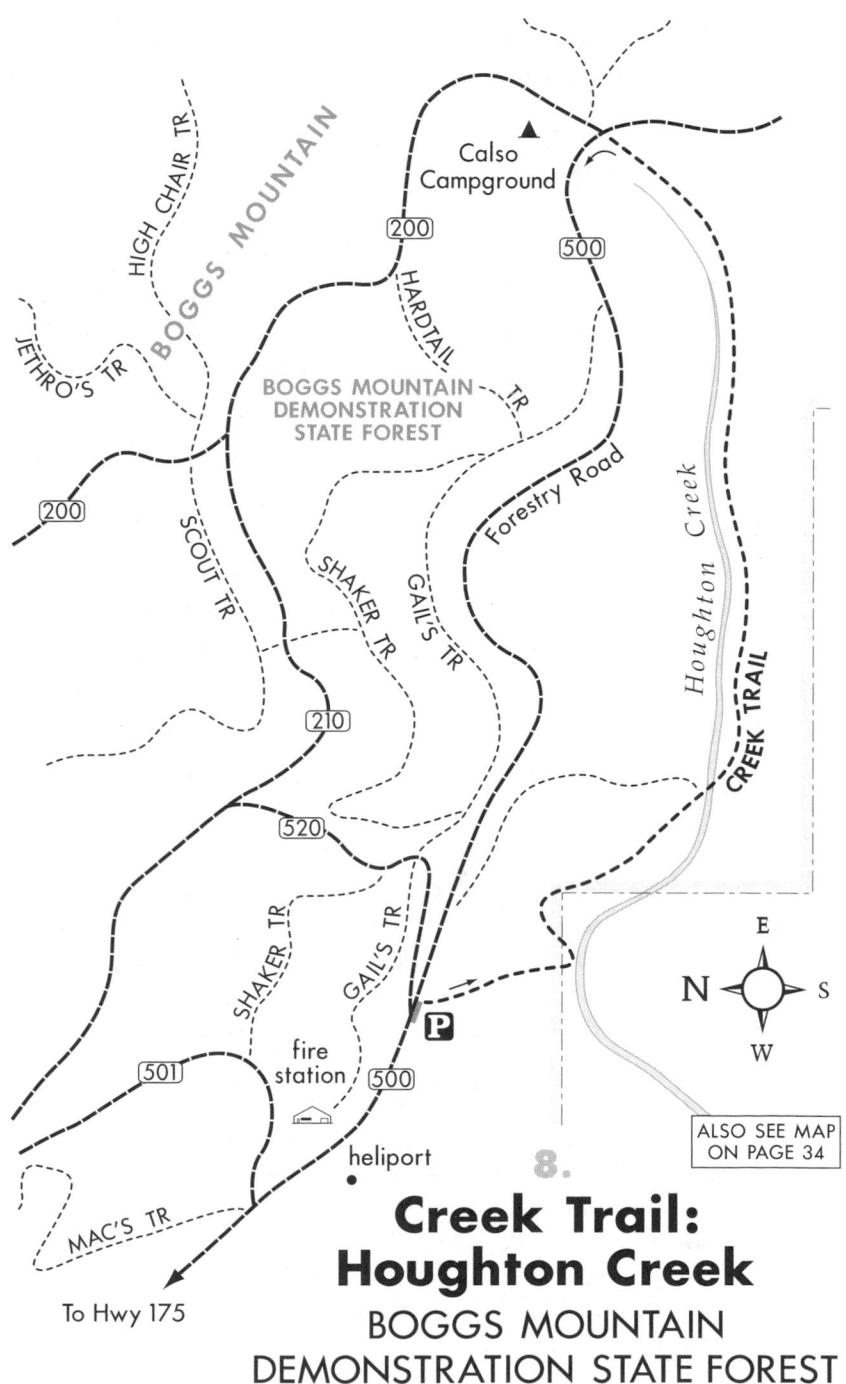

HIGH CHAIR TR

JETHRO'S TR

BOGGS MOUNTAIN

Calso Campground

200

500

HARDTAIL TR

BOGGS MOUNTAIN DEMONSTRATION STATE FOREST

200

SCOUT TR

SHAKER TR

GAIL'S TR

Forestry Road

Houghton Creek

CREEK TRAIL

210

520

SHAKER TR

GAIL'S TR

E
N ⟡ S
W

fire station

501

500

P

heliport

MAC'S TR

To Hwy 175

ALSO SEE MAP ON PAGE 34

8.

Creek Trail:
Houghton Creek
BOGGS MOUNTAIN
DEMONSTRATION STATE FOREST

With elevations ranging from 2,400 feet to 3,750 feet, the diverse trail system explores meadows, ridgetops, dense forests, and riparian corridors. The forests are thick with ponderosa pine, sugar pine, California black oaks, Douglas firs, western red cedar, dogwoods, and big-leaf maples. This seldom-traveled area is a great place to hike, away from the crowds. Hobergs Loop sits on the northwest end of the state forest and weaves through the arboreal terrain to an overlook.

Driving directions: From downtown Calistoga, drive 17 miles north on Highway 29 (which is Lincoln Avenue in town) over the winding mountain road to Highway 175 in the town of Middletown. Turn left on Highway 175, and continue 10.2 miles to Entrance Road. The signed turnoff is located 1.8 miles past the town of Cobb in the hamlet of Hobergs. Turn right on Entrance Road, and drive 0.1 mile to the trailhead and parking area on the right.

Hiking directions: Take the signed Hobergs Loop on the left side of the metal gate. Traverse the forested hillside 80 yards to a posted junction. Begin the loop on the right fork, straight ahead. Climb up the slope through Douglas fir and manzanita to a marked junction with Mac's Trail on the right. Stay left on Hobergs Loop to an unmarked Y-fork. Veer right and steadily gain elevation at a gentle grade. Switchback to the right and continue uphill through pines and firs. Top a minor slope in a clearing to a posted junction. Continue 100 yards straight ahead to the Boggs Ridge Trail at 0.9 miles. Detour right on the Boggs Ridge Trail, and meander through the forest at a level grade. At a quarter mile is Vista Point, an overlook on the left with tree-obscured views of Seigler Mountain and the surrounding peaks. Return to Hobergs Loop Trail and continue to the right (north). Gradually descend and curve around the north end of Boggs Mountain, completing the loop.■

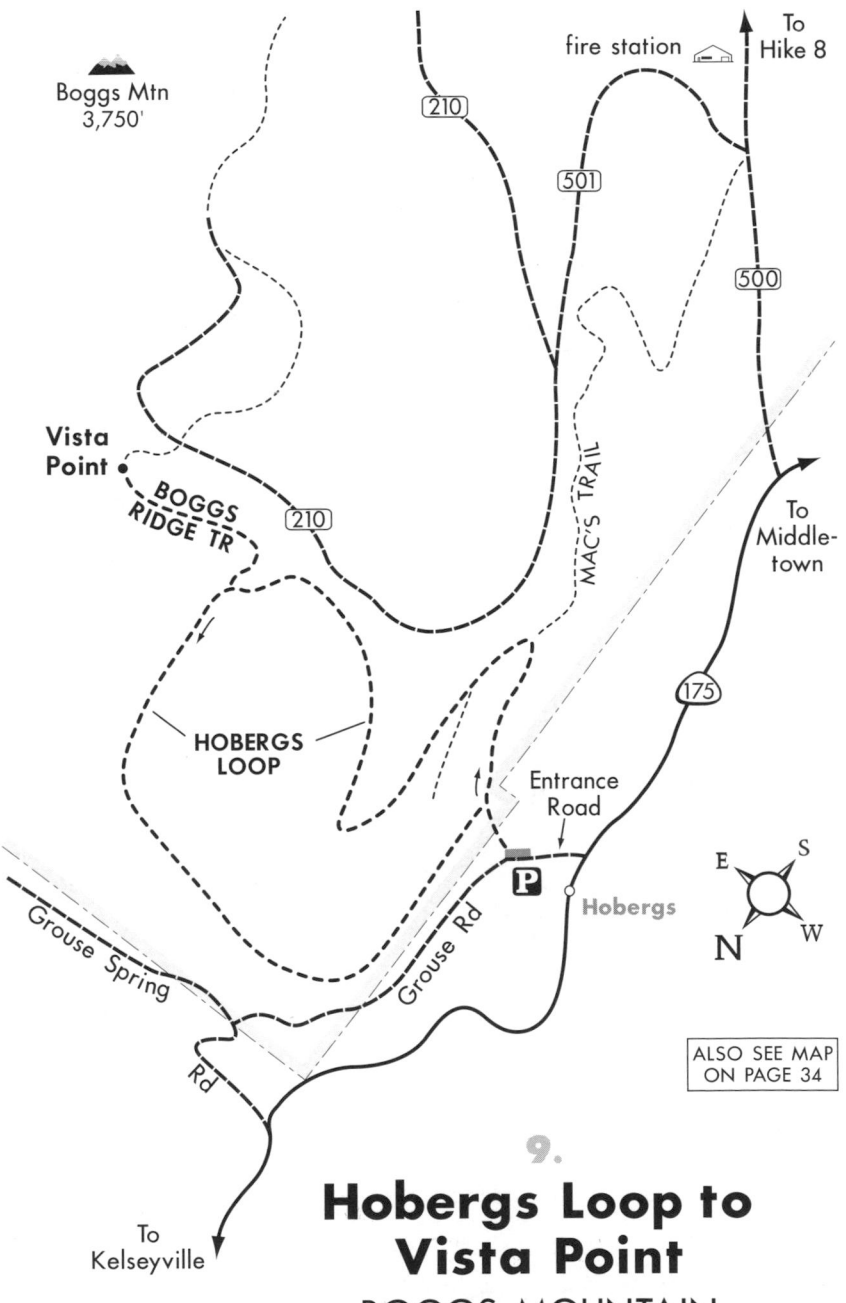

Hobergs Loop to Vista Point

BOGGS MOUNTAIN
DEMONSTRATION STATE FOREST

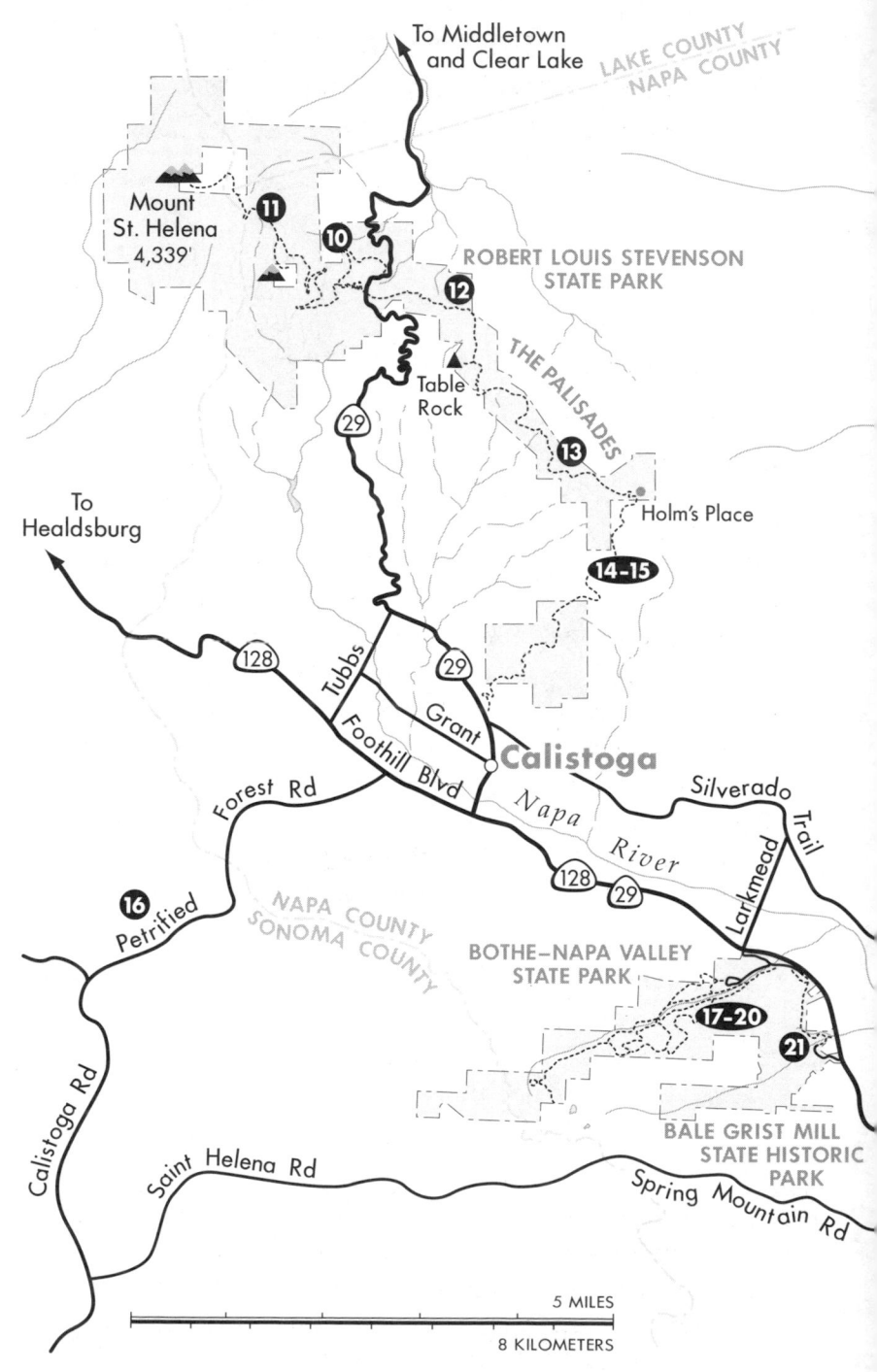

North Napa Valley

CALISTOGA • ST. HELENA • ANGWIN

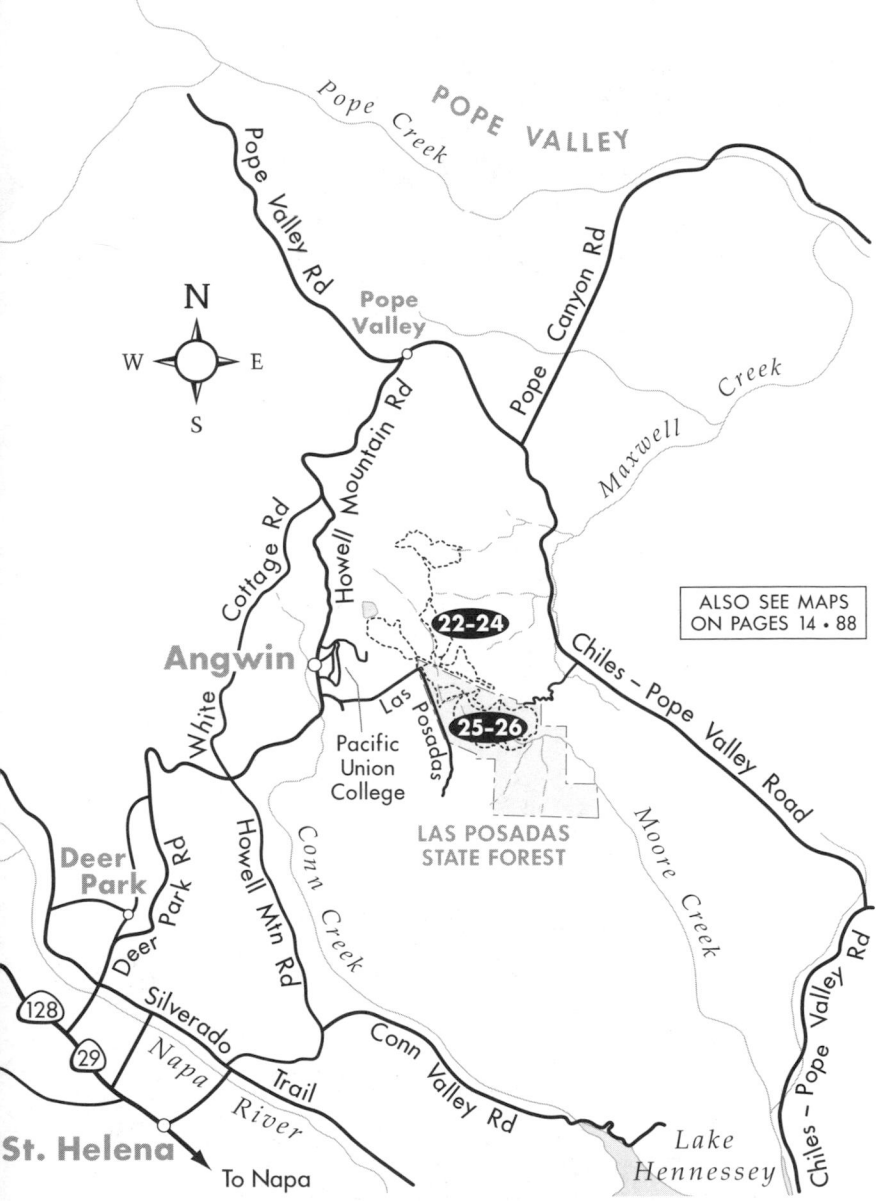

POPE VALLEY

Pope Creek

Pope Valley Rd

Pope Valley

Pope Canyon Rd

Maxwell Creek

N
W E
S

Howell Mountain Rd

Cottage Rd

22-24

ALSO SEE MAPS
ON PAGES 14 • 88

Angwin

White

Las Posadas

25-26

Chiles – Pope Valley Road

Pacific
Union
College

LAS POSADAS
STATE FOREST

Moore Creek

Deer
Park

Deer Park Rd

Howell Mtn Rd

Conn Creek

128

Silverado

29

Napa River

Trail

Conn Valley Rd

Lake
Hennessey

Chiles – Pope Valley Rd

St. Helena

To Napa

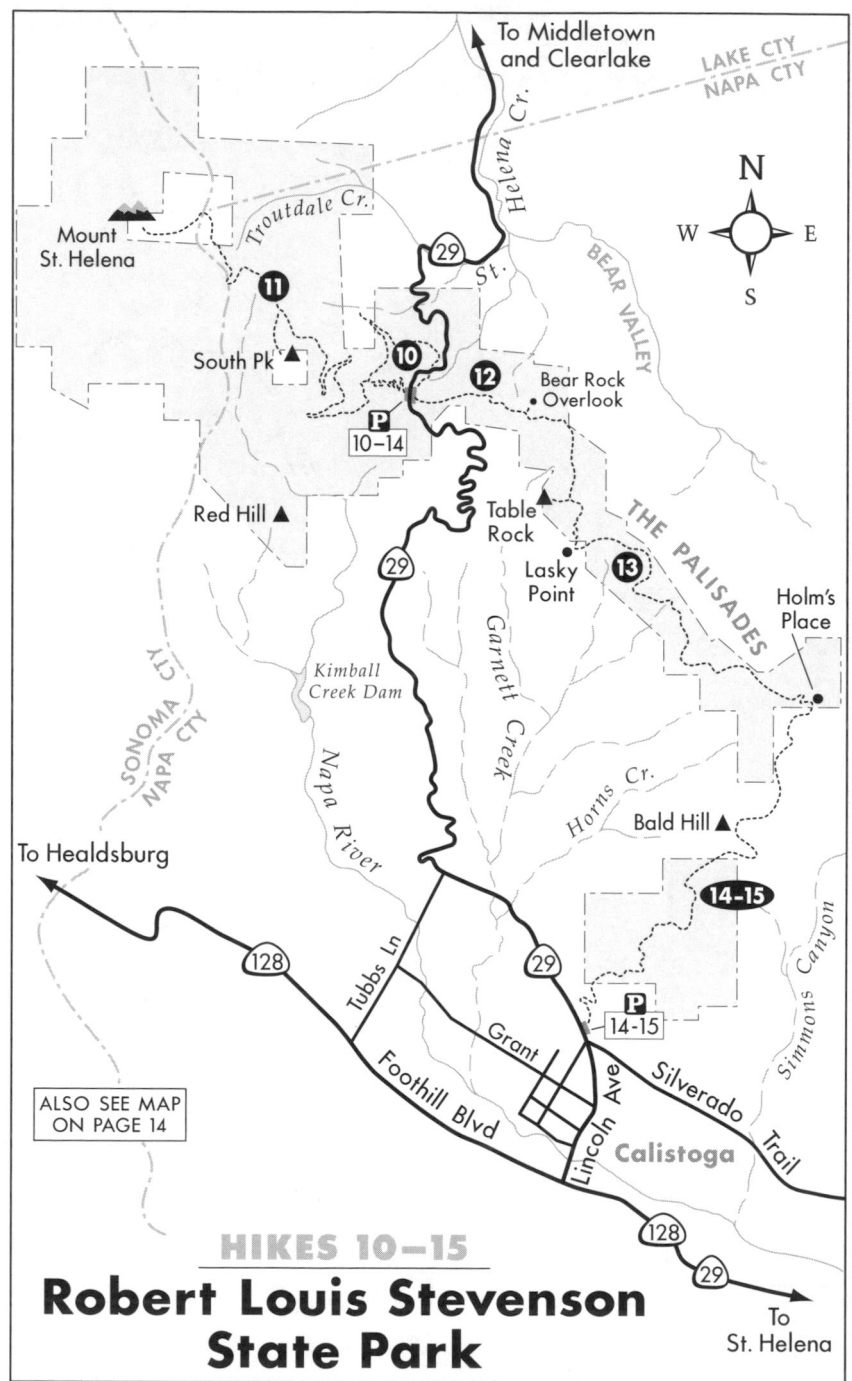

ALSO SEE MAP
ON PAGE 14

HIKES 10–15
Robert Louis Stevenson State Park

10. Stevenson Memorial Trail
ROBERT LOUIS STEVENSON STATE PARK

Hiking distance: 1.4 miles round trip or 2.2-mile loop
Hiking time: 1 hour
Elevation gain: 500 feet
Dogs: not allowed
Maps: U.S.G.S. Detert Reservoir
       Bothe–Napa Valley/Robert Louis Stevenson State Parks

map
page 47

Summary of hike: Robert Louis Stevenson State Park encompasses 5,272 acres in the Mayacamas Mountains above Calistoga. The immense park straddles Sonoma, Napa, and Lake Counties. The centerpiece of the park is Mount Saint Helena, the highest peak in Sonoma County (Hike 11). This hike makes a loop along the lower portion of the trail to the Stevenson Memorial. In the summer of 1880, Robert Louis Stevenson, author of *Treasure Island* and *Kidnapped*, honeymooned for several months in an abandoned, two-story bunkhouse near the Silverado Mine. Stevenson wrote about this time in his book *Silverado Squatters*. A memorial marker identifies the site of the abandoned mine building. The memorial, unveiled in 1911, has a quartz base and an open, book-shaped Scotch granite cap inscribed with a Stevenson poem. This short loop hike zigzags up the hillside under the shade of Douglas fir, live oak, madrone, tanbark oak, and manzanita.

Driving directions: Robert Louis Stevenson State Park is located northeast of Calistoga on Highway 29: From Highway 29/Lincoln Avenue in downtown Calistoga, drive 8.5 miles northeast on Lincoln Avenue (Highway 29) through town and up the winding mountain road. Park in the parking area on the left at the road's summit. Additional parking is available in the larger parking area directly across the road.

Hiking directions: Walk up the steps to a flat, grassy picnic area and posted trailhead. Head up the forested hillside on the rock-embedded path. Six switchbacks zigzag up the forested mountain. In a shady flat at 0.7 miles is the Stevenson Memorial, a stone monument by a mossy rock formation. This is the turn-around spot for a 1.4-mile round-trip walk. For the 2.2-mile loop hike, climb two more switchbacks to the Mount Saint Helena Trail—a T-junction with a service road at 0.85 miles. The trail to Mount Saint Helena goes left and climbs 1,600 feet over the next 4.5 miles (Hike 11). For this hike, go to the right and steadily descend northward. Cross under power lines at a right U-bend and head southeast. Near Highway 29, pass through a metal gate to the road. Carefully cross the highway and descend 40 yards into the forest to a footpath. Bear right and climb 0.3 miles through the forest to the highway, directly across from the trailhead. Cautiously cross the road, completing the loop.■

11. Mount Saint Helena Trail
ROBERT LOUIS STEVENSON STATE PARK

Hiking distance: 10.6 miles round trip
Hiking time: 5 to 6 hours
Elevation gain: 2,100 feet
Dogs: not allowed
Maps: U.S.G.S. Detert Reservoir and Mount Saint Helena
Bothe—Napa Valley/Robert Louis Stevenson State Parks

*map
page 49*

Summary of hike: Mount Saint Helena, in Robert Louis Stevenson State Park, is the tallest peak in Sonoma County at 4,339 feet. A 5.3-mile trail winds through the undeveloped park to the volcanic mountain's North Peak. It is a long, sinuous fire road on a south-facing slope, exposed to sun and wind. The popular hiking and biking route steadily climbs but is never steep. The long distance and substantial elevation gain, however, make it a strenuous hike. Throughout the hike, the views are spectacular. From the summit are 360-degree vistas extending across Napa Valley to Mount Tamalpais, including the twin peaks of Mount Diablo and San Francisco in the south, Mount Lassen and Snow Mountain in the north, the Vaca Mountains in the east, and the coastal ranges to the ocean in the west.

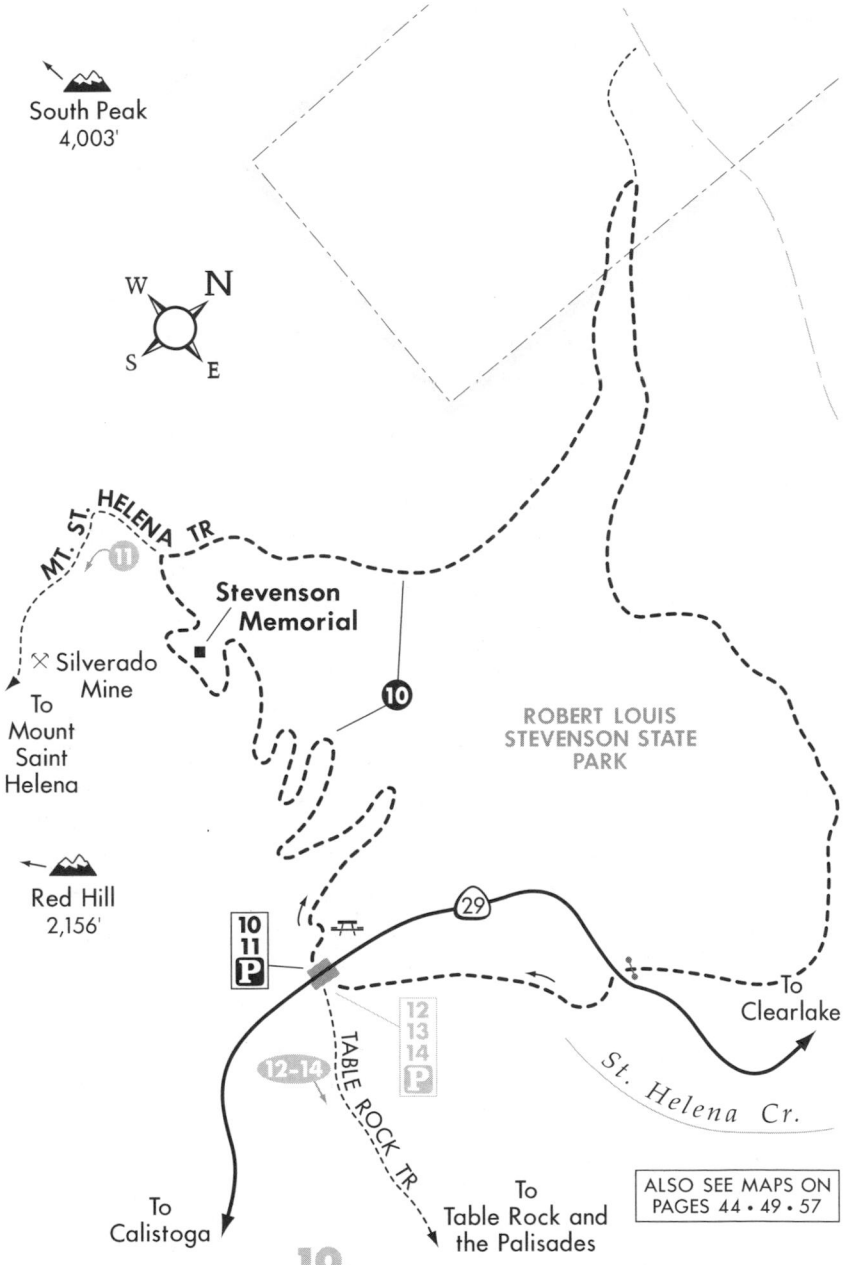

South Peak
4,003'

W **N** S E

MT. ST. HELENA TR

Stevenson Memorial

⑪

⚒ Silverado Mine

To Mount Saint Helena

10

ROBERT LOUIS STEVENSON STATE PARK

Red Hill
2,156'

29

10 11 P

🍽

12 13 14 P

12-14

TABLE ROCK TR

St. Helena Cr.

To Clearlake

To Calistoga

To Table Rock and the Palisades

ALSO SEE MAPS ON PAGES 44 • 49 • 57

10.
Stevenson Memorial Trail
ROBERT LOUIS STEVENSON STATE PARK

Driving directions: Robert Louis Stevenson State Park is located northeast of Calistoga on Highway 29: From Highway 29/Lincoln Avenue in downtown Calistoga, drive 8.5 miles northeast on Lincoln Avenue (Highway 29) through town and up the winding mountain road. Park in the parking area on the left at the road's summit. Additional parking is available in the larger parking area directly across the road.

Hiking directions: Follow the hiking directions for Hike 10 to the T-junction with the service road at 0.8 miles, shortly after the Stevenson Memorial. The right fork weaves down the hillside back to Highway 29. For this hike, go to the left, as views open up of Napa Valley and the surrounding mountains. The trail passes above Silverado Mine, but it is not visible. At 1.6 miles, on a horseshoe right bend, is weather-chiseled Bubble Rock, a pockmarked igneous formation that is popular with rock climbers. Continue up the well-graded road cut into the chaparral-covered slope, with views across Napa County and Sonoma County. The exposed terrain is dotted with manzanita, small oaks, knobcone pines, bay laurel, and greasewood. Make a sweeping left bend at 2.25 miles, passing fractured rock columns. Cross under power lines and continue a half mile to a road junction on a saddle at 3.6 miles. The left branch leads 0.5 miles to 4,003-foot South Peak, the lower summit. Continue north—straight ahead—between North and South Peaks, with a view of Lake Berryessa on the right. Continue to a ridge at 4.5 miles. Veer left, entering Sonoma County, and head west toward the peak. Pass through groves of sugar pines and Douglas firs, then leave the forest for the final ascent. At the summit, pass a group of communication structures to the rocky north face above Rattlesnake and Bradford canyons. After savoring the views, return along the same route. ∎

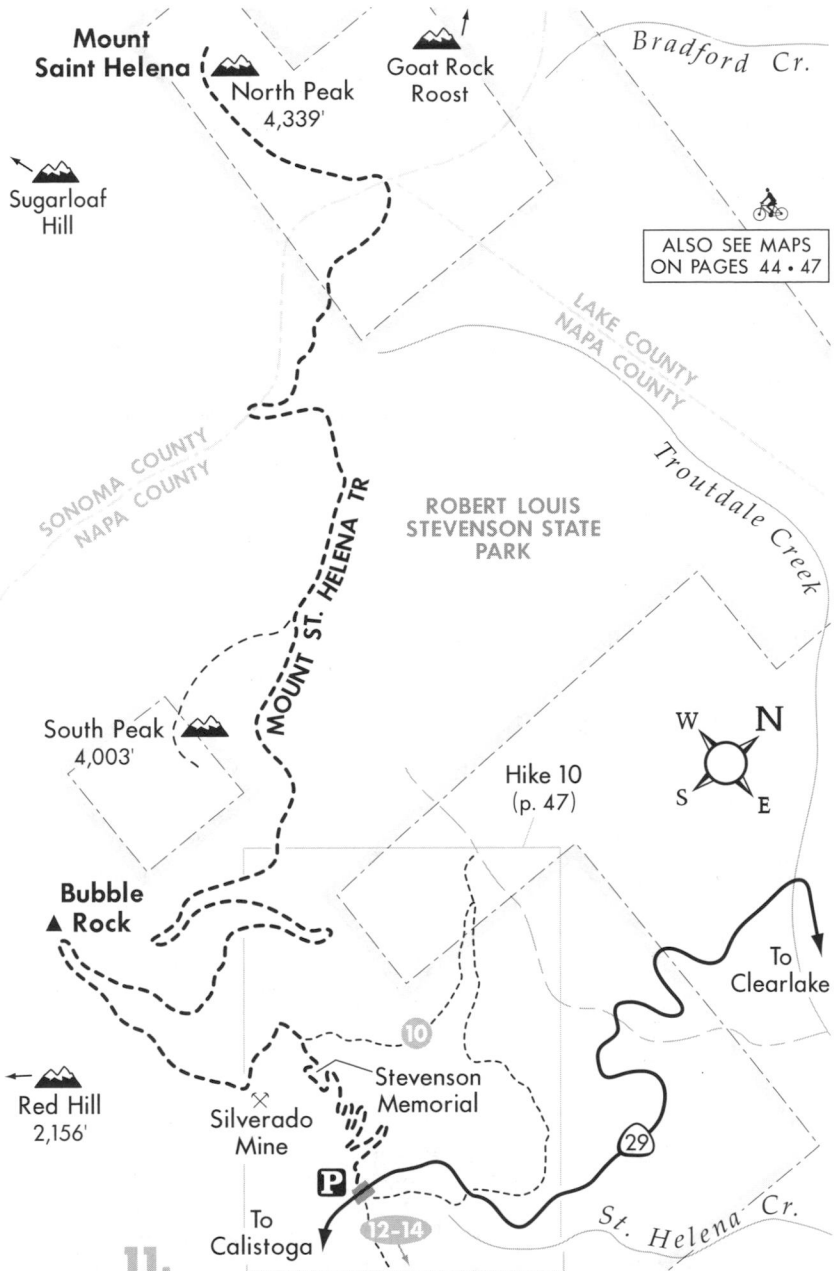

11.
Mount Saint Helena Trail
ROBERT LOUIS STEVENSON STATE PARK

12. Table Rock Trail
ROBERT LOUIS STEVENSON STATE PARK

Hiking distance: 4.4 miles round trip
Hiking time: 2 hours
Elevation gain: 500 feet
Dogs: not allowed
Maps: U.S.G.S. Detert Reservoir
　　　　Bothe-Napa Valley/Robert Louis Stevenson State Parks

Summary of hike: Hikes 12—14 head east through Robert Louis Stevenson State Park from the summit at Highway 29. The hikes are three segments of the entire trail from the Table Rock trailhead to the Historic Oat Hill Mine Road. This first segment— the Table Rock Trail—follows an abandoned utility road and a single-tread path. The trail leads 2.2 miles through the forest to spectacular overlooks, crossing a ridge to prominent Table Rock. The massive formation sits at the head of Garnett Canyon at an elevation of 2,462 feet. It is the largest rock mass in the area.

Driving directions: From Highway 29/Lincoln Avenue in downtown Calistoga, drive 8.5 miles northeast on Lincoln Avenue (Highway 29) through town and up the winding mountain road. Park in the parking area on the right at the road's summit. It is directly across the trailhead parking lot for Mount St. Helena.

Hiking directions: Pass the Table Rock Trail sign, and head up the forested hillside to an old dirt road. Bear left to the end of the road to an overlook of Saint Helena Creek Canyon and the surrounding mountains at 0.4 miles. Veer right on the trail through a mixed forest of oaks, Douglas fir, maple, and bay laurel while the vistas extend into Napa Valley. Steadily climb to the posted Bear Rock Overlook at one mile, with an eastward view into Bear Valley. Go right and descend a hundred yards, passing gorgeous rock outcroppings. Descend on the loose gravel path, using careful footing. Continue through a flat in a garden of lava rock on a rock-lined path. The trail heads downhill on another steep section to seasonal Garnett Creek. Cross the creek and ascend the

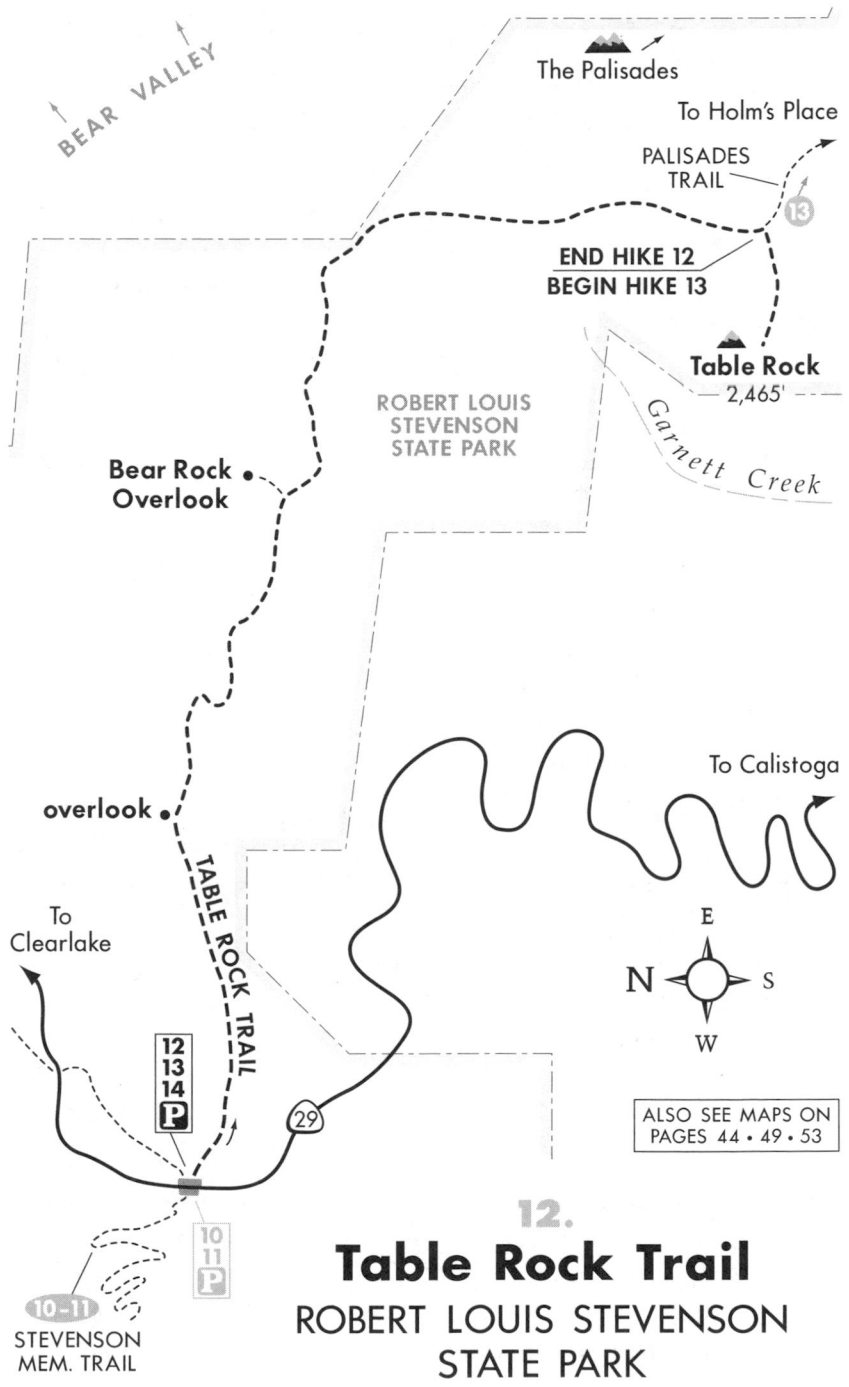

BEAR VALLEY

The Palisades

To Holm's Place

PALISADES TRAIL

13

END HIKE 12
BEGIN HIKE 13

Table Rock
— 2,465' — —

ROBERT LOUIS
STEVENSON
STATE PARK

Garnett Creek

Bear Rock
Overlook

overlook

To Calistoga

To
Clearlake

TABLE ROCK TRAIL

12
13
14
P

29

E
N — S
W

ALSO SEE MAPS ON
PAGES 44 • 49 • 53

10
11
P

10-11
STEVENSON
MEM. TRAIL

12.
Table Rock Trail
ROBERT LOUIS STEVENSON
STATE PARK

hillside to another natural display of volcanic rock sculptures. Climb through the rocks to a signed junction with the Palisades Trail on the left at 2.1 miles. Detour 0.2 miles to the right, staying on the Table Rock Trail. Scramble up the loosely defined path to the edge of the volcanic cliffs atop Table Rock. After taking in the views, return to the Palisades Trail junction, the turn-around point for this hike.

To extend the hike on the Palisades Trail, continue with Hike 13, the next hike.■

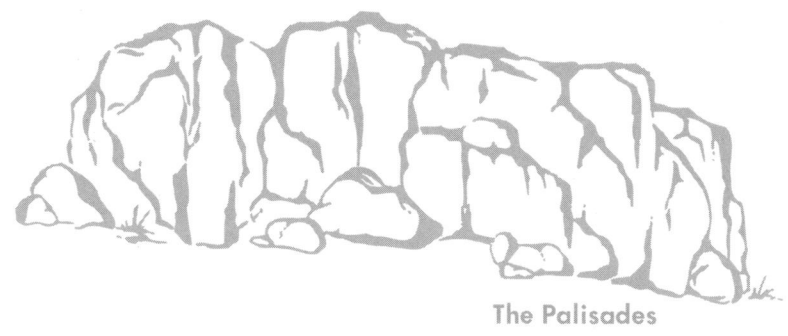

The Palisades

13. Table Rock Trail—Palisades Trail to Holm's Place
ROBERT LOUIS STEVENSON STATE PARK

Hiking distance: 12 miles round trip
Hiking time: 7 hours
Elevation gain: 700 feet
Dogs: not allowed
Maps: U.S.G.S. Detert Reservoir and Calistoga
Bothe-Napa Valley/Robert Louis Stevenson State Parks

Summary of hike: The rugged Palisades (cover photo) are precipitous volcanic cliffs that stretch southeast from Mount Saint Helena. The Palisades property was acquired in 1993, raising the Robert Louis Stevenson State Park acreage to 5,272 acres. The Palisades Trail, arguably among the best hikes in Napa County,

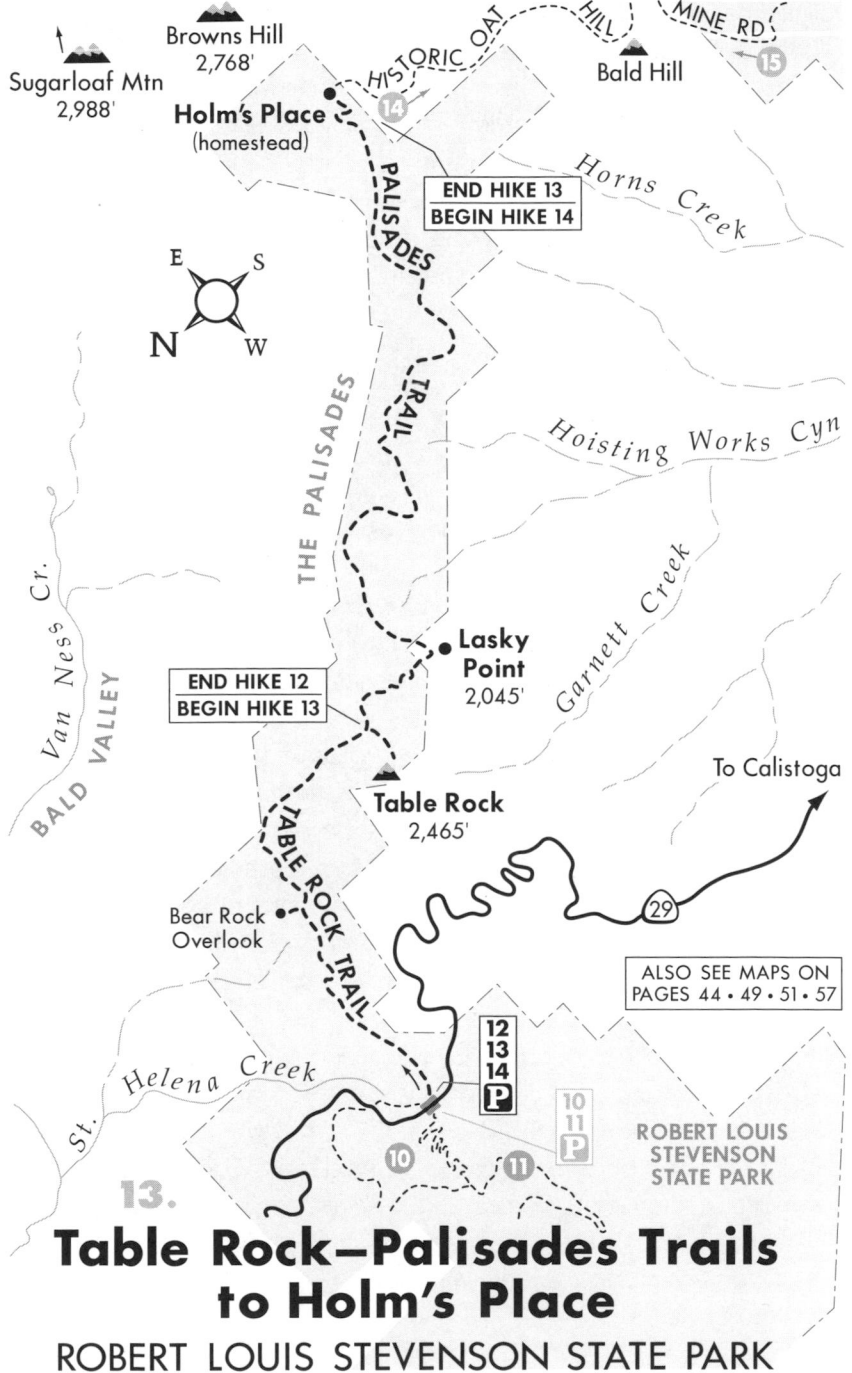

Sugarloaf Mtn
2,988'

Browns Hill
2,768'

HISTORIC OAT HILL

MINE RD
15

Holm's Place
(homestead)

14

Bald Hill

Horns Creek

PALISADES

END HIKE 13
BEGIN HIKE 14

E
S
N
W

THE PALISADES

TRAIL

Hoisting Works Cyn

Van Ness Cr.

BALD VALLEY

Lasky
Point
2,045'

Garnett Creek

END HIKE 12
BEGIN HIKE 13

TABLE ROCK TRAIL

Table Rock
2,465'

To Calistoga

Bear Rock
Overlook

29

ALSO SEE MAPS ON
PAGES 44 • 49 • 51 • 57

St. Helena Creek

12
13
14
P

10
11
P

10

11

ROBERT LOUIS
STEVENSON
STATE PARK

13.
Table Rock—Palisades Trails
to Holm's Place
ROBERT LOUIS STEVENSON STATE PARK

links the Table Rock Trail (Hike 12) with the Historic Oat Hill Mine Road (Hikes 14 and 15). The trail begins by Table Rock at the east end of the Table Rock Trail and ends at Karl Holm's homestead among old foundations, remnants of two stone houses, and a small apple orchard. En route, the trail skirts the base of the dramatic volcanic cliffs, passing awesome rocky outcroppings and cliffs on the sun-exposed slope. Peregrine falcons are frequently spotted from the trail. Bring an ample supply of drinking water, as the long hike can be hot.

Driving directions: Same as Hike 12.

Hiking directions: Begin from the end of Hike 12—at the signed Palisades Trail–Table Rock Trail junction at 2.1 miles. Take the Palisades Trail and head uphill, with views of Table Rock and Mt. Saint Helena. Emerge on the west-facing slope overlooking Napa Valley, the Mayacamas Mountains, and the Sonoma County coastal range. Zigzag down the steep hillside with the aid of rock steps. Temporarily leave the state park, and enter the Lasky Property on a quarter-mile trail easement. The trail leads to 2,045-foot Lasky Point at 2.7 miles, where there is a bird's-eye view of Calistoga. A plaque in the volcanic rock thanks Moses Lasky, a mountain climber and owner of the land, for sharing his land with hikers. Continue traversing the mountain, and reenter Robert Louis Stevenson State Park on the southwest face of the mountain. Follow the contours of the mountain, with awesome views of The Palisades, Garnett Canyon, and Napa Valley. Alternate between exposed grassy chaparral and stream-fed forested pockets with moss-covered boulders. At 4.6 miles, pass close to the towering lava formations and a few trickling streams. Walk under an overhanging rock grotto to a view of the Historic Oat Hill Mine Road (Hike 15), traversing the east-west cliffs. Descend on two switchbacks amid mossy boulders to the remains of the Holm's homestead in a shaded oak and bay laurel forest at 6 miles. This is the turn-around point for Hike 13.

If you are hiking the one-way shuttle, continue with Hike 14, the next hike.■

14. Table Rock—Palisades—Oat Hill Mine
ONE-WAY SHUTTLE HIKE
ROBERT LOUIS STEVENSON STATE PARK

Hiking distance: 10.6-mile one-way shuttle
Hiking time: 6 hours
Elevation gain: 700 feet
Elevation loss: 1,900 feet
Dogs: not allowed
Maps: U.S.G.S. Detert Reservoir and Calistoga
    Bothe-Napa Valley/Robert Louis Stevenson State Parks

map
page 57

Summary of hike: This one-way shuttle hike combines Hikes 12, 13 and 15. The trail begins eight miles north of Calistoga at the summit of Highway 29 and ends on the edge of Calistoga, less than a half mile from downtown. The hike combines the Table Rock Trail, the Palisades Trail, and the Historic Oat Hill Mine Road. Highlights of the trail include the Bear Rock Overlook, a garden of lava rock and volcanic cliffs, Garnett Creek, Table Rock, Lasky Point, a rock grotto, and the old Holm's Place homestead. This hike follows the sun-exposed slope and requires ample drinking water.

Driving directions: From Highway 29/Lincoln Avenue in downtown Calistoga, drive 8.5 miles northeast on Lincoln Avenue (Highway 29) through town and up the winding mountain road. Park in the parking area on the right at the road's summit. It is directly across from the trailhead parking lot to Mount St. Helena.

SHUTTLE CAR: Leave the shuttle car at the intersection of Lincoln Avenue (Highway 29) and Silverado Trail, located a half mile north of downtown Calistoga. (Follow the driving directions to Hike 15.)

Hiking directions: Follow the hiking directions for Hikes 12 and 13. Begin this hike from the 6-mile point by Holm's Place—at the end of Hike 13. From the remains of the stone houses in the shaded oak and bay laurel forest, walk gently downhill. Veer right on the rock-embedded path through the beautiful lava formations and sweeping views of The Palisades. Steadily descend along the towering rock wall on the left. Curve left and cross the ridge, continuing downhill on the brushy slope overlooking Napa Valley. Watch for wagon wheel ruts embedded in the slab rock. Skirt the east side of Bald Hill, overlooking forested Simmons Canyon. Loop clockwise around Bald Hill through oak groves, evergreens, and manzanita. Near the bottom are views of Calistoga, vineyards, and the sounds of civilization. Pass the gated trailhead at the junction of Highway 29 and Silverado Trail, a half mile north of downtown Calistoga. ■

15. Historic Oat Hill Mine Road to Holm's Place
ROBERT LOUIS STEVENSON STATE PARK

Hiking distance: 9 miles round trip
Hiking time: 5 hours
Elevation gain: 1,900 feet
Dogs: not allowed
Maps: U.S.G.S. Calistoga
Bothe-Napa Valley / Robert Louis Stevenson State Parks

map
page 59

Summary of hike: The Historic Oat Hill Mine Road is an old mining road between the town of Calistoga and Pope Valley. This hiking-biking section of the trail is the reverse of the Hike 14 shuttle, for those who wish to walk only this end of the trail up to Holm's Place. The remote county-built road, completed in 1893, was used by freight wagons hauling quicksilver from the mines to the railroad in Calistoga. Grooves in the rockbed from the wagon wheels are still visible. The rocky, rutted road (closed in 1979) rigorously climbs from 400 feet to 2,300 feet. The road leads to Holm's Place—the old Karl Holm homestead in a shaded oak and bay laurel forest. At the 160-acre homestead are remnants of two stone houses and a small apple orchard. The scenic,

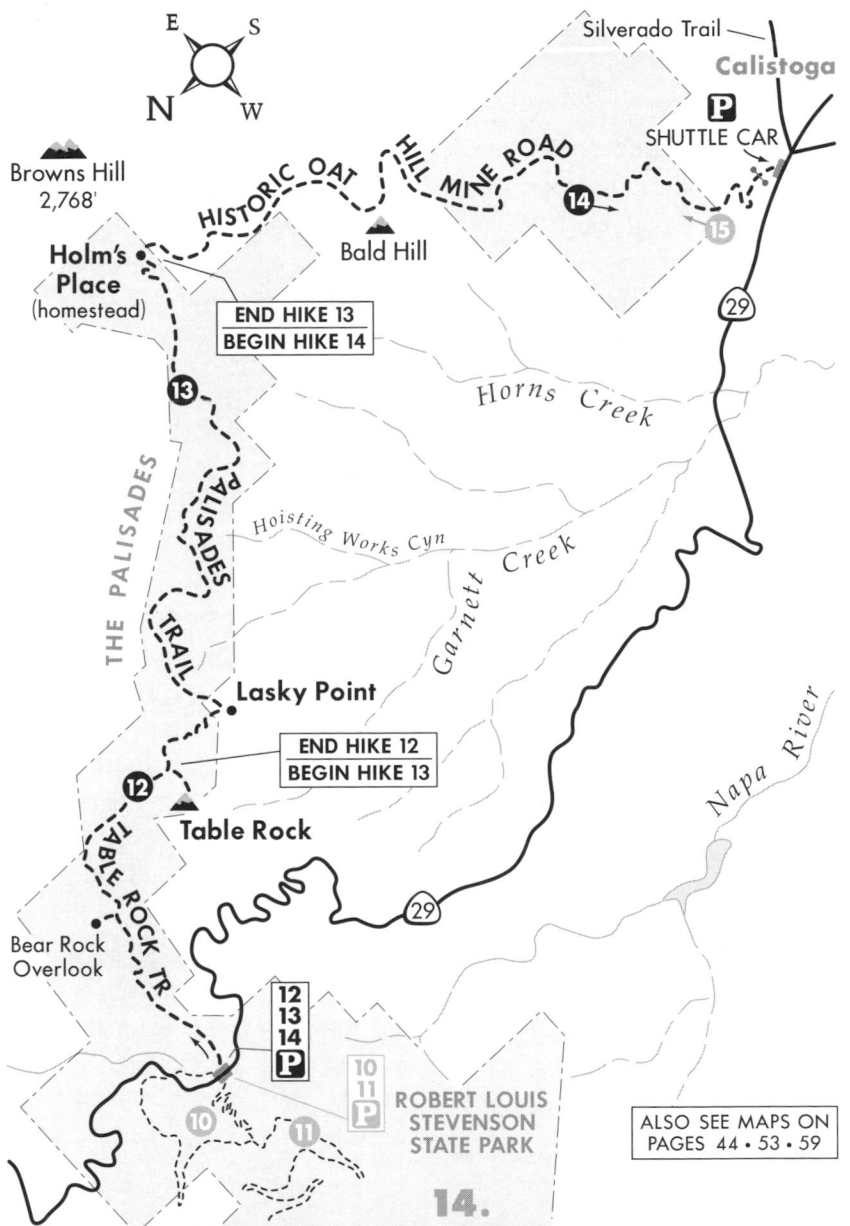

ALSO SEE MAPS ON
PAGES 44 · 53 · 59

14.

Table Rock–Palisades–
Oat Hill Mine shuttle
ROBERT LOUIS STEVENSON STATE PARK

backcountry road offers great views of The Palisades (cover photo) and upper Napa Valley. The trail is open to bicyclists to Holm's Place. Pack lots of drinking water.

Driving directions: From Highway 29/Lincoln Avenue in downtown Calistoga, drive one mile northeast on Lincoln Avenue (Highway 29) through town to Silverado Trail. Drive through the intersection and park in the spaces on the right at the trailhead. If the few parking spaces are taken, park in the large dirt area on the diagonal side of the intersection by Lake Street.

Hiking directions: Walk past the trail sign and metal gate. Gently climb the slope, parallel to Highway 29. Curve away from the highway under a canopy of oaks, pines, and toyon to vistas of vineyards and the town of Calistoga. Continue climbing, curving around the contours of the hill, as the vistas down Napa Valley constantly change. Steadily climb through oak groves, stands of evergreens, and manzanita that repose a thousand feet above Simmons Canyon. Loop around Bald Hill on a brush-lined slope, where old wagon wheel ruts were once carved into the rocky road. Cross a ridge and continue uphill along the towering rock wall on the right. The rock-embedded path heads through beautiful lava formations and sweeping views of The Palisades. The trail leads 4.5 miles to the remnants of two stone houses and a barn at Holm's Place, the old homestead of Karl Holm in a shady oak and bay laurel forest.

To extend the hike to an overlook of the Historic Oat Hill Mine Road, the trail climbs two switchbacks amid mossy boulders on the Palisades Trail. The Palisades Trail then continues 3.3 miles to Lasky Point, 3.9 miles to Table Rock, and 6 miles to the Table Rock Trailhead. (Reference Hikes 12 and 13.) ■

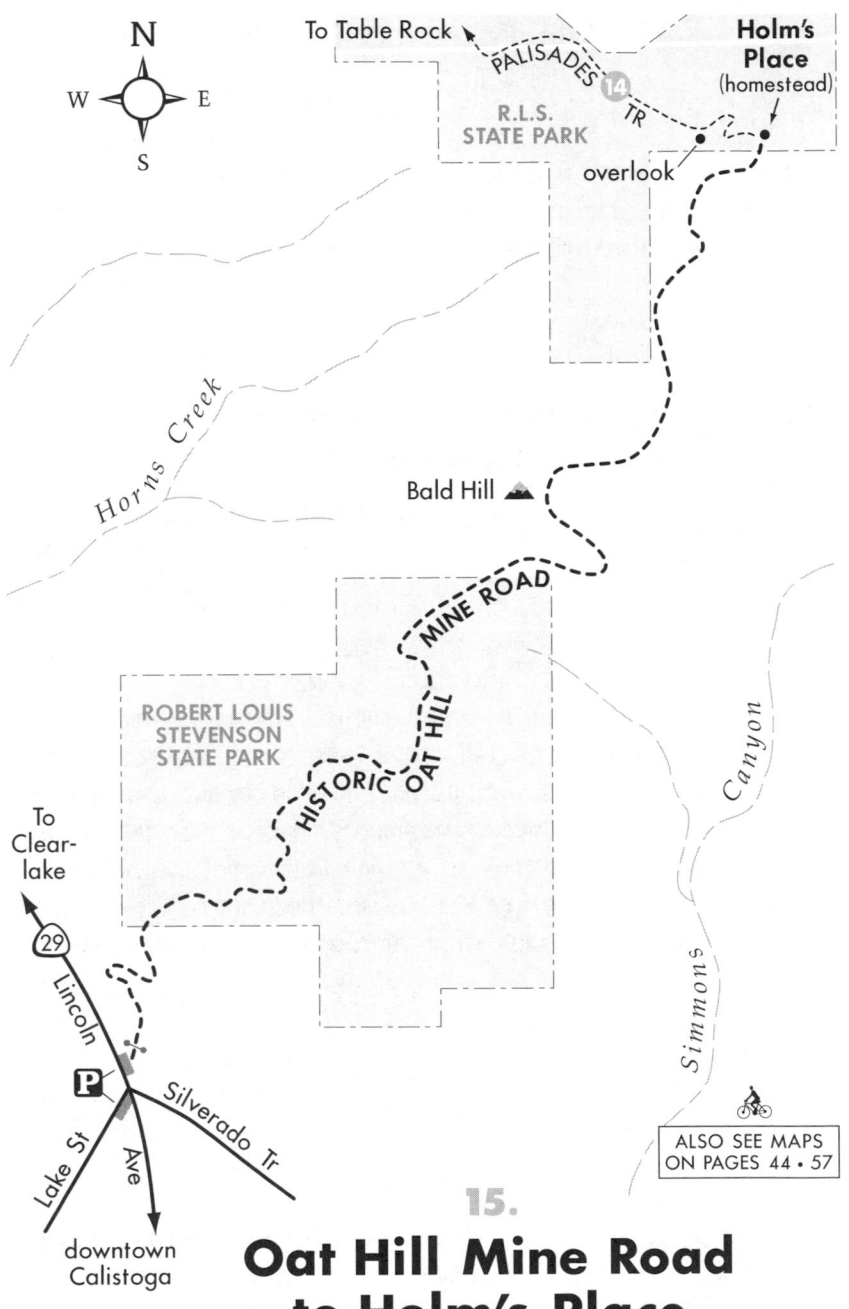

N
W E
S

To Table Rock
Holm's Place (homestead)

PALISADES TR

14

R.L.S. STATE PARK

overlook

Horns Creek

Bald Hill

MINE ROAD

ROBERT LOUIS STEVENSON STATE PARK

HISTORIC OAT HILL

Canyon

To Clear-lake

29

Lincoln

Simmons

P

Silverado Tr

Lake St

Ave

ALSO SEE MAPS ON PAGES 44 • 57

downtown Calistoga

15.

Oat Hill Mine Road to Holm's Place

ROBERT LOUIS STEVENSON STATE PARK

16. The Petrified Forest

4100 Petrified Forest Road · Calistoga
Open Daily: Winter 9—5 · Summer 9—7 · (707) 942-6667

Hiking distance: 0.5-mile loop plus 0.5-mile spur trail
Hiking time: 40 minutes
Elevation gain: 100 feet
Dogs: allowed
Maps: U.S.G.S. Mark West Springs
The Petrified Forest trail map

Summary of hike: The Petrified Forest is a massive forest of stone trees in the hills of eastern Sonoma County near Calistoga. Sitting at an elevation of 1,000 feet, the fossilized redwood forest resulted from volcanic ash blanketing the area 3.4 million years ago. The trees all point in a southwest direction, but researchers cannot agree on the origin of the magma blast. The buried trees were saturated with water containing silica. The silica seeped into the decomposing wood fibers, slowly replacing the organic material cell by cell. It eventually led to their petrifaction, resulting in one of the best Pliocene fossil forests in the world.

In the 1870s, Charlie Evans, a friend of Jack London and Robert Louis Stevenson, discovered the geological wonder while tending his cows. He became known as Petrified Charlie. Uplift, erosion, and excavation have exposed the giant petrified redwoods, creating the natural museum we see today. Within the spectacular fossils are deposits of minerals, crystal, obsidian, wood opal, and silica. Out of the rock trees grow oaks, Douglas firs, red-bark manzanitas, bay laurels, toyons, and madrones.

A half-mile trail loops through the natural displays of all the major tree exposures. Interpretive signs describe the preservation process of how living trees evolve into stone. On weekend mornings, a guided Meadow Walk is available. This extended hike leads to an area closed to the public. It departs from The Giant and heads northwest through a locked gate into the upper meadow. The trail visits an overlook of Mount Saint Helena and the 100-foot-high Ash Fall. The ash fall is rich with volcanic material, including tuff, iron, obsidian, pumice, and petrified wood chunks. The walk can extend to a fern and redwood forest by a tributary of Mark West Springs. Call for tour times.

The privately owned park, declared a Historical Landmark in 1978, includes a museum, gift shop, and picnic areas. Leashed dogs are allowed on the trails.

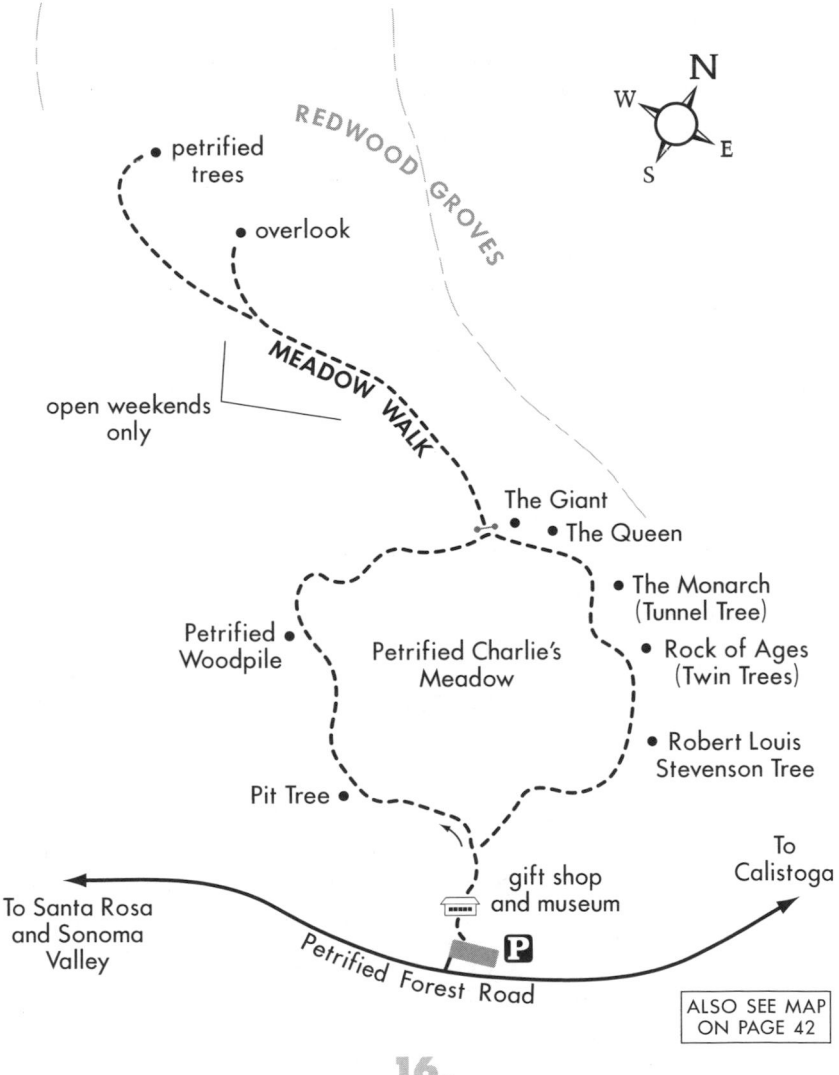

ALSO SEE MAP ON PAGE 42

16.

The Petrified Forest

Driving directions: From Lincoln Avenue and Highway 128 in Calistoga, drive one mile northwest on Highway 128 to Petrified Forest Road. Turn left and continue 3.8 miles to the signed entrance on the right. An entrance fee is required.

Hiking directions: Walk through the gift shop to the trailhead by the massive trunk of an 850-year-old coastal live oak that blew over in 2004. Veer left onto the trail, passing the 43-foot-long Pit Tree on the left, the only petrified pine in the park. Up ahead is Petrified Woodpile, a pile of broken fragments covered with moss and embedded with lichen. Stroll through the mixed evergreen forest among oak, pine, fir, and madrone. At the top of the trail, across from Petrified Charlie's Meadow, are a group of well-preserved petrified redwoods with viewing platforms. Among these are The Giant, a 60-foot-long tree with deeply ribbed bark, and the Queen, with an 8-foot diameter and a giant root ball. The Queen has a live oak growing through it. Pass an area where new excavation has exposed two more fossilized trees. Walk through the 105-foot-long Monarch (Tunnel Tree) on the left, the largest known intact petrified tree in the world. Next is the Rock of Ages Tree, a double tree that is also known as Twin Trees. The last major tree on the loop is the Robert Louis Stevenson Tree, mentioned by the author in the book *The Silverado Squatters*. Descend the slope and complete the loop back at the gift shop.

The Meadow Walk meets at The Giant on weekend mornings. With a guide, walk through the locked gate. Weave through manzanita and madrone groves, oak-lined meadows, and past outcroppings from the ancient lava flows to a knoll. From the knoll is a great view of Mount Saint Helena. If your guide is willing, continue past the knoll to an ash flow with lava, pumice, obsidian, and bits of petrified wood. Two hundred yards ahead, on the backside of the hill, are undisturbed petrified trees still in place. A nature trail continues a half mile north into the shaded forest to the fern-covered canyon floor and a stand of redwood trees by a seasonal drainage of Mark West Springs. ▪

17. Coyote Peak
Redwood—Coyote—Ritchey Canyon Trails
BOTHE—NAPA VALLEY STATE PARK

Hiking distance: 4.5-mile loop
Hiking time: 2.5 hours
Elevation gain: 850 feet
Dogs: not allowed
Maps: U.S.G.S. Calistoga
Bothe-Napa Valley/Robert Louis Stevenson State Parks

map
page 65

Summary of hike: Bothe—Napa Valley State Park (pronounced *bo-thay*) sits in the heart of Napa Valley between Calistoga and Saint Helena. The rugged state park was founded in 1960. Before 1960, the park was a private resort owned by Reinhold Bothe. The diverse geography includes heavily forested north-facing slopes and canyons, while the sunny south-facing slopes are covered with brush, oaks, and manzanita. The easternmost stands of coastal redwoods grow in the lush riparian habitats near the creeks and springs. This hike begins in lower Ritchey Canyon along Ritchey Creek under big-leaf maples, oaks, madrones, and redwoods (Hike 18). The Coyote Peak Trail leaves the creek and moderately climbs to the 1,170-foot summit of Coyote Peak. En route to the tree-covered peak are views of Napa Valley and upper Ritchey Canyon.

Driving directions: Bothe-Napa Valley State Park is located along Highway 29 between Calistoga and St. Helena.

FROM HIGHWAY 29/LINCOLN AVENUE IN CALISTOGA: Drive 3.5 miles south on Highway 29 to the posted state park entrance on the right. Turn right and drive 0.4 miles to the posted Ritchey Creek Trailhead and parking area on the right.

FROM HIGHWAY 29 IN ST. HELENA: Drive 4.5 miles north on Highway 29 to the posted state park entrance on the left. Turn left and drive 0.4 miles to the posted Ritchey Creek Trailhead and parking area on the right.

Hiking directions: Pass the trailhead sign and enter the forest. Cross a service road to the banks of Ritchey Creek. Curve left, heading upstream, and follow the south side of the creek to a trail split at 0.4 miles. The Ritchey Canyon Trail crosses the creek to the right, our return route. Begin the loop to the left on the Redwood Trail, across the creek from the campground. Traverse the moist, north-facing slope with an understory of ferns, thimbleberry, and wild rose bushes. The signed Coyote Peak Trail is on the left at 0.9 miles. Bear left and head up the picturesque stream-fed side canyon. Weave through the shady side canyon, and cross the drainage on a U-shaped right bend. Steadily gain elevation, contouring around the slope of the peak. Traverse the hillside path among California bays to a clearing and a trail split. Detour left on the rock-embedded path 0.1 miles to Coyote Peak, a rounded summit with a tree-obscured view. En route are views into Ritchey Canyon, with the tops of the redwoods towering over the forest canopy, and a northern view of Mount Saint Helena.

After resting, return to the trail junction, and descend into Ritchey Canyon. Rock hop over a tributary stream and stroll through a redwood grove to a posted T-junction with the South Fork Trail at 2.4 miles. The trail is an old skid road used by early loggers to haul out the redwoods. The right fork returns for a shorter loop. For this hike, bear left and traverse the hillside. Atop a minor ridge, an unmarked side path on the right detours 60 yards to an overlook of Ritchey Canyon. Continue the descent down the South Fork Trail to a junction with the Spring Trail. The left fork leads up canyon to the Traverso Homestead (Hike 20). Bear right on the serpentine road, and gently descend through the forest. Cross a concrete spillway over the creek to the Redwood Trail on the right. Continue straight ahead on the Vineyard Trail along the edge of Ritchey Creek. At a Y-fork, the Vineyard Trail veers left. Curve to the right on the Ritchey Canyon Trail, and follow the north side of the creek. Pass the creek crossing on the right that connects to the Redwood Trail. Continue straight, reaching the Hitchcock homesite on the right by a wood barn with a tin roof. Pass a campground access path on the left, and ford the creek to the right, completing the loop. Bear left and return 0.4 miles to the trailhead.■

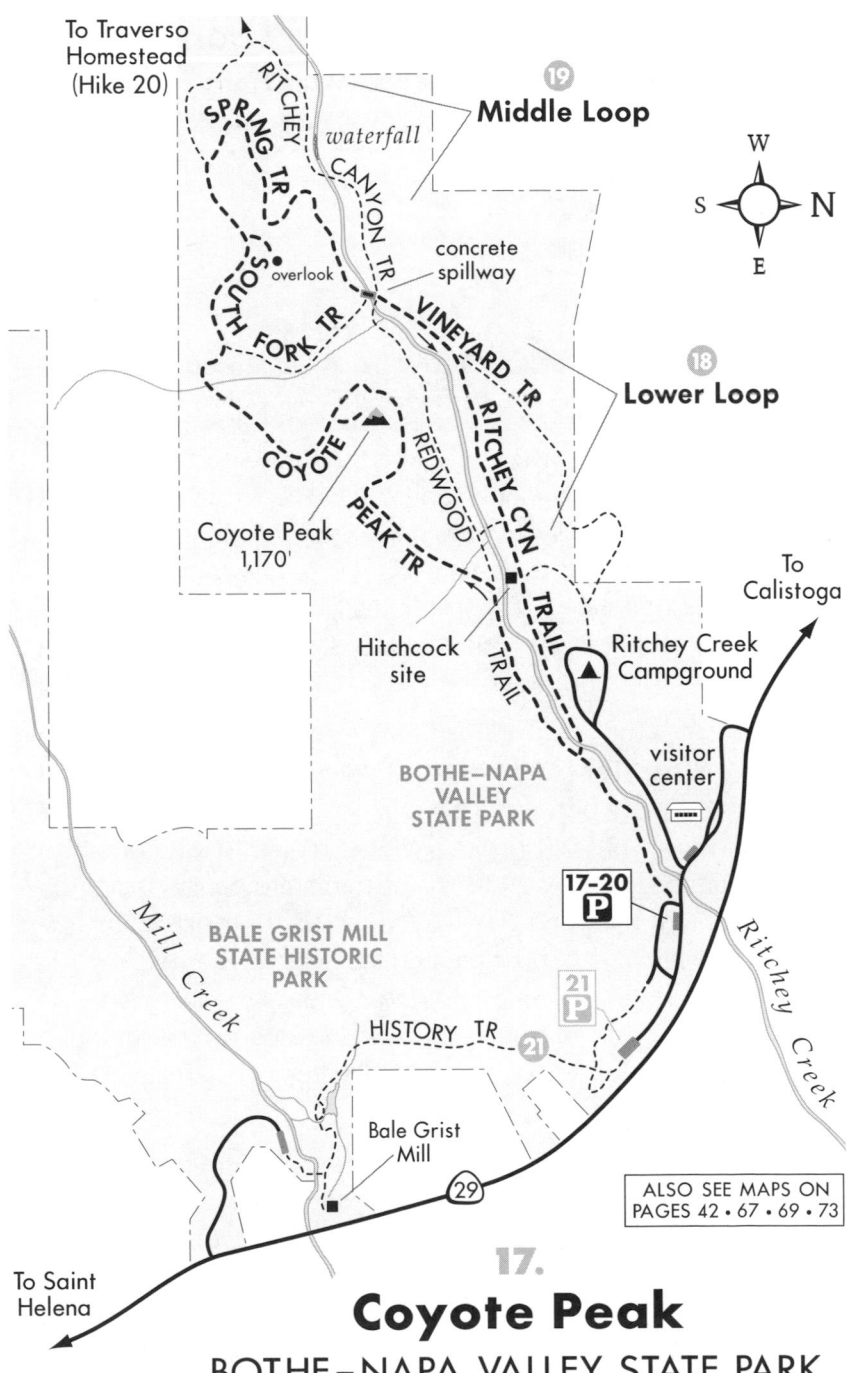

To Traverso Homestead (Hike 20)

RITCHEY SPRING TR.

waterfall

⑲ **Middle Loop**

SOUTH FORK TR.

overlook

CANYON TR.

concrete spillway

VINEYARD TR.

⑱ **Lower Loop**

COYOTE

REDWOOD

RITCHEY CYN.

PEAK TR.

Coyote Peak 1,170'

Hitchcock site

TRAIL

TRAIL

To Calistoga

Ritchey Creek Campground

visitor center

BOTHE–NAPA VALLEY STATE PARK

17-20 P

BALE GRIST MILL STATE HISTORIC PARK

Mill Creek

Ritchey Creek

21 P

HISTORY TR.

㉑

Bale Grist Mill

㉙

ALSO SEE MAPS ON PAGES 42 • 67 • 69 • 73

To Saint Helena

17.

Coyote Peak
BOTHE–NAPA VALLEY STATE PARK

W N E S

18. Lower Ritchey Canyon Loop
Redwood—Ritchey Canyon Trails
BOTHE—NAPA VALLEY STATE PARK

Hiking distance: 3-mile loop
Hiking time: 1.5 hours
Elevation gain: 400 feet
Dogs: not allowed
Maps: U.S.G.S. Calistoga
Bothe—Napa Valley/Robert Louis Stevenson State Parks

Summary of hike: The 1,900-acre Bothe—Napa Valley State Park stretches along perennial Ritchey Creek and Mill Creek, reaching west into Sonoma County. The popular park offers camping, picnicking, swimming, horseback riding, and hiking on more than 10 miles of trails. Hikes 18—20 follow the lush riparian habitat along Ritchey Creek, a tributary of the Napa River, in a redwood-lined drainage. This hike loops around the lower portion of the park and visits the old Hitchcock homesite, dating back to the 1870s.

Driving directions: Bothe—Napa Valley State Park is located along Highway 29 between Calistoga and Saint Helena.
FROM HIGHWAY 29/LINCOLN AVENUE IN CALISTOGA: Drive 3.5 miles south on Highway 29 to the posted state park entrance on the right. Turn right and drive 0.4 miles to the posted Ritchey Creek Trailhead and parking area on the right.
FROM HIGHWAY 29 IN ST. HELENA: Drive 4.5 miles north on Highway 29 to the posted state park entrance on the left. Turn left and drive 0.4 miles to the posted Ritchey Creek Trailhead and parking area on the right.

Hiking directions: Pass the trailhead sign and enter the forest. Cross a service road to the banks of Ritchey Creek. Curve left, heading upstream, and follow the south side of the creek to a trail split at 0.4 miles. The Ritchey Canyon Trail crosses the creek to the right, our return route. Begin the loop to the left on the Redwood Trail, across the creek from the campground. Traverse

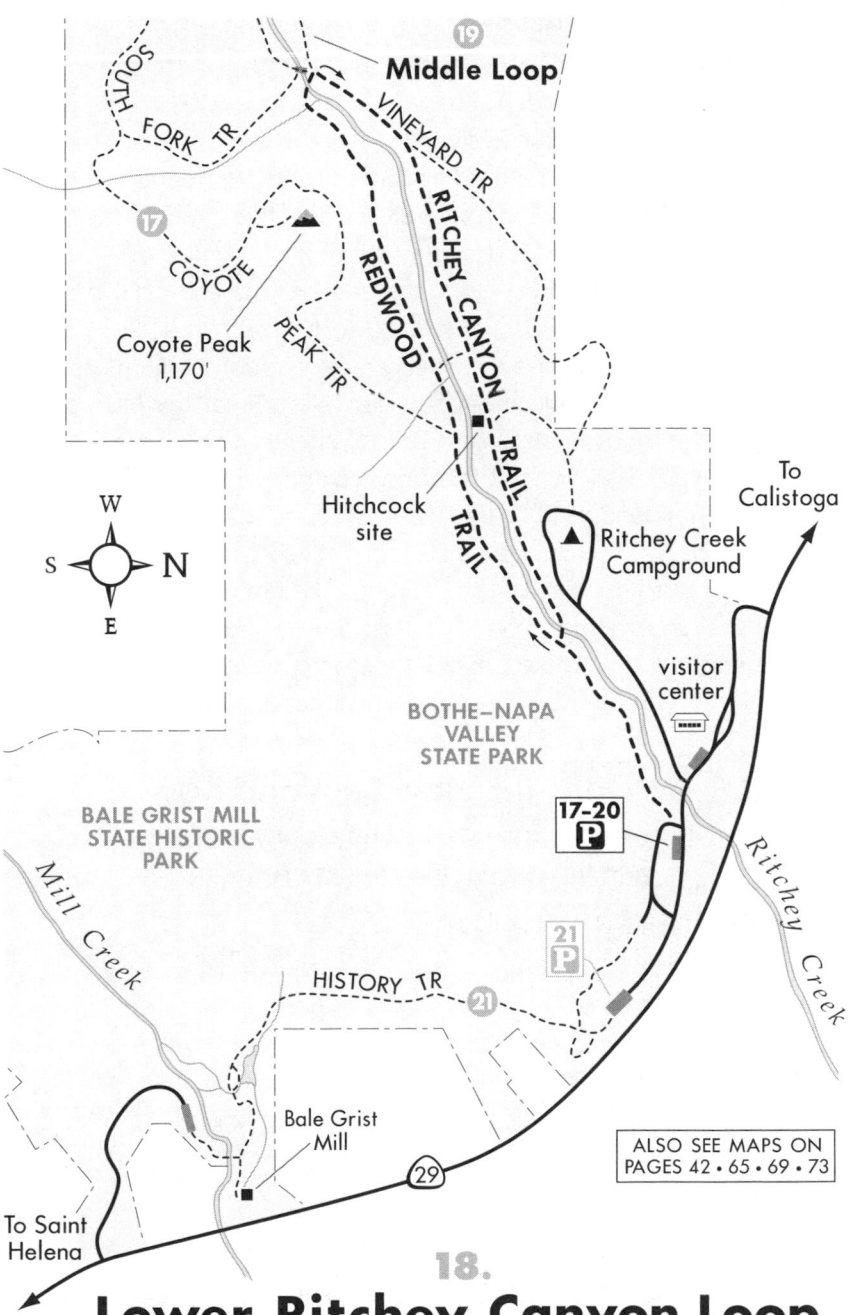

19 **Middle Loop**

SOUTH FORK TR

VINEYARD TR

RITCHEY CANYON TRAIL

17

COYOTE

REDWOOD TRAIL

PEAK TR

Coyote Peak
1,170'

Hitchcock
site

To
Calistoga

▲ Ritchey Creek
Campground

W
S — N
E

visitor
center

BOTHE–NAPA
VALLEY
STATE PARK

**BALE GRIST MILL
STATE HISTORIC
PARK**

Mill Creek

17-20
P

21
P

Ritchey Creek

HISTORY TR 21

Bale Grist
Mill

ALSO SEE MAPS ON
PAGES 42 • 65 • 69 • 73

29

To Saint
Helena

18.

Lower Ritchey Canyon Loop
BOTHE–NAPA VALLEY STATE PARK

the moist, north-facing slope to a second fork at 0.9 miles. The 1.5-mile Coyote Peak Trail veers left and climbs 700 feet through upland forest and chaparral to a 1,170-foot peak (Hike 17). Stay in the lush canyon on the Redwood Trail. Cross a tributary stream, and walk 100 yards to a third junction on the right—a connector trail to the Ritchey Canyon Trail across the creek. Continue straight, staying on the hiking-only section of the Redwood Trail. Weave through the forest along the creek as the canyon narrows. The Redwood Trail ends in a shaded redwood forest. Rock hop over Ritchey Creek to a dirt road and a junction at 1.5 miles. To extend the hike, continue on the Hike 19 loop. For this hike, bear right on the Vineyard Trail, and follow Ritchey Creek to a Y-fork. The Vineyard Trail veers left. Curve to the right on the Ritchey Canyon Trail, and follow the north side of the creek. Pass the creek crossing on the right that connects to the Redwood Trail. Continue straight, reaching the Hitchcock home site on the right by a wood barn with a tin roof. Pass a campground access path on the left, and ford the creek to the right, completing the loop. Bear left and return 0.4 miles to the trailhead.∎

19. Middle Ritchey Canyon Loop
Redwood—Spring—Ritchey Canyon Trails
BOTHE—NAPA VALLEY STATE PARK

Hiking distance: 4.5-mile double loop
Hiking time: 2.5 hours
Elevation gain: 850 feet
Dogs: not allowed
Maps: U.S.G.S. Calistoga
Bothe—Napa Valley/Robert Louis Stevenson State Parks

Summary of hike: Bothe—Napa Valley State Park lies along rugged volcanic terrain ranging from 300 to 2,000 feet, producing diverse vegetation. The northern slopes and canyons are filled with an evergreen and hardwood forest. The southern, exposed slopes are covered with chaparral and brush. Ritchey Creek flows through the heart of the state park. A network of trails fol-

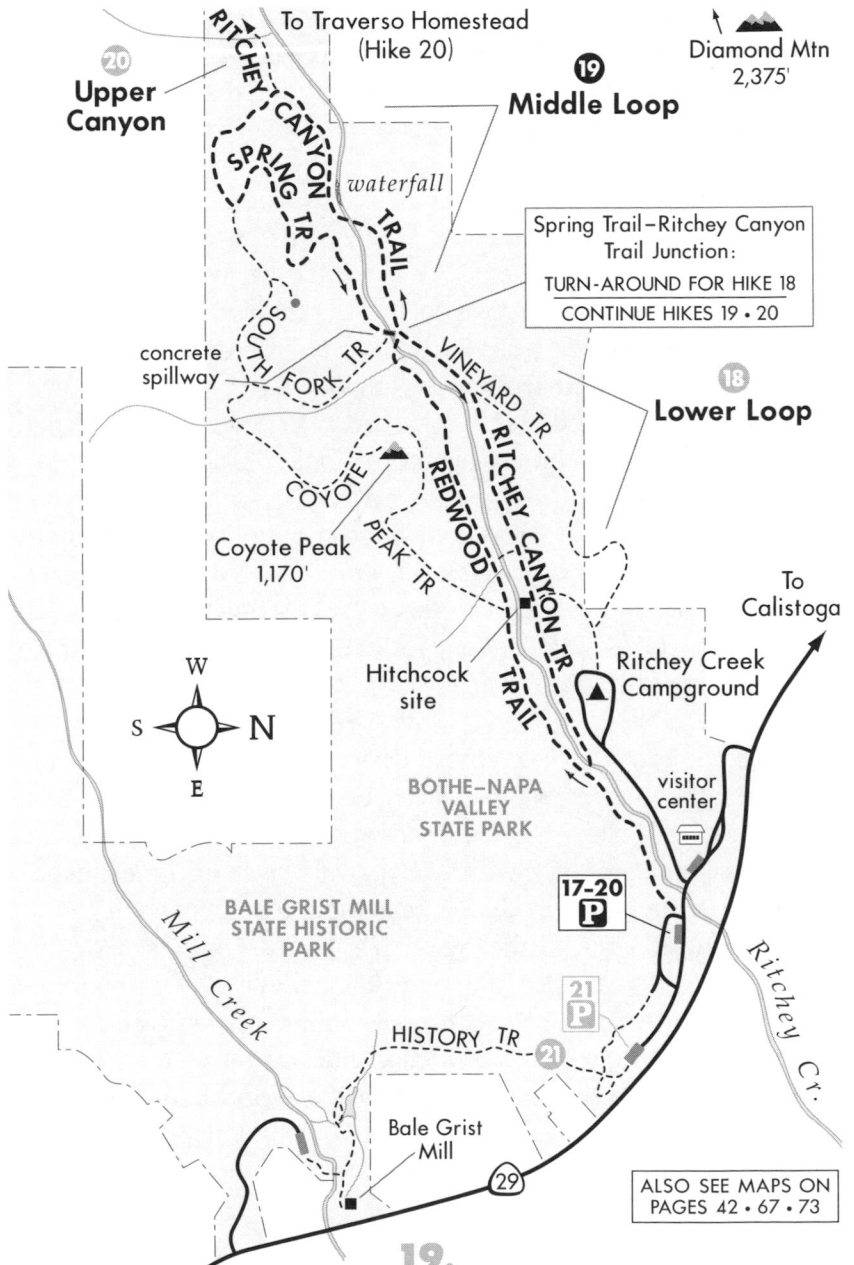

To Traverso Homestead
(Hike 20)

⑳ Upper Canyon

Diamond Mtn
2,375'

⑲ Middle Loop

waterfall

RITCHEY CANYON TRAIL

SPRING TR.

concrete spillway

SOUTH FORK TR.

VINEYARD TR.

Spring Trail–Ritchey Canyon
Trail Junction:
TURN-AROUND FOR HIKE 18
CONTINUE HIKES 19 · 20

⑱ Lower Loop

COYOTE PEAK TR.

REDWOOD TRAIL

RITCHEY CANYON TRAIL

Coyote Peak
1,170'

Hitchcock
site

Ritchey Creek
Campground

To Calistoga

visitor center

BOTHE–NAPA
VALLEY
STATE PARK

W · N · E · S

BALE GRIST MILL
STATE HISTORIC
PARK

Mill Creek

17-20 P

21 P

HISTORY TR.

㉑

Bale Grist
Mill

㉙

Ritchey Cr.

ALSO SEE MAPS ON
PAGES 42 · 67 · 73

19.

Middle Ritchey Canyon Loop
BOTHE–NAPA VALLEY STATE PARK

lows the riparian corridor through stands of coastal redwoods and ferns. This hike climbs into the secluded middle canyon and explores a sampling of the park's natural features. The hike continues from the lower canyon—Hike 18.

Driving directions: Same as Hike 18.

Hiking directions: Take the Redwood Trail, following the hiking directions for Hike 18. Continue to the junction with the Spring Trail and Ritchey Canyon Trail at 1.5 miles (noted on the map). The Spring Trail goes left, our return route. Cross the road and take the posted Ritchey Canyon Trail. Climb the hillside and descend back to the creek. Rock hop over the creek, passing a cascading waterfall on the right. Climb again, cross three feeder streams, and pass a moss-covered rock cave. Climb steadily (with a few short, steep sections) to an open flat and a posted junction at 2.3 miles. Views of upper Ritchey Canyon and Diamond Mountain extend to the west. The right fork leads 1.2 miles into Upper Ritchey Canyon, continuing to a fruit orchard and meadow at the Traverso Homestead site from the 1880s (Hike 20). Take the Spring Trail straight ahead, and slowly descend through a mixed forest. Curve left on a dirt road among towering redwoods, and pass a junction with the South Fork Trail on a U-bend. Follow the serpentine road on a gentle but steady downhill grade. Cross a concrete spillway over the creek, completing the upper loop by the Redwood Trail. Continue straight ahead on the edge of the creek to a Y-fork. The Vineyard Trail veers left. Curve to the right on the Ritchey Canyon Trail, and follow the north side of the creek. Pass the creek crossing on the right leading to the Redwood Trail. Continue straight, reaching the Hitchcock home site on the right by the wood barn with a tin roof. Pass a campground access path on the left, and ford the creek to the right, completing the loop. Bear left and return 0.4 miles to the trailhead.■

20. Upper Ritchey Canyon to Traverso Homestead
Redwood—Spring—Ritchey Canyon Trails
BOTHE—NAPA VALLEY STATE PARK

Hiking distance: 7 miles round trip
Hiking time: 3.5 hours
Elevation gain: 1,100 feet
Dogs: not allowed
Maps: U.S.G.S. Calistoga
Bothe-Napa Valley/Robert Louis Stevenson State Parks

map
page 73

Summary of hike: The Ritchey Canyon Trail in Bothe—Napa Valley State Park runs nearly 4 miles along Ritchey Creek to the Traverso Homestead site in a pastoral meadow. The old homestead, located at the upper west end of the state park, dates back to the 1880s. A small fruit orchard still remains. En route, the shaded path weaves along a riparian habitat between volcanic rock cliffs, passing through groves of big-leaf maples, Douglas firs, oaks, and redwoods.

Driving directions: Bothe—Napa Valley State Park is located along Highway 29 between Calistoga and Saint Helena.

FROM HIGHWAY 29/LINCOLN AVENUE IN CALISTOGA: Drive 3.5 miles south on Highway 29 to the posted state park entrance on the right. Turn right and drive 0.4 miles to the posted Ritchey Creek Trailhead and parking area on the right.

FROM HIGHWAY 29 IN ST. HELENA: Drive 4.5 miles north on Highway 29 to the posted state park entrance on the left. Turn left and drive 0.4 miles to the posted Ritchey Creek Trailhead and parking area on the right.

Hiking directions: Take the Redwood Trail, following the hiking directions for Hike 18. Continue to the junction with the Spring Trail and Ritchey Canyon Trail at 1.5 miles (noted on the map). The Spring Trail goes left, our return route. Cross the road and take the posted Ritchey Canyon Trail. Climb the hillside and descend back to the creek. Rock hop over the creek, passing a cascading waterfall on the right. Climb again, crossing three feeder streams, and pass a moss-covered rock cave. Steadily gain elevation (with a few short, steep sections) to an open flat and a posted junction at 2.3 miles. Views of upper Ritchey Canyon and Diamond Mountain extend to the west. The left fork, the Spring Trail, is the upper end of the return route. For now go to the right, staying on the Ritchey Canyon Trail. Gently descend through the forest on the north-facing canyon wall. Cross a stair-stepping tributary stream, and pass redwood fairy rings, maple trees, and ferns. Follow the undulating path, emerging from the dense forest to chaparral, grasslands, and an unsigned junction at 3.5 miles. The left fork makes a horseshoe left bend and climbs the south canyon wall. The right fork crosses the drainage at the Traverso Homestead in a clearing with old rusted debris and a fruit orchard. It is a pastoral setting, but it takes some imagination to visualize the homestead.

Return to the junction with Spring Trail. Stay to the right on the Spring Trail, and slowly descend through a mixed forest. Curve left on a dirt road among towering redwoods, and pass a junction with the South Fork Trail on a U-bend. Follow the serpentine road on a gentle but steady downhill grade. Cross the concrete spillway over the creek, completing the upper loop by the Redwood Trail. Continue straight ahead on the Vineyard Trail along the edge of the creek to a Y-fork. The Vineyard Trail veers left. Curve to the right on the Ritchey Canyon Trail, and follow the north side of the creek. Pass the creek crossing on the right that connects to the Redwood Trail. Continue straight, reaching the Hitchcock homesite on the right by a wood barn with a tin roof. Pass a campground access path on the left, and ford the creek to the right, completing the loop. Bear left and return 0.4 miles to the trailhead.■

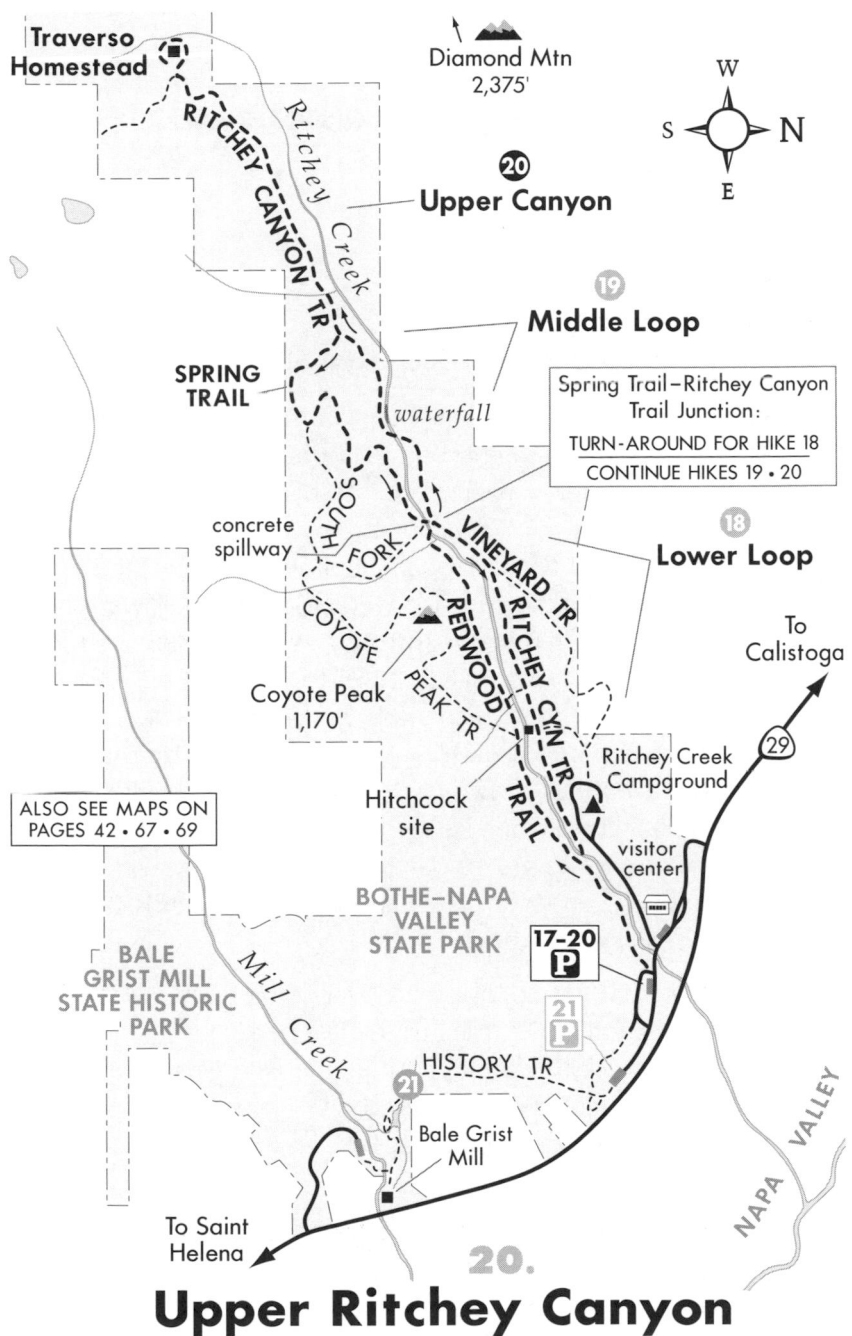

Traverso Homestead

Diamond Mtn
2,375'

W · N · E · S *(compass)*

⁲⁰ Upper Canyon

RITCHEY CANYON TR

Ritchey Creek

ⁱ⁹ Middle Loop

SPRING TRAIL

waterfall

| Spring Trail–Ritchey Canyon Trail Junction: |
| TURN-AROUND FOR HIKE 18 |
| CONTINUE HIKES 19 · 20 |

concrete spillway

SOUTH FORK

COYOTE

VINEYARD TR

RITCHEY CYN TR

¹⁸ Lower Loop

To Calistoga

REDWOOD TRAIL

PEAK TR

Coyote Peak 1,170'

Hitchcock site

Ritchey Creek Campground

29

visitor center

ALSO SEE MAPS ON PAGES 42 · 67 · 69

BALE GRIST MILL STATE HISTORIC PARK

Mill Creek

BOTHE–NAPA VALLEY STATE PARK

17-20 P

21 P

HISTORY TR

21

Bale Grist Mill

NAPA VALLEY

To Saint Helena

20.
Upper Ritchey Canyon
BOTHE–NAPA VALLEY STATE PARK

21. History Trail
BOTHE—NAPA VALLEY STATE PARK to
BALE GRIST MILL STATE HISTORIC PARK

Hiking distance: 2.4 miles round trip
Hiking time: 1.5 hours
Elevation gain: 200 feet
Dogs: not allowed
Maps: U.S.G.S. Calistoga
          Bothe—Napa Valley/Robert Louis Stevenson State Parks

Summary of hike: Dr. Edward Bale had the Bale Grist Mill built in 1846. It was used for grinding grain (grist) into wheat flour. Water from Mill Creek was diverted into Mill Pond and delivered by redwood flumes to the top of the waterwheel. The weight of the water turned the 20-foot wheel, which turned the mill-stones, which ground the grist. The water-powered mill was used until 1905. The mill has been restored with a larger 36-foot diameter wheel. Bale Grist Mill State Historic Park is adjacent to Bothe—Napa Valley State Park. The parks are connected by Highway 29 and the 1.2-mile History Trail. This hike begins from the east end of Bothe—Napa Valley State Park and leads to the Bale Grist Mill State Historic Park. The trail passes an old pioneer cemetery with marked graves dating back to the mid-1800s. The hike climbs a ridge under a forest canopy, then descends into the Mill Creek drainage and the mill.

Driving directions: Follow the driving directions to Hike 17, then continue another 0.3 miles to the last parking lot.

To hike the trail in reverse, park at the Bale Grist Mill State Historic Park. The entrance is located on Highway 29—1.6 miles south of Bothe—Napa Valley State Park and 2.9 miles north of Saint Helena.

Hiking directions: From the picnic area, take the posted path south, parallel to Highway 29. Curve right, away from the highway, to an open meadow and the historic White Church Cemetery. A side path on the left leads to the rock headstones. Back on the main trail, enter the forest of madrone, Douglas fir, and oaks. Climb the shaded hillside to the ridge. Follow the ridge, topping out in a half mile. The serpentine path slowly descends into the Mill Creek drainage to a tributary stream. Cross the stream and follow its west bank downstream to a posted junction at 0.9 miles. The left fork detours along the creek to the site of the old Mill Pond and the dam built in 1859. The History Trail crosses a wooden bridge over a seasonal stream to a trail split at Mill Creek. The left fork leads to the historic Grist Mill buildings. The right fork crosses a long wooden bridge over Mill Creek to the Bale Grist Mill parking lot. After exploring the mill and granary, return by retracing your steps. ■

BALE GRIST MILL STATE HISTORIC PARK

Mill Cr.

P

Bale Grist Mill and granary

Mill Pond

29

White Church Cemetery

HISTORY TRAIL

BOTHE–NAPA VALLEY STATE PARK

S
E — W
N

ALSO SEE MAPS ON PAGES 42 • 73

Hikes 17–20

17–20 P

P

To Hwy 29

21.

History Trail
BOTHE–NAPA VALLEY STATE PARK
BALE GRIST MILL STATE HISTORIC PARK

22. Observatory—Cow Pond Loop
PACIFIC UNION COLLEGE

Hiking distance: 2-mile loop
Hiking time: 1 hour
Elevation gain: 150 feet
Dogs: allowed
Maps: U.S.G.S. St Helena
　　　　Pacific Union College trail map

Summary of hike: Pacific Union College is nestled in the hills above Napa Valley in the heart of Angwin. The college is surrounded on the north and east by Howell Mountain and is adjacent to Las Posadas State Forest. The trail system, popular with mountain bikers, is a maze of fire roads and rolling single tracks that weave through Howell Mountain and down into Pope Valley. This trail loops around the west end of the open space above Mill Valley. The hike begins on a wide dirt road and loops around a large cow pasture, passing a man-made pond and an observatory. Keep in mind that these trails are on private land and hiking privileges can be revoked at any time. Please be respectful to insure that the trails remain open for public use.

Driving directions: From Silverado Trail and Deer Park Road—north of Saint Helena—drive 5.4 miles north on Deer Park Road to Cold Springs Road in the town of Angwin. (En route, Deer Park Road becomes Howell Mountain Road.) Turn right on Cold Springs Road, and continue 1.1 miles (staying straight onto Las Posadas Road) to a right bend in the road. Park in the pullouts on the side of the road at the bend.

Hiking directions: Pass through the metal vehicle gate, and head north on the wide, forested road. Pass through a second gate at a junction with a dirt road on the right. Continue straight through the mixed forest of oak, Douglas fir, gray pine, madrone, and manzanita. Pass a lush cow pasture rimmed by the forested hills on the left to a fenced corner with two gates. Straight ahead is Mill Valley. Instead, walk through the gate on the left and head up the hillside. Pass through another gate at the Young

Observatory. Just past the observatory, curve left past Cow Pond, a huge man-made pond on the right. As the road curves left (above the Angwin Airport) take the dirt path on the left through the gate. Descend to the cow pasture and curve right, skirting the edge of the pasture. Walk through a gate and circle the pasture, completing the loop. ■

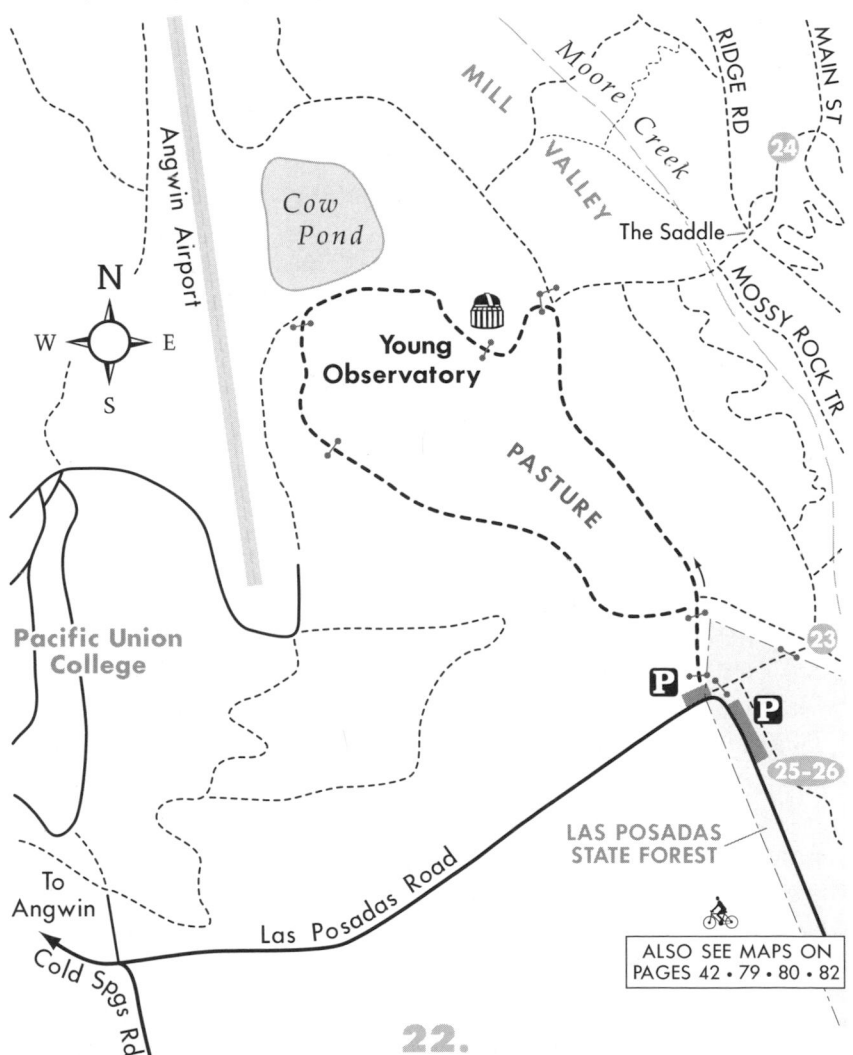

22.
Observatory–Cow Pond Loop
PACIFIC UNION COLLEGE

23. Whoop De Dogs—Flat Rock Loop
PACIFIC UNION COLLEGE

Hiking distance: 2.2-mile loop
Hiking time: 1 hour
Elevation gain: 300 feet
Dogs: allowed
Maps: U.S.G.S. St Helena
Pacific Union College trail map

Summary of hike: Above the vineyards of Napa Valley in the town of Angwin is a network of trails on Howell Mountain. The privately owned (but open to the public) land is a hidden jewel. A complex tapestry of trails winds many miles through the shaded forest. This hike forms a loop on the south edge of the open space along the border of Las Posadas State Forest. The undulating trail loops through an arboreal canopy of redwoods, oaks, gray pine, Douglas fir, manzanita, and madrones.

Driving directions: Same as Hike 22.

Hiking directions: Pass the trailhead gate and head east, straight ahead. Walk 175 yards and pass through a wooden gate to an unsigned junction. Take the right fork and continue east on the Whoop De Dogs Trail. As the road curves left, follow the footpath straight ahead, staying on the Whoop De Dogs Trail. Climb up the slope through a mixed forest, dropping down and climbing out of three consecutive gulches. As the main trail curves left, again continue straight, skirting the edge of Las Posadas State Forest. Head uphill and descend again. Climb one more hill and curve left at the far east end of the loop. Descend under the shade of the forest to a T-junction with the Chute Trail. Go to the right and stroll at a level grade to a Y-fork. Veer left on the Flat Rock Trail, and head up the slope to where slabs of rock are embedded in the trail. Climb another short hill and stay left at a trail split. Complete the loop a short distance ahead. Pass through the wooden gate, and return 175 yards back to the trailhead.■

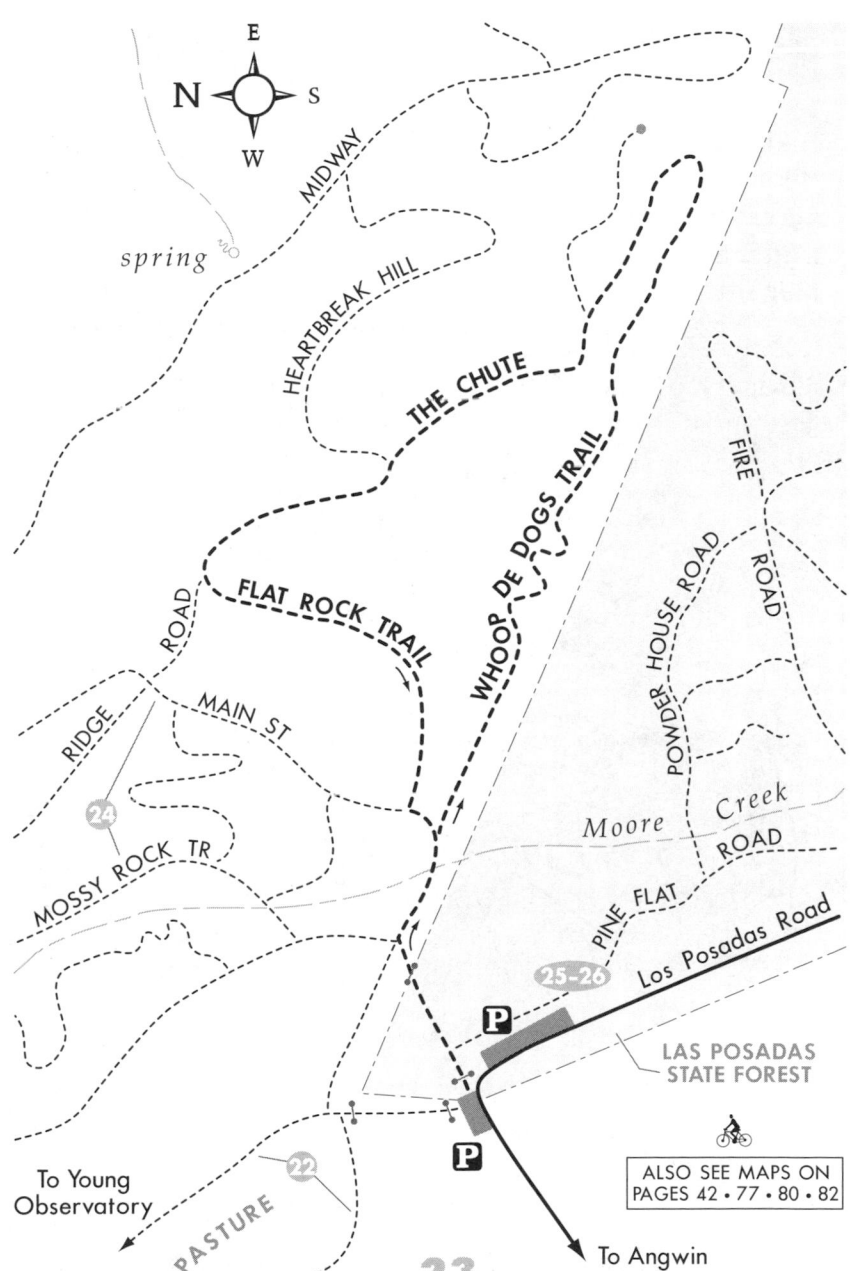

N E S W

spring

MIDWAY

HEARTBREAK HILL

THE CHUTE

WHOOP DE DOGS TRAIL

FLAT ROCK TRAIL

FIRE ROAD

POWDER HOUSE ROAD

RIDGE ROAD

MAIN ST

24

MOSSY ROCK TR

Moore Creek

ROAD

PINE FLAT

25-26 Los Posadas Road

LAS POSADAS STATE FOREST

To Young Observatory

PASTURE

22

To Angwin

ALSO SEE MAPS ON PAGES 42 • 77 • 80 • 82

23.

Whoop De Dogs—Flat Rock Loop
PACIFIC UNION COLLEGE

24. Inspiration Point and Redwood Flat
PACIFIC UNION COLLEGE

Hiking distance: 5 miles round trip
Hiking time: 2.5 hours
Elevation gain: 800 feet
Dogs: allowed
Maps: U.S.G.S. St Helena
  Pacific Union College trail map

map
page 82

Summary of hike: The Pacific Union College open space is great cross-country terrain that spreads across ridges and val-

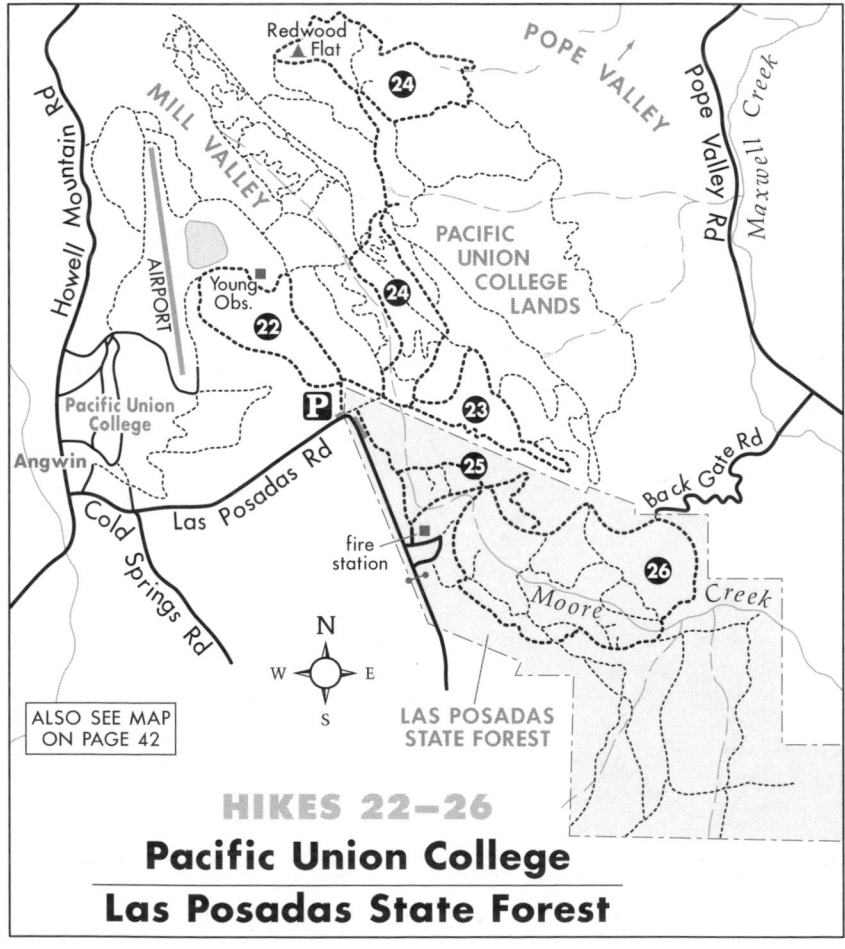

HIKES 22–26
Pacific Union College
Las Posadas State Forest

leys. This hike explores the northern end of the arborous trail system through the open space. The trail loops around Redwood Flat, a campground at 1,600 feet in a cool, shaded grove of redwoods. En route, the hike passes Inspiration Point, a huge cliff with beautiful vistas across Pope Valley.

Driving directions: Same as Hike 22.

Hiking directions: Pass the trailhead gate and head east, straight ahead. Walk 175 yards and pass through a wooden gate to an unsigned junction. Go straight through the junction, and continue a short distance to the unmarked Mossy Rock Trail on the right. Curve right on the Mossy Rock Trail, and weave through a dense forest with mixed trees and mossy rocks. Follow the canyon floor to a T-junction with a dirt road. Bear right on the old road, and climb to a 5-way junction on The Saddle. Cross the ridge and follow the sign towards Inspiration Point. Descend to an open flat. Cross the flat and walk 30 yards to the Inspiration Point junction on the right. Detour 20 yards on this trail to a rail-lined overlook of Pope Valley and the mountains of eastern Napa County. Return to the main trail, and head north on Main Street through a redwood forest with giant madrones and an understory of ferns. Stay to the right, past a posted junction with the Angwish Hill Trail, to Four Corners. Bear left and begin the loop. Walk a few hundred yards and enter Redwood Flat. Loop around the camp, passing groves of redwoods and fairy rings. Head east and descend towards Pope Valley. Watch for the unmarked Sand Climb Trail on the right before reaching the valley floor. Take the trail right, and steadily climb the east-facing hillside to a T-junction. Bear right and traverse the hillside 340 yards, completing the loop at Four Corners. Retrace your steps on Main Street to Inspiration Point. Continue straight on Main Street, parallel to a rock wall on the right. Slowly gain elevation through the dense forest, and weave downhill to a junction by the wooden gate, completing a second loop. Bear left, pass through the gate, and return 175 yards to the trailhead. ■

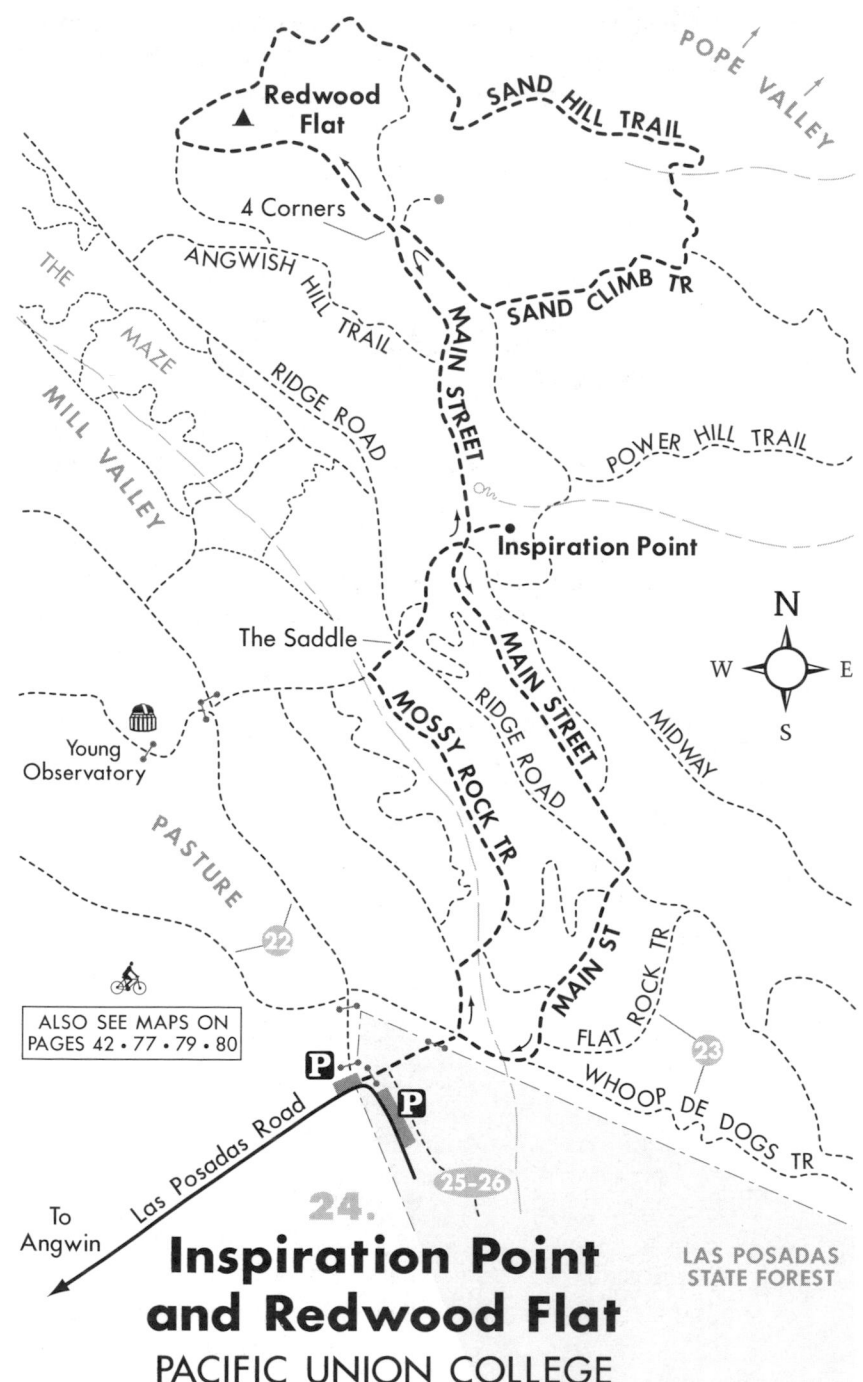

24.
Inspiration Point and Redwood Flat
PACIFIC UNION COLLEGE

Map labels:

POPE VALLEY

Redwood Flat

SAND HILL TRAIL

4 Corners

ANGWISH HILL TRAIL

SAND CLIMB TR

MAIN STREET

POWER HILL TRAIL

THE MAZE

MILL VALLEY

RIDGE ROAD

Inspiration Point

The Saddle

N · W · E · S

MAIN STREET

MIDWAY

Young Observatory

MOSSY ROCK TR

RIDGE ROAD

PASTURE

22

ALSO SEE MAPS ON PAGES 42 · 77 · 79 · 80

MAIN ST

FLAT ROCK TR

23

P

P

Las Posadas Road

25-26

WHOOP DE DOGS TR

To Angwin

LAS POSADAS STATE FOREST

25. Pine Flat—Roosevelt— Powder House Loop

LAS POSADAS STATE FOREST

755 Las Posadas Road · Angwin

Hiking distance: 2.2-mile loop
Hiking time: 1 hour
Elevation gain: 200 feet
Dogs: allowed
Maps: U.S.G.S. St Helena
Las Posadas trail map

map
page 85

Summary of hike: Las Posadas State Forest is one of eight demonstration forests in California. The 796-acre forest was acquired as a gift to the state. It is dedicated for the purposes of study and research to improve forest management practices, environmental stewardship, timber production, and public recreation. The rolling, forested hills are located above the town of Angwin, east of Napa Valley and Saint Helena. The diverse trail system includes forested dirt roads and shaded single tracks through redwood groves, tunnels of manzanita, natural rock gardens, overlooks with views of vineyards, and the mountains and valleys of eastern Napa County.

Driving directions: From Silverado Trail and Deer Park Road—north of Saint Helena—drive 5.4 miles north on Deer Park Road to Cold Springs Road in the town of Angwin. (En route, Deer Park Road becomes Howell Mountain Road.) Turn right on Cold Springs Road, and continue 1.1 miles (staying straight onto Las Posadas Road) to a right bend in the road. Park in the pullouts on the side of the road at the bend.

Hiking directions: Pass through the narrow trailhead gate, and head south (right) on the unsigned Pine Flat Road, parallel to Las Posadas Road. Stroll through an oak, Douglas fir, and madrone forest to a trail split at 0.2 miles. Stay to the right, reaching a second junction at a half mile. The right fork leads to the fire station. Bear left on the Fire Road through a grove of massive pines and firs to a 4-way junction. Begin a loop straight ahead on the Roosevelt Road. Gently climb through the shade of the forest, and veer right at the fenced park boundary. Stroll through the forest and pass a grove of redwoods on the left. Steadily descend and curve left. Soon afterwards, make a horseshoe right bend to a T-junction with the Fire Road. The left fork continues to Moore Creek and a historic cemetery (Hike 26). For this hike, go to the right and climb back to the 4-way junction, completing the loop.

For the return loop, walk straight through the junction on Powder House Road. Weave through the forest, passing a meadow with lichen-covered boulders on the left. A footpath meanders through the meadow. Continue on Powder House Road, then curve right on Pine Flat Road, completing the second loop. Return to the trailhead on the right. ■

26. Wilderness—Cemetery— Full Moon Rock Loop
LAS POSADAS STATE FOREST
755 Las Posadas Road · Angwin

Hiking distance: 4.4-mile loop
Hiking time: 2.5 hours
Elevation gain: 400 feet
Dogs: allowed
Maps: U.S.G.S. St Helena
Las Posadas trail map

map
page 87

Summary of hike: This large loop hike through Las Posadas State Forest visits the site of the Las Posadas Pioneer Cemetery atop Graveyard Knoll. Seven members of the John Morris family, owners of this land, were buried on the knoll in the 1800s. Inscribed stone markers date back to 1880. For centuries prior to this, it was a Native American resting spot.

The rounded knoll offers 360-degree vistas through the trees. The trail also explores redwood groves with fairy rings. (A fairy ring is a circular group of redwoods growing out of an ancestral

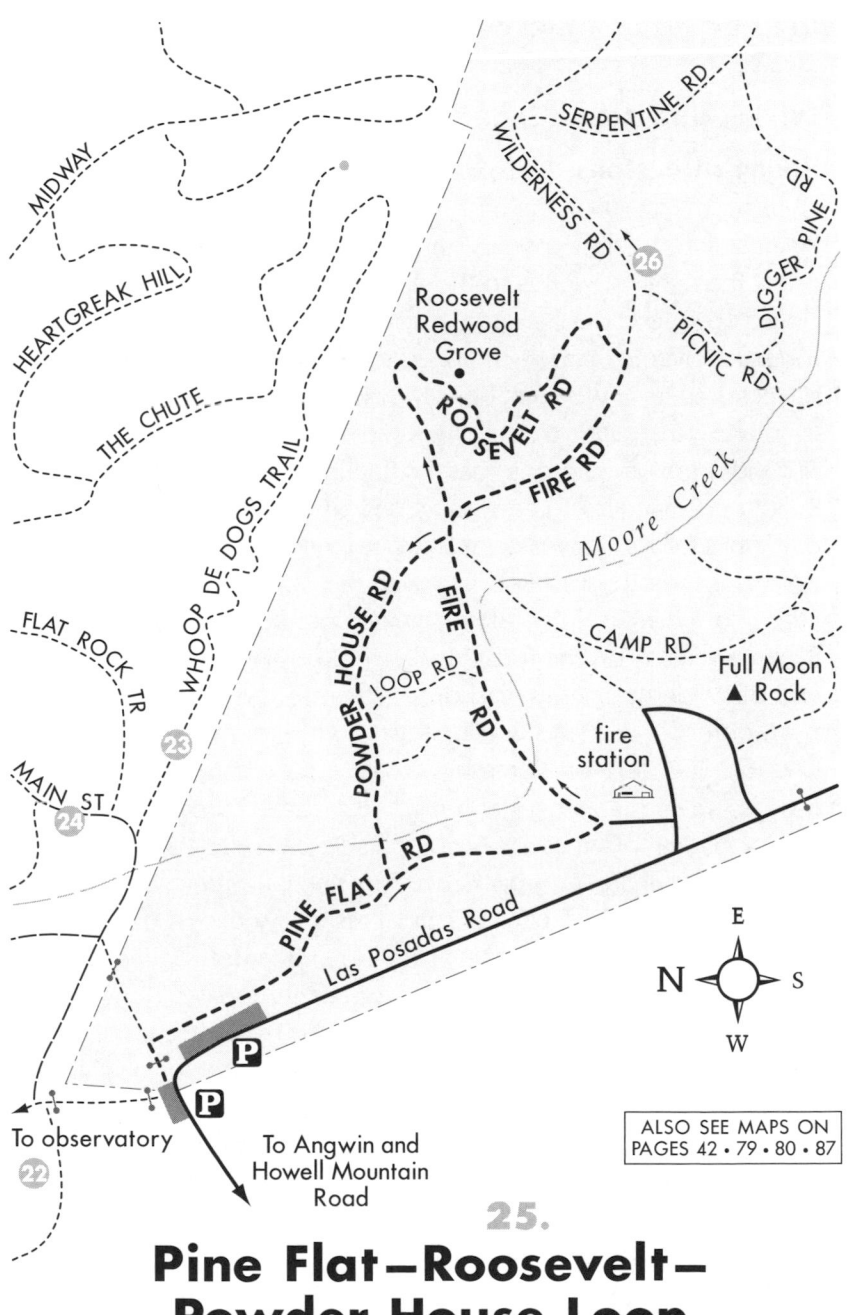

ALSO SEE MAPS ON
PAGES 42 • 79 • 80 • 87

25.

Pine Flat–Roosevelt–
Powder House Loop
LAS POSADAS STATE FOREST

tree.) The land is leased by the 4-H Club. Be respectful of the area so that it remains open to the public.

Driving directions: Same as Hike 25.

Hiking directions: Pass through the narrow trailhead gate, and head south (right) on the unsigned Pine Flat Road, parallel to Las Posadas Road. Enter a shady mixed forest to a junction at 0.2 miles. The right fork leads to the fire station. Veer left on Powder House Road, and pass a side path on the right that leads through a lichen-covered garden of boulders. Stay left at a Y-fork, and descend to a 4-way junction with Roosevelt Road. Begin the loop and go straight on the Fire Road. Descend through Douglas firs and a redwood grove, passing the lower ends of Roosevelt Road and Picnic Road. Leave the shade of the fir trees, and enter a forest of oaks, gray pine, manzanita, and madrones. The vistas extend across the rolling hills. At a road split, Serpentine Road heads to the right. Stay left on Wilderness Road, passing gated Back Gate Road on the left. Curve right, looping around the east end of Wilderness Road, and drop down to the canyon bottom by Moore Creek. Head uphill, staying on Wilderness Road to a junction. Bear left on Cemetery Road and cross a bridge over Moore Creek. Curve right and climb the forested hillside to Las Posadas Pioneer Cemetery. A posted side path leads 50 yards up to the stone markers atop Graveyard Knoll. Return to the main trail and go straight on Camp Road. Pass a few cabins below on the right to the signed Full Moon Rock Trail. Bear left on the footpath, and wind uphill through a grove of redwoods to Dogwood Road, a narrow dirt road. Cross the road and traverse the hillside, passing a massive rock formation on the left. Return to Camp Road and continue uphill to a horseshoe left bend. On the bend, veer right on a distinct footpath. Cross the hillside path and emerge at the 4-way junction with Roosevelt Road, completing the loop. Cross through the junction and retrace your steps on Powder House Road. ■

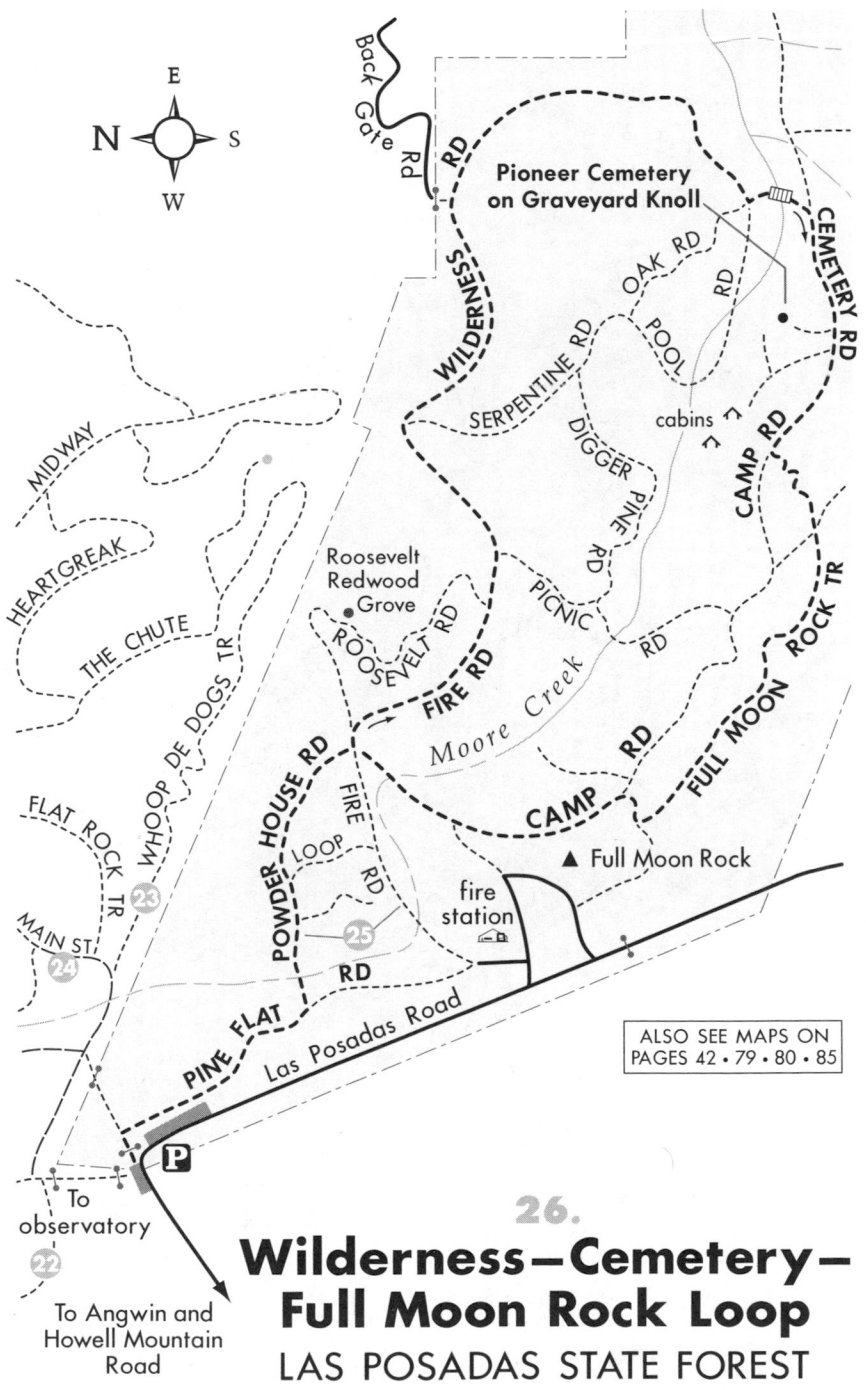

N E S W

Back Gate Rd

WILDERNESS RD

Pioneer Cemetery on Graveyard Knoll

CEMETERY RD

OAK RD

RD

POOL RD

SERPENTINE RD

DIGGER PINE RD

cabins

CAMP RD

MIDWAY

HEARTGREAK

THE CHUTE

WHOOP DE DOGS TR

Roosevelt Redwood Grove

ROOSEVELT RD

FIRE RD

PICNIC RD

Moore Creek

POWDER HOUSE RD

FIRE LOOP RD

CAMP RD

FULL MOON ROCK TR

FLAT ROCK TR

23

MAIN ST

24

25

▲ Full Moon Rock

fire station

PINE FLAT RD

Las Posadas Road

ALSO SEE MAPS ON PAGES 42 • 79 • 80 • 85

P

To observatory

22

To Angwin and Howell Mountain Road

26.
Wilderness–Cemetery– Full Moon Rock Loop
LAS POSADAS STATE FOREST

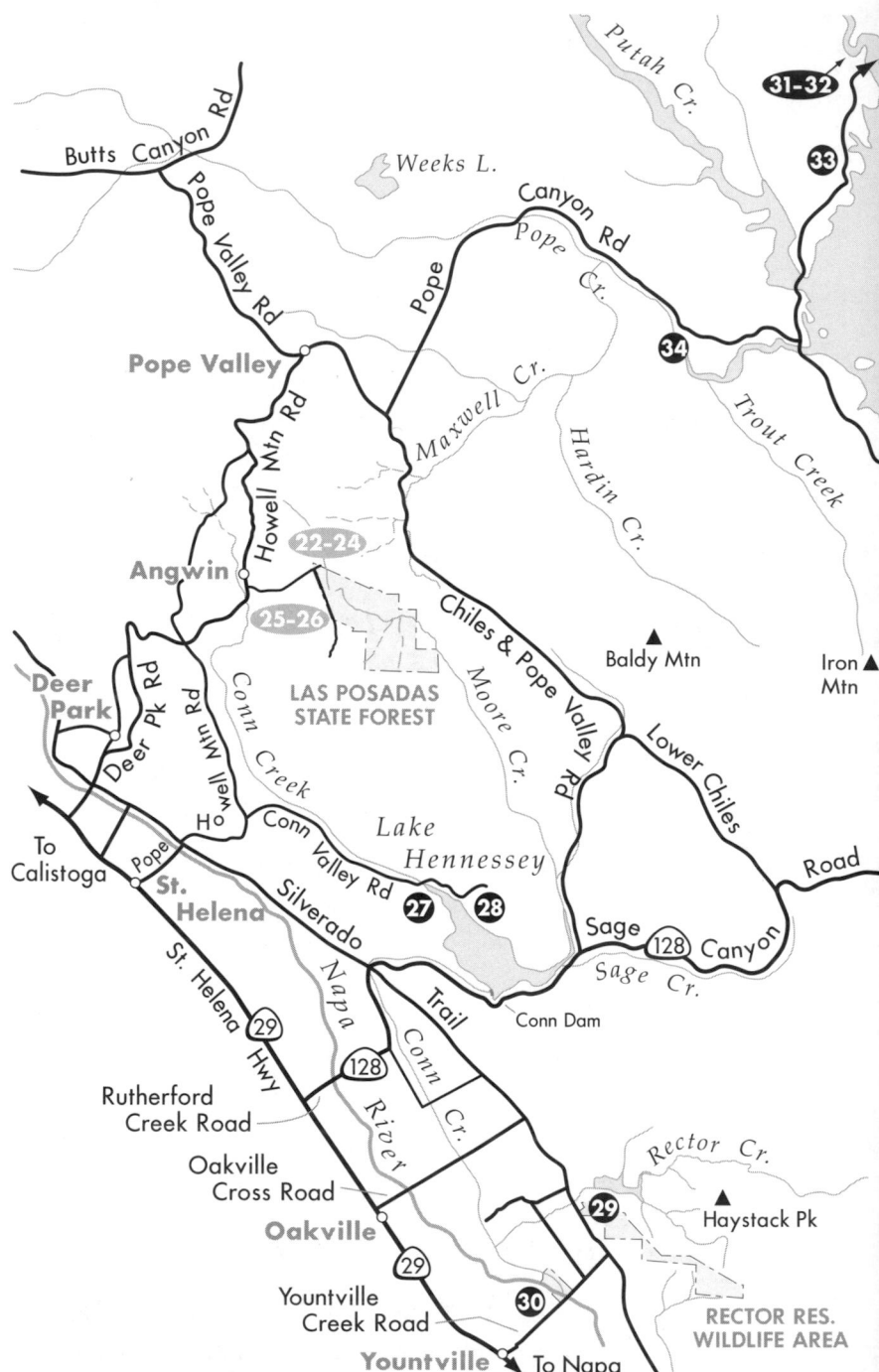

Central Napa Valley
and the Eastern Mountains
RUTHERFORD • YOUNTVILLE •
LAKE BERRYESSA

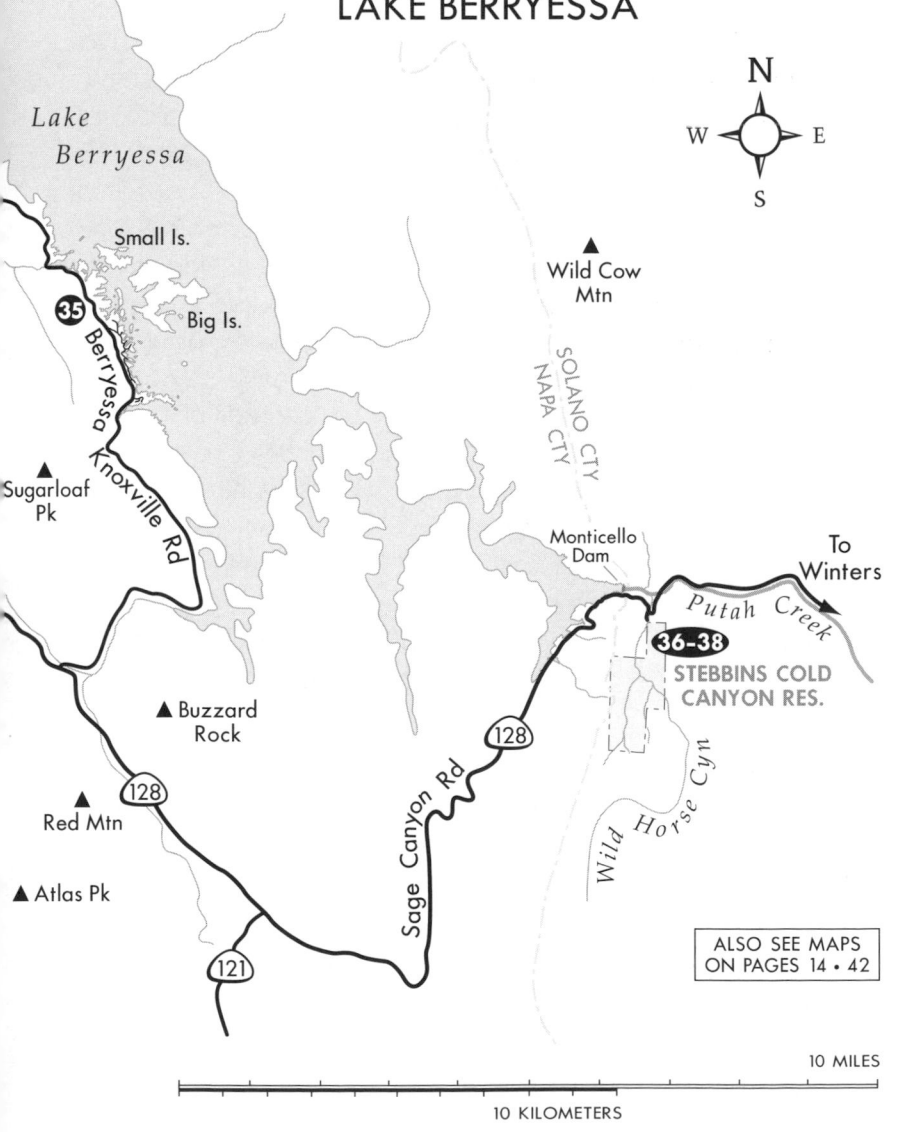

To Knoxville
Wildlife Area

HIKES
27-38

N
W E
S

*Lake
Berryessa*

Small Is.

35

Berryessa

Big Is.

Wild Cow
Mtn

SOLANO CTY
NAPA CTY

▲
Sugarloaf
Pk

Knoxville Rd

Monticello
Dam

To
Winters

Putah Creek

36-38

STEBBINS COLD
CANYON RES.

▲ Buzzard
Rock

128

Sage Canyon Rd

Wild Horse Cyn

128
▲
Red Mtn

▲ Atlas Pk

121

ALSO SEE MAPS
ON PAGES 14 • 42

10 MILES

10 KILOMETERS

27. Northwest Shoreline Trail
LAKE HENNESSEY

Hiking distance: 3 miles round trip
Hiking time: 1.5 hours
Elevation gain: Level
Dogs: allowed
Maps: U.S.G.S. St. Helena and Rutherford

map
next page

Summary of hike: Lake Hennessey is nestled in the hills on the east side of Napa Valley midway between Napa and Calistoga. The 850-acre man-made reservoir, measuring 2 miles long by 1.5 miles wide, sits at an elevation of 331 feet. The lake was dammed in 1945 to supply water for the city of Napa. It is fed by Sage Creek, Moore Creek, Chiles Creek, and Conn Creek. Sloping hills surround the secluded and quiet reservoir. The pristine mountain lake is also used for fishing, boating, wildlife viewing, picnicking, and is among the best year-round birding areas in the county. The lake is on the Pacific Flyway and is home to hundreds of species of resident and migratory birds. Potential sightings include bald eagles, golden eagles, hawks, osprey, great blue herons, white egrets, woodpeckers, and loons.

This hike begins on the east end of Conn Valley at the northwest tip of Lake Hennessey. The trail follows the shoreline through a mixed forest with views of the lake and surrounding hills. Dogs are allowed on the trail but not in the lake.

Driving directions: From Silverado Trail and Pope Street—east of Saint Helena—drive 1.2 miles east on Howell Mountain Road to Conn Valley Road. Continue straight on Conn Valley Road, and drive 3.1 miles to the trailhead on the right at the northwest corner of Lake Hennessey. Park in the dirt pullout on the left.

Hiking directions: Pass the trailhead gate and the "rules" signs. Stroll through the oak woodland on the dirt road. Skirt the northwest edge of Lake Hennessey in a mixed forest of gray pine, maple, manzanita, and oaks draped with lace lichen. At a quarter mile, views open up across Lake Hennessey and the mountains to the east. With every bend in the road, new sections of Lake Hennessey and the surrounding mountains come into view. Loop around a large bay lined with reeds, and pass three holding ponds on the right. Descend to a private road leading to the water treatment plant at 1.5 miles, the turn-around spot. It is not possible to walk around the entire lake. Return by retracing your steps. ■

28. Northeast Shoreline Trail
LAKE HENNESSEY

Hiking distance: 4.4 miles round trip
Hiking time: 2 hours
Elevation gain: Level
Dogs: allowed
Maps: U.S.G.S. St. Helena, Rutherford, and Yountville

map
next page

Summary of hike: This hike follows the northeast shoreline of Lake Hennessey, opposite of Hike 27. The trail winds along the wooded shore of the lake in an uncrowded, tranquil setting. It is a great spot for bird watching, with shoreline reeds, sandbars, and sand beaches backed by the rolling, forested hills. En route, the hike passes a shady stream-fed canyon and oak groves. Dogs are allowed on the trail but not in the lake.

Driving directions: From Silverado Trail and Pope Street— east of Saint Helena—drive 1.2 miles east on Howell Mountain Road to Conn Valley Road. Continue straight on Conn Valley Road, and drive 4.1 miles to the trailhead at the end of the road by the entrance to Moore Ranch. Park in the dirt pullout on the left, across the road from the signed trailhead.

Hiking directions: Cross the entrance road and take the dirt road past the trailhead gate and signs. Walk south along the Moore Ranch boundary, passing a grove of stately oaks, to a Y-fork at a hundred yards. The left fork is a gated ranch road. Stay

Lake Hennessey

HIKE 27

Northwest Shoreline Trail

HIKE 28

Northeast Shoreline Trail

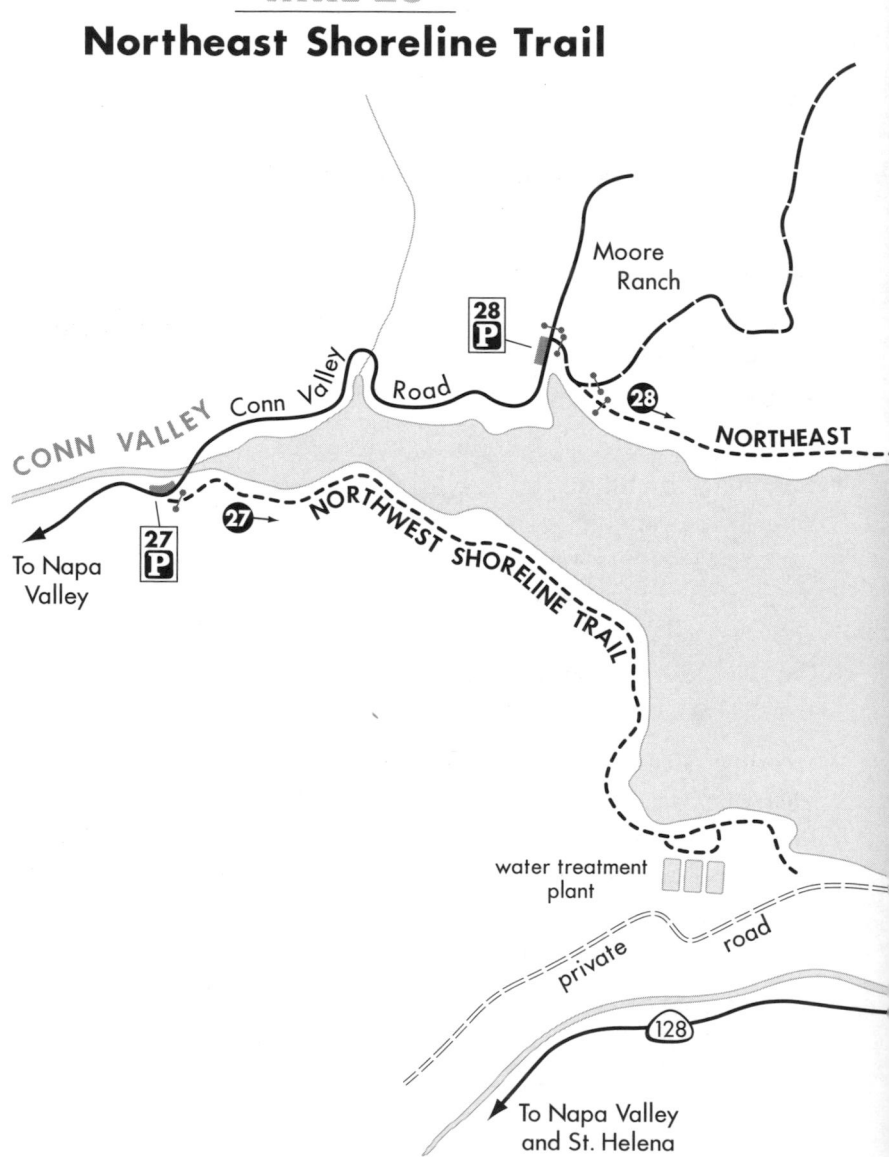

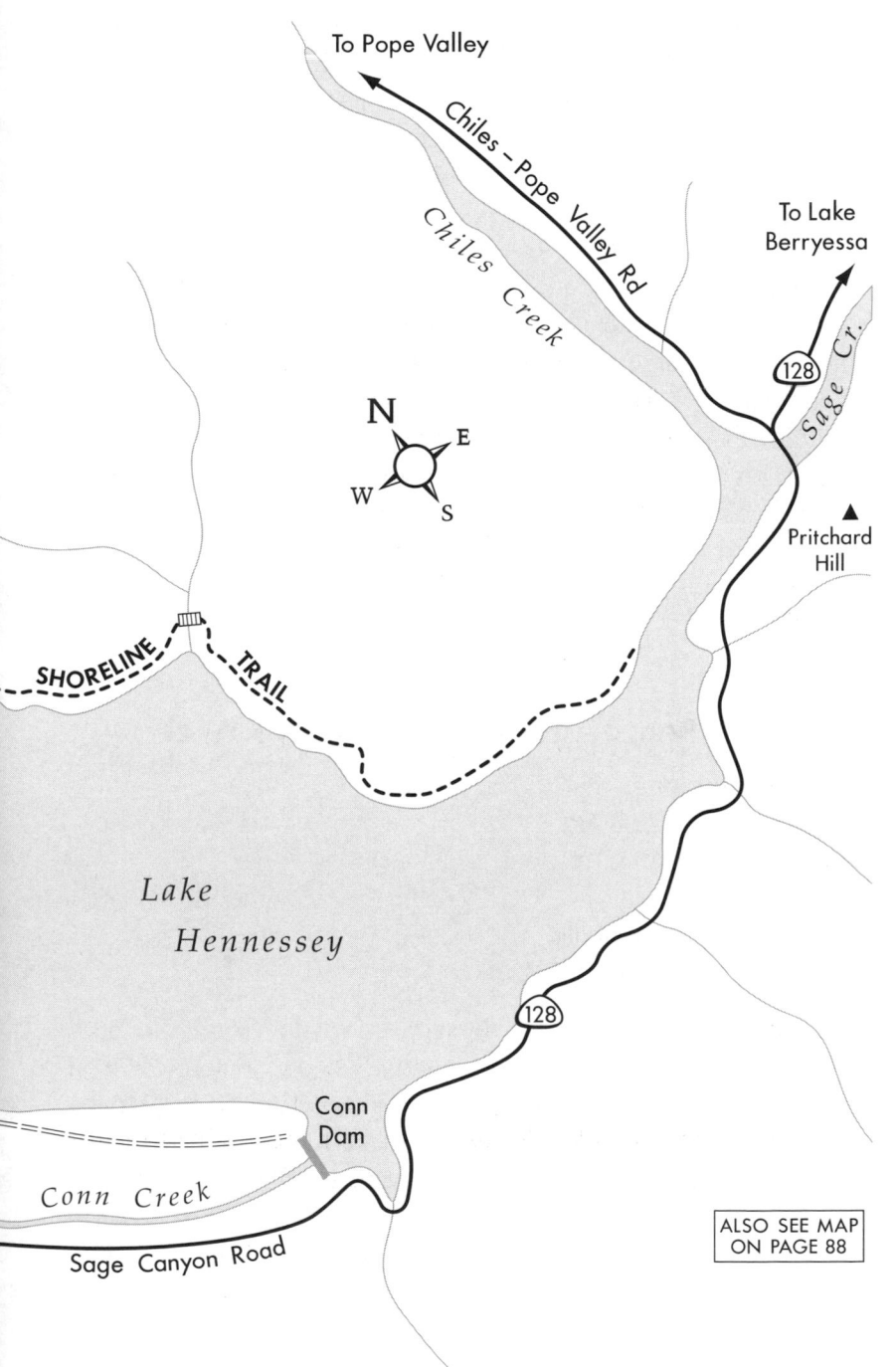

To Pope Valley

Chiles – Pope Valley Rd

Chiles Creek

To Lake
Berryessa

128

Sage Cr.

N
E
W
S

▲
Pritchard
Hill

SHORELINE TRAIL

Lake
Hennessey

128

Conn
Dam

Conn Creek

Sage Canyon Road

ALSO SEE MAP
ON PAGE 88

to the right past a second trail gate to the shore of Lake Hennessey. Follow the northwest tip of the lake, with gorgeous views of the surrounding mountains. Curve left as vistas of the entire lake come into view. Follow the serpentine dirt road, passing sandbars and a reed-filled wetland on the edge of the lake. At 1.2 miles, curve around an inlet and a forested stream-fed canyon. Cross a bridge over the seasonal drainage, and pass through a shady oak grove with lace lichen hanging from the trees. Continue through the grasslands, with full views of Lake Hennessey, Conn Dam, and the spillway. Curve around the contours of the hillside and lake to a view of the vineyards on Pritchard Hill across the lake to the east. Enter another live oak grove on the south-facing hillside 40 feet above the lake. Pass a pocket beach, climb a hill, and slowly descend to the end of the trail on the banks of the lake at 2.2 miles. Return along the same route.■

29. Rector Reservoir Wildlife Area

Hiking distance: 5 miles round trip
Hiking time: 2.5 hours
Elevation gain: 1,000 feet
Dogs: allowed
Maps: U.S.G.S. Yountville
       Rector Reservoir Wildlife Area

Summary of hike: Rector Reservoir Wildlife Area, located east of Yountville, covers 415 rugged acres on the south side of Rector Reservoir. The oblong reservoir was formed in 1946 by damming Rector Creek. The lake is tucked into the hills on the western slope of Haystack Peak near the mouth of Rector Canyon. The area, managed by the California Department of Fish and Game, consists of oak woodland and chaparral. Elevations range from 200 feet to 1,900 feet. This seldom-hiked trail climbs a ridge to an overlook of Rector Reservoir, then continues up to

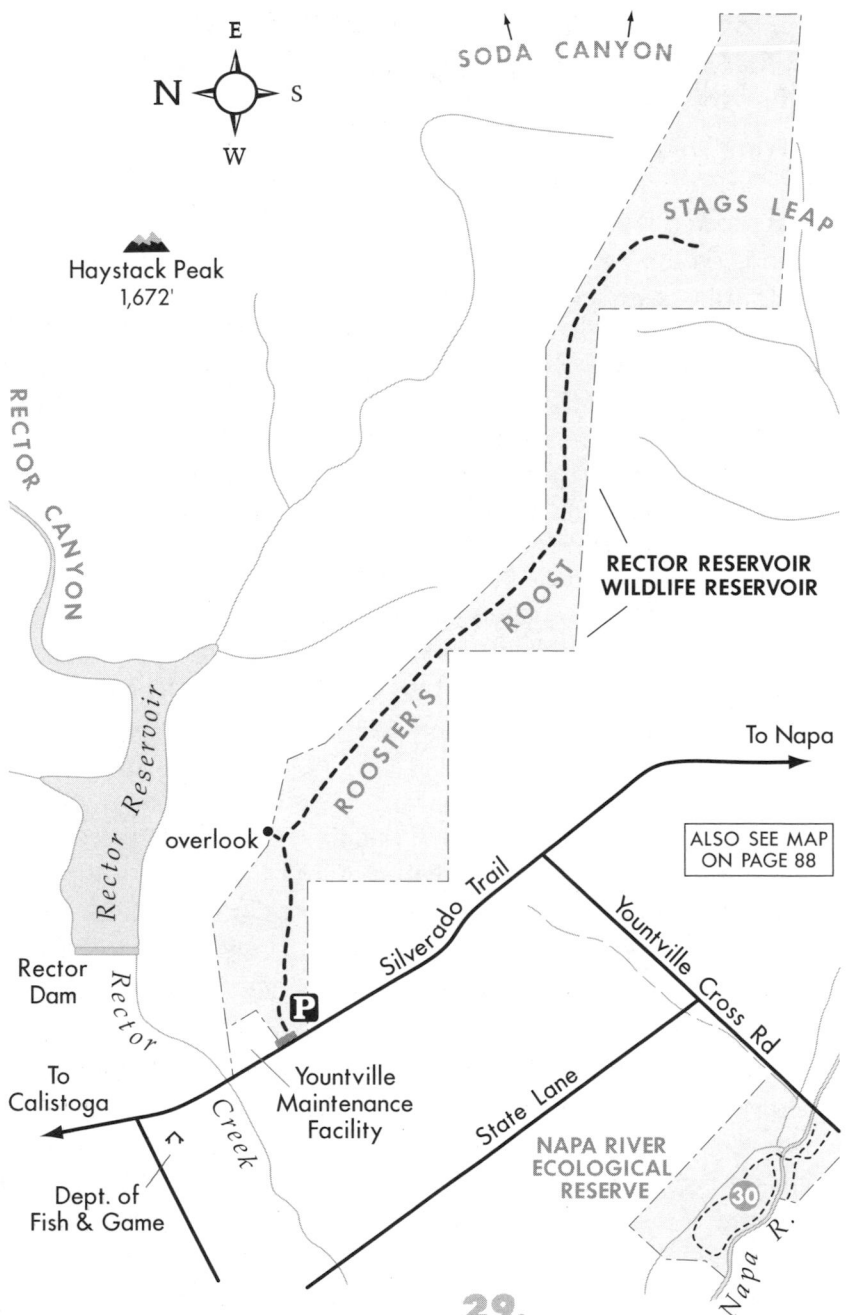

SODA CANYON

STAGS LEAP

Haystack Peak
1,672'

RECTOR CANYON

Rector Reservoir

RECTOR RESERVOIR
WILDLIFE RESERVOIR

ROOSTER'S ROOST

To Napa

ALSO SEE MAP
ON PAGE 88

overlook

Silverado Trail

Yountville Cross Rd

Rector
Dam

Rector Creek

P

Yountville
Maintenance
Facility

State Lane

To
Calistoga

NAPA RIVER
ECOLOGICAL
RESERVE

30

Napa R.

Dept. of
Fish & Game

29.
Rector Reservoir Wildlife Area

the sheer volcanic cliffs of the Stags Leap palisades after climbing a thousand feet. From Stags Leap are incredible views into Soda Canyon and across Napa Valley.

Driving directions: From Silverado Trail—east of Yountville—the hard-to-spot trailhead is located 1.6 miles south of Oakville Cross Road and 0.8 miles north of Yountville Cross Road. The trailhead is on the east side of the highway, 0.3 miles south of the California Department of Fish and Game, and on the south edge of the Napa County Yountville Maintenance Facility. Park in the wide pullout on the east side of the road by the "Park Off Pavement" sign.

Hiking directions: Head up the footpath, skirting the south edge of the gated Yountville Maintenance Facility. Walk through the open grasslands dotted with blue oaks, then head uphill. Pass fields of lichen-colored rocks and vistas of the vineyards below. The path temporarily levels out on an open slope to a Y-fork near the ridge. Detour on the left fork, climbing 70 yards to the ridge overlooking Rector Canyon, Rector Reservoir, the dam, and distinct Haystack Peak to the east. Return to the main trail and continue east to the ridge, which is locally referred to as Rooster's Roost. Follow the ridge uphill, with spectacular views across Napa Valley. The rock-embedded path levels out and crosses a narrow ridge with far-reaching vistas in every direction. Cross a peak by a jumble of rocks, and follow the narrow spine to another peak on a grassy oak-covered slope. Skirt the fenced east border along the ridge, gradually gaining elevation. Top the slope at Stags Leap, a 1,200-foot ridge with views into Soda Canyon. The path fades and becomes obscure on Stags Leap. Return by retracing your steps. ■

30. Napa River Ecological Reserve

Hiking distance: 1.2-mile loop
Hiking time: 45 minutes
Elevation gain: Level
Dogs: allowed
Maps: U.S.G.S. Yountville

map
page 99

Summary of hike: The Napa River Ecological Reserve is an important wildlife habitat that straddles the Napa River east of Yountville. The 73-acre oasis, surrounded by vineyards, is managed by the California Department of Fish and Game. The Napa River and Conn Creek flow through the heart of the reserve. This level trail loops through an old-growth woodland on the east side of the Napa River and along Conn Creek. It is a popular spot for hiking, fishing, and bird watching.

The lush vegetation supports a diverse wildlife population, acting as a residence and migratory stopover with food, water, and shelter. The flood-plain habitat is rich with more than 230 plant species, including the dominant oaks draped with lace lichen, California bay, Oregon ash, cottonwood, willow, buckeye, twisting grapevines, and thickets of blackberry shrubs. Approximately 150 species of birds have been sited, such as woodpeckers, Steller's and western scrub jays, ducks, swallows, owls, hawks, and hummingbirds.

Driving directions: From the north end of Yountville on Highway 29, turn east on Madison Street. Drive a quarter mile to Yount Street. Turn left and quickly turn right on Yountville Cross Road. Continue 0.9 miles to the posted trailhead and parking area on the left.

Hiking directions: From the posted trailhead and information board, walk 100 yards northwest through the open field to the levee and the majestic oak grove. Climb the levee to an overlook of the Napa River, then descend to the river. Follow the riparian path to the left for a short distance upstream through a tangle of vegetation to a seasonal footbridge. Cross over the Napa River and veer left to a Y-fork. Begin the loop to the right. Stroll through a meadow and the lush greenery under towering oaks with lace lichen hanging from the oak branches. Skirt the west edge of Conn Creek on the forested footpath. Curve left at the far north end of the reserve to a sitting bench. Loop back under a canopy of massive bay laurel trees on the east bank of the Napa River. Continue downstream, overlooking the river, and complete the loop by the meadow. Return across the bridge over the river, and climb to the top of the levee.

To extend the hike, bear right and follow the ridge atop the twisted, oak-covered levee. The levee ends in less than a quarter mile at a vineyard. ■

31. Zim Zim Creek Trail
KNOXVILLE WILDLIFE AREA

Hiking distance: 6 miles round trip
Hiking time: 3 hours
Elevation gain: 250 feet
Dogs: allowed
Maps: U.S.G.S. Knoxville
Calif. Dept. of Fish and Game, Knoxville Wildlife Area

map
page 101

Summary of hike: The Knoxville Wildlife Area is north of Lake Berryessa near the Yolo County line. The rugged terrain stretches over 20,000 acres, with elevations ranging from 1,000 feet to 2,200 feet. The diverse habitat forms the western slope of Blue Ridge between the Cache Creek drainage and the Putah Creek Drainage. It is a critical wildlife corridor for animals such as bears, mountain lions, and golden and bald eagles. The land also contains some of the state's most biologically important habitats, including oak woodlands and serpentine chaparral, two threatened vegetation types in California.

This hike follows remote Zim Zim Creek as it meanders and tumbles through the isolated meadows just southwest of the wildlife area. The nearly level hike has ten creek crossings and leads to the remains of an old burned cabin, where the hike ends.

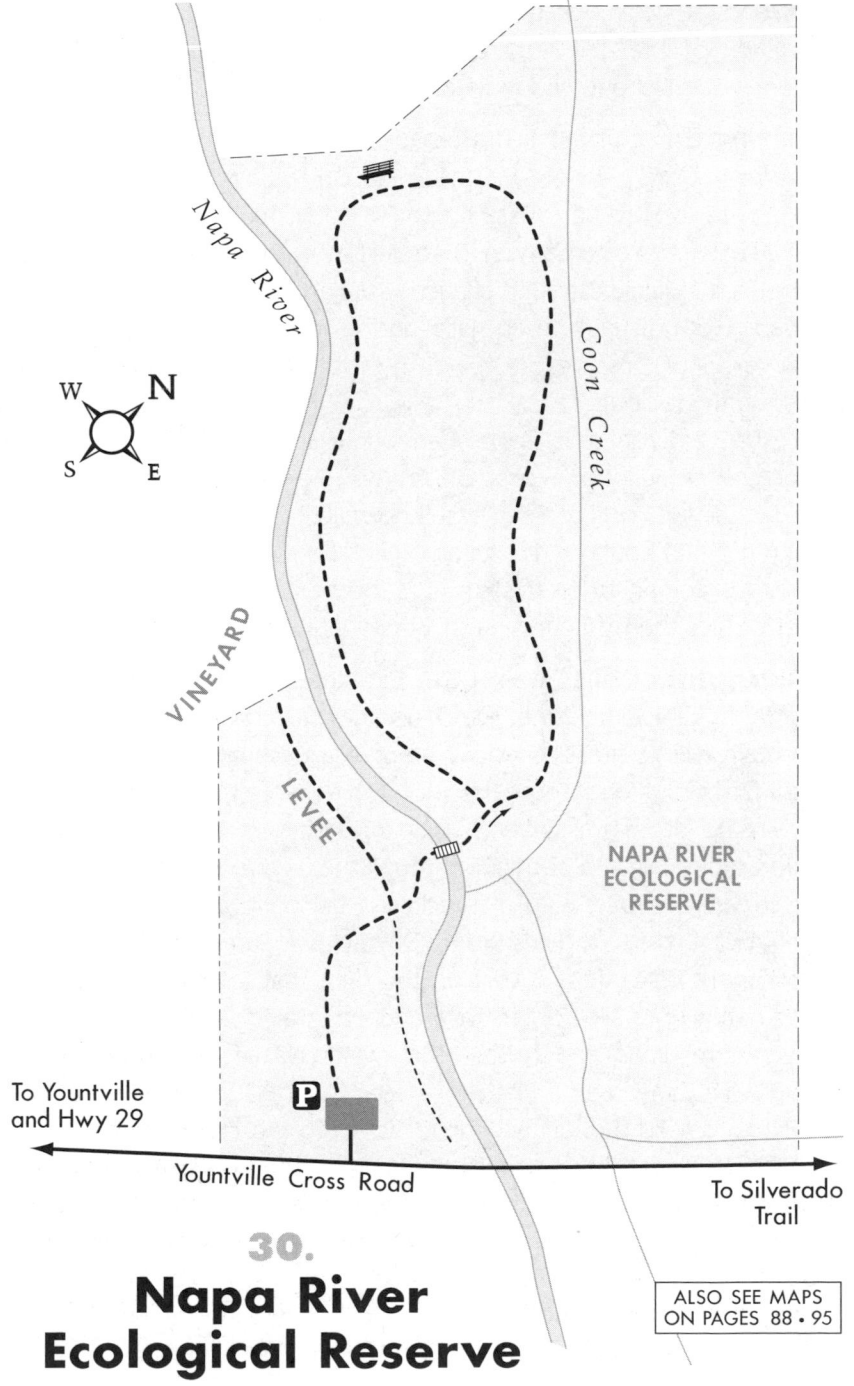

W **N** E
S

Napa River

Coon Creek

VINEYARD

LEVEE

NAPA RIVER
ECOLOGICAL
RESERVE

To Yountville
and Hwy 29

Yountville Cross Road

To Silverado
Trail

30.
Napa River
Ecological Reserve

ALSO SEE MAPS
ON PAGES 88 • 95

Beyond the cabin site, the trail climbs a ridge to Zim Zim Falls. This portion of the trail requires some tenacity to follow, as it is steep, washed out, and indistinct.

Driving directions: RUTHERFORD: From the Silverado Trail east of Rutherford, drive 11.2 miles east on Sage Canyon Road (Highway 128) to Berryessa Knoxville Road. Turn left and continue 13 miles to Pope Canyon Road, just after crossing Pope Creek. Continue 11.1 miles straight ahead—staying on Berryessa Knoxville Road—to a distinct green gate on the left. It is located at mile marker 24.00, just before the fifth crossing over Eticuera Creek. Park in the pullout.

ANGWIN: From the Pope Canyon Road and Chiles & Pope Valley Road junction—east of Angwin—drive 9.3 miles east on Pope Canyon Road to Berryessa Knoxville Road at Lake Berryessa. Turn left and continue 11.1 miles on Berryessa Knoxville Road to a distinct green gate on the left. It is located at mile marker 24.00, just before the fifth crossing of Eticuera Creek. Park in the pullout.

Hiking directions: Walk past the green gate on the south edge of Zim Zim Creek. Head up the old dirt road, and pass through a large grass meadow along the base of the hills. Cross Zim Zim Creek and enter the mouth of the canyon. The canyon opens up into a grassy valley dotted with oaks. Hop across Zim Zim Creek again and continue through the meadow. Cross a feeder stream, and pass an unmarked road on the left that climbs the southwest hills to Adams Ridge. Drop down and cross the creek four more times. Pass a trail on the right that crosses the creek and heads up a side drainage. Continue straight, cross the creek two more times, and follow the west side of the creek. Hop over Zim Zim Creek a ninth time, and walk 80 yards uphill to a Y-fork. Stay to the left and drop down to the creek, where the dirt road ends. Make a tenth crossing of the creek, and follow the cliff-hugging footpath uphill. Zim Zim Falls is around the bend to the left. Due to erosion, reaching the falls entails continuing up a steep cliff thick with brush and some rock scrambling. Beyond this point the trail is not recommended, as it is indistinct and the footing is treacherous. Return by retracing your steps. ■

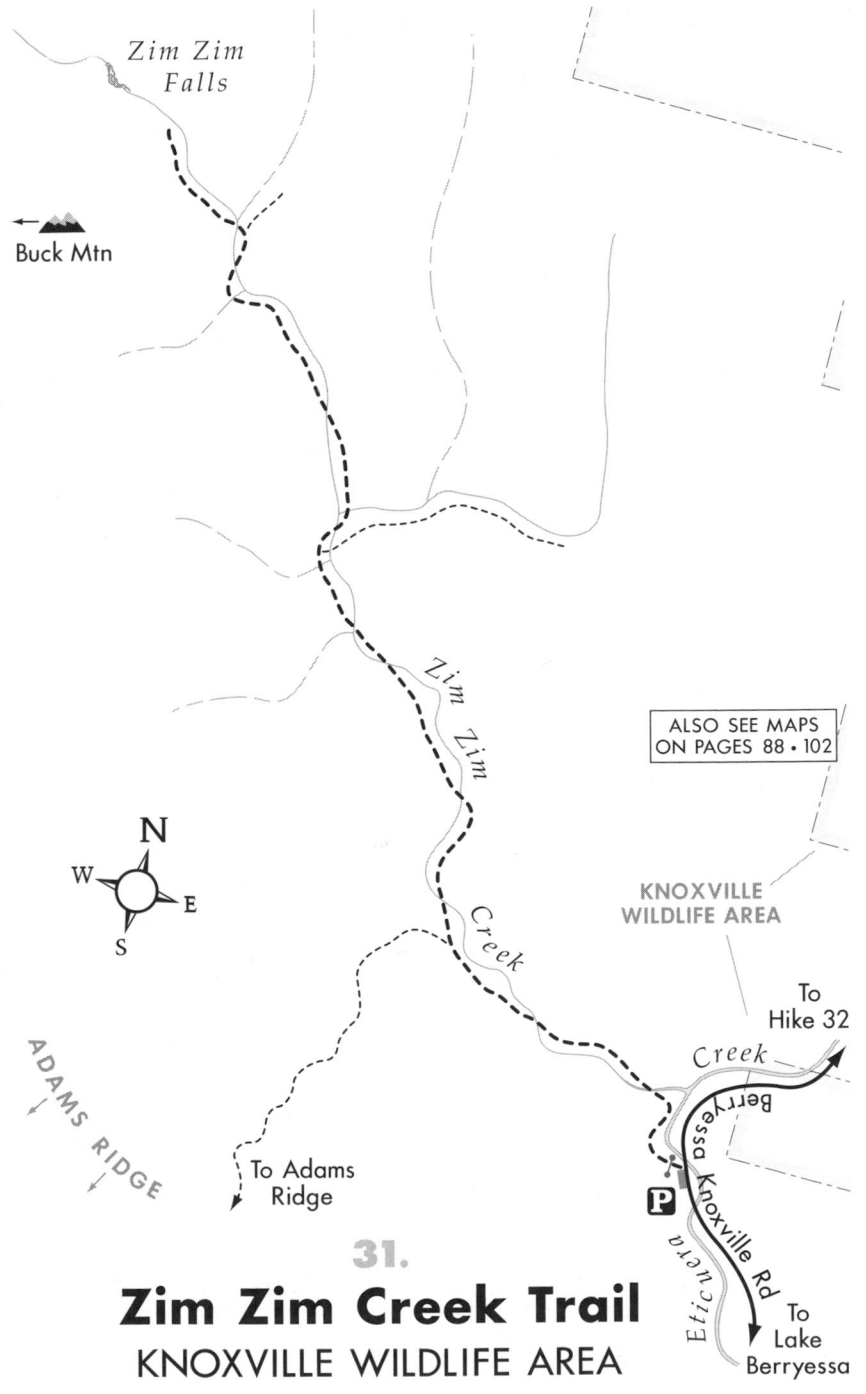

Zim Zim
Falls

Buck Mtn

Zim Zim

Creek

N
W E
S

ALSO SEE MAPS
ON PAGES 88 · 102

KNOXVILLE
WILDLIFE AREA

To
Hike 32

Creek

Berryessa

ADAMS RIDGE

To Adams
Ridge

P

Knoxville Rd

Eticuera

To
Lake
Berryessa

31.

Zim Zim Creek Trail
KNOXVILLE WILDLIFE AREA

32. Long Canyon
KNOXVILLE WILDLIFE AREA

Hiking distance: 3.8-mile loop
Hiking time: 2 hours
Elevation gain: 500 feet
Dogs: allowed
Maps: U.S.G.S. Knoxville
Calif. Dept. of Fish and Game, Knoxville Wildlife Area

Summary of hike: The Knoxville Wildlife Area is part of the Eticuera Creek watershed, a major feeder stream of Lake Berryessa a few miles to the south. Access to the remote area is from Berryessa Knoxville Road, which requires driving through shallow Eticuera Creek numerous times. The wildlife area offers hike-in access only. Recreational uses include fishing, primitive camping, hunting and hiking, with a gorgeous display of wildflowers in the spring. Old ranch roads and dirt trails course through the hilly, winding lands.

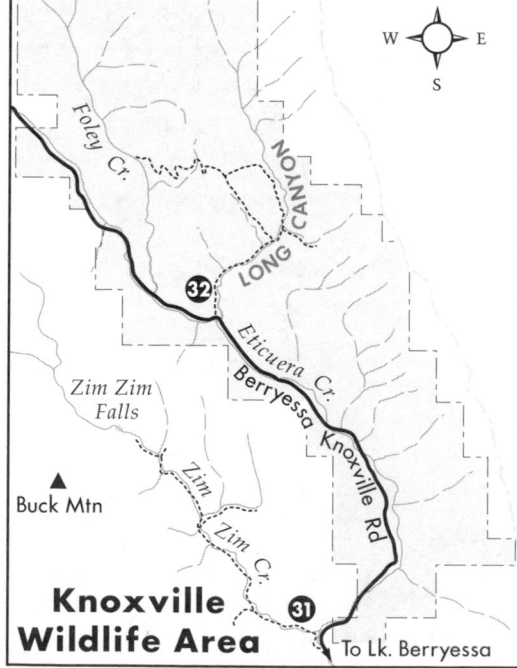

Long Canyon is a four-mile-long canyon that lies along the western base of Blue Ridge. This hike follows a portion of the serpentine canyon along a tributary of Eticuera Creek. The route climbs to a ridge above Foley Canyon with spectacular views, then loops back to the floor of Long Canyon.

Driving directions:
RUTHERFORD: From the Silverado Trail east of

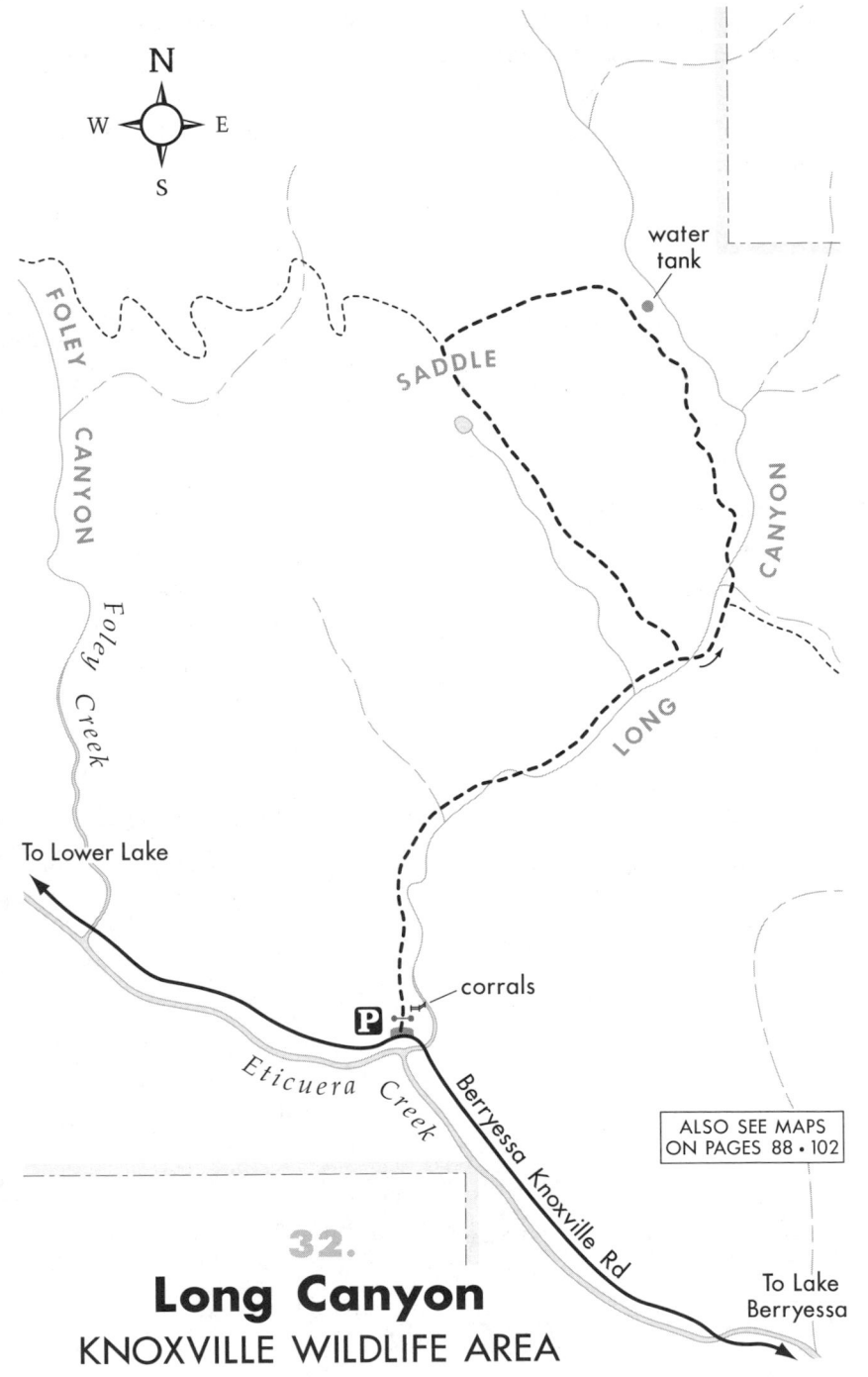

N
W · E
S

water tank

SADDLE

FOLEY CANYON

Foley Creek

CANYON

LONG

To Lower Lake

corrals

P

Eticuera Creek

Berryessa Knoxville Rd

ALSO SEE MAPS ON PAGES 88 · 102

To Lake Berryessa

32.

Long Canyon
KNOXVILLE WILDLIFE AREA

Rutherford, drive 11.2 miles east on Sage Canyon Road (Highway 128) to Berryessa Knoxville Road. Turn left and continue 13 miles to Pope Canyon Road, just after crossing over Pope Creek. Continue 15.4 miles straight ahead—staying on Berryessa Knoxville Road—to a wide parking area with a green gate on the right. It is located on a sweeping left bend in the road by mile marker 28.25.

ANGWIN: From the Pope Canyon Road and Chiles & Pope Valley Road junction—east of Angwin—drive 9.3 miles east on Pope Canyon Road to Berryessa Knoxville Road at Lake Berryessa. Turn left and continue 15.4 miles to a wide parking area with a green gate on the right. It is located on a sweeping left bend in the road by mile marker 28.25.

Hiking directions: Climb over the trailhead gate, and follow the grassy path past corrals on the right. Enter the mouth of Long Canyon, and traverse the west slope above the ephemeral creek. Stroll through oak groves and grassland meadows. Curve right, following the curve of the canyon. Cross Long Creek two consecutive times, and weave up canyon to a third creek crossing. A path on the left veers into a side canyon—our return route. Begin the loop to the right. Cross the creekbed as the canyon begins to narrow. Blue Ridge towers 1,300 feet above the trail. Follow the drainage to a Y-fork. The right fork climbs up a side canyon to the east. Stay in Long Canyon on the left fork, and cross the creek a fourth time after 60 yards. Head up the west canyon slope, climbing high above the canyon floor. Curve left as views open to upper Long Canyon. Walk along the level, grassy slope with ever-changing vistas. Pass a metal watertank and curve left into a side canyon. Continue up the side canyon, following the hillside contours to a grassy flat and a junction. The right fork leaves Long Canyon and leads into the Foley Creek drainage. Bear left 50 yards to a saddle. Descend from the saddle, and pass a large pond on the right. Head down the canyon on a grassy footpath above and parallel to the drainage. Slowly descend to a T-junction on the floor of Long Canyon, completing the loop. Bear right and retrace your steps back to the trailhead. ▪

33. Barton Hill
LAKE BERRYESSA

Hiking distance: 0.9-mile loop
Hiking time: 30 minutes
Elevation gain: 80 feet
Dogs: allowed
Maps: U.S.G.S. Walter Springs

map
page 107

Summary of hike: Lake Berryessa is a man-made reservoir on the rural and wild eastern side of Napa County. Prior to the inundation of the reservoir, Berryessa Valley was a productive agricultural region. Monticello, the main town in the valley, was abandoned in order to construct the reservoir. Monticello Dam, built in 1957, rises to a height of 304 feet and spans over a thousand feet across Devil's Gate Canyon on Putah Creek at the southern end of the reservoir. The 26-mile-long lake covers 19,250 acres and is among the largest lakes in California.

The lake is nestled between Blue Ridge and Cedar Roughs. It is surrounded by nearly 29,000 acres of federally owned or managed lands. Oak woodlands and chaparral-covered slopes surround the steep and rocky southern end of the lake. The shallow north end has a grassy shoreline with gentle, sloping banks.

Barton Hill is a rounded, 500-foot grassy knoll dotted with oaks on the northwest shore of Lake Berryessa. Located between the inlet streams of Putah Creek and Eticuera Creek, Barton Hill juts out into the lake. This easy hike circles the scenic knoll, overlooking inlets and coves populated with migratory birds and shorebirds. Throughout the hike are gorgeous vistas up and across the lake to the surrounding mountains.

Driving directions: RUTHERFORD: From the Silverado Trail east of Rutherford, drive 11.2 miles east on Sage Canyon Road (Highway 128) to Berryessa Knoxville Road. Turn left and continue 13 miles to Pope Canyon Road, just after crossing over Pope Creek. Continue 3 miles straight ahead—staying on Berryessa Knoxville Road—to the posted Barton Hill Trail on the right by mile marker 15.87. Park in the pullout on the right by the trailhead.

ANGWIN: From the Pope Canyon Road and Chiles & Pope Valley Road junction—east of Angwin—drive 9.3 miles east on Pope Canyon Road to Berryessa Knoxville Road at Lake Berryessa. Turn left and continue 3 miles to the posted Barton Hill Trail on the right by mile marker 15.87. Park in the pullout on the right by the trailhead.

Hiking directions: Walk down wooden steps past the Barton Hill trail sign to the oak-dotted hillside. Head down the sloping meadow overlooking Lake Berryessa and the rugged eastern mountains across the lake. Near the shoreline, at the base of the Barton Hill, veer left and follow the footpath to the east end of the promontory. Go left and head north along the base of Barton Hill, skirting the edge of the cliffs above a rocky beach. Descend to the beach in a deep cove. Cross the beach or take the parallel footpath along the edge of the hillside cliff. Continue to the protected calm water at the west end of the cove. Walk up Gibson Flat, an open grassland rimmed with oaks. Pass through the Gibson Flat trailhead gate at Berryessa Knoxville Road. Walk 0.15 miles left on the road, completing the loop at the Barton Hill trailhead.■

34. Pope Canyon Trail

Hiking distance: 2.4 miles round trip
Hiking time: 1.5 hours
Elevation gain: 200 feet
Dogs: allowed
Maps: U.S.G.S. Chiles Valley
       Pope Canyon trail map

map
page 109

Summary of hike: Pope Canyon lies on the north edge of Cedar Roughs, one of the creeks that feeds Lake Berryessa from the west. It is a highly scenic agricultural area that is rapidly becoming dominated by vineyards. Cedar Roughs, a federally designated Wilderness Study Area, is a forested area with a high concentration of shrubby Sargent and McNabb cypress trees.

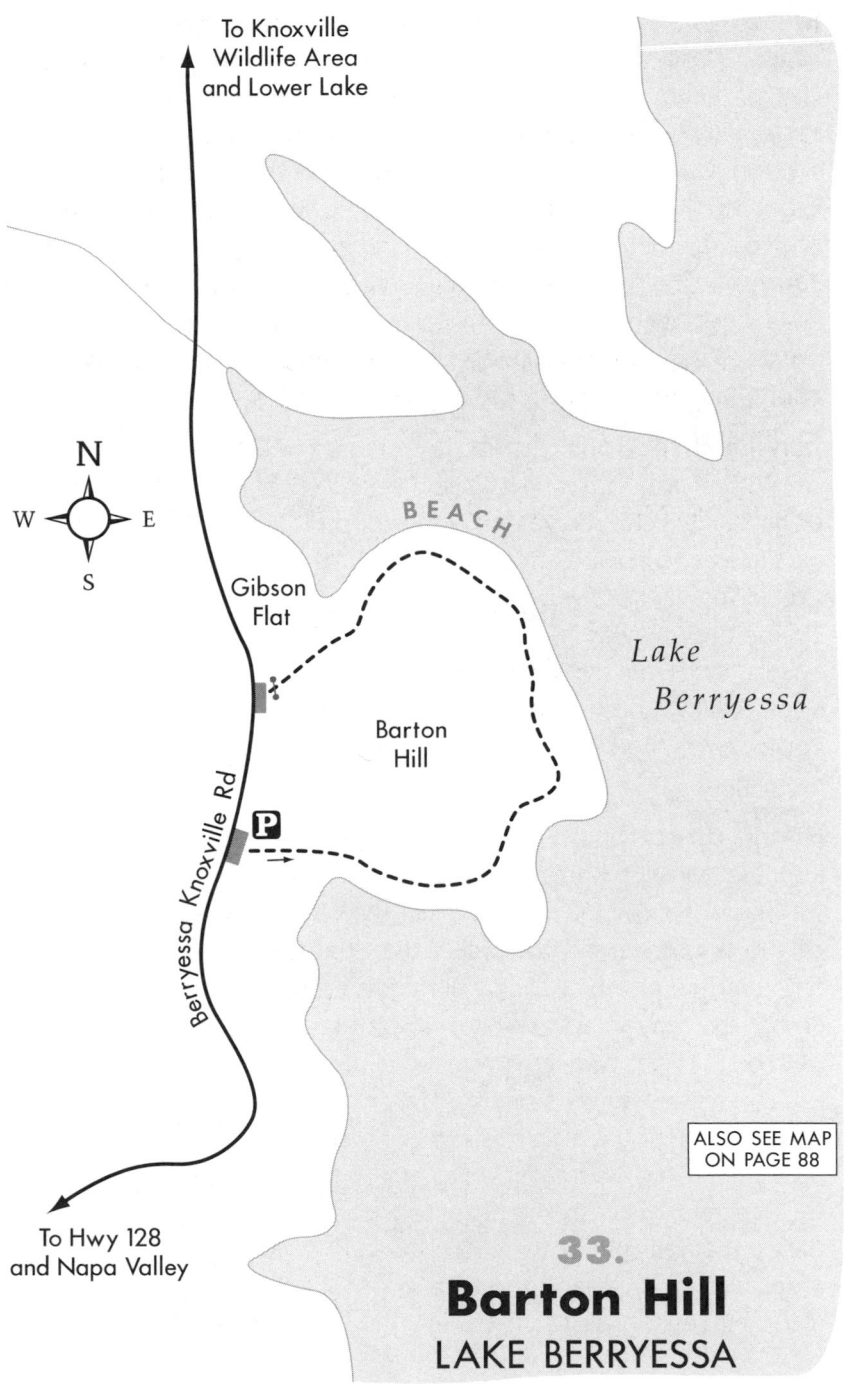

To Knoxville
Wildlife Area
and Lower Lake

N
W · E
S

Gibson
Flat

B E A C H

Lake
Berryessa

Barton
Hill

Berryessa Knoxville Rd

P

ALSO SEE MAP
ON PAGE 88

To Hwy 128
and Napa Valley

33.
Barton Hill
LAKE BERRYESSA

Sargent cypress groves occur only in California, and this is the largest stand in the state, stretching over 3,000 acres. Pope Canyon Road winds along Pope Creek from Lake Berryessa to Pope Valley. The Pope Canyon Trail follows the original Pope Canyon Road, a wide dirt road along the north side of Pope Creek at the northern base of Cedar Roughs. The trail begins above the creek and descends to the Pope Canyon arm of Lake Berryessa. The route leads to a grassy area on the shoreline amid large oaks, scenic rock outcroppings, and cliffs angling directly down to the water. The deep canyon is a great area for spotting osprey and western grebes.

Driving directions: RUTHERFORD: From the Silverado Trail east of Rutherford, drive 11.2 miles east on Sage Canyon Road (Highway 128) to Berryessa Knoxville Road. Turn left and continue 13 miles to Pope Canyon Road, just after crossing over Pope Creek. Turn left and drive 2.4 miles to the dirt pullout on the left by the brown metal gate.

ANGWIN: From the junction of Pope Canyon Road and Chiles & Pope Valley Road—east of Angwin—drive 7.1 miles east on Pope Canyon Road to the dirt pullout on the right by the brown metal gate.

Hiking directions: Pass the brown metal gate and descend into the oak-filled grassland. Curve left, parallel to Pope Creek far below. Follow the north wall of the canyon, passing a couple of old landslides and traversing the contours of the cliffs. The trail overlooks vertical rock walls covered in lichen, forested hills across the canyon, and pools in Pope Creek. At 0.7 miles, a side path on the right weaves down the hillside through oaks, bay laurel, and manzanita to a sloping beach on the edge of the wide creek. Return to the main trail and continue southeast, with a view up a stream-fed side canyon. Pass through an old fence, and gently descend beneath the forested hills to the banks of Pope Creek. The trail ends at the shoreline and a sweeping elbow in the creek, where it widens into an arm of Lake Berryessa. Return by retracing your steps.■

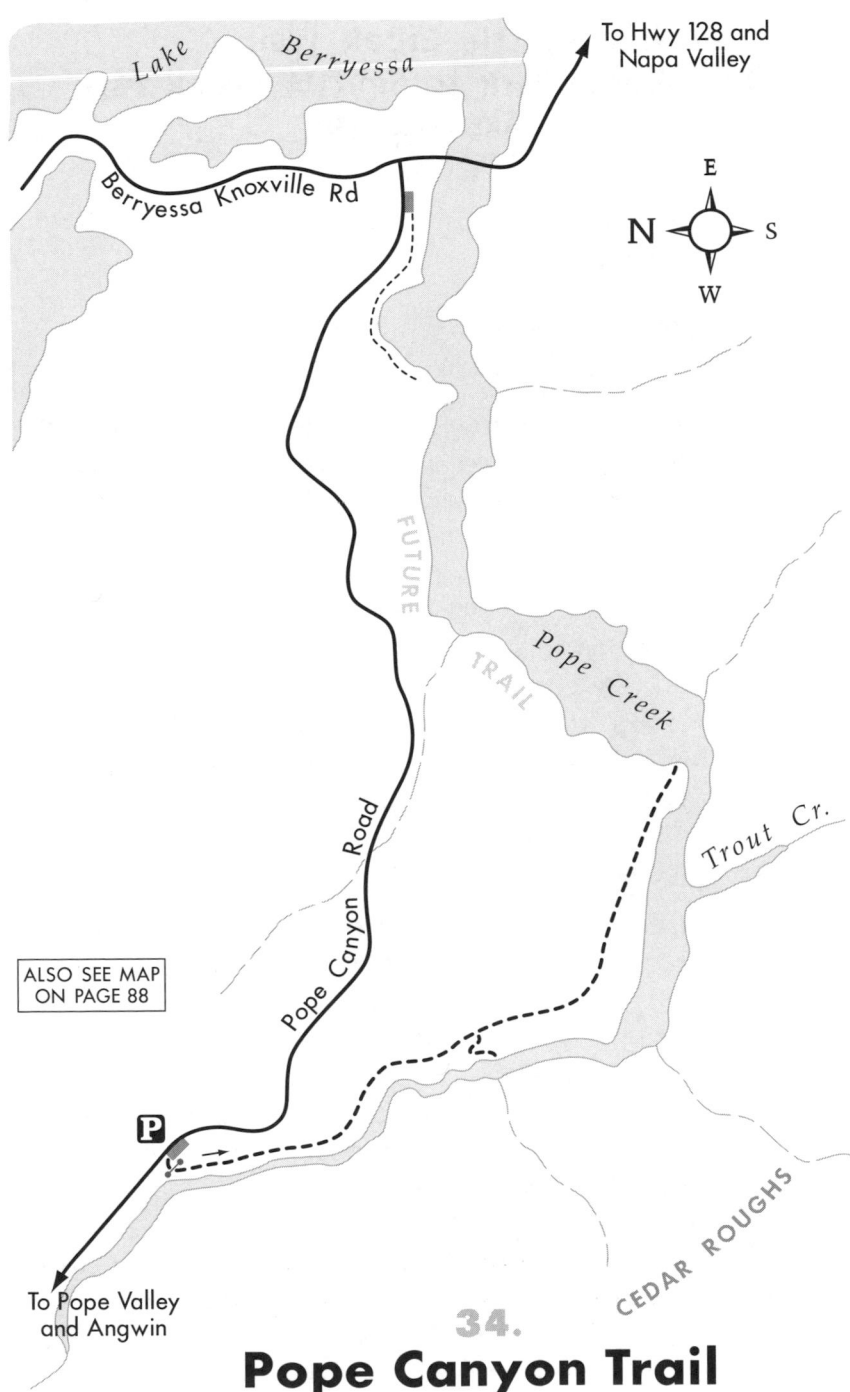

Lake Berryessa

To Hwy 128 and Napa Valley

Berryessa Knoxville Rd

E
N — S
W

FUTURE

TRAIL

Pope Creek

Trout Cr.

Pope Canyon Road

ALSO SEE MAP ON PAGE 88

P

CEDAR ROUGHS

To Pope Valley and Angwin

34.
Pope Canyon Trail

35. Smittle Creek Trail:
Oak Shores Park to Smittle Creek Park
LAKE BERRYESSA

Hiking distance: 5 miles round trip
Hiking time: 2.5 hours
Elevation gain: 100 feet
Dogs: allowed
Maps: U.S.G.S. Lake Berryessa
Smittle Creek trail map

Summary of hike: Berryessa Knoxville Road parallels the west shore of Lake Berryessa and offers access to marinas, campgrounds, beaches, and the park headquarters. Oak Shores Park and Smittle Creek Park sit on the west shore of Lake Berryessa. The large day-use parks are popular recreation areas with sandy beaches, picnic areas, and fishing sites. Oak Shores Park has eight different recreation areas with a hundred picnic sites. The two lakefront parks are connected by the Smittle Creek Trail, a 2.6-mile trail that follows the shoreline of Lake Berryessa (back cover photo). The trail explores gorgeous inlets, quiet coves, and crosses over oak-covered knolls. Throughout the hike are close-up views of Big Island and Small Island, where bald eagles are frequently sighted.

Driving directions: RUTHERFORD: From the Silverado Trail east of Rutherford, drive 11.2 miles east on Sage Canyon Road (Highway 128) to Berryessa Knoxville Road. Turn left and continue 7.5 miles to the Oak Shores Day Use Area on the right. (It is located 0.8 miles past the visitor center.) Turn right to the entrance kiosk. From the kiosk, turn left and drive 0.8 miles, following the signs to Coyote Knolls. Park in the paved lot by the Smittle Creek Trail sign and kiosk on the right.

NAPA: From the Silverado Trail and Trancas Street in Napa, drive 12.5 miles northeast on Highway 121 (Monticello Road) to a T-junction with Highway 128. Turn left and continue 4.8 miles to Berryessa Knoxville Road. Turn right and continue 7.5 miles to the Oak Shores Day Use Area, following the directions above.

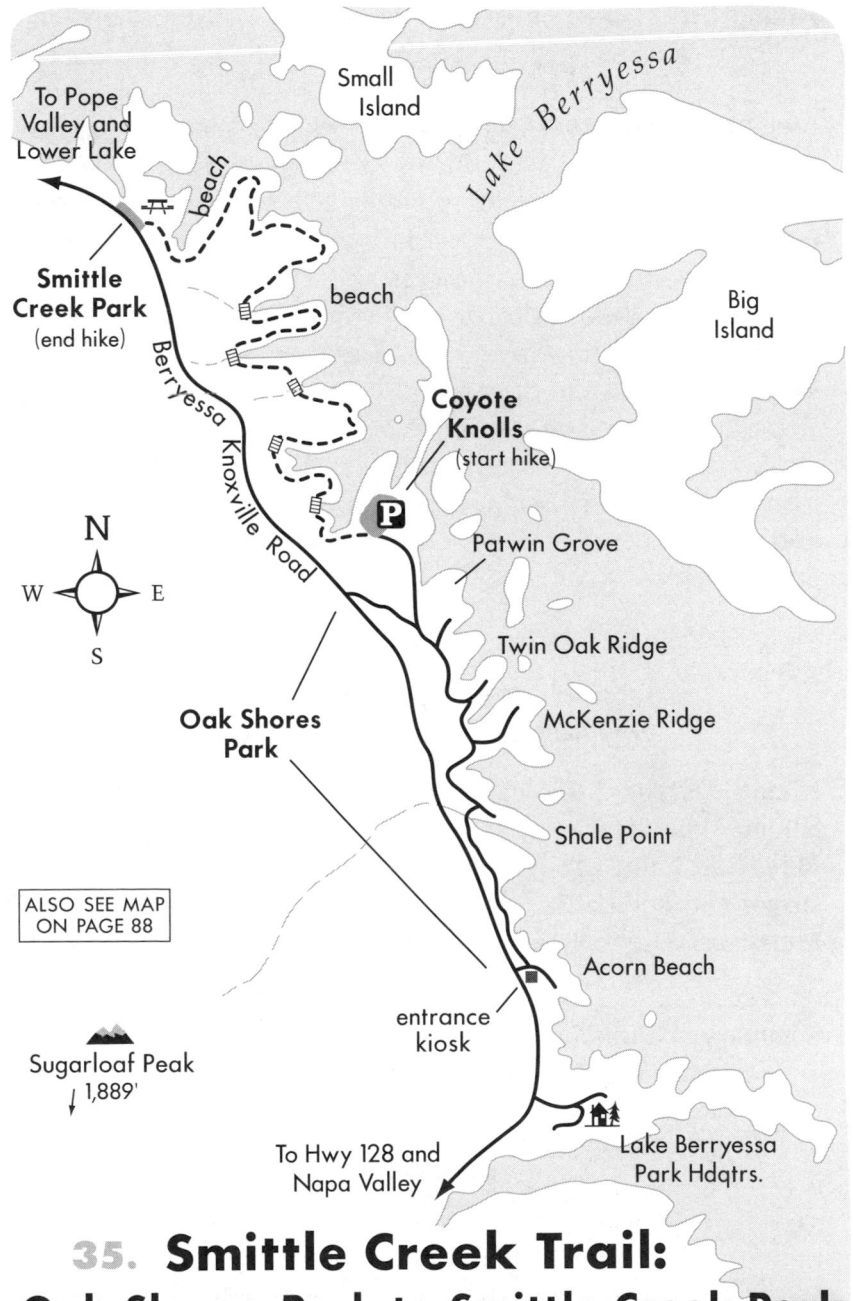

Small Island

Lake Berryessa

To Pope Valley and Lower Lake

beach

Smittle Creek Park
(end hike)

beach

Big Island

Berryessa Knoxville Road

Coyote Knolls
(start hike)

P

Patwin Grove

N
W — E
S

Twin Oak Ridge

Oak Shores Park

McKenzie Ridge

Shale Point

ALSO SEE MAP ON PAGE 88

Acorn Beach

entrance kiosk

Sugarloaf Peak
↓ 1,889'

To Hwy 128 and Napa Valley

Lake Berryessa Park Hdqtrs.

35. **Smittle Creek Trail:**
Oak Shores Park to Smittle Creek Park
LAKE BERRYESSA

Hiking directions: Take the well-defined path northbound, and loop around a finger of the lake. Staying close to the water, loop around a second finger through groves of live oak, manzanita, and grassland. Leave the two-fingered inlet, and skirt a small bay overlooking the two oak-studded islands of Big Island and Small Island. Follow the edge of the main body of Lake Berryessa, and loop around another finger of the lake. Cross a wooden footbridge over the seasonal drainage. Zigzag up the hillside and descend through the forest to the back end of another cove. Cross a bridge over the drainage and climb a couple of switchbacks. Return to the edge of the lake, and continue on the sloping hillside to a beach on the main body of the lake. Climb steps, traverse the hill, and loop around another inlet. Walk over a bridge and cross over two consecutive hills, passing two more inlets. The trail ends at a picnic area with sandy beaches at the Smittle Creek picnic area. ■

36. Homestead Trail
STEBBINS COLD CANYON RESERVE

Hiking distance: 2 miles round trip
Hiking time: 1 hour
Elevation gain: 350 feet

map
page 116

Dogs: not allowed
Maps: U.S.G.S. Monticello Dam and Mt. Vaca
     Stebbins Cold Canyon Reserve trail map

Summary of hike: Lake Berryessa sits in the mountainous eastern side of Napa County about 40 minutes from Napa Valley. Monticello Dam, located 9 miles west of Winters on Putah Creek, restrains Lake Berryessa. Prior to 1957 (before the dam was built), it was the site of Monticello Valley and the small farming community of Monticello. The remains of the townsite are deep beneath the surface of the lake. Just downstream from Monticello Dam lies Stebbins Cold Canyon Reserve, a holding in the University of California Natural Reserve System. The area is named for a world-renowned plant geneticist, naturalist, and professor at UC Davis and Berkeley.

The Homestead Trail begins at the mouth of the canyon and gently climbs along the canyon bottom to the old Vlahos homestead and a cold storage area from the mid-1930s. Stone foundations of the former farmhouse still remain. The trail ends in a shady glen under big-leaf maples on the banks of Cold Creek by a waterfall and the old cold storage foundations. This hike can be combined with Hike 37 for a rugged 5-mile loop hike.

Driving directions: RUTHERFORD: From the Silverado Trail east of Rutherford, drive 26.8 miles east on Sage Canyon Road (Highway 128) to the Stebbins–Cold Canyon parking pullout on the right by a metal gate on a sweeping left bend. The pullout is 0.4 miles past the Monticello Dam. If the pullout is full, drive 100 yards farther to a large parking area on the left.

NAPA: From the Silverado Trail and Trancas Street in Napa, drive 12.5 miles northeast on Highway 121 (Monticello Road) to a T-junction with Highway 128. Turn right and continue 10.8 miles to the Stebbins–Cold Canyon parking pullout on the right by a metal gate on a sweeping left bend. Continue with the directions above.

Hiking directions: Pass through the trailhead gate to a junction. The left fork leads to Pleasants Ridge (Hike 38). Take the right fork to the canyon floor. Parallel the east side of seasonal Cold Creek, passing the sign-in station and information kiosk. Head up the canyon on a gentle grade beneath Blue Ridge to the west, which straddles the Napa–Solano county line. Cross transient Cold Creek in a forest of gray pines, passing pools in the bedrock as the trail continues up canyon along the creek. Walk across a wooden footbridge, and continue uphill through scrub oak and buckbrush chaparral to a view of Wild Horse Canyon, which merges with Cold Canyon from the east (left). Pass low stone foundations and scattered remains, including wood boards and rusted metal remnants from the Vlahos homestead on the right, an old goat farm. (Hike 37 continues up the wood steps on the hillside.) After exploring the open area around the farmhouse, descend into a cool, shaded oasis with large big-leaf maple trees and California bay. Ford the creek to another rock foundation used by the Vlahos family as a cold storage area. Beneath the shade of the trees is a small waterfall pouring over boulders into a pool. This is the end of the trail. Return by retracing your steps.

To extend the hike into a steep 5-mile loop, continue with Hike 37.■

37. Blue Ridge Loop Trail
STEBBINS COLD CANYON RESERVE

Hiking distance: 5-mile loop
Hiking time: 3 hours
Elevation gain: 1,500 feet
Dogs: allowed, but not recommended
Maps: U.S.G.S. Monticello Dam and Mt. Vaca
     Stebbins Cold Canyon Reserve trail map

map
page 116

Summary of hike: Stebbins Cold Canyon Reserve encompasses 576 acres in the Vaca Mountains just east of Napa County in Solano County. The reserve lies in the steep canyons of the northern coastal range and includes the drainages of Cold Canyon and Wild Horse Canyon. Most of the land bordering the reserve is public, adding approximately 4,000 acres of protected rugged wildlands (predominantly U.S. Bureau of Land Management and California Department of Fish and Game land). The undisturbed habitats include valley and foothill grasslands, blue oak woodlands, chaparral-covered slopes, and mixed riparian woodlands with year-round springs and intermittent streams.

The Blue Ridge Loop Trail explores the western ridgeline atop Blue Ridge, connecting to the Cold Canyon floor via the old Homestead Trail (Hike 36). From the rolling ridge are overlooks of Cold Canyon, Lake Berryessa, Putah Creek Valley, and the surrounding mountains. This hike will test your endurance. Although dogs are allowed on the trail, it is not recommended. The trail is rocky and steep; the footing is unstable along the crumbly sandstone. Pack ample water.

Driving directions: RUTHERFORD: From the Silverado Trail east of Rutherford, drive 26.8 miles east on Sage Canyon Road (Highway 128) to the Stebbins–Cold Canyon parking pullout on the right by a metal gate on a sweeping left bend. The pullout is 0.4 miles past the Monticello Dam. If the pullout is full, drive 100 yards farther to a large parking area on the left.

NAPA: From the Silverado Trail and Trancas Street in Napa, drive 12.5 miles northeast on Highway 121 (Monticello Road) to a T-junction with Highway 128. Turn right and continue 10.8 miles to the Stebbins–Cold Canyon parking pullout on the right by a metal gate on a sweeping left bend. Continue with the directions above.

Hiking directions: From the end of Hike 36—by the Vlahos family cold storage foundation and the waterfall—return to the homestead foundation. Climb the wood steps to the west and head up the hillside. Traverse the hill on the narrow, undulating footpath. Climb a long, steep series of wood steps, zigzagging up the mountain. Near Blue Ridge, northern vistas reveal layers of ridges and canyons. Descend a short distance and curve right. Climb up Blue Ridge to a level area with an unmarked junction on the right at 1.9 miles. Straight ahead, the trail climbs 0.8 miles to a minor ridge and private property boundary. Instead, bear right along the loop and climb to a view of Lake Berryessa and Cold Canyon. The east-facing views extend across Pleasants Ridge and down Putah Creek Valley to Central Valley. Contour north, up and down the rock-embedded spine of Blue Ridge on a demanding roller coaster route with five summits. The fourth peak at 3 miles is covered with a lichen-encrusted jumble of boulders. After ascending the fifth peak, descend on the lake-facing slope to great views that include Monticello Dam, the gorge at the head of Putah Canyon (known as Devil's Gate), and the vertical sandstone cliffs. Veer right and steeply descend into Cold Canyon. The path levels out, weaves through an oak grove, and drops into the shade of the canyon forest. At 4.5 miles, pass through the trailhead gate to Highway 128. Bear right 80 yards on the highway, completing the loop at the parking area. ■

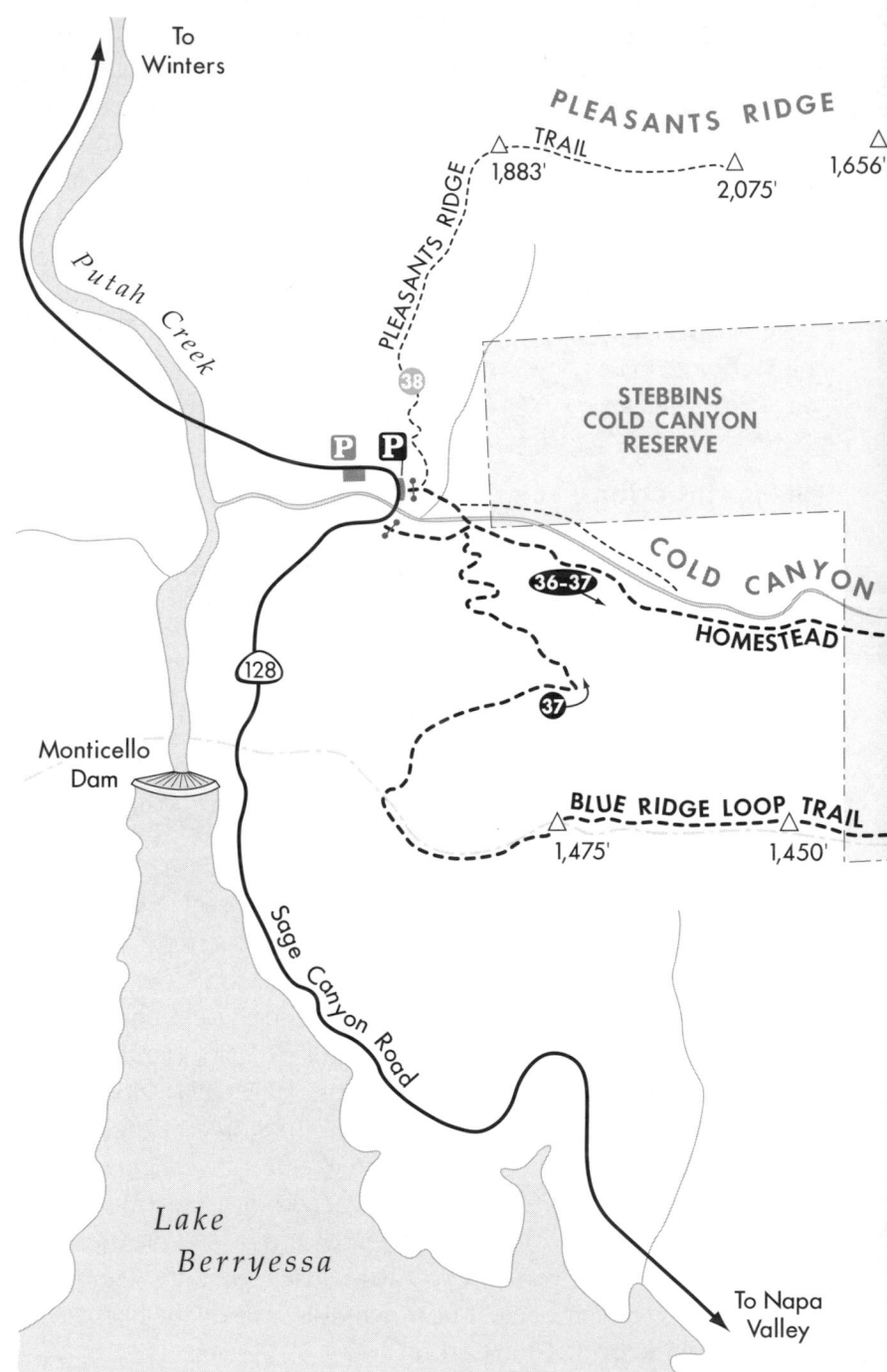

To
Winters

PLEASANTS RIDGE

PLEASANTS RIDGE TRAIL
△ 1,883'   △ 2,075'   △ 1,656'

Putah Creek

38 (P)

P P

STEBBINS
COLD CANYON
RESERVE

COLD CANYON

36-37

HOMESTEAD

128

37

BLUE RIDGE LOOP TRAIL
△ 1,475'   △ 1,450'

Monticello
Dam

Sage Canyon Road

Lake
Berryessa

To Napa
Valley

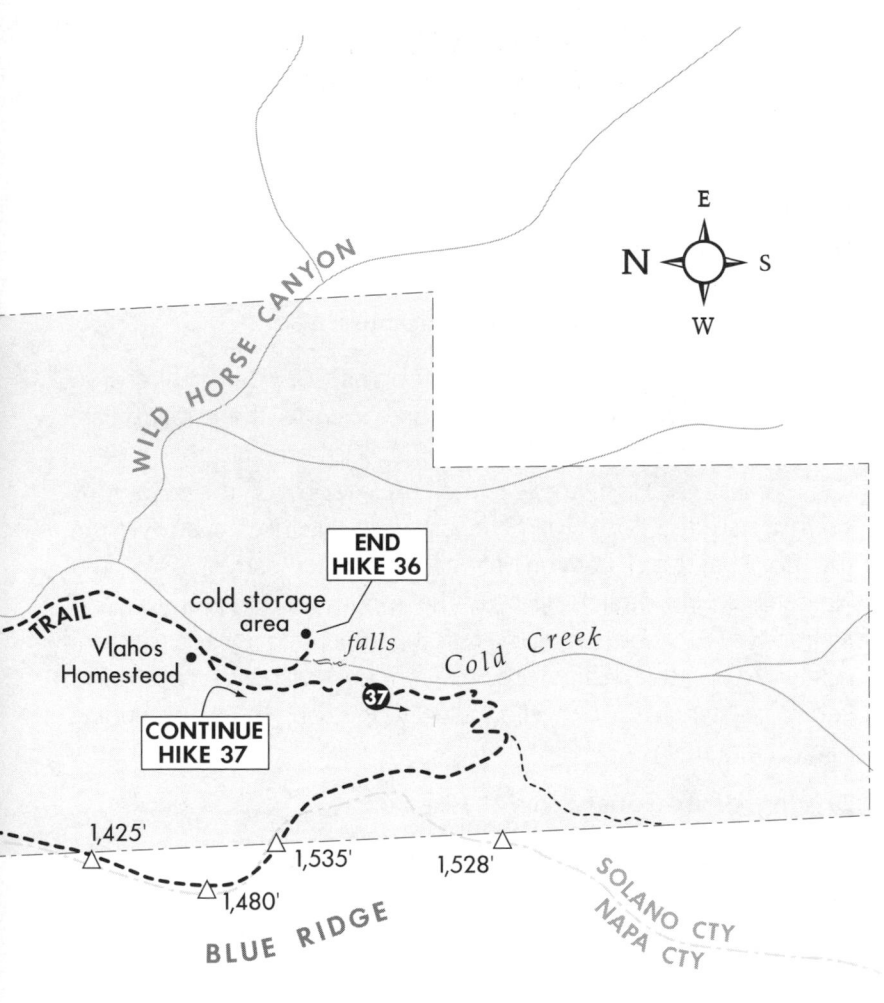

Stebbins Cold Canyon Reserve

HIKE 36
Homestead Trail

HIKE 37
Blue Ridge Loop Trail

38. Pleasants Ridge Trail
STEBBINS COLD CANYON RESERVE

Hiking distance: 2 miles round trip
Hiking time: 1 hour
Elevation gain: 1,500 feet
Dogs: not allowed
Maps: U.S.G.S. Monticello Dam and Mt. Vaca
Stebbins Cold Canyon Reserve trail map

Summary of hike: The trails in Stebbins Cold Canyon Reserve (a UC Davis ecological study area) are open to the public year-round. Access to the trails is at the northern mouth of Cold Canyon, just off Highway 128. The topography of the reserve is primarily steep, sloping land. Pleasants Ridge rises sharply from the floor of Cold Canyon, forming the east canyon wall. The Pleasants Ridge Trail begins at the mouth of the canyon and aggressively climbs the spine of the mountain to the eastern ridge. Atop the ridge are magnificent vistas across Lake Berryessa, Putah Creek Valley, Blue Ridge, and the surrounding rugged mountains.

Driving directions: Same as Hike 36.

Hiking directions: Pass through the trailhead gate to a junction. The right fork leads up to the old Vlahos homestead and Blue Ridge (Hikes 36 and 37). Take the left fork straight ahead. Climb up the south slope of the tree-filled canyon, and ascend the steep ridge through savanna dominated by blue oaks. Halfway up, traverse the south-facing slope below the ridge. Return to the ridge and climb to the 1,883-foot north summit that overlooks Monticello Dam, Lake Berryessa, the surrounding mountains, the town of Winters, and Central Valley. The path climbs another half mile south to the 2,075-foot summit. Return along the same route. ■

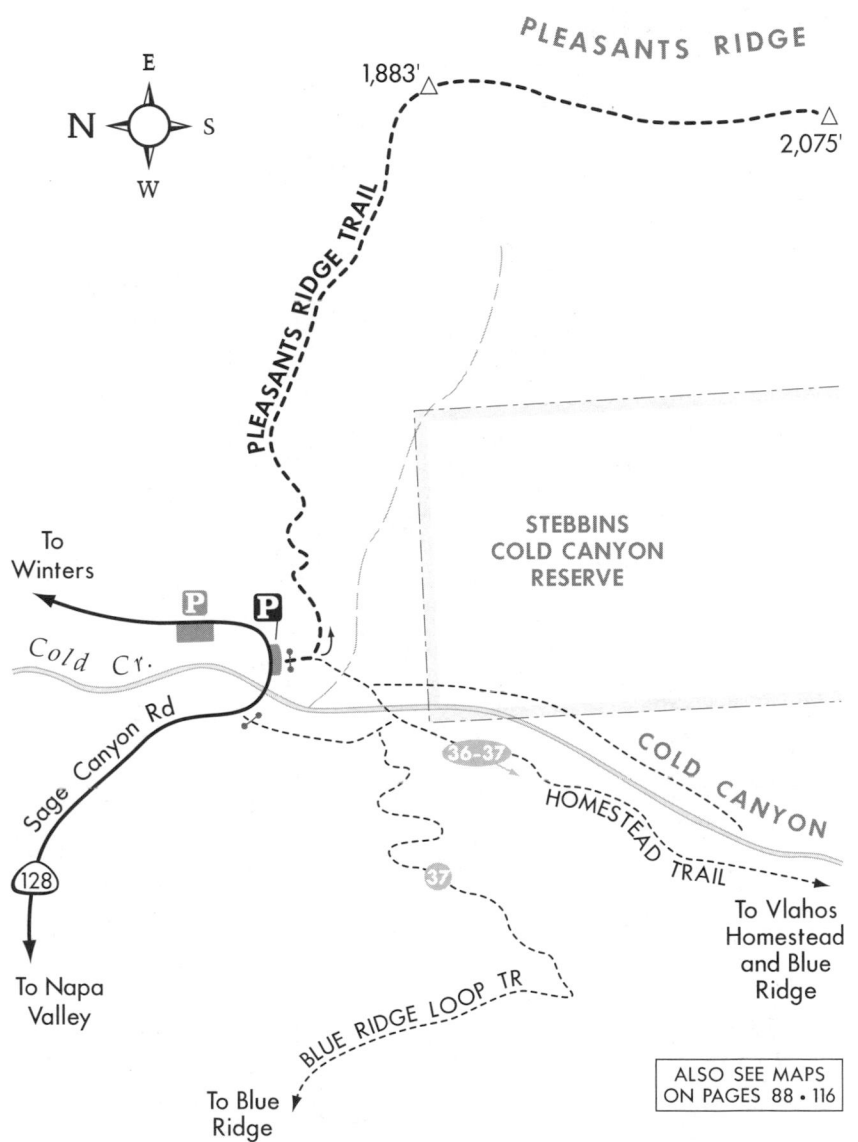

PLEASANTS RIDGE

1,883'
2,075'

PLEASANTS RIDGE TRAIL

N E S W

To Winters

STEBBINS COLD CANYON RESERVE

Cold Cr.

Sage Canyon Rd

128

To Napa Valley

36-37

37

COLD CANYON

HOMESTEAD TRAIL

To Vlahos Homestead and Blue Ridge

BLUE RIDGE LOOP TR

To Blue Ridge

ALSO SEE MAPS ON PAGES 88 • 116

38.

Pleasants Ridge Trail
STEBBINS COLD CANYON RESERVE

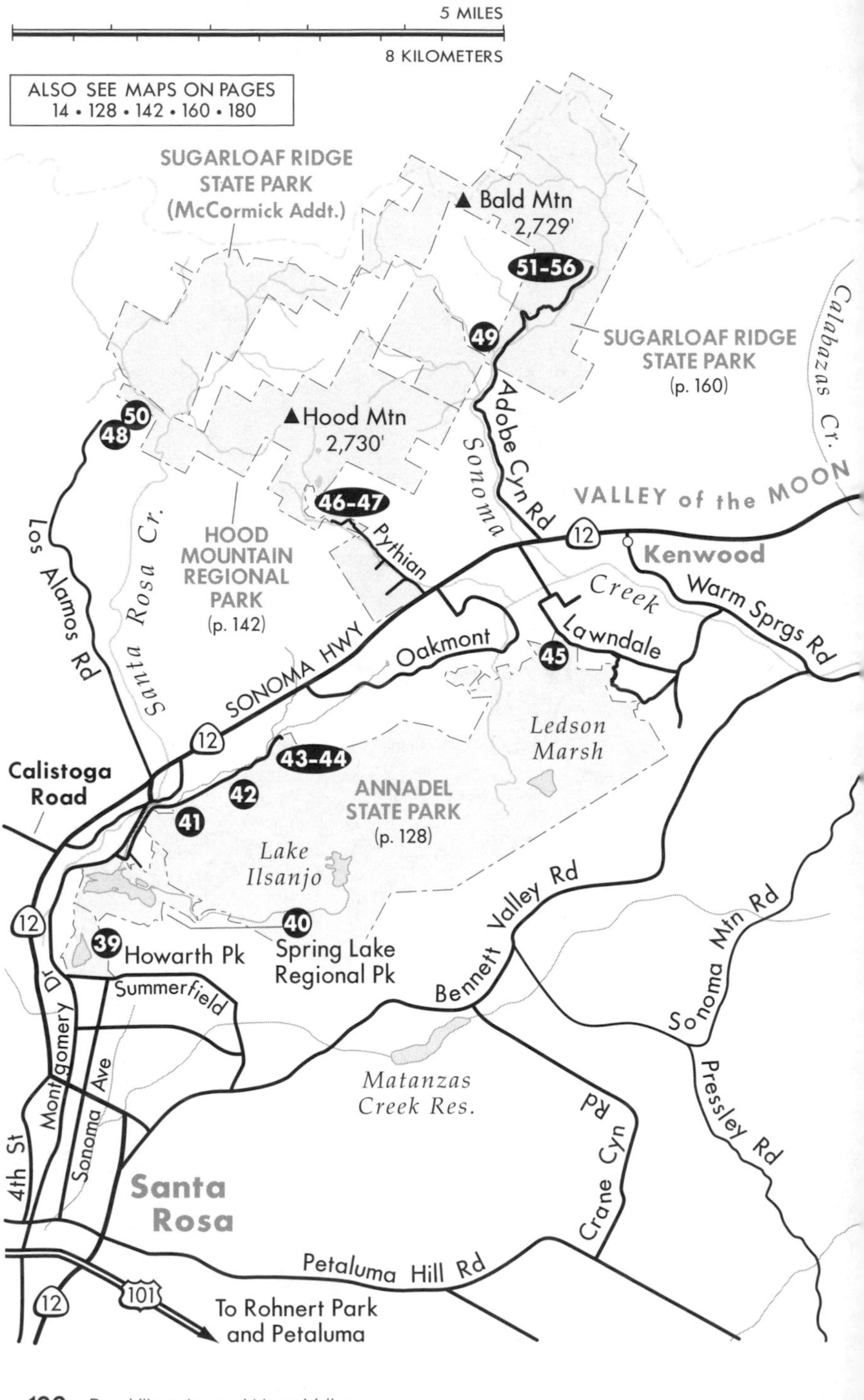

ALSO SEE MAPS ON PAGES
14 • 128 • 142 • 160 • 180

SUGARLOAF RIDGE
STATE PARK
(McCormick Addt.)

▲ Bald Mtn
2,729'

51-56

49

SUGARLOAF RIDGE
STATE PARK
(p. 160)

Calabazas Cr.

50
48

▲ Hood Mtn
2,730'

Sonoma

Adobe Cyn Rd

VALLEY of the MOON

Los Alamos Rd

Santa Rosa Cr.

HOOD
MOUNTAIN
REGIONAL
PARK
(p. 142)

46-47

Pythian

Sonoma

Creek

12

Kenwood

Warm Sprgs Rd

SONOMA HWY

Oakmont

Lawndale

45

Ledson
Marsh

12

Calistoga
Road

43-44

42

41

ANNADEL
STATE PARK
(p. 128)

Lake
Ilsanjo

Bennett Valley Rd

Sonoma Mtn Rd

12

39 Howarth Pk

40
Spring Lake
Regional Pk

Summerfield

Bennett

Pressley Rd

Montgomery Dr

Sonoma Ave

Matanzas
Creek Res.

Crane Cyn Rd

4th St

**Santa
Rosa**

Petaluma Hill Rd

12

101

To Rohnert Park
and Petaluma

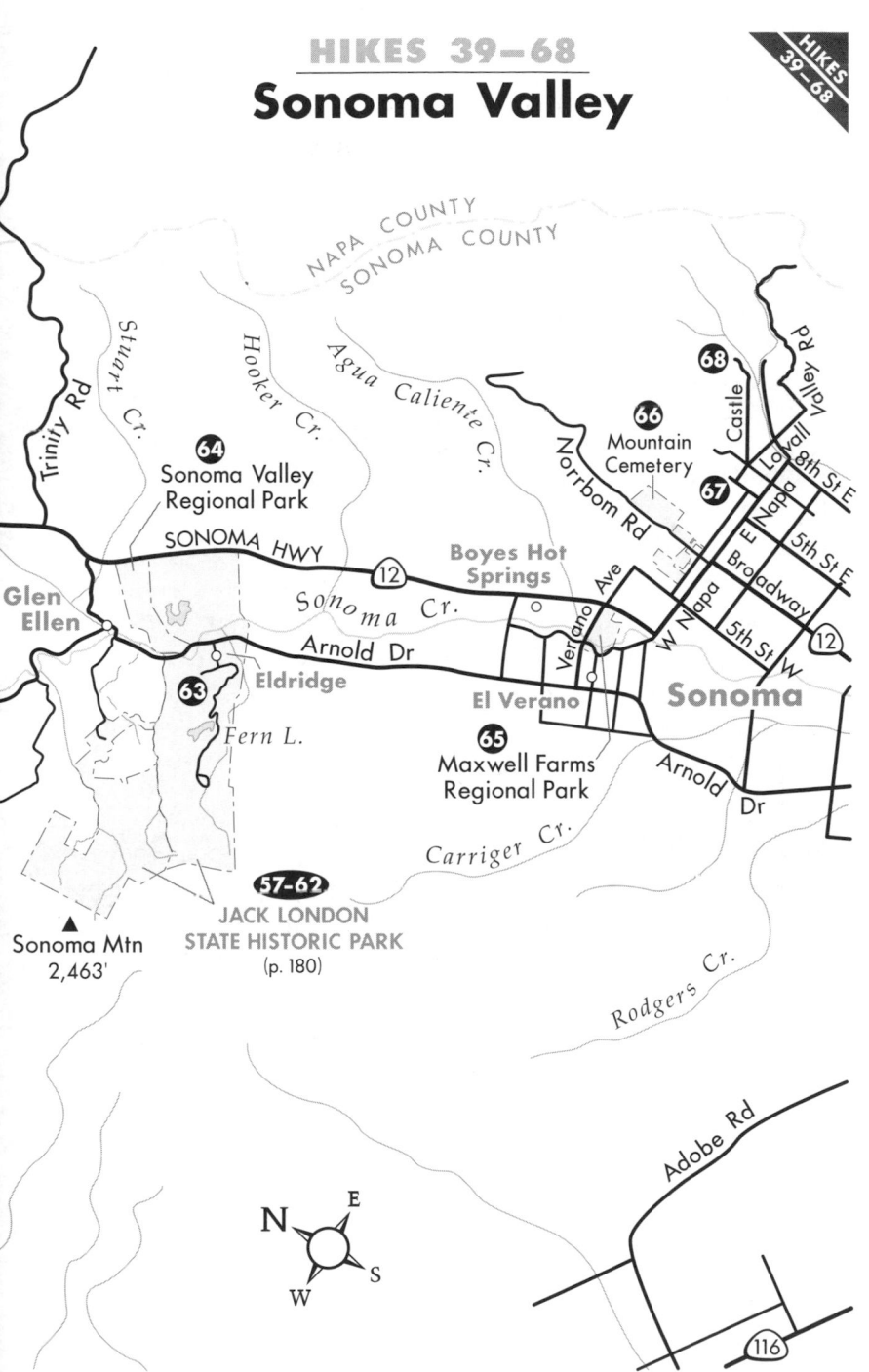

39. Howarth Park
Old Fisherman's—Eagle Scout Loop
around Lake Ralphine

630 Summerfield Road · Santa Rosa

Hiking distance: 0.9-mile loop
Hiking time: 30 minutes
Elevation gain: Level
Dogs: allowed
Maps: U.S.G.S. Santa Rosa
         Howarth Park Map and Trail Guide

map
page 124

Summary of hike: Howarth Park lies adjacent to Spring Lake Regional Park on the east side of Santa Rosa. The diverse 152-acre community park is one of the city's oldest and largest parks. It includes tennis courts; a softball field; a climbing wall; an amusement area with a train, carousel, and animal barn; and a 25-acre lake with boat rentals. Hiking and biking trails surround Lake Ralphine in the center of the park. The trails connect with Spring Lake Regional Park (Hike 40) and continue into Annadel State Park (Hikes 41—45). This hike loops around Lake Ralphine under stands of oaks.

Driving directions: NORTH SONOMA VALLEY: From Highway 12 and Calistoga Road on the northwest end of Sonoma Valley, drive 1.1 miles southeast on Highway 12 (Sonoma Highway) to Los Alamos Road. Turn right and drive 0.2 miles to Melita Road. Turn right and immediately veer left onto Montgomery Drive. Continue 2.2 miles to Summerfield Road. Turn left and go a quarter mile to the signed park entrance. Turn left into the park, and drive 0.2 miles to the parking lot at Lake Ralphine.

KENWOOD: From the town of Kenwood in Sonoma Valley, drive 5.8 miles northwest on Highway 12 (Sonoma Highway) to Los Alamos Road on the left. Turn left and continue with the directions above.

Hiking directions: From the south end of Lake Ralphine, take the paved Old Fisherman's Trail, a segment of the Bay Area Ridge

Trail. Follow the east side of the lake to a fork at 0.1 mile. Curve left onto a dirt path. Meander through oak trees and a mixed riparian forest with willows, manzanita, and madrones. Pass short side paths leading to the lakeshore. At the north tip of the lake is a junction. The right fork leads 50 yards to the paved path and continues into Spring Lake Regional Park. Descend on the left fork—the Eagle Scout Trail—and cross a wooden bridge over the lake's inlet stream. Continue on the north side of the lake, staying close to the shoreline. Traverse the forested hillside above the lake toward the dam. Bear left and cross a bridge over the outlet stream channel. Walk across Lake Ralphine Dam, completing the loop.■

40. Spring Lake Regional Park
Spring Lake Loop
393 Violetti Road · Santa Rosa

Hiking distance: 2.6-mile loop
Hiking time: 1.5 hours
Elevation gain: 50 feet
Dogs: allowed
Maps: U.S.G.S. Santa Rosa
Spring Lake Regional Park map

map
page 125

Summary of hike: Spring Lake Regional Park sits in the foothills of eastern Santa Rosa between Howarth Park (Hike 39) and Annadel State Park (Hikes 41—45). The 320-acre park is among the most popular parks in Santa Rosa. The centerpiece of the park is Spring Lake, a 72-acre lake constructed in 1962 as a flood control reservoir. The lake is used for sailing, canoeing, and fishing (bass, bluegill, and trout). The expansive park also has a campground, picnic area, a three-acre spring-fed swimming lagoon, and miles of multi-use trails. A paved biking path and a dirt equestrian trail intertwine around the lake. This hike circles the lake counter-clockwise. Connector paths join the loop from numerous other locations. Bikes are allowed on this paved loop.

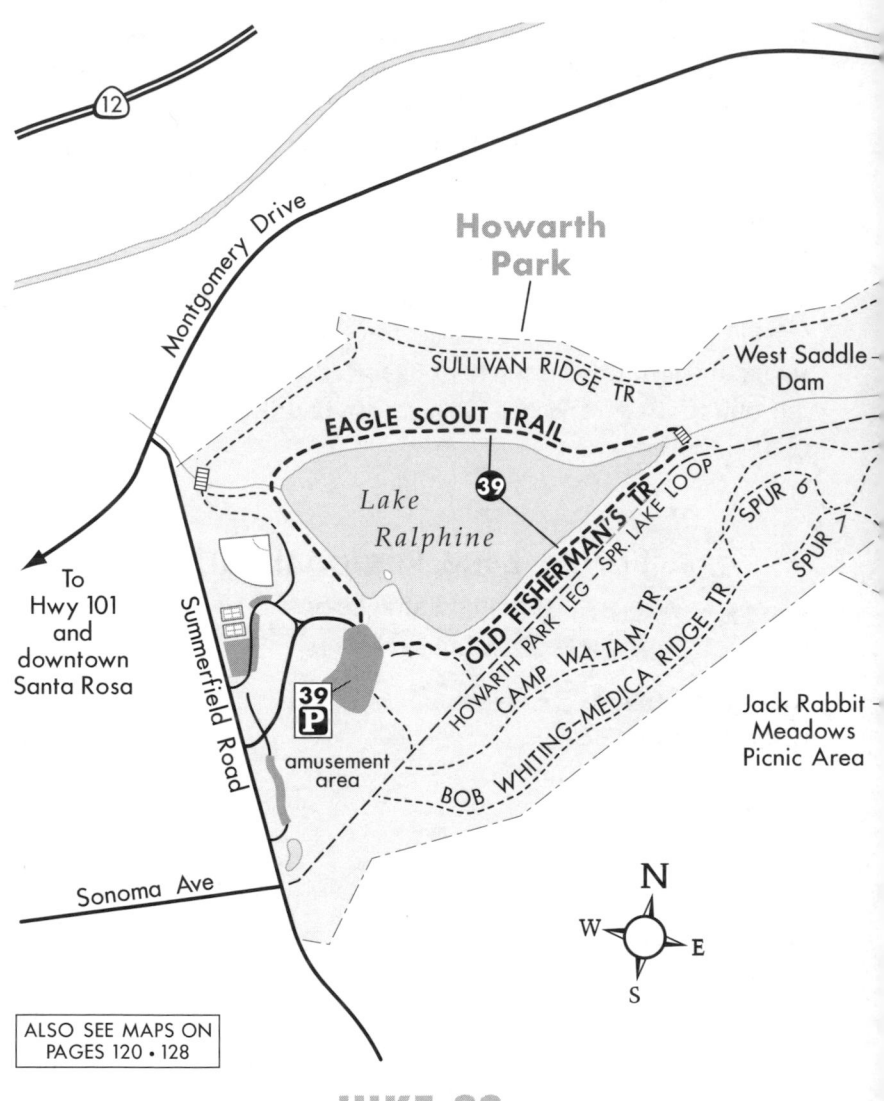

To
Hwy 101
and
downtown
Santa Rosa

Howarth
Park

SULLIVAN RIDGE TR

West Saddle
Dam

EAGLE SCOUT TRAIL

Lake
Ralphine

39

OLD FISHERMAN'S TR

HOWARTH PARK LEG - SPR. LAKE LOOP

SPUR 6

SPUR 7

CAMP WA-TA-M TR

MEDICA RIDGE TR

Jack Rabbit
Meadows
Picnic Area

Montgomery Drive

Summerfield Road

39 P

amusement
area

BOB WHITING

Sonoma Ave

N
W ✦ E
S

ALSO SEE MAPS ON
PAGES 120 • 128

ALSO SEE MAPS ON PAGES 120 • 128

HIKE 39
Howarth Park
LAKE RALPHINE LOOP

HIKE 40
Spring Lake Regional Park
SPRING LAKE LOOP

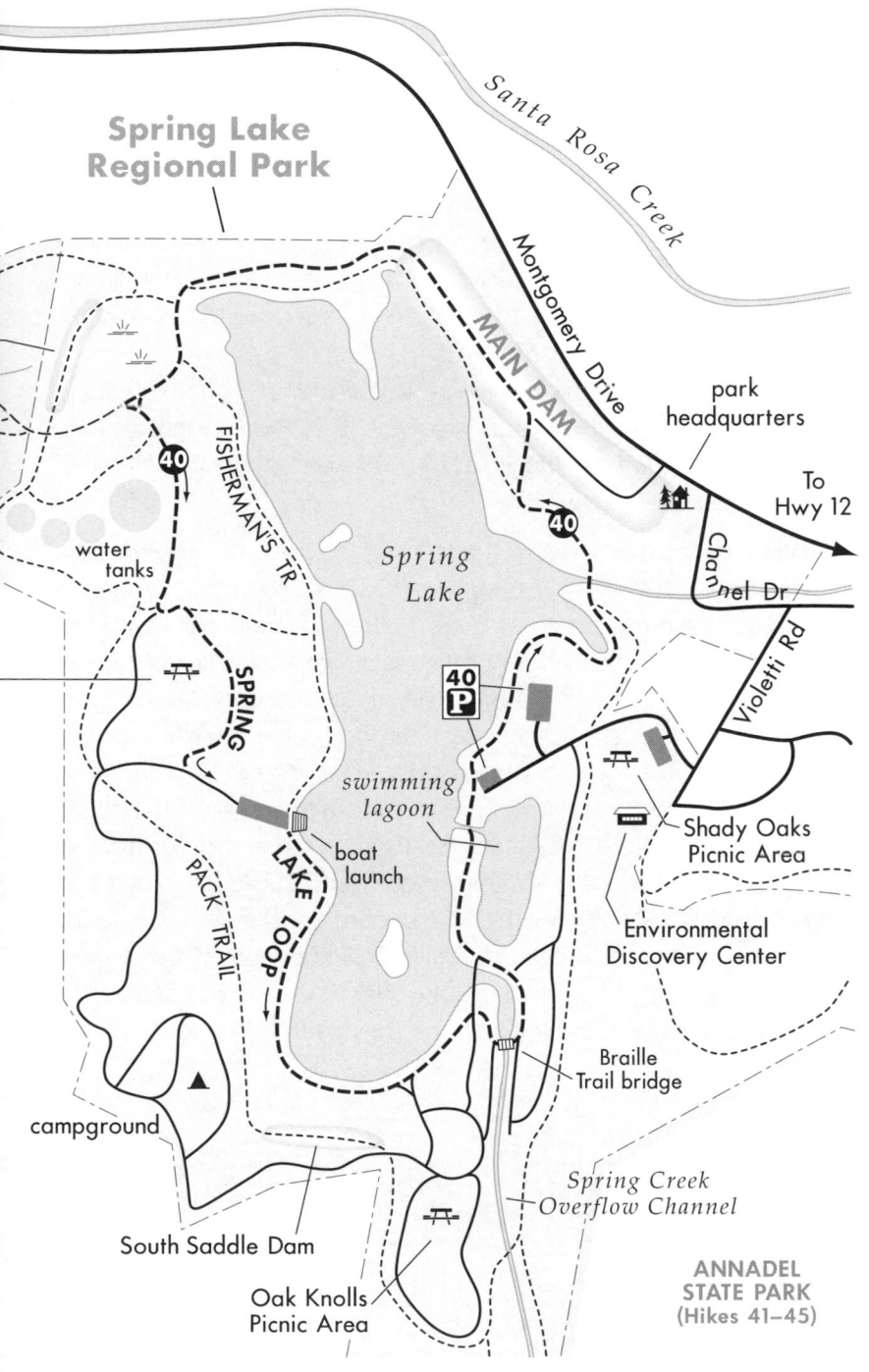

Spring Lake Regional Park

Santa Rosa Creek

Spring Lake Regional Park

Montgomery Drive

MAIN DAM

park headquarters

To Hwy 12

FISHERMAN'S TR

water tanks

Spring Lake

Channel Dr

Violetti Rd

SPRING

40 P

swimming lagoon

boat launch

Shady Oaks Picnic Area

LAKE LOOP

PACK TRAIL

Environmental Discovery Center

Braille Trail bridge

campground

South Saddle Dam

Spring Creek Overflow Channel

ANNADEL STATE PARK (Hikes 41–45)

Oak Knolls Picnic Area

Driving directions: NORTH SONOMA VALLEY: From Highway 12 and Calistoga Road on the northwest end of Sonoma Valley, drive 1.1 miles southeast on Highway 12 (Sonoma Highway) to Los Alamos Road. Turn right and drive 0.2 miles to Melita Road. Turn right and immediately veer left onto Montgomery Drive. Continue a half mile to Channel Drive. Turn left and go 0.2 miles to Violetti Road. Turn right and drive 0.2 miles to the posted park entrance. Turn right, passing the entrance station, and drive straight ahead 0.2 miles to the parking lot at Spring Lake and the swimming lagoon. A parking fee is required.

KENWOOD: From the town of Kenwood in Sonoma Valley, drive 5.8 miles northwest on Highway 12 (Sonoma Highway) to Los Alamos Road on the left. Turn left and continue with the directions above.

Hiking directions: From the parking lot, take the paved path to the right, following the edge of Spring Lake. Loop around a finger of the lake, and cross over the Santa Rosa Creek Diversion Channel. Head up to the top of the main dam, and walk northwest across the dam. After crossing, slowly descend, following the north end of the lake. Curve south through oak groves to a posted trail split. The right fork leads to Lake Ralphine in Howarth Park (Hike 39). Curve left, passing water storage tanks on the right. Weave into Jack Rabbit Meadows Picnic Area and down to the boat launch. Follow the shoreline south, and curve left along the south end of Spring Lake beneath South Saddle Dam. Continue along the shoreline. Cross the Braille Trail Bridge over the Spring Creek Overflow Channel. Skirt the west side of the swimming lagoon, completing the loop at the trailhead parking lot. ■

Annadel State Park

map
next page

HIKES 41—45

6201 Channel Drive • Santa Rosa

Annadel State Park lies on the eastern edge of Santa Rosa at the north end of the Sonoma Mountains. The largely undeveloped park covers 5,000 pristine acres of oak woodlands, Douglas fir and redwood forests, and exposed chaparral slopes. The state park includes broad meadows, rolling hills, narrow ridges, stream-fed canyons, creeks, old cobblestone quarries, a 26-acre lake, and a wetland marsh. More than 35 miles of interconnecting hiking, jogging, biking, and horseback riding trails weave through the park's diverse habitats. Hikes 41—45 explore the wide range of terrain and landscape found at Annadel State Park.

41. Cobblestone—Orchard Loop
ANNADEL STATE PARK

Hiking distance: 4.7-mile loop
Hiking time: 2.5 hours
Elevation gain: 400 feet
Dogs: not allowed
Maps: U.S.G.S. Santa Rosa
　　　　Annadel State Park

map
page 131

Summary of hike: This hike forms a loop on the Cobblestone and Orchard Trails in Annadel State Park. The Cobblestone Trail is named for the basalt cobblestones that were mined out of the area's quarries. The stones were once used for paving roads. The old cobblestones can still be seen on the streets of San Francisco and Sacramento. The trail passes the Wymore Quarry, where a gravity-powered tram transported cobblestones to a railroad line at Channel Drive. The return route on the Orchard Trail runs through the remains of an old orchard. The loop travels through several diverse habitats and landscapes, including oak and manzanita savanna, open meadows, and a stream-fed draw. En route, the trail crosses a narrow ridge and leads to vistas of upper Sonoma Valley and the Santa Rosa Plain.

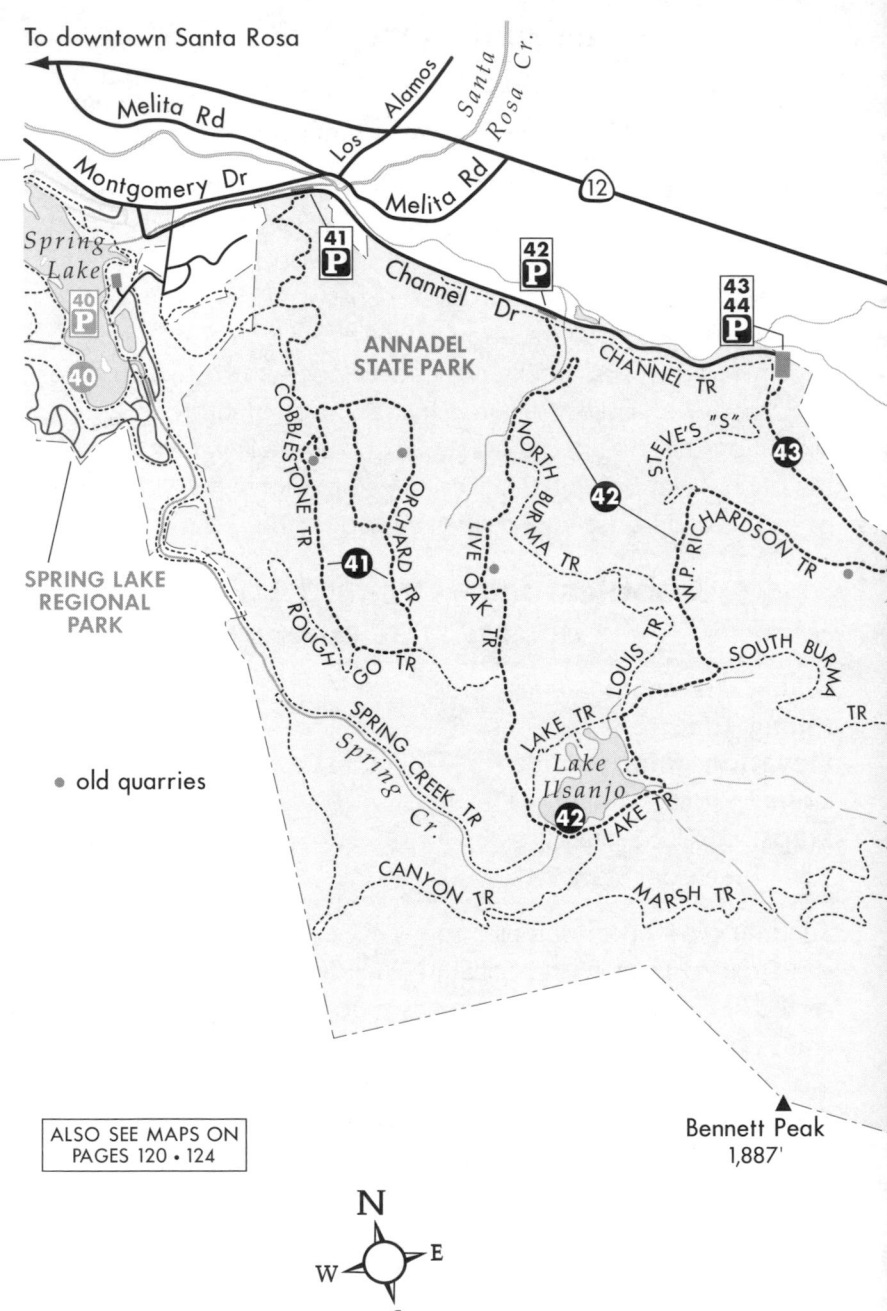

To downtown Santa Rosa

Melita Rd

Los Alamos

Santa Rosa Cr.

Montgomery Dr

Melita Rd

12

Spring Lake

41 P

Channel Dr

42 P

43 44 P

40 P

40

ANNADEL STATE PARK

CHANNEL TR

STEVE'S "S"

COBBLESTONE TR

NORTH BURMA TR

W.P. RICHARDSON TR

43

42

SPRING LAKE REGIONAL PARK

ORCHARD TR

41

LIVE OAK TR

ROUGH GO TR

LAKE TR

LOUIS TR

SOUTH BURMA TR

• old quarries

SPRING CREEK TR

Spring Cr.

Lake Ilsanjo

42

LAKE TR

CANYON TR

MARSH TR

ALSO SEE MAPS ON
PAGES 120 • 124

Bennett Peak
1,887'

N
W E
S

Annadel State Park

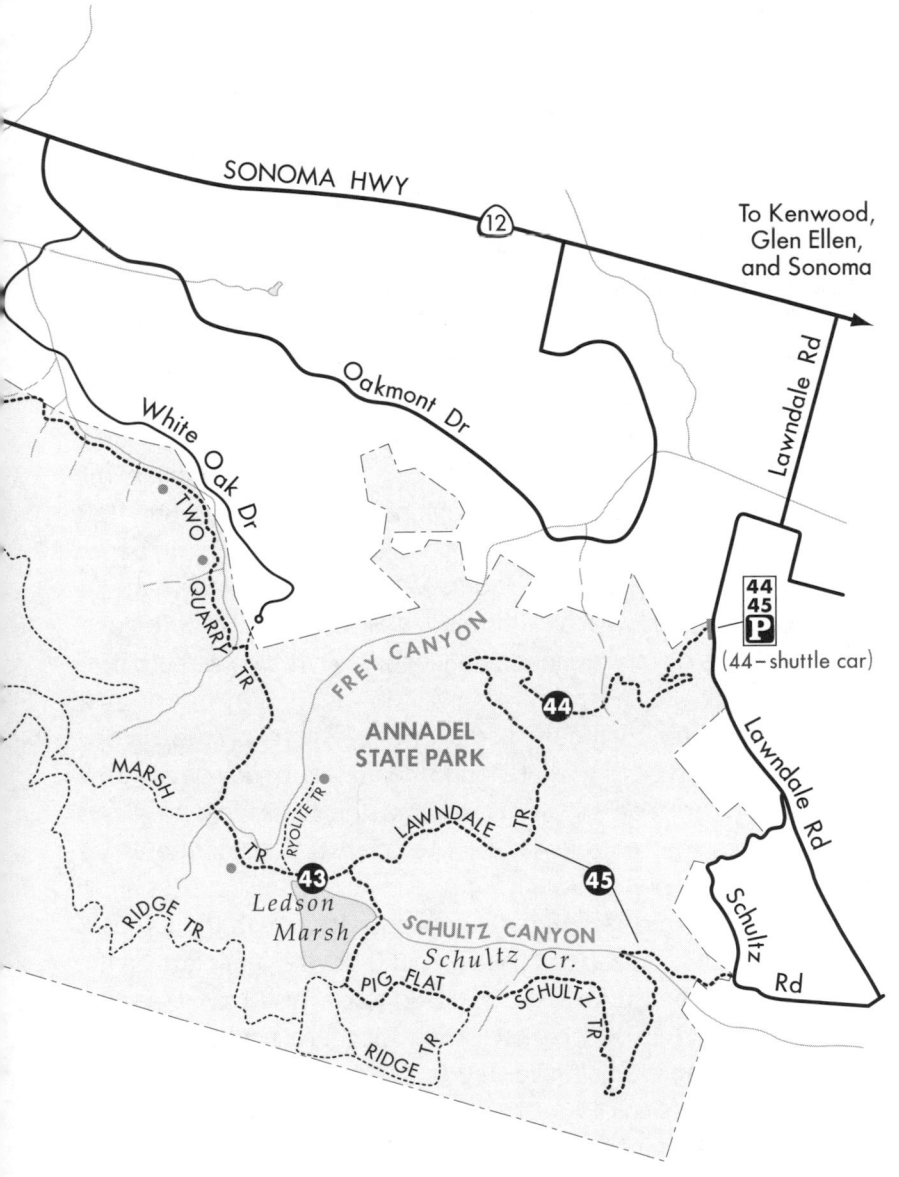

Driving directions: NORTH SONOMA VALLEY: From Highway 12 and Calistoga Road on the northwest end of Sonoma Valley, drive 1.1 miles southeast on Highway 12 (Sonoma Highway) to Los Alamos Road. Turn right and drive 0.2 miles to Melita Road. Turn right and immediately veer left onto Montgomery Drive. Drive a half mile to Channel Drive. Turn left and go 0.6 miles to the posted Cobblestone Trail on the right. Park in the pullout on the left.

KENWOOD: From the town of Kenwood in Sonoma Valley, drive 5.8 miles northwest on Highway 12 (Sonoma Highway) to Los Alamos Road on the left. Turn left and continue with the directions above.

Hiking directions: Walk past the map kiosk on the Cobblestone Trail, entering the shady forest with moss-covered rocks. Pass through an oak and manzanita grassland, and weave up the north-facing hillside. Head up a draw and level out in a wide, open meadow. Skirt the west edge of the meadow, then curve left and cross through the grassland to a junction at 0.7 miles. The right fork leads to Spring Lake Regional Park (Hike 40). Stay left and reenter the mixed forest. Continue climbing to a sitting bench and an overlook of upper Sonoma Valley. Cross a minor ridge to a second junction with a path that leads to Spring Lake Regional Park. A short distance ahead is a junction with the Orchard Trail at 1.2 miles. Begin the loop to the right, staying on the Cobblestone Trail. Cross the narrow ridge, with two steep drop-offs. Make a sweeping right bend, then a left bend, passing the Wymore Quarry on the left. Traverse the hillside, with views west across the Santa Rosa Plain, to a posted T-junction at 2.2 miles. Bear left on the Rough Go Trail. Walk 0.2 miles, passing an open meadow rimmed with oaks, to a junction with the Orchard Trail. The right fork leads to Lake Ilsanjo (Hike 42). Bear left on the Orchard Trail, and follow the west edge of False Lake Meadow to a junction. The two paths form a loop around the knoll just ahead, rejoining in a half mile. The left fork is slightly shorter. The right fork passes an old quarry. Both paths rejoin at 3.4 miles and lead a short distance to the Cobblestone Trail, completing the loop. Return 1.2 miles to the right.■

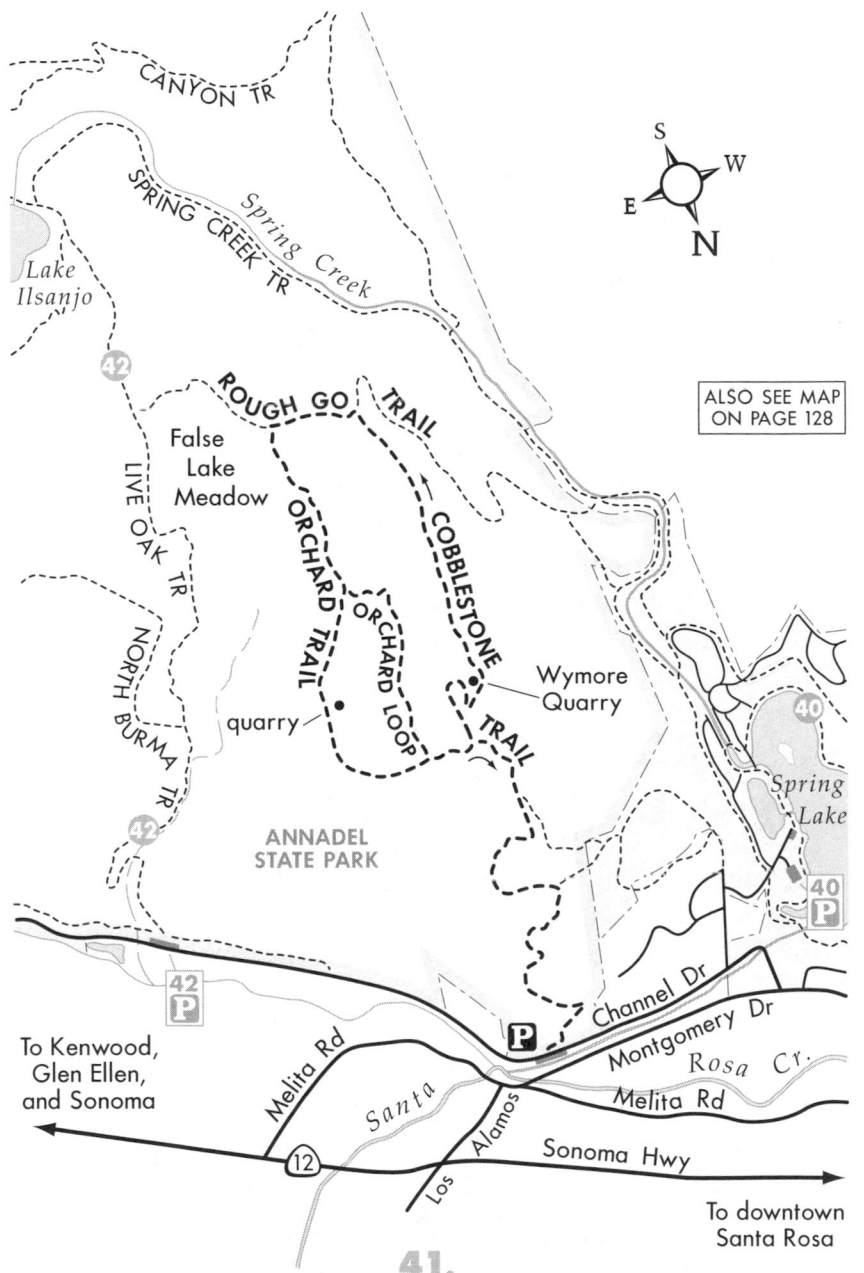

ALSO SEE MAP
ON PAGE 128

41.

Cobblestone – Orchard Loop
ANNADEL STATE PARK

42. Lake Ilsanjo
ANNADEL STATE PARK

Hiking distance: 6.2-mile loop
Hiking time: 3.5 hours
Elevation gain: 600 feet
Dogs: not allowed
Maps: U.S.G.S. Santa Rosa and Kenwood
       Annadel State Park

Summary of hike: In the 1930s, Joe Coney bought the land that is now Annadel State Park. In the 1950s he built Lake Ilsanjo on Spring Creek and named it after himself and his wife Ilse. Joe used the 26-acre lake as a hunting and fishing retreat for his friends. Lake Ilsanjo is now the heart of the park, popular with picnickers, cyclists, joggers, equestrians, hikers, and anglers hoping to catch bluegill and bass. This hike leads to Lake Ilsanjo, surrounded by meadows filled with wildflowers. The trail skirts the lakeshore and returns via the Richardson Trail, an old ranch road shaded by redwoods and mixed oak woodlands.

Driving directions: NORTH SONOMA VALLEY: From Highway 12 and Calistoga Road on the northwest end of Sonoma Valley, drive 1.1 miles southeast on Highway 12 (Sonoma Highway) to Los Alamos Road. Turn right and drive 0.2 miles to Melita Road. Turn right and immediately veer left onto Montgomery Drive. Drive a half mile to Channel Drive. Turn left and go 1.5 miles to the posted North Burma Trail and Channel Trail. Park along the right side of the road. A parking fee is required.

KENWOOD: From the town of Kenwood in Sonoma Valley, drive 5.8 miles northwest on Highway 12 (Sonoma Highway) to Los Alamos Road on the left. Turn left and continue with the directions above.

Hiking directions: Head up the forested slope on the North Burma Trail. Follow the west side of a stream, originating from False Lake Meadow. Rock-hop over the creek and climb two switchbacks. Pass a 15-foot cataract, reaching a posted trail split on a flat at 0.7 miles. The North Burma Trail goes left. Stay straight

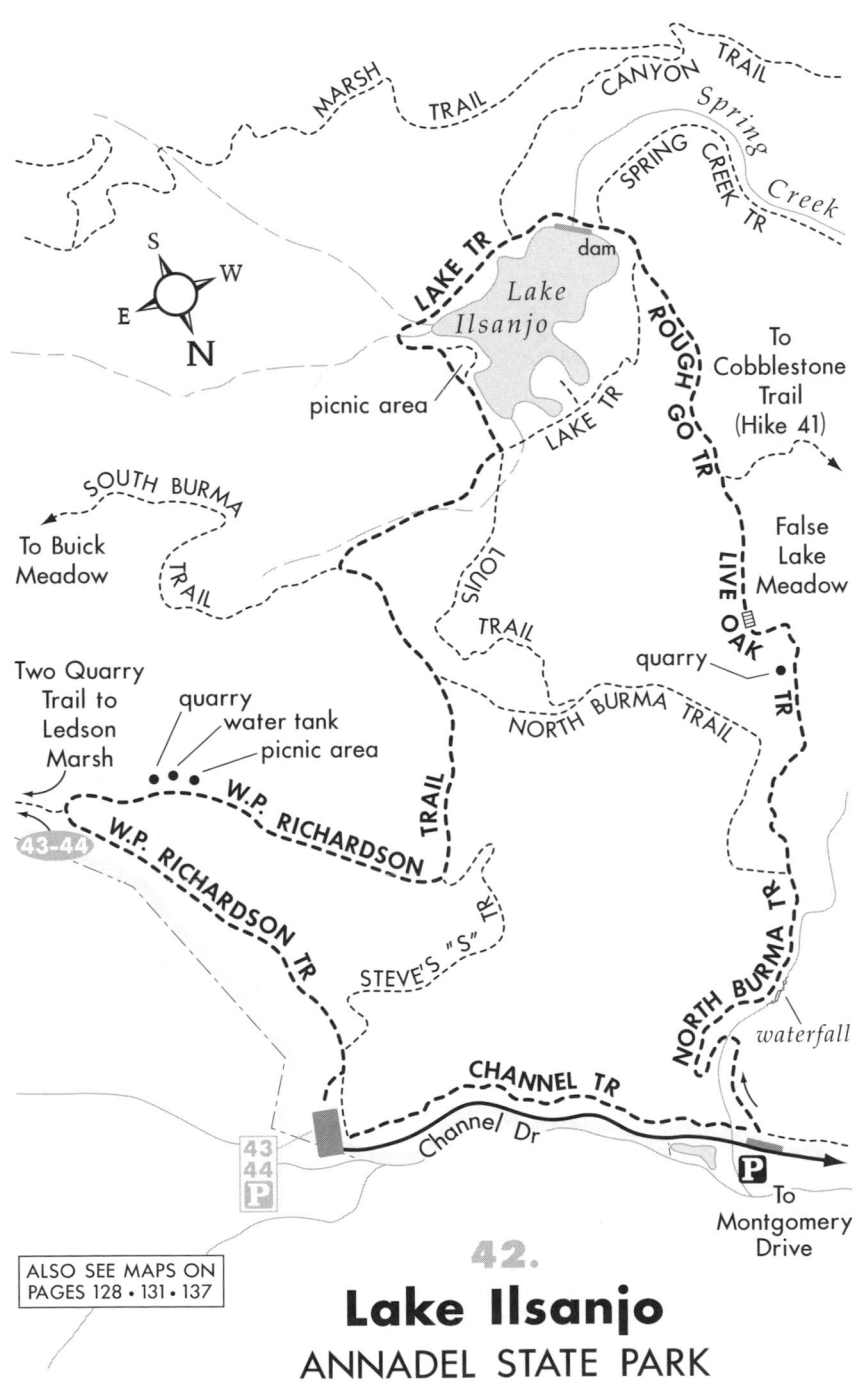

S W E N (compass)

MARSH TRAIL

CANYON TRAIL

Spring Creek

SPRING CREEK TR

LAKE TR

dam

Lake Ilsanjo

ROUGH GO TR

To Cobblestone Trail (Hike 41)

picnic area

LAKE TR

False Lake Meadow

LIVE OAK TR

SOUTH BURMA TRAIL

To Buick Meadow

LOUIS TRAIL

quarry

NORTH BURMA TRAIL

Two Quarry Trail to Ledson Marsh

quarry
water tank
picnic area

W.P. RICHARDSON TRAIL

43-44

W.P. RICHARDSON TR

STEVE'S "S" TR.

NORTH BURMA TR

waterfall

CHANNEL TR

Channel Dr

43 44 P

P To Montgomery Drive

ALSO SEE MAPS ON PAGES 128 • 131 • 137

42.
Lake Ilsanjo
ANNADEL STATE PARK

on the Live Oak Trail and traverse the hillside, skirting the east side of grassy False Lake Meadow. At the summit, pass the site of an old quarry on the left. Gradually descend and cross a small bridge, emerging from the shady oak forest into False Lake Meadow. Cross the tree-rimmed grasslands to a junction with the Rough Go Trail at 1.6 miles. Follow the Rough Go Trail straight ahead through the rocky grassland. At just over 2 miles, the Rough Go Trail ends at a junction with the Lake Trail on the west side of Lake Ilsanjo. Both directions circle the lake. For this hike, curve right, crossing the dam and spillway. Loop around the south and east sides of the picturesque lake. Cross two of the lake's feeder streams and a picnic area with a side loop on the left. At the north end of the lake is a 4-way junction at 3 miles. The left fork loops back to the Rough Go Trail. The Louis Trail continues straight ahead for a shorter 5.1-mile hike. For this hike, bear right on the W.P. Richardson Trail, an old ranch road. Head up the dirt road, staying left past a junction with the South Burma Trail. Traverse the hill, passing the North Burma Trail. Begin an easy descent through a forest of redwoods, Douglas fir, and coast live oak, passing Steve's "S" Trail at 3.9 miles. Pass a picnic area, water tank, and wood steps to a quarry site, all on the right. At 4.6 miles, pass the Two Quarry Trail (Hike 43) on a horseshoe left bend. Continue down to the parking lot at the east end of Channel Drive at 5.5 miles. Head left and walk 0.7 miles on forested Channel Drive or the Channel Trail back to the trailhead. ■

43. Two Quarry Trail to Ledson Marsh
ANNADEL STATE PARK

Hiking distance: 7 miles round trip
Hiking time: 4 hours
Elevation gain: 800 feet
Dogs: not allowed
Maps: U.S.G.S. Kenwood
       Annadel State Park

map
page 137

Summary of hike: Ledson Marsh sits in a large 1,100-foot-high circular depression on the quieter, southeast side of the park. The marsh was built as a reservoir to water eucalyptus trees. It is now overgrown with cattails, tules, and native grasses. It is a popular bird observation site with more than 100 species of birds. The Two Quarry Trail, named for two basalt quarry sites along the trail, leads into the eastern portion of the park to Ledson Marsh. The hike begins on the Warren Richardson Trail at the east end of Channel Drive and joins with the Two Quarry Trail. This hike may be combined with Hike 44 for a 6.4-mile shuttle hike.

Driving directions: NORTH SONOMA VALLEY: From Highway 12 and Calistoga Road on the northwest end of Sonoma Valley, drive 1.1 miles southeast on Highway 12 (Sonoma Highway) to Los Alamos Road. Turn right and drive 0.2 miles to Melita Road. Turn right and immediately veer left onto Montgomery Drive. Drive a half mile to Channel Drive. Turn left and go 2.2 miles to the large parking lot at the end of the road. A parking fee is required.

KENWOOD: From the town of Kenwood in Sonoma Valley, drive 5.8 miles northwest on Highway 12 (Sonoma Highway) to Los Alamos Road on the left. Turn left and continue with the directions above.

Hiking directions: From the far end of the parking lot, take the hikers-only footpath to the W.P. Richardson Trail, a wide dirt road. Bear left and head up the old boulder-studded ranch road to an oak-rimmed meadow with a view of Sugarloaf Ridge. At 0.9 miles, on a horseshoe right bend, is a picnic area and junction. Leave the road and take the Two Quarry Trail to the left. Cross a stream and head east on the footpath through bay laurel and towering Douglas fir trees. Traverse the hillside, parallel to the creek on the left, and cross three small feeder streams. Pass a rock quarry on the right, where the trail begins to climb. Head up the lush canyon, rising above, then returning to the creek. Pass a second distinct quarry on the right, and curve away from the creek. Stroll through the quiet forest, cross another tributary stream, and return to the creek by a series of small waterfalls and pools. Hop over the creek to a T-junction at 2.4 miles. The left fork leaves the park to White Oak Drive, a private road. Go to the right, staying on the Two Quarry Trail, which is now a dirt road.

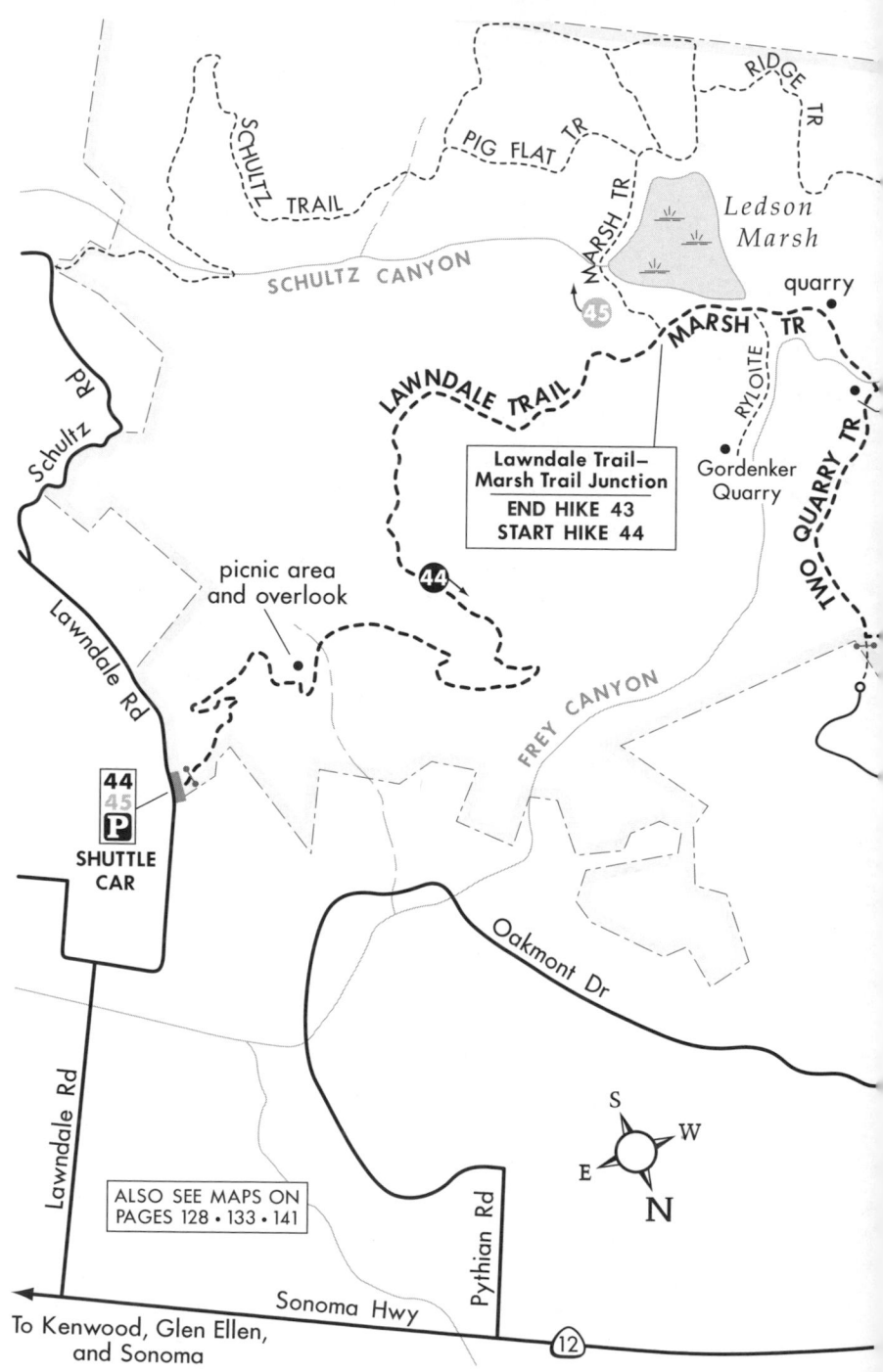

SCHULTZ TRAIL

PIG FLAT TR

RIDGE TR

MARSH TR

Ledson Marsh

quarry

SCHULTZ CANYON

45

MARSH TR

LAWNDALE TRAIL

RYLOITE

TWO QUARRY TR

Schultz Rd

Lawndale Rd

Lawndale Trail–Marsh Trail Junction
END HIKE 43
START HIKE 44

Gordenker Quarry

picnic area and overlook

44

FREY CANYON

44
45
P
SHUTTLE CAR

Oakmont Dr

Lawndale Rd

ALSO SEE MAPS ON
PAGES 128 • 133 • 141

Pythian Rd

S W
E N

Sonoma Hwy

To Kenwood, Glen Ellen,
and Sonoma

12

Two Quarry Trail to Ledson Marsh

Two Quarry–Lawndale shuttle

ANNADEL STATE PARK

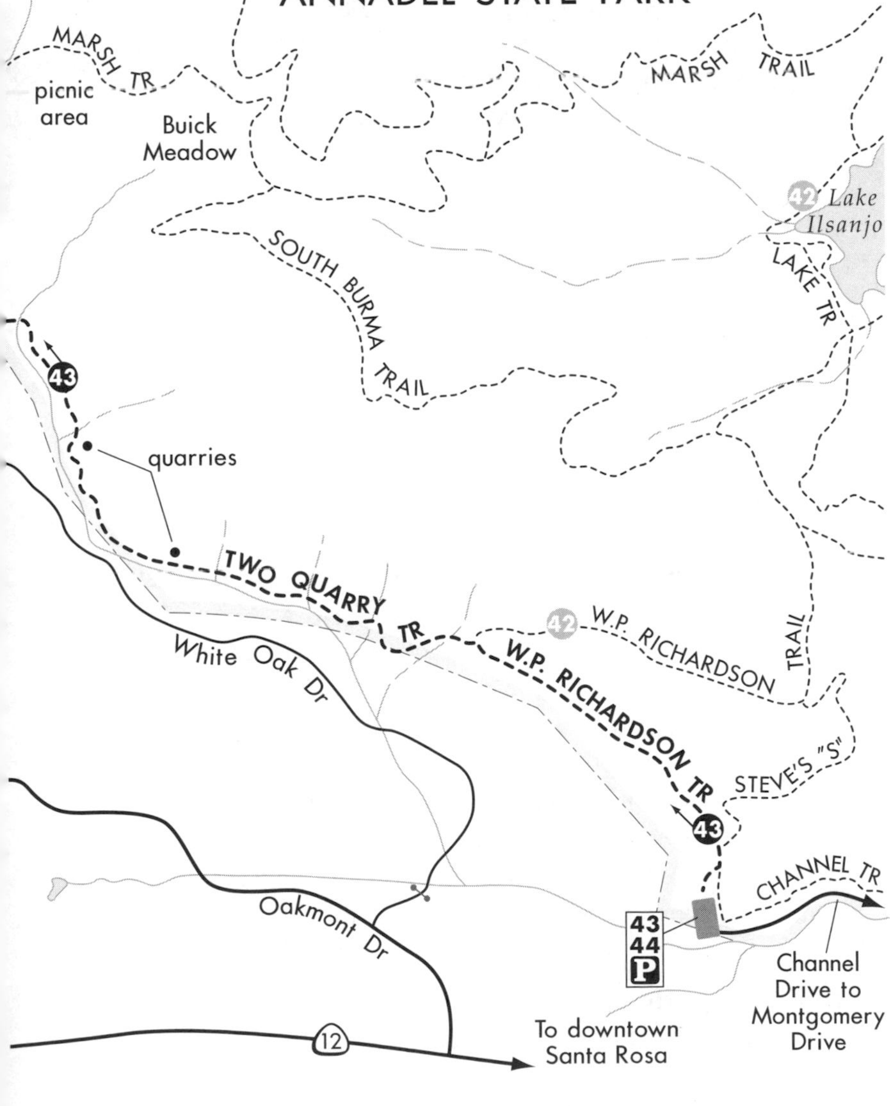

MARSH TR

picnic area

Buick Meadow

MARSH TRAIL

SOUTH BURMA TRAIL

42 Lake Ilsanjo

LAKE TR

43

quarries

TWO QUARRY TR

White Oak Dr

42 W.P. RICHARDSON

W.P. RICHARDSON TR

TRAIL

STEVE'S "S"

43

CHANNEL TR

Oakmont Dr

43 44 P

Channel Drive to Montgomery Drive

12

To downtown Santa Rosa

Steadily gain elevation through the dense forest, weaving along the contours of the canyon wall. Leave the canyon to an expansive meadow with a picnic area and posted junction. Bear left on the Marsh Trail, crossing a stream. Pass remnants of another quarry on the right to the northwest corner of Ledson Marsh at 3.3 miles. Follow the north edge of the reed-covered marsh a quarter mile to a junction with the Lawndale Trail, the turn-around point for this hike. The Marsh Trail continues to the right along the east side of Ledson Marsh. Straight ahead—Hike 44—descends almost 3 miles to Lawndale Road at the northeast corner of Annadel State Park. For the 6.4-mile shuttle hike to Lawndale Road, continue with Hike 44. ■

44. Two Quarry—Lawndale Shuttle
ANNADEL STATE PARK

Hiking distance: 6.4-mile one-way shuttle
Hiking time: 3.5 hours
Elevation gain: 800 feet
Dogs: not allowed
Maps: U.S.G.S. Kenwood
       Annadel State Park

map
page 136

Summary of hike: Between 1870 and 1920, Italian stone-cutters worked in the basalt quarries of present-day Annadel State Park. The cobblestones were used for paving streets throughout northern California. The Two Quarry Trail leads into the quieter eastern portion of the park towards Ledson Marsh, joining with the Marsh Trail and the Lawndale Trail. This hike continues from Hike 43, utilizing a shuttle car at the Lawndale Trailhead. After passing the quarries, the hike descends from Ledson Marsh to Lawndale Road, weaving through redwood and Douglas fir forests to vistas of Sonoma Valley and the surrounding mountains. The quarries have since been reclaimed by moss.

Driving directions: Same as Hike 43.
SHUTTLE CAR: Same as Hike 45 (Lawndale Trailhead).

Hiking directions: Begin at the end of Hike 43—on the north edge of Ledson Marsh at the Lawndale Trail–Marsh Trail junction. The Marsh Trail follows the east side of Ledson Marsh. For this hike, continue straight ahead on the Lawndale Trail at a level grade. Descend through oak trees into the canyon. Traverse the canyon walls under a forest canopy of firs and redwoods. Head downhill to a right bend under powerlines. The vistas extend across Sonoma Valley to Sugarloaf Ridge, Bald Mountain, and Red Mountain. Continue traversing the steep hillside and make a sharp left bend, crossing over a seasonal drainage. Emerge from the forest to a grassy knoll and picnic area overlooking Sonoma Valley. Loop around the knoll and curve left over another drainage. Zigzag down two switchbacks, crossing a drainage on the second bend. Wind down to the base of the mountain and the trailhead on Lawndale Road.■

45. Lawndale Trail— Schultz Canyon Loop
ANNADEL STATE PARK

Hiking distance: 7-mile loop
Hiking time: 4 hours
Elevation gain: 700 feet
Dogs: not allowed
Maps: U.S.G.S. Kenwood
      Annadel State Park

map
page 141

Summary of hike: The Lawndale Trail begins at the eastern end of Annadel State Park in Sonoma Valley. The trail is an old road once used by stonecutters working in the basalt quarries. The road follows a stream drainage, climbs to knolls with overlooks, weaves under a canopy of redwoods and Douglas firs, and emerges at Ledson Marsh above 1,100 feet. The water collected in Ledson Marsh overflows into Schultz Canyon. The hike returns down the remote canyon, following the forested watercourse.

Driving directions: NORTH SONOMA VALLEY: From Highway 12 and Calistoga Road on the northwest end of Sonoma Valley, drive 5.5 miles southeast on Highway 12 (Sonoma Highway) to Lawndale Road. Turn right and go 1.1 miles to the trailhead parking lot on the right at the base of the mountains.

KENWOOD: From the town of Kenwood in Sonoma Valley, drive 1.4 miles northwest on Highway 12 (Sonoma Highway) to Lawndale Road on the left. Turn left and go 1.1 miles to the trailhead parking lot on the right at the base of the mountains.

Hiking directions: Walk past the trailhead gate, and head up the grassy slope dotted with oak, madrone, and buckeye trees. Loop around a lush, stream-fed canyon and continue up the hillside through moss-covered valley oaks and manzanita. Curve right, crossing the drainage, and emerge to a grassy knoll with a picnic area and open vistas. The views extend across Sonoma Valley to Sugarloaf Ridge, Hood Mountain, Bald Mountain, and Red Mountain. Loop left around the knoll, and reenter a cool Douglas fir and redwood forest with several species of ferns covering the forest floor. Cross two more seasonal drainages, steadily climbing on a gentle grade. After gaining 500 feet in elevation, the trail switchbacks to the left beneath power lines. Top a minor ridge and slowly curve right around a hill. Cross under the power lines, where the trail levels out. Continue to a junction with the Marsh Trail at 2.9 miles. Bear left on the Marsh Trail, and cross a bridge over Schultz Creek, the outlet stream of Ledson Marsh. Skirt the east edge of the reed-filled marsh to a signed junction with a picnic area overlooking the wetland at 3.3 miles. Bear left on the Pig Flat Trail, and cross the flat through oaks and manzanita to a staggered junction at 3.8 miles. To the right is the Ridge Trail. Twenty yards ahead, bear left and head east on the Schultz Trail. Cross a tributary of Schultz Creek, and meander through the forest down the south wall of Schultz Canyon. Curve out of the canyon and switchback left to vistas down Sonoma Valley. Pass a picnic area and overlook on the left, and return into Schultz Canyon. At the canyon floor, follow the creek downstream 150 yards and hop over the creek. Traverse the hill to the east edge of Annadel State Park, reaching the gate at Schultz Road. Bear left on Schultz Road, and climb 0.8 miles up the narrow, winding road to Lawndale Road. Go to the left and continue a half mile downhill to the trailhead at the base of the mountain. ∎

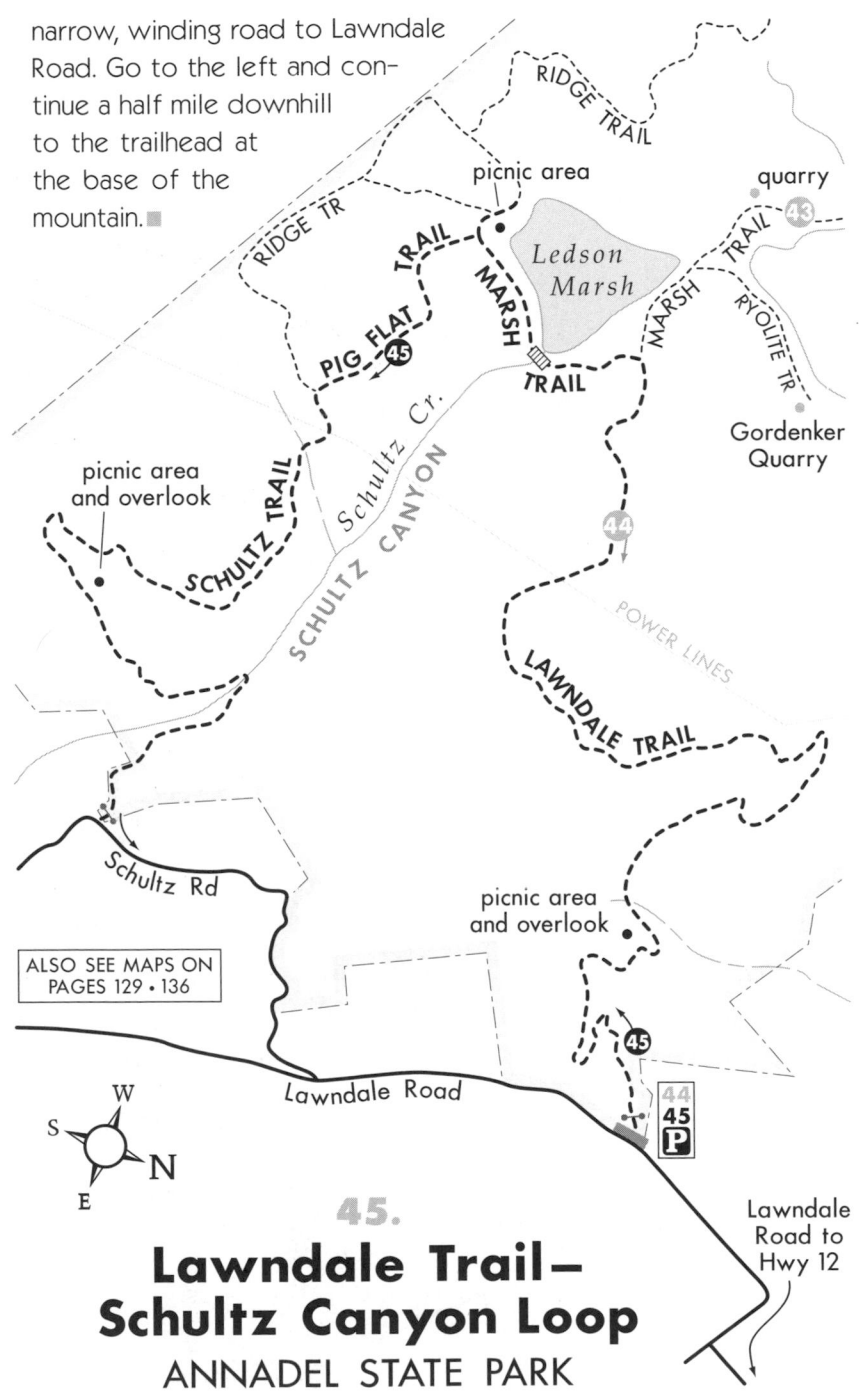

picnic area

quarry

RIDGE TRAIL

RIDGE TR

Ledson Marsh

MARSH TRAIL

PIG FLAT TRAIL

45

TRAIL

MARSH TRAIL

RYOLITE TR

43

Gordenker Quarry

picnic area and overlook

SCHULTZ TRAIL

Schultz Cr.

SCHULTZ CANYON

44

POWER LINES

LAWNDALE TRAIL

Schultz Rd

picnic area and overlook

ALSO SEE MAPS ON PAGES 129 · 136

45

44
45
P

Lawndale Road

Lawndale Road to Hwy 12

W
S   N
E

45.

Lawndale Trail—
Schultz Canyon Loop
ANNADEL STATE PARK

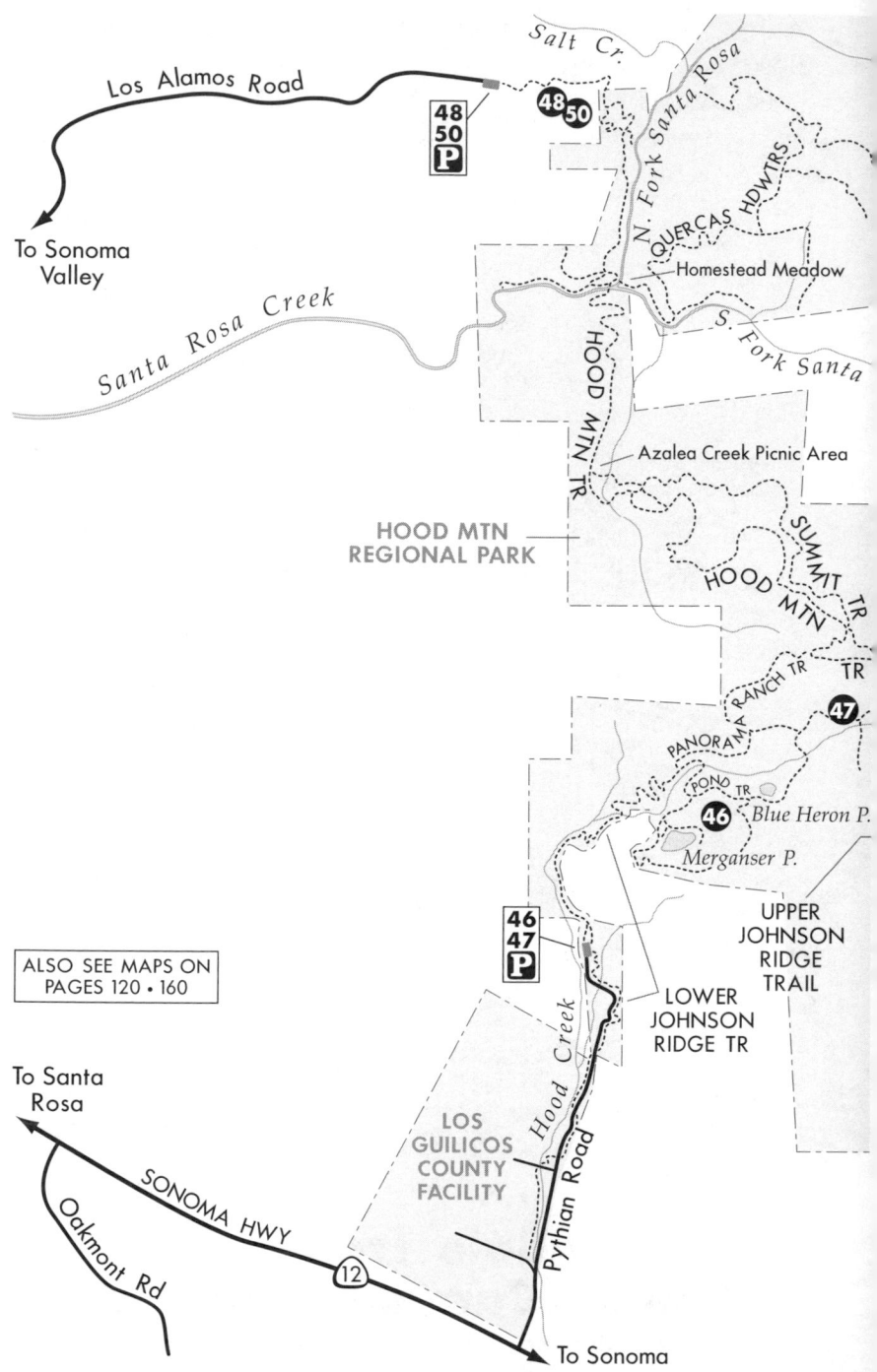

Los Alamos Road

48 50 P

48 50

Salt Cr.

N. Fork Santa Rosa

QUERCAS HDWTRS.

Homestead Meadow

To Sonoma Valley

Santa Rosa Creek

S. Fork Santa

HOOD MTN TR

Azalea Creek Picnic Area

HOOD MTN REGIONAL PARK

SUMMIT TR

HOOD MTN TR

PANORAMA RANCH TR

TR

47

POND TR

46 Blue Heron P.

Merganser P.

UPPER JOHNSON RIDGE TRAIL

46 47 P

LOWER JOHNSON RIDGE TR

ALSO SEE MAPS ON PAGES 120 • 160

Hood Creek

To Santa Rosa

SONOMA HWY

Oakmont Rd

LOS GUILICOS COUNTY FACILITY

Pythian Road

12

To Sonoma

Hood Mountain
Regional Park

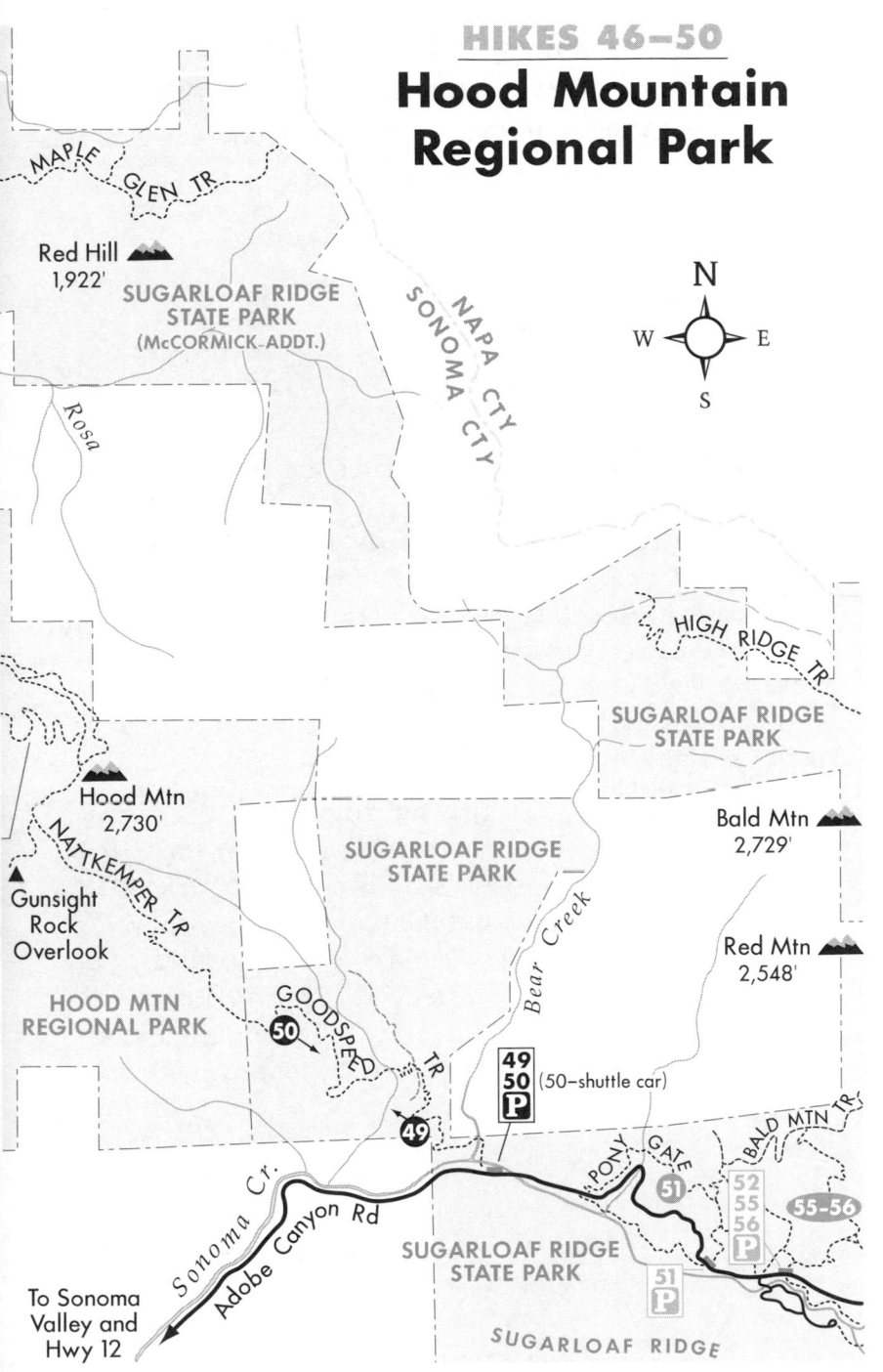

MAPLE GLEN TR

Red Hill 1,922'

SUGARLOAF RIDGE
STATE PARK
(McCORMICK-ADDT.)

Rosa

NAPA CTY
SONOMA CTY

N
W   E
S

HIGH RIDGE TR

SUGARLOAF RIDGE
STATE PARK

Hood Mtn
2,730'

NATTKEMPER TR

Gunsight
Rock
Overlook

SUGARLOAF RIDGE
STATE PARK

Bald Mtn
2,729'

Bear Creek

Red Mtn
2,548'

HOOD MTN
REGIONAL PARK

GOODSPEED TR

50

49
50
P (50-shuttle car)

BALD MTN TR

49

PONY GATE

51

52
55
56
P

55-56

Sonoma Cr.

Adobe Canyon Rd

SUGARLOAF RIDGE
STATE PARK

51
P

To Sonoma
Valley and
Hwy 12

SUGARLOAF RIDGE

46. Lower Johnson Ridge Trail to Merganser Pond and Blue Heron Pond

HOOD MOUNTAIN REGIONAL PARK

Pythian Road · Kenwood

Hiking distance: 4-mile loop
Hiking time: 2 hours
Elevation gain: 1,000 feet
Dogs: allowed
Maps: U.S.G.S. Kenwood
      Hood Mountain Regional Park

Summary of hike: This hike begins from the newest addition to Hood Mountain Regional Park on the western base of Hood Mountain. The 247-acre Lawson Property, along with the Johnson property, now provides public access from the Sonoma Valley floor, from Pythian Road to the crest of Hood Mountain. This hike follows the Lower Johnson Ridge Trail to Merganser Pond and Blue Heron Pond while overlooking Hood Creek Canyon. The trail winds halfway up Hood Mountain through mixed woodland forests and grassland habitats.

Driving directions:

NORTH SONOMA VALLEY: From Highway 12 and Calistoga Road on the north end of Sonoma Valley, drive 4.6 miles southeast on Highway 12 (Sonoma Highway) to Pythian Road. Turn left and continue 1.3 miles to the trailhead parking lot on the right at the end of the public road. A parking fee is required.

KENWOOD: From the town of Kenwood in Sonoma Valley, drive 2 miles north on Highway 12 (Sonoma Highway) to Pythian Road on the right. Turn right and continue with the directions above.

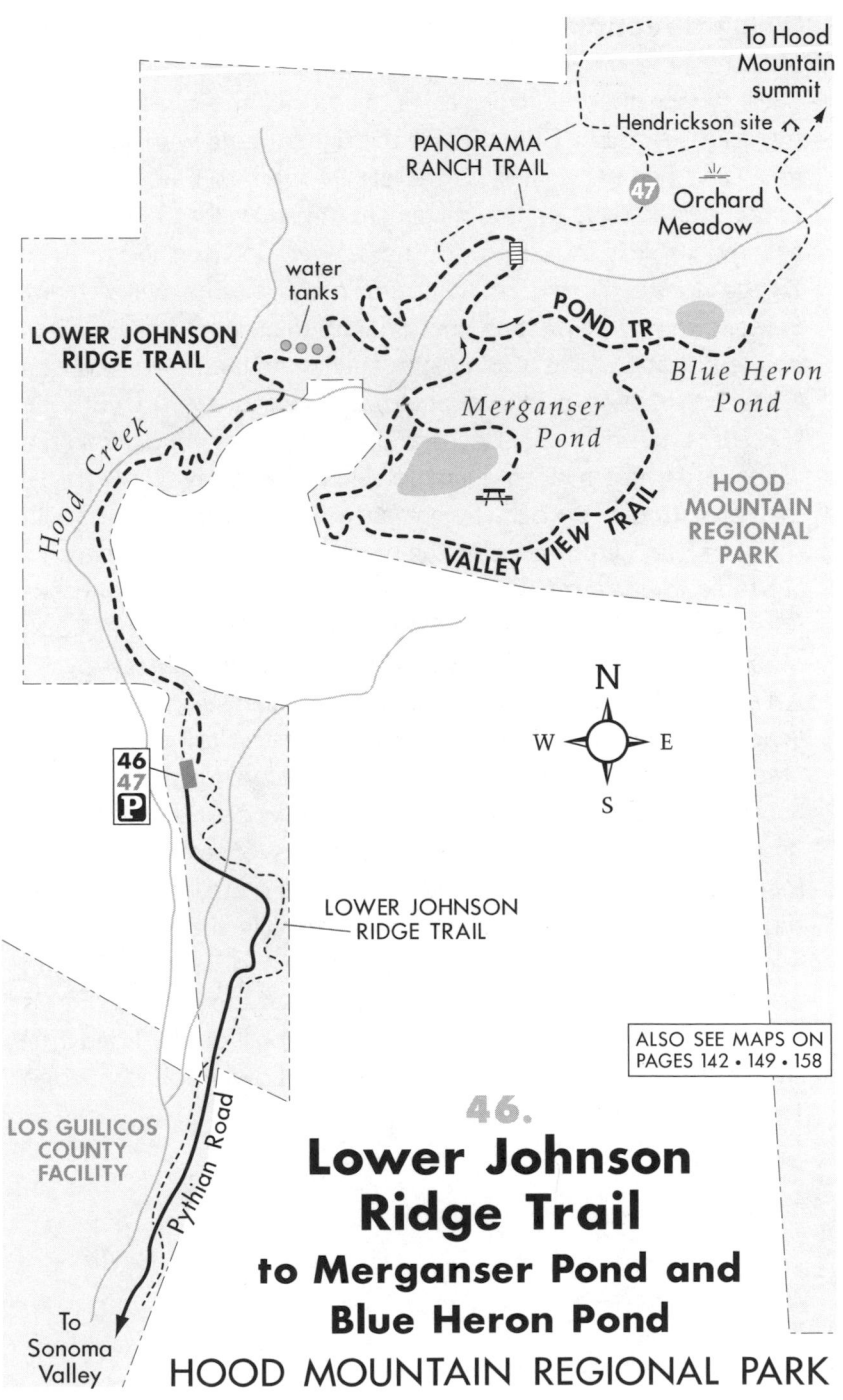

To Hood Mountain summit

Hendrickson site

PANORAMA RANCH TRAIL

47 Orchard Meadow

water tanks

LOWER JOHNSON RIDGE TRAIL

POND TR

Blue Heron Pond

Hood Creek

Merganser Pond

VALLEY VIEW TRAIL

HOOD MOUNTAIN REGIONAL PARK

N
W E
S

46 47 P

LOWER JOHNSON RIDGE TRAIL

ALSO SEE MAPS ON PAGES 142 • 149 • 158

LOS GUILICOS COUNTY FACILITY

Pythian Road

To Sonoma Valley

46.

Lower Johnson Ridge Trail
to Merganser Pond and Blue Heron Pond
HOOD MOUNTAIN REGIONAL PARK

Hiking directions: Walk north up the hill, passing a mileage sign, into the mixed forest on the Lower Johnson Ridge Trail. Stroll among the oak, Douglas fir, madrone, and big-leaf maple trees. Pass a couple of homes on the right. Merge with an asphalt road, and head 0.3 miles up the steep road, high above Hood Creek. Curve right as the pavement ends. Walk 40 yards and switchback left, returning to the Lower Johnson Ridge Trail. Zigzag up the hill on the footpath, passing three water tanks. Steadily climb to a posted junction with the Panorama Ranch Trail on the left at 1.5 miles. Curve right, staying on the Lower Johnson Ridge Trail. Cross a bridge over Hood Creek to a Y-fork with the Pond Trail. The right fork descends to Merganser Pond. Begin the loop on the left fork to a junction with the Valley View Trail— the return route. Detour straight ahead 100 yards to the south shore of Blue Heron Pond. At the north end of the pond is a picnic table under a mature walnut tree. The Pond Trail continues north and joins the Upper Johnson Ridge Trail to the Hood Mountain summit and the Gunsight Rock Overlook (Hike 47). After enjoying the pastoral site, return to the Valley View Trail. Bear left and descend, overlooking Sonoma Valley and Annadel State Park. Loop around the canyon, high above Merganser Pond, to an overlook of the valley above Kenwood and Glen Ellen. Drop down on a couple of switchbacks to a junction near Merganser Pond. The right fork leads 50 yards to the southwest shore. The side path follows a berm on the edge of the pond and rejoins the main trail at a junction with the Pond Trail. A side path on the right loops around to the east side of the pond and ends by picnic tables. From the junction, head uphill on the Pond Trail and veer left, completing the loop at the Lower Johnson Ridge Trail. Bear left and retrace your steps.■

47. Lower and Upper Johnson Ridge Trails

Route 1: Hood Mountain Summit and Gunsight Rock

HOOD MOUNTAIN REGIONAL PARK

Pythian Road · Kenwood

Hiking distance: 7.2 miles round trip
Hiking time: 4 hours
Elevation gain: 1,900 feet
Dogs: allowed
Maps: U.S.G.S. Kenwood
  Hood Mountain Regional Park

map
page 149

Summary of hike: Three routes climb to the summit of Hood Mountain and the Gunsight Rock Overlook: the Hood Mountain Trail from the north end of Hood Mountain Regional Park (Hike 48); the Goodspeed–Nattkemper Trail from Sugarloaf Ridge State Park (Hike 49); and the Lower and Upper Johnson Ridge Trails via Sonoma Valley off of Pythian Road (this hike), which begins near the western base of Hood Mountain. The trail climbs to the 2,730-foot summit and continues to the Gunsight Rock Overlook, an extensive rock formation with a notch. From the perch are expansive views of Sonoma Valley, Annadel State Park, Sonoma Mountain, Santa Rosa, and the coastal mountains. The hike accesses several trails en route to the summit, passing through Hood Creek Canyon, the headwaters of Hood Creek, a dense coniferous woodland, a freshwater wetland, and the Hendrickson Homestead site. The trail then follows the crest of Hood Mountain to its summit; the Gunsight Rock Trail continues to the overlook on a vertical rock perch.

Driving directions: NORTH SONOMA VALLEY: From Highway 12 and Calistoga Road on the north end of Sonoma Valley, drive 4.6 miles southeast on Highway 12 (Sonoma Highway) to Pythian Road. Turn left and continue 1.3 miles to the trailhead parking lot on the right at the end of the public road. A parking fee is required.

KENWOOD: From the town of Kenwood in Sonoma Valley, drive 2 miles north on Highway 12 (Sonoma Highway) to Pythian Road on the right. Turn right and continue with the directions above.

Hiking directions: Walk north up the hill, passing a mileage sign, into the mixed forest on the Lower Johnson Ridge Trail. Stroll among the oak, Douglas fir, madrone, and big-leaf maple trees. Pass a couple of homes on the right. Merge with an asphalt road, and head 0.3 miles up the steep road, high above Hood Creek. Curve right as the pavement ends. Walk 40 yards and switchback left, returning to the Lower Johnson Ridge Trail. Zigzag up the hill on the footpath, passing three water tanks on the right. Steadily climb to a posted junction with the Panorama Ranch Trail on the left at 1.5 miles. The right fork leads to Blue Heron Pond and Merganser Pond (Hike 46). For this hike, go left on the Panorama Ranch Trail and steadily climb. Skirt Orchard Meadow on the right to a junction. Bear right on the Orchard Meadow Trail, and walk 0.15 miles to a junction with Upper Johnson Ridge Trail. Bear left past the Hendrickson Historical Homesite on the left. (The site includes two old wood houses, a stone root cellar, and a brick chimney.) Head north, zigzagging up the mountain and passing Knight's Retreat Trail, to the Hood Mountain Trail atop the ridge. Go to the right and climb 0.2 miles through the shaded forest to the Hood Mountain summit at just over 3 miles. From the summit, descend 0.2 miles on the Nattkemper Trail through manzanita and multi-colored lava rock outcroppings to the signed Gunsight Rock Trail. The left fork leads through Sugarloaf Ridge State Park to Adobe Canyon Road (Hike 49). Veer right on the Gunsight Rock Trail, and walk 0.2 miles to a massive jumble of rocks overlooking Sonoma Valley. The vistas extend to San Pablo Bay and the Santa Rosa Valley, Sonoma Mountain to Mount Tamalpais in Marin County, and Mount Diablo in Contra Costa County. Return by retracing your route. ■

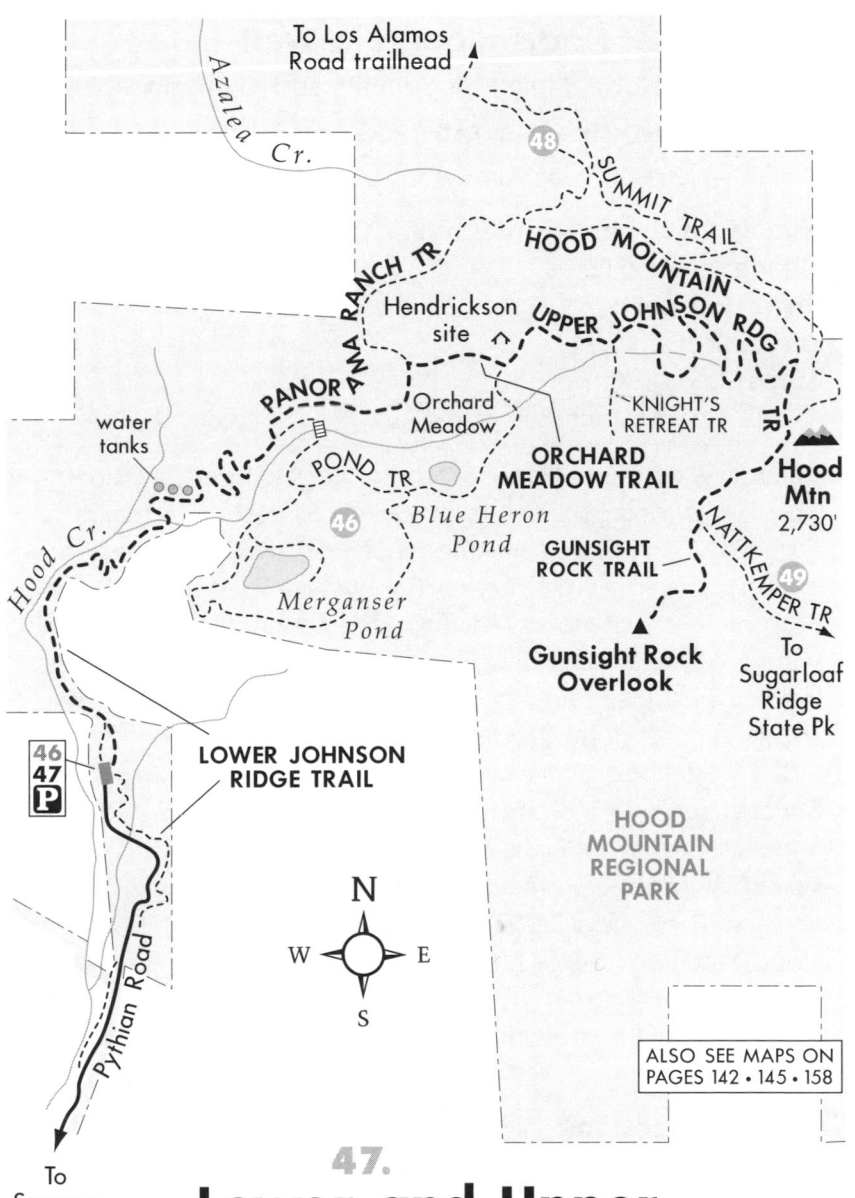

To Los Alamos
Road trailhead

Azalea Cr.

48

SUMMIT TRAIL

HOOD MOUNTAIN

PANORAMA RANCH TR

Hendrickson site

UPPER JOHNSON RDG

KNIGHT'S RETREAT TR

water tanks

Orchard Meadow

ORCHARD MEADOW TRAIL

Hood Cr.

POND TR

46

Blue Heron Pond

Merganser Pond

GUNSIGHT ROCK TRAIL

NATTKEMPER TR

Hood Mtn 2,730'

49

Gunsight Rock Overlook

To Sugarloaf Ridge State Pk

46
47
P

LOWER JOHNSON RIDGE TRAIL

N
W · E
S

HOOD MOUNTAIN REGIONAL PARK

Pythian Road

To Sonoma Valley

ALSO SEE MAPS ON PAGES 142 · 145 · 158

47.

Lower and Upper Johnson Ridge Trails

Hood Mountain summit • Gunsight Rock

HOOD MOUNTAIN REGIONAL PARK

48. Hood Mountain Trail
Route 2: Hood Mountain Summit and Gunsight Rock
HOOD MOUNTAIN REGIONAL PARK
3000 Los Alamos Road · Santa Rosa

Hiking distance: 11.8 miles round trip
Hiking time: 6 hours
Elevation gain: 2,100 feet
Dogs: allowed
Maps: U.S.G.S. Kenwood
       Hood Mountain Regional Park

Summary of hike: Hood Mountain Regional Park sits in the Mayacamas Mountains five miles east of Santa Rosa, adjacent to Sugarloaf Ridge State Park. The 5,800-acre wilderness park has elevations ranging from 650 feet above sea level to 2,730 feet atop the crest of Hood Mountain. The park contains the headwaters of Santa Rosa Creek and tributaries that feed Sonoma Creek. The diverse park includes rolling meadows, deep canyons, sheer wooded slopes, and dramatic rock outcroppings.

Gunsight Rock, a massive jumble of rocks, sits high above Sonoma Valley. The prominent rock face can be seen along the Sonoma Highway. From the overlook are spectacular vistas of the valley. On a clear day, the Golden Gate Bridge, the Pacific Ocean, and the Sierra Nevada Range are visible. This hike follows the Hood Mountain Trail (a fire road) to the 2,730-foot summit of Hood Mountain, the highest peak between Sonoma Valley and Napa Valley. The trail then continues to the Gunsight Rock Overlook.

Driving directions: NORTH SONOMA VALLEY: From Highway 12 and Calistoga Road on the north end of Sonoma Valley, drive 1.1 miles southeast on Highway 12 (Sonoma Highway) to Los Alamos Road. Turn left and drive 4.7 miles up the narrow, winding mountain road to the road gate and trailhead parking area on the right. A parking fee is required.

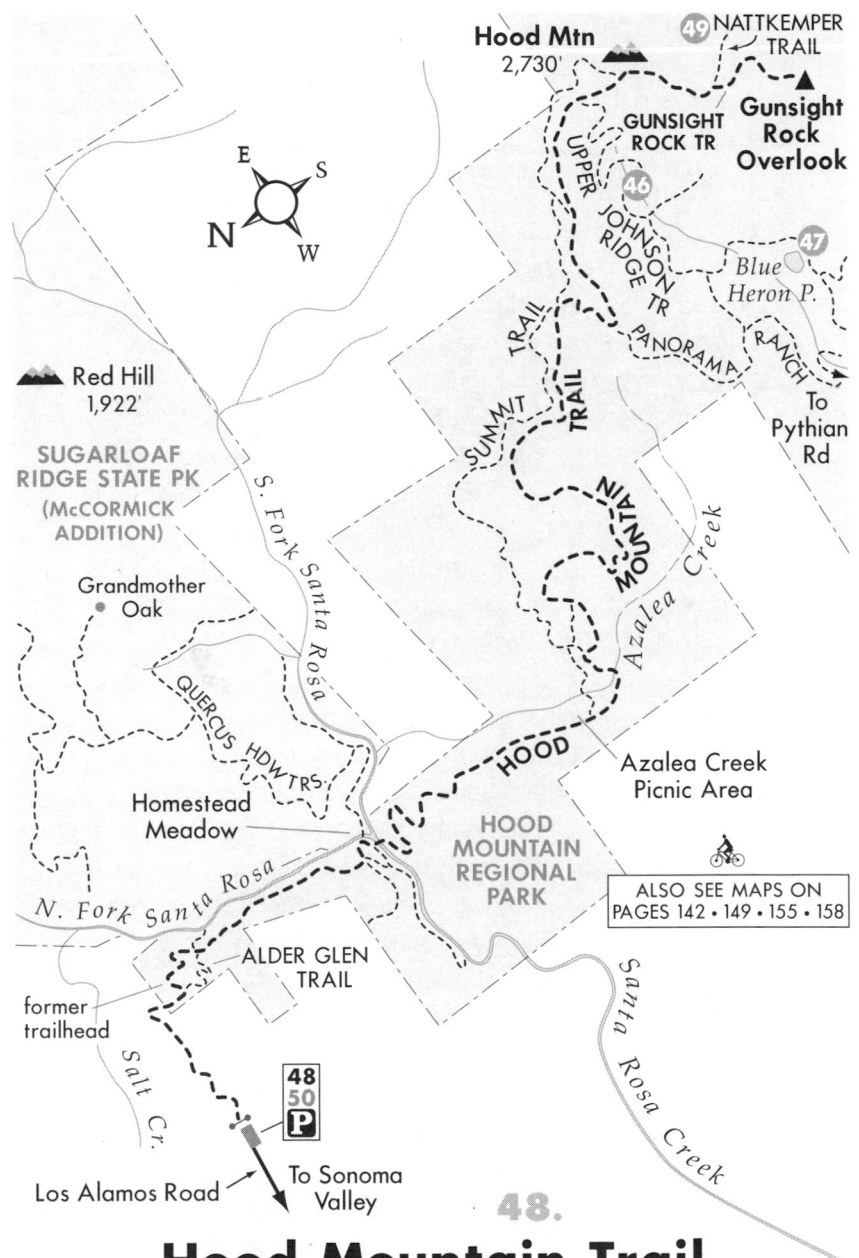

Hood Mtn
2,730'

NATTKEMPER TRAIL
49

GUNSIGHT ROCK TR

Gunsight Rock Overlook

46

UPPER JOHNSON RIDGE TR

PANORAMA

47

Blue Heron P.

RANCH

To Pythian Rd

E S N W

Red Hill
1,922'

SUGARLOAF RIDGE STATE PK
(McCORMICK ADDITION)

SUMMIT TRAIL

HOOD MOUNTAIN TRAIL

Grandmother Oak

S. Fork Santa Rosa

Azalea Creek

QUERCUS HDW TRS

Homestead Meadow

N. Fork Santa Rosa

HOOD

Azalea Creek Picnic Area

HOOD MOUNTAIN REGIONAL PARK

ALSO SEE MAPS ON
PAGES 142 • 149 • 155 • 158

ALDER GLEN TRAIL

former trailhead

Salt Cr.

48
50
P

Los Alamos Road

To Sonoma Valley

Santa Rosa Creek

48.

Hood Mountain Trail
Hood Mountain summit • Gunsight Rock
HOOD MOUNTAIN REGIONAL PARK

KENWOOD: From the town of Kenwood in Sonoma Valley, drive 5.5 miles north on Highway 12 (Sonoma Highway) to Los Alamos Road on the right. Turn right and continue with the directions above.

Hiking directions: Pass the trailhead gate, and walk down the paved road on the south wall of Salt Creek Canyon. Pass the slide area from the torrential winter storms of 2005 that closed this road. Steadily descend through a forest of evergreens, maples, oaks, bays, figs, and madrones. Pass the Alder Glen Trail to the old trailhead parking and picnic area at 0.6 miles. Weave down the wide, forested path on the Hood Mountain Trail. Follow the west canyon wall into Homestead Meadow, engulfed by the surrounding mountains, to the picnic area and T-junction at 1.1 miles. The right fork is a service road. Bear left and drop down 100 yards to a signed trail split. The left fork enters the 1,200-acre McCormick Addition of Sugarloaf Ridge State Park. Stay to the right for 30 yards to Santa Rosa Creek amid alders and bays. Rock hop over the creek, and head up the slope among horsetail ferns. The long, steady climb leads to the posted Azalea Creek Picnic Area on the left and restrooms on the right at 2.5 miles. Climb a short distance, passing the Summit Trail. Cross over Azalea Creek, and climb to vistas of Mount St. Helena and the coastal range. Pass a few more junctions with the Summit Trail, a parallel footpath that traverses through a pygmy forest. Both routes head east and merge on a flat circular clearing atop the 2,730-foot summit of Hood Mountain at 5.5 miles.

From the summit, descend on the Nattkemper Trail through manzanita and colorful lava outcrops for 0.2 miles to the signed Gunsight Rock Trail. The left fork leads into Sugarloaf Ridge State Park to Adobe Canyon Road (Hike 49). Veer right on the Gunsight Rock Trail and walk 0.2 miles, passing volcanic outcroppings to a massive block of rocks overlooking Sonoma Valley. The vistas extend to San Pablo Bay and the Santa Rosa Valley, Sonoma Mountain to Mount Tamalpais in Marin County, and Mount Diablo in Contra Costa County. Return by retracing your route, or take the alternate Summit Trail back to the Azalea Creek Picnic Area.■

49. Goodspeed—Nattkemper Trails
Route 3: Hood Mountain Summit and Gunsight Rock

**SUGARLOAF RIDGE STATE PARK and
HOOD MOUNTAIN REGIONAL PARK**

2605 Adobe Canyon Road · Kenwood

Hiking distance: 7 miles round trip

Hiking time: 4 hours

**map
page 155**

Elevation gain: 2,100 feet

Dogs: not allowed Sugarloaf Ridge/allowed Hood Mountain

Maps: U.S.G.S. Kenwood
Sugarloaf Ridge State Park
Hood Mountain Regional Park

Summary of hike: This is the third route to the Hood Mountain summit and the Gunsight Rock Overlook. The trail begins on the west side of the mountain in Sugarloaf Ridge State Park. The hike utilizes the Goodspeed and Nattkemper Trails, overlooking Sonoma Valley while crossing the southwest-facing, sun-exposed slope of Hood Mountain. En route, the trail enters Hood Mountain Regional Park, leading to the 2,730-foot summit and the Gunsight Rock Overlook, a distinctive formation of massive rocks perched on the cliffs just beneath the summit. The views from the overlook are fantastic.

Driving directions: NORTH SONOMA VALLEY: From Highway 12 and Calistoga Road on the north end of Sonoma Valley, drive 6 miles southeast on Highway 12 (Sonoma Highway) to Adobe Canyon Road. Turn left and continue 2.3 miles up the winding mountain road to the dirt parking area on the left.

KENWOOD: From the town of Kenwood in Sonoma Valley, drive 0.9 miles north on Highway 12 (Sonoma Highway) to Adobe Canyon Road on the right. Turn right and continue 2.3 miles up the winding mountain road to the dirt parking area on the left.

Hiking directions: Take the posted Goodspeed Trail from the lower west end of the parking area. Immediately enter a lush redwood grove, and cross a wooden bridge over Sonoma Creek. Loop clockwise around a hill among moss-covered rocks, ferns, and big-leaf maples. Cross a bridge over Bear Creek, a tributary of Sonoma Creek. Follow the creek a short distance, and curve left up the hillside through a predominant Douglas fir forest. Climb at a moderate grade on the rock-embedded path. The views extend from forested Adobe Canyon to volcanic Sugarloaf Ridge. Zigzag up the mountain through chaparral and manzanita, with views of Bald Mountain, Red Mountain, Brushy Peaks, and Sonoma Mountain across the valley. Cross a gravel road at 0.9 miles. Descend via four switchbacks, and cross a boulder-filled tributary of Sonoma Creek. Ascend the mountainside, leaving the chaparral, and enter the shade of a Douglas fir forest with manzanita. Make a horseshoe right bend, and steadily climb up the exposed, rock-strewn ridge. Cross a seasonal stream in a pocket of trees to the open, southwest-facing slope. Traverse the grassland with amazing vistas, continuing to the posted Hood Mountain Regional Park boundary and a map kiosk at 2 miles. Head across the open grasslands on the Nattkemper Trail. (The Goodspeed Trail becomes the Nattkemper Trail at the boundary.) Pass a bench and memorial plaque to Clark Nattkemper (1914—2001), with views stretching to San Pablo Bay. Continue climbing to a posted junction with the Gunsight Overlook Trail on the left. The Nattkemper Trail continues 0.2 miles straight ahead through thickets of live oak to the 2,730-foot Hood Mountain summit in a circular clearing. Take the left fork on the Gunsight Rock Trail, and walk 0.2 miles to a massive jumble of rocks overlooking Sonoma Valley to San Pablo Bay and the Santa Rosa Plain. The vistas extend to Mount Diablo and over Sonoma Mountain to Mount Tamalpais. Return by retracing your route.■

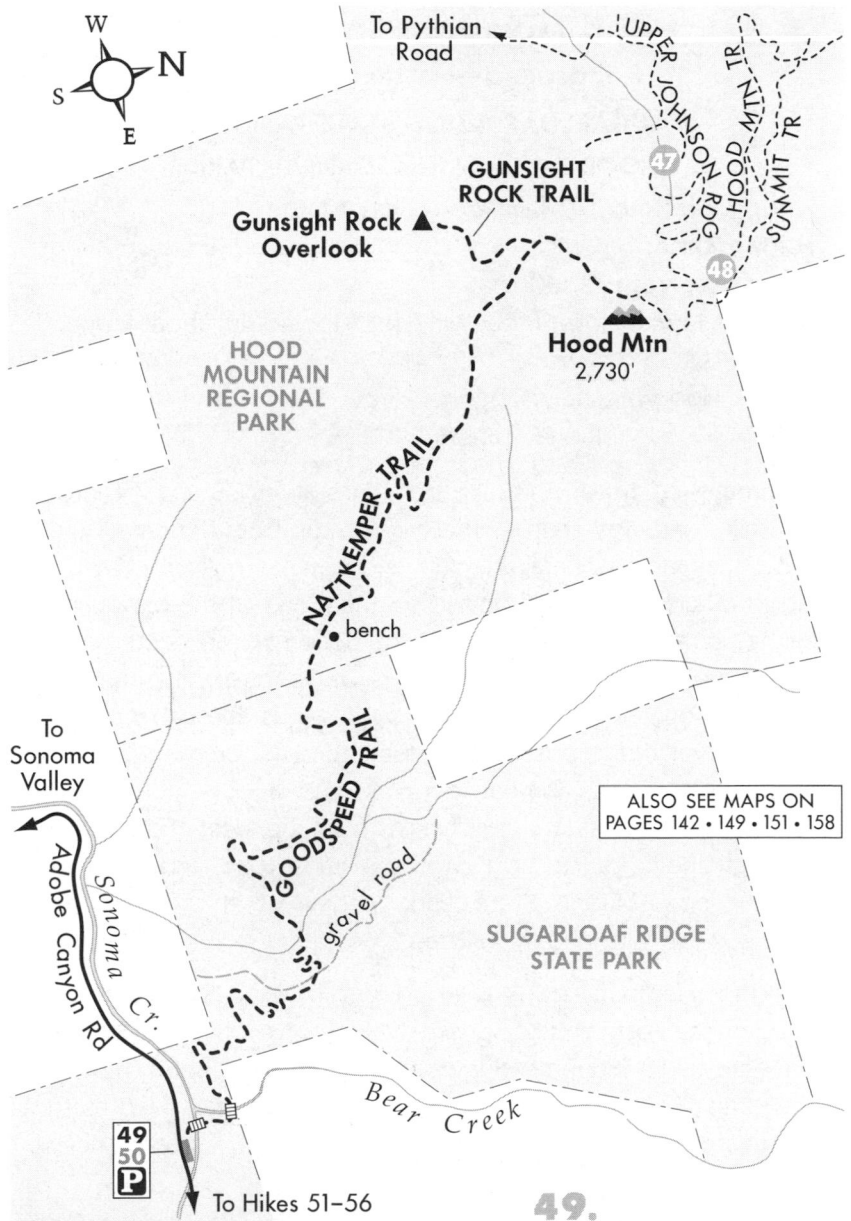

W N S E

To Pythian Road

GUNSIGHT ROCK TRAIL

Gunsight Rock Overlook ▲

UPPER JOHNSON RDG

47

HOOD MTN TR

SUMMIT TR

48

HOOD MOUNTAIN REGIONAL PARK

Hood Mtn 2,730'

NATTKEMPER TRAIL

• bench

To Sonoma Valley

GOODSPEED TRAIL

gravel road

Adobe Canyon Rd

Sonoma Cr.

ALSO SEE MAPS ON PAGES 142 • 149 • 151 • 158

SUGARLOAF RIDGE STATE PARK

Bear Creek

49 50 P

To Hikes 51–56

49.

Goodspeed–Nattkemper Trails
Hood Mountain summit • Gunsight Rock
HOOD MOUNTAIN • SUGARLOAF RIDGE

50. Hood Mountain Shuttle Hike
Goodspeed—Nattkemper Trails

SUGARLOAF RIDGE STATE PARK and
HOOD MOUNTAIN REGIONAL PARK

Hiking distance: 9.4-mile one-way shuttle
Hiking time: 5 hours
Elevation gain: 2,100 feet

map page 158

Dogs: allowed Hood Mountain/not allowed Sugarloaf Ridge
Maps: U.S.G.S. Kenwood
       Hood Mountain Regional Park
       Sugarloaf Ridge State Park

Summary of hike: This hike combines Hikes 48 and 49 into a 9.4-mile, one-way shuttle. The hike climbs from Sonoma Valley, up to the Hood Mountain summit, and down into Adobe Canyon. Hood Mountain, located on the southern end of the Mayacamas Range, is the highest peak along the Sonoma–Napa county line. Along the hike are expansive views of Sonoma Valley and the coastal mountains. The diverse route winds through canyons; climbs over ridgetops; and passes through open grasslands, mixed woodlands, Sargent cypress, and a pygmy forest of Mendocino cypress. The hike begins from the west end of Hood Mountain Regional Park, off of Los Alamos Road, and continues into Sugarloaf Ridge State Park, ending at the Goodspeed Trailhead on Adobe Canyon Road.

Driving directions: TRAILHEAD: From Highway 12 and Calistoga Road on the north end of Sonoma Valley, drive 1.1 miles southeast on Highway 12 (Sonoma Highway) to Los Alamos Road. Turn left and drive 4.7 miles up the narrow, winding mountain road to the road gate and trailhead parking area on the right. A parking fee is required.

From the town of Kenwood in Sonoma Valley, drive 5.5 miles north on Highway 12 (Sonoma Highway) to Los Alamos Road on the right. Turn right and continue with the directions above.

SHUTTLE CAR: From Highway 12 and Calistoga Road on the north end of Sonoma Valley, drive 6 miles southeast on Highway 12 (Sonoma Highway) to Adobe Canyon Road. Turn left and continue 2.3 miles up the winding mountain road to the dirt parking area on the left.

From the town of Kenwood in Sonoma Valley, drive 0.9 miles north on Highway 12 (Sonoma Highway) to Adobe Canyon Road on the right. Turn right and continue 2.3 miles up the winding mountain road to the dirt parking area on the left.

Hiking directions: Follow the hiking directions of Hike 48 to the Gunsight Rock Overlook. After enjoying the views from the overlook, head back up the Gunsight Rock Trail and continue southeast on the Nattkemper Trail. Cross the open grasslands with world-class views. Pass a bench and memorial plaque to Clark Nattkemper (1914-2001). At 7 miles, the trail reaches Sugarloaf Ridge State Park by a map kiosk. The Nattkemper Trail becomes the Goodspeed Trail at the boundary. Continue on the Goodspeed Trail and pass through a pocket of fir trees. Cross a seasonal stream and steadily descend on the rock-strewn, southwest-facing slope. Enter the shade of a Douglas fir forest, and cross a boulder-filled tributary of Sonoma Creek. Climb via four switchbacks to a gravel road. Cross the road and zigzag down the mountain through chaparral and manzanita, with views of Bald Mountain, Red Mountain, Brushy Peaks, and Sugarloaf Ridge forming the heart of Sugarloaf Ridge State Park. Curve right through a predominant Douglas fir forest to Bear Creek. Cross a wooden footbridge over the creek. Loop around a hill among moss-covered rocks and through a lush redwood grove to Sonoma Creek. Cross a bridge over the creek, and ascend the slope to the shuttle car parking area at Adobe Canyon Road.■

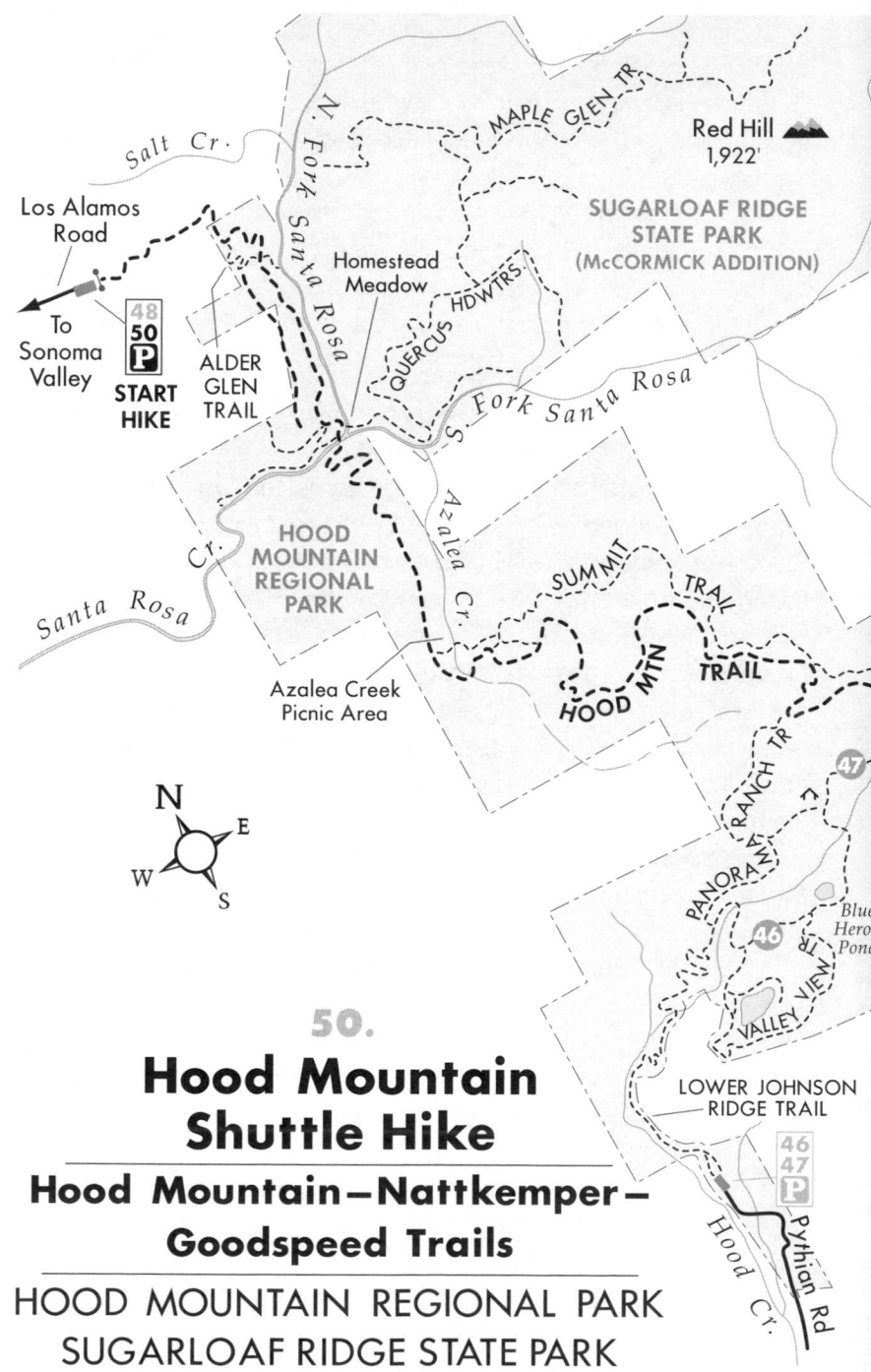

Red Hill ▲▲
1,922'

SUGARLOAF RIDGE
STATE PARK
(McCORMICK ADDITION)

MAPLE GLEN TR.

N. Fork Santa Rosa

Salt Cr.

Los Alamos
Road

To
Sonoma
Valley

48
50 P
START HIKE

ALDER
GLEN
TRAIL

Homestead
Meadow

QUERCUS HDWTRS

S. Fork Santa Rosa

Azalea Cr.

Cr.

HOOD
MOUNTAIN
REGIONAL
PARK

Santa Rosa

Azalea Creek
Picnic Area

SUMMIT TRAIL

HOOD MTN TRAIL

PANORAMA RANCH TR.

47

46

Blue
Heron
Pond

VALLEY VIEW TR.

LOWER JOHNSON
RIDGE TRAIL

46 47 P

Hood Cr.

Pythian Rd.

N
E
W
S

50.
Hood Mountain
Shuttle Hike

Hood Mountain–Nattkemper–
Goodspeed Trails

HOOD MOUNTAIN REGIONAL PARK
SUGARLOAF RIDGE STATE PARK

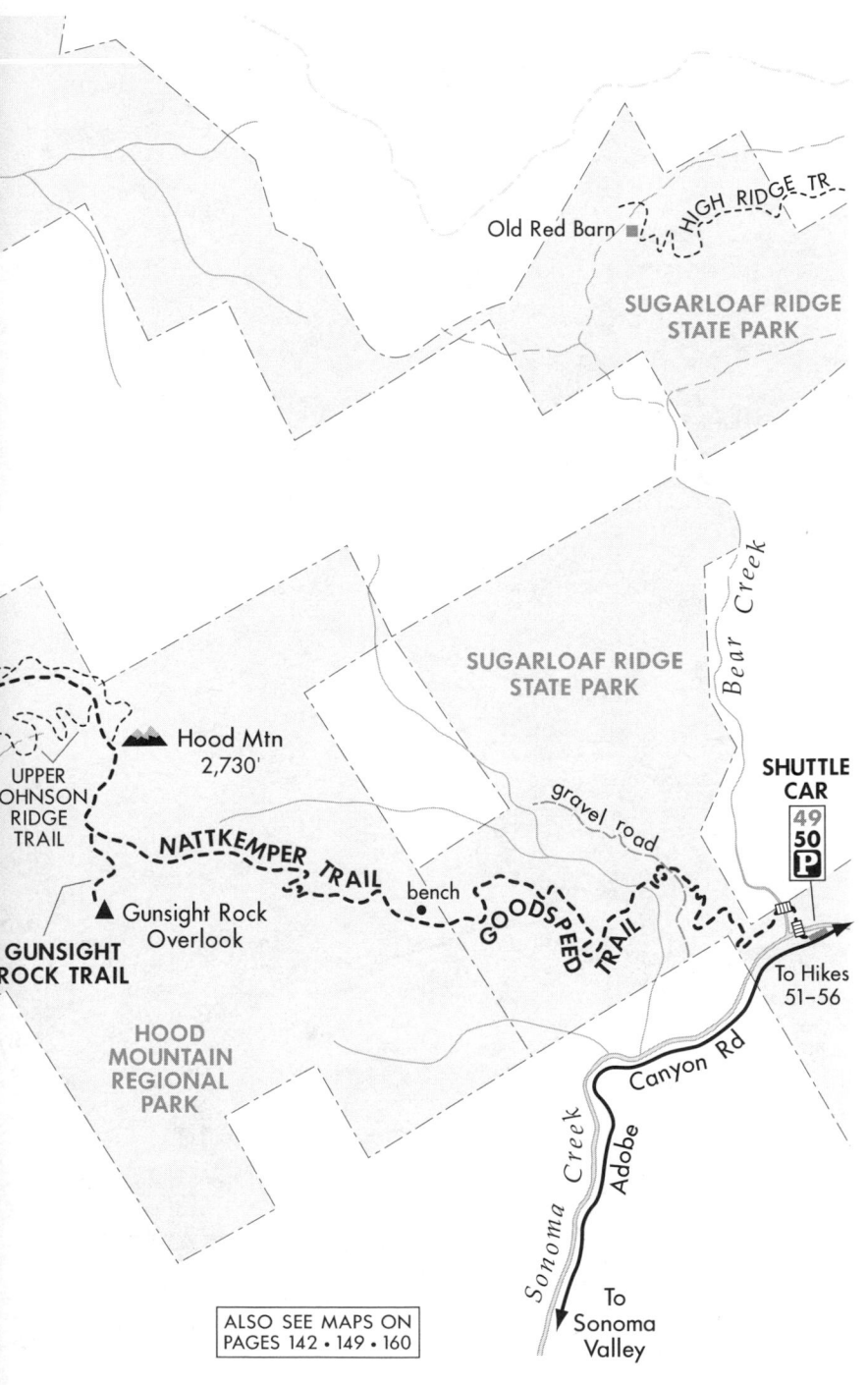

Old Red Barn ■ HIGH RIDGE TR

SUGARLOAF RIDGE
STATE PARK

Bear Creek

SUGARLOAF RIDGE
STATE PARK

Hood Mtn
2,730'

UPPER
JOHNSON
RIDGE
TRAIL

NATTKEMPER TRAIL

bench

GOODSPEED TRAIL

SHUTTLE
CAR

49
50
P

To Hikes
51–56

▲ Gunsight Rock
Overlook

GUNSIGHT
ROCK TRAIL

HOOD
MOUNTAIN
REGIONAL
PARK

gravel road

Canyon Rd

Sonoma Creek

Adobe

To
Sonoma
Valley

ALSO SEE MAPS ON
PAGES 142 • 149 • 160

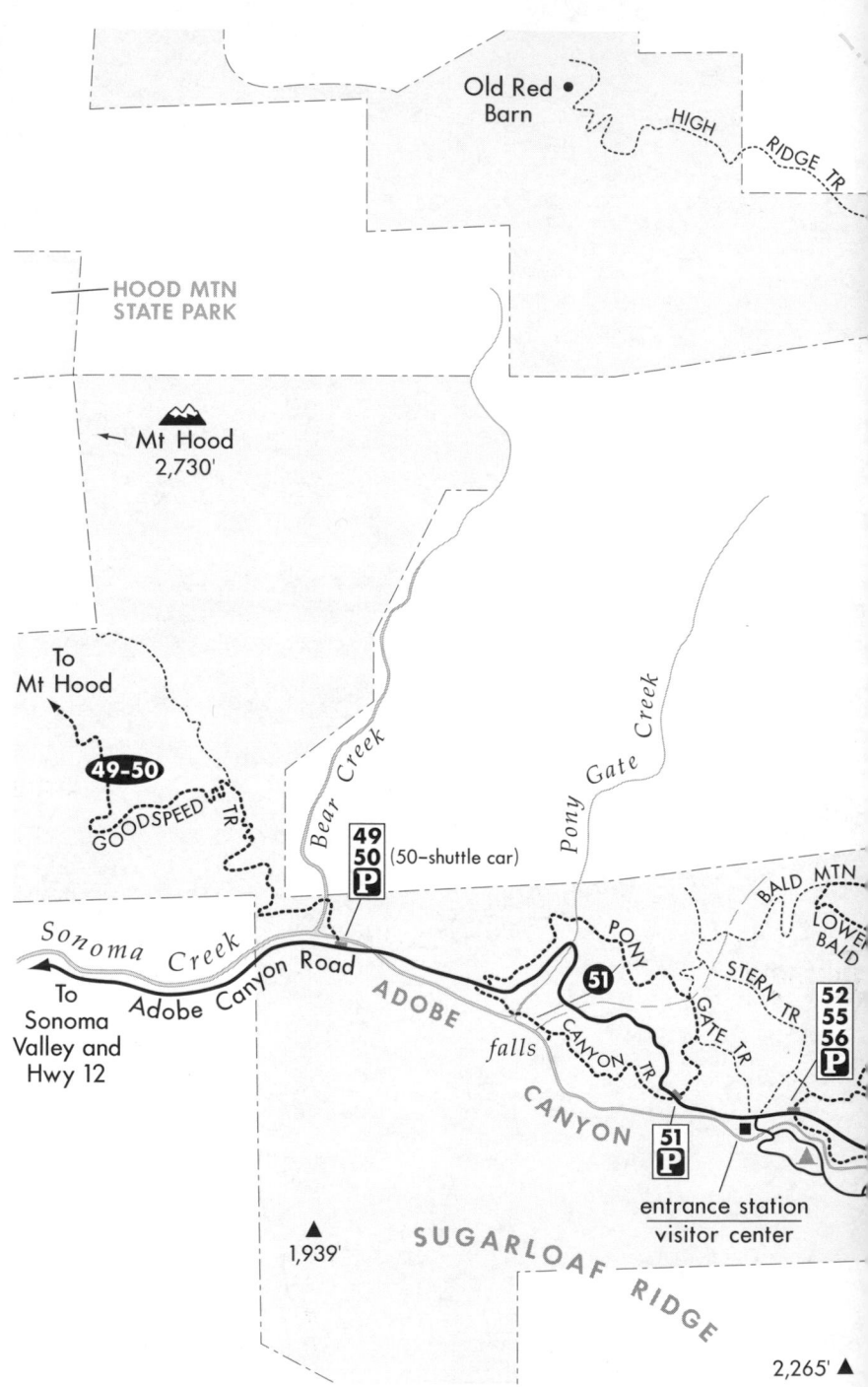

Sugarloaf Ridge State Park

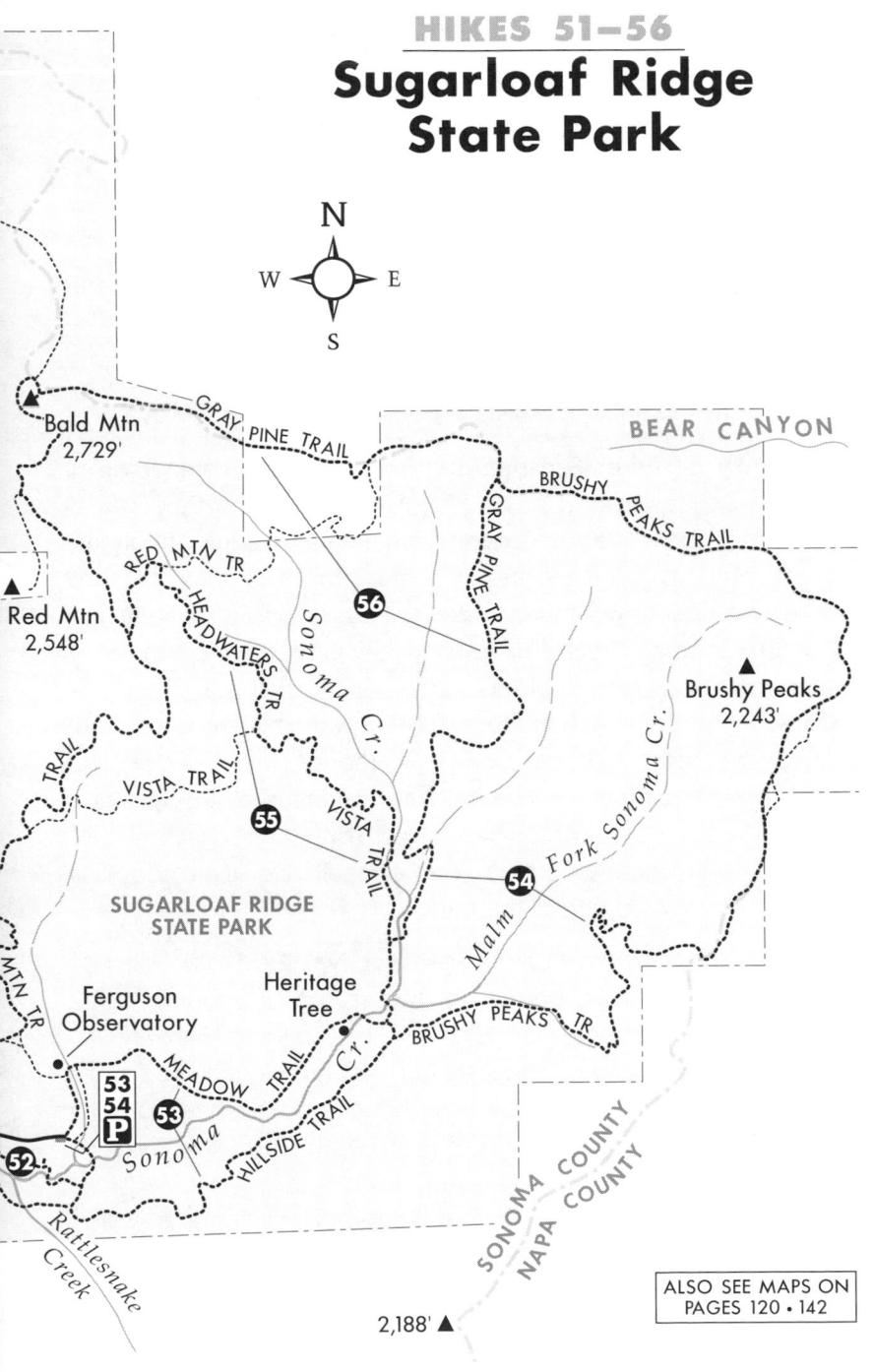

N
W — E
S

Bald Mtn
2,729'

GRAY PINE TRAIL

BEAR CANYON

BRUSHY PEAKS TRAIL

GRAY PINE TRAIL

RED MTN TR

56

HEADWATERS TR

Red Mtn
2,548'

Sonoma Cr.

Brushy Peaks
2,243'

Fork Sonoma Cr.

TRAIL

VISTA TRAIL

55

VISTA TRAIL

54

SUGARLOAF RIDGE
STATE PARK

Malm

Ferguson
Observatory

Heritage
Tree

BRUSHY PEAKS TR

MTN TR

MEADOW TRAIL

Sonoma Cr.

53
54
P

53

HILLSIDE TRAIL

52

Sonoma

Rattlesnake Creek

SONOMA COUNTY
NAPA COUNTY

2,188' ▲

ALSO SEE MAPS ON
PAGES 120 • 142

51. Pony Gate—Canyon Loop to Sonoma Creek Falls

SUGARLOAF RIDGE STATE PARK

2605 Adobe Canyon Road · Kenwood

Hiking distance: 1.7-mile loop
Hiking time: 1 hour
Elevation gain: 450 feet
Dogs: not allowed
Maps: U.S.G.S. Kenwood
Sugarloaf Ridge State Park

Summary of hike: Sugarloaf Ridge State Park is named for its distinct conical-shaped ridge of volcanic rock. The 2,200-foot ridge rises above Adobe Canyon from the south edge of Sonoma Creek. Sonoma Creek forms on the upper slopes of Bald Mountain and flows through the grassy meadow into Adobe Canyon. Sonoma Creek Falls plunges 25 feet over a jumble of huge, moss-covered boulders in the forested shade of Adobe Canyon. The Canyon Trail leads to the waterfall through a lush forest of redwood, oak, bay, sycamore, maple, alder, and madrone trees. The Pony Gate Trail traverses a grassy slope above Sonoma Creek through a mixed forest of coast live oak, laurel, and fir. These two trails form a scenic and diverse loop in the lower west corner of the park.

Driving directions: NORTH SONOMA VALLEY: From Highway 12 and Calistoga Road on the northwest end of Sonoma Valley, drive 6 miles southeast on Highway 12 (Sonoma Highway) to Adobe Canyon Road on the left. Turn left and continue 3.2 miles up the winding mountain road to the posted trailhead parking area on the left. It is located 0.2 miles shy of the park entrance station.

KENWOOD: From the town of Kenwood in Sonoma Valley, drive 0.9 miles northwest on Highway 12 (Sonoma Highway) to Adobe Canyon Road on the right. Turn right and continue with the directions above.

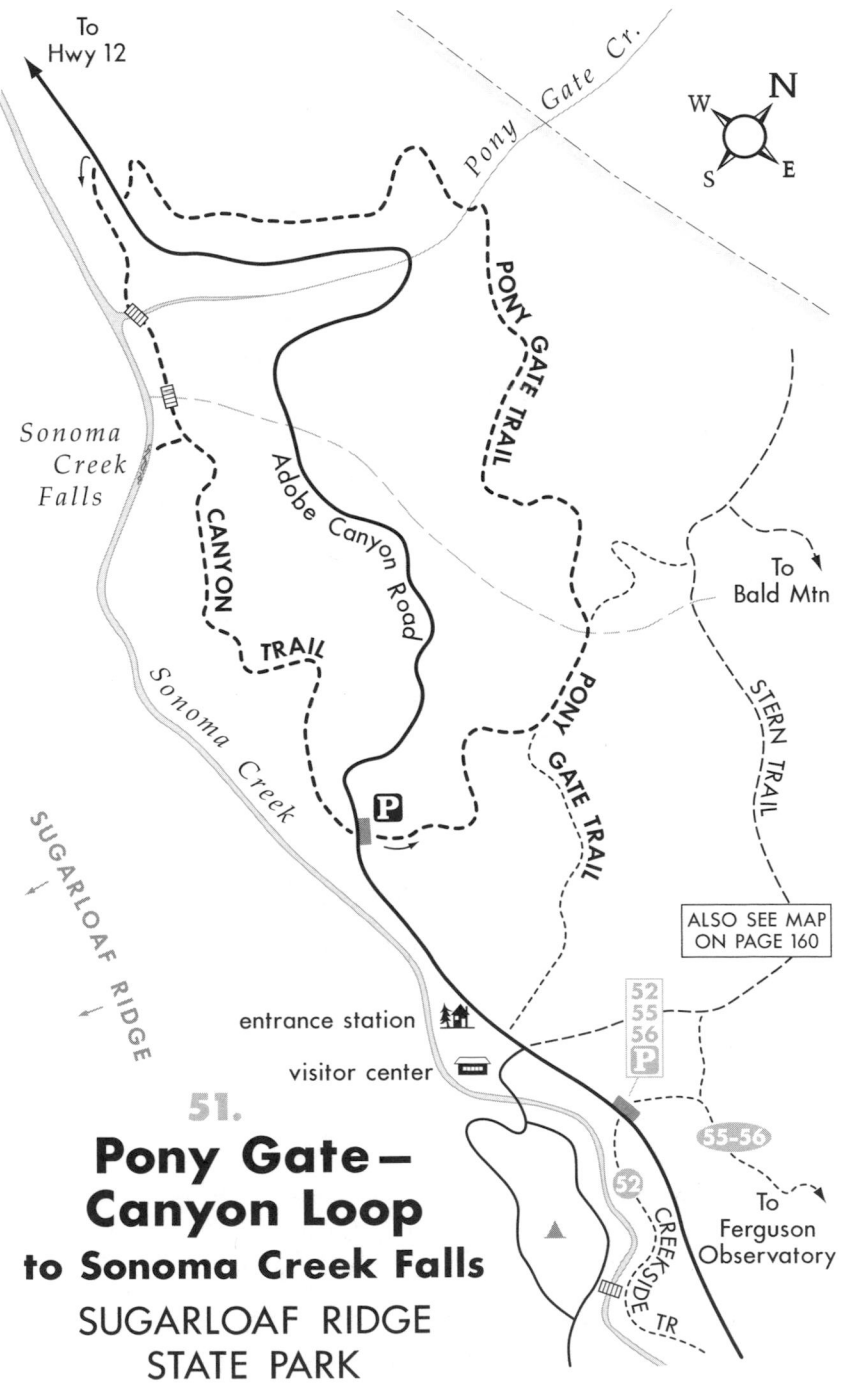

To Hwy 12

Pony Gate Cr.

N
W   E
S

PONY GATE TRAIL

Sonoma Creek Falls

Adobe Canyon Road

CANYON TRAIL

To Bald Mtn

Sonoma Creek

PONY GATE TRAIL

STERN TRAIL

P

ALSO SEE MAP ON PAGE 160

SUGARLOAF RIDGE

52 55 56 **P**

entrance station

visitor center

55-56

52

To Ferguson Observatory

CREEKSIDE TR

51.
Pony Gate — Canyon Loop
to Sonoma Creek Falls
SUGARLOAF RIDGE STATE PARK

Hiking directions: Take the posted trail from the upper east end of the parking area, and head up the forested hillside. The vistas extend across Adobe Canyon to the forested wall of Sugarloaf Ridge and across Sonoma Valley to Sonoma Mountain. Traverse the hillside to a junction with the Pony Gate Trail at 0.2 miles. Bear left and cross a tributary of Sonoma Creek to a Y-fork. Stay to the left and descend under a canopy of oaks, pines, and madrones to Pony Gate Creek. Follow the cascading creek 20 yards downstream, and rock-hop across the gulch. Climb up the hill and weave through the shady forest. Steadily descend to Adobe Canyon Road at 1.1 mile. Cautiously walk 50 yards down the road to the posted Canyon Trail on the left. Descend steps into a redwood, oak, and fern-filled forest. Head southeast in lush Adobe Canyon above Sonoma Creek. Follow the creek upstream, and cross a wooden footbridge over Pony Gate Creek. Cross a second bridge over the tributary stream to a junction at 1.3 miles. Detour 50 yards to the right to Sonoma Creek Falls, tumbling through a rocky ravine amid redwoods, Douglas firs, and moss-covered boulders. After enjoying the falls, return to the main trail. Climb steps, steadily gaining elevation through the dense forest. Emerge from the forest at Adobe Canyon Road across from the trailhead, completing the loop.■

52. Creekside Nature Trail
SUGARLOAF RIDGE STATE PARK
2605 Adobe Canyon Road · Kenwood

Hiking distance: 0.75-mile loop
Hiking time: 30 minutes
Elevation gain: 100 feet
Dogs: not allowed
Maps: U.S.G.S. Kenwood
      Sugarloaf Ridge State Park
      Creekside Nature Trail interpretive guide

Summary of hike: The Creekside Nature Trail is an easy 0.75-mile loop on the valley floor of Sugarloaf Ridge State Park. The

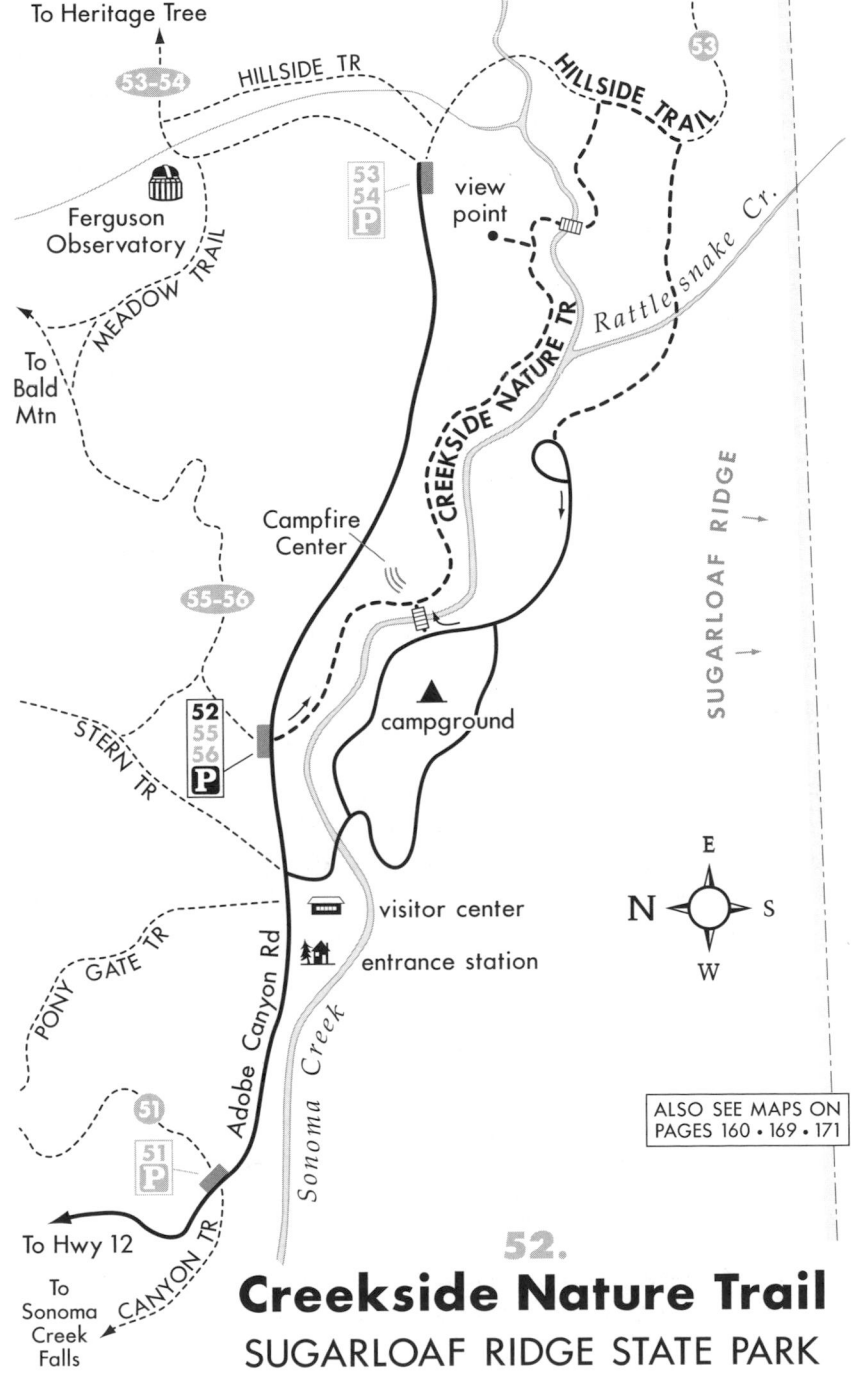

To Heritage Tree

53-54

HILLSIDE TR

HILLSIDE TRAIL

53

view point

Ferguson Observatory

53 54 P

MEADOW TRAIL

CREEKSIDE NATURE TR

Rattlesnake Cr.

SUGARLOAF RIDGE

To Bald Mtn

Campfire Center

55-56

STERN TR

52 55 56 P

campground

E

N ☆ S

W

PONY GATE TR

visitor center

entrance station

Adobe Canyon Rd

Sonoma Creek

51

51 P

To Hwy 12

To Sonoma Creek Falls

CANYON TR

ALSO SEE MAPS ON PAGES 160 • 169 • 171

52.

Creekside Nature Trail
SUGARLOAF RIDGE STATE PARK

trail meanders along the banks of Sonoma Creek and Rattlesnake Creek through a forest of coast live oak, white oak, black oak, Douglas fir, California bay laurel, coyote brush, and Oregon ash. En route are overlooks of Hood Mountain, Red Mountain, Bald Mountain, and Sugarloaf Ridge. The nature trail has 17 numbered posts that correspond with a free pamphlet available from the ranger station by the park entrance.

Driving directions: NORTH SONOMA VALLEY: From Highway 12 and Calistoga Road on the north end of Sonoma Valley, drive 6 miles southeast on Highway 12 (Sonoma Highway) to Adobe Canyon Road. Turn left and continue 3.5 miles up the winding mountain road to the large trailhead parking area on the left. It is located 0.1 miles past the park entrance station. A parking fee is required.

KENWOOD: From the town of Kenwood in Sonoma Valley, drive 0.9 miles north on Highway 12 (Sonoma Highway) to Adobe Canyon Road on the right. Turn right and continue with the directions above.

Hiking directions: Cross the road to the picnic area and signed Creekside Nature Trail. Follow the log-rail fence above Sonoma Creek, and pass the picnic area on the right. Stroll through the lush forest with coast live oak, white oak, Douglas fir, white alder, and coyote brush. Traverse the hillside, passing scattered serpentine rock. Cross a wood footbridge and skirt the Campfire Center amphitheater on the left. Veer left on the gravel path, passing interpretive stations. At signpost 11, take a 45-yard detour to the left. Climb the knoll to a bench and huge black oak tree with views of Hood Mountain, Bald Mountain, and Red Mountain. Return to the main trail and continue east. At signpost 12, cross a wood bridge over Sonoma Creek, and climb to a junction with the Hillside Trail (Hike 53). Bear right and follow the Hillside Trail 80 yards. Bear right again, continuing on the Creekside Nature Trail, with a view of volcanic Sugarloaf Ridge to the south. Descend past a water tank on the right, and rock-hop over Rattlesnake Creek. Traverse the northern base of Sugarloaf

Ridge, and enter the campground at site 25. Follow the campground road in a tree-rimmed meadow. Cross the bridge over Sonoma Creek by campsite 12, completing the loop back at the Campfire Center. Curve left, cross the footbridge, and return to the left.■

53. Meadow—Hillside Loop

SUGARLOAF RIDGE STATE PARK

2605 Adobe Canyon Road · Kenwood

Hiking distance: 2.2-mile loop
Hiking time: 1 hour
Elevation gain: 250 feet
Dogs: not allowed
Maps: U.S.G.S. Kenwood and Rutherford
Sugarloaf Ridge State Park

map
page 169

Summary of hike: Sugarloaf Ridge State Park encompasses 2,700 acres of steep, rugged hills ranging in elevation from 600 to 2,729 feet. The park includes a campground, primitive campsites, picnic areas, rolling meadows, an observatory with three telescopes, and 25 miles of hiking and equestrian trails. The Meadow Trail strolls along the north side of Sonoma Creek in a scenic, grassy meadow. The path leads to Heritage Tree, a massive big-leaf maple tree in a creekside picnic area. The Hillside Trail traverses the forested hills on the opposite side of Sonoma Creek at the foot of Sugarloaf Ridge. These two trails form an easy loop in the heart of the park.

Driving directions: NORTH SONOMA VALLEY: From Highway 12 and Calistoga Road on the north end of Sonoma Valley, drive 6 miles southeast on Highway 12 (Sonoma Highway) to Adobe Canyon Road. Turn left and continue 3.8 miles up the winding mountain road to the end of the road. It is located 0.4 miles past the park entrance station. Park in the posted area on the right. A parking fee is required.

KENWOOD: From the town of Kenwood in Sonoma Valley, drive 0.9 miles north on Highway 12 (Sonoma Highway) to Adobe Canyon Road on the right. Turn right and continue with the directions above.

Hiking directions: Walk past the vehicle gate and observatory sign, following the wide gravel road along a stream. Pass the Robert Ferguson Observatory on its right side, and walk through the trail gate. Cross over the stream and pass the Hillside Trail. Skirt the north edge of the large meadow to Sonoma Creek at a half mile. En route, interpretive signs about the sun, Mars, Jupiter, and Saturn line the trail. (The trail is part of the Planet Walk—Hike 54.) Follow the creek upstream through towering oaks and bay laurel. At 0.9 miles, pass the sprawling Heritage Tree in a picnic area on the banks of Sonoma Creek. Cross the wood bridge over the creek to a junction with the Gray Pine Trail on the left (Hikes 54—56), then the Brushy Peaks Trail on the left. Stay to the right both times, and head southwest on the Hillside Trail along the edge of the meadow. Gradually climb the hillside toward Sugarloaf Ridge. Traverse the slope through grasslands and a forest of Douglas fir, California bay, and coast live oak. Weave up the hill to 1,450 feet, the trail's highest point. Head downhill past two wooden water tanks and a picnic area overlook to a posted junction with the Creekside Nature Trail (Hike 52). Bear right, staying on the Hillside Trail, and continue downhill. Pass a second junction with the Creekside Nature Trail. Hop over Sonoma Creek and complete the loop at the trailhead. ■

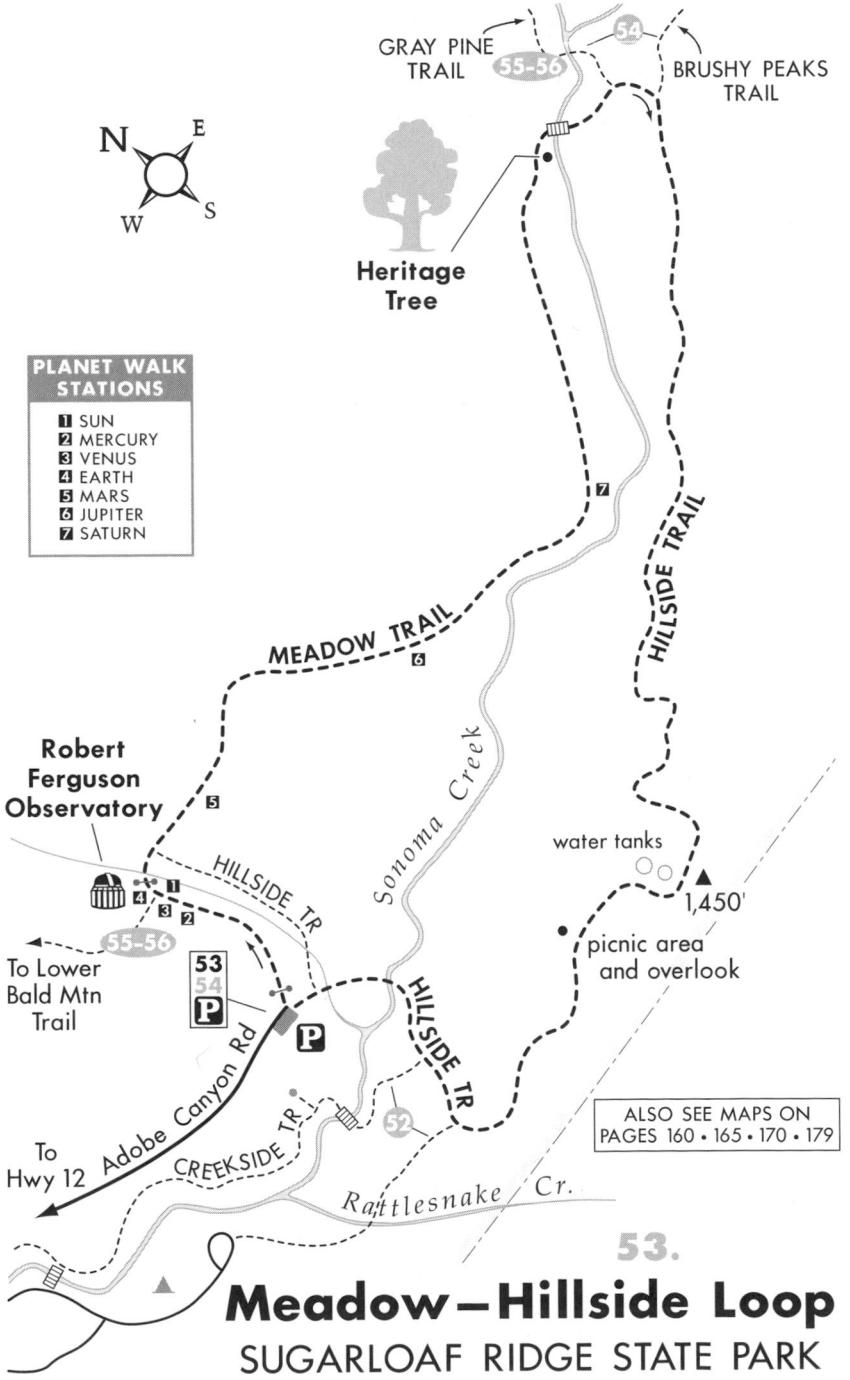

N E W S

GRAY PINE TRAIL 55-56

54

BRUSHY PEAKS TRAIL

Heritage Tree

PLANET WALK STATIONS

1 SUN
2 MERCURY
3 VENUS
4 EARTH
5 MARS
6 JUPITER
7 SATURN

7

MEADOW TRAIL 6

HILLSIDE TRAIL

Robert Ferguson Observatory

5

Sonoma Creek

water tanks

1,450'

picnic area and overlook

HILLSIDE TR

1 4 3 2

HILLSIDE TR

55-56

To Lower Bald Mtn Trail

53
54
P

P

HILLSIDE TR

52

ALSO SEE MAPS ON PAGES 160 • 165 • 170 • 179

To Hwy 12

Adobe Canyon Rd

CREEKSIDE TR

Rattlesnake Cr.

53.
Meadow–Hillside Loop
SUGARLOAF RIDGE STATE PARK

54. Brushy Peaks—Gray Pine Loop including the Planet Walk

SUGARLOAF RIDGE STATE PARK

2605 Adobe Canyon Road · Kenwood

Hiking distance: 6.5-mile loop
Hiking time: 3.5 hours
Elevation gain: 1,000 feet
Dogs: not allowed
Maps: U.S.G.S. Kenwood and Rutherford
      Sugarloaf Ridge State Park

Summary of hike: Sugarloaf Ridge State Park contains three distinct ecological systems. In Sonoma Creek Canyon are riparian redwood forests that also include Douglas fir, gray pines, big-

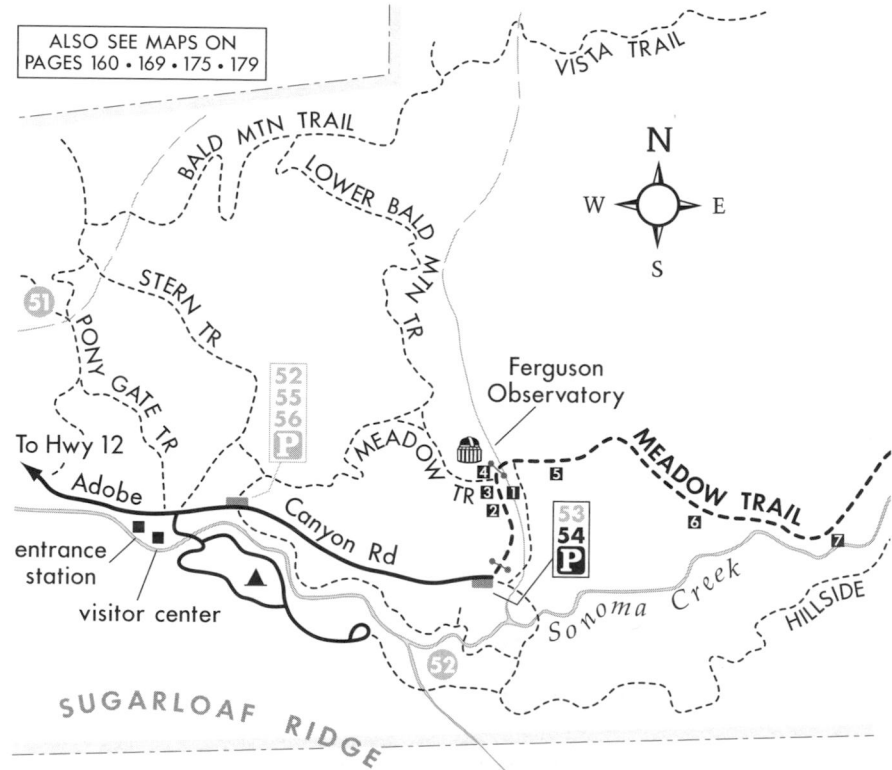

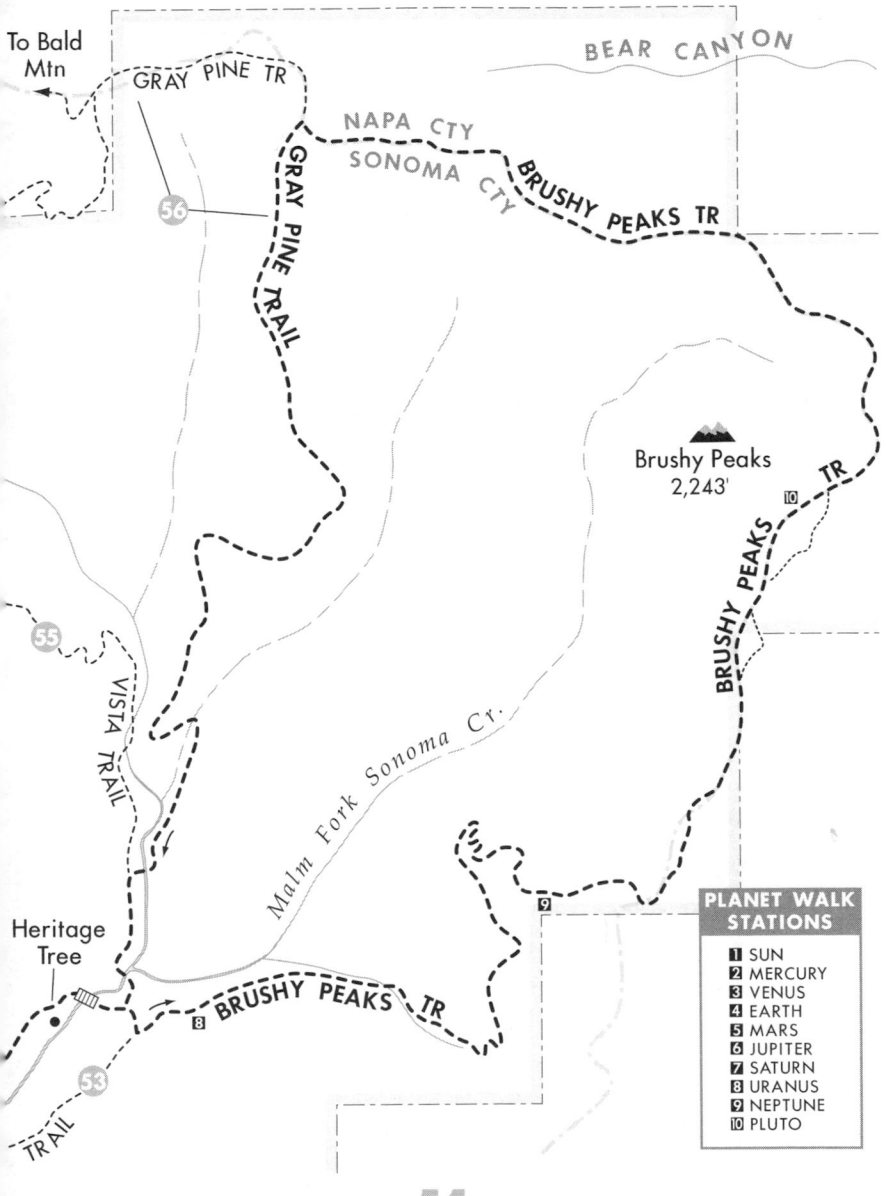

PLANET WALK STATIONS

1. SUN
2. MERCURY
3. VENUS
4. EARTH
5. MARS
6. JUPITER
7. SATURN
8. URANUS
9. NEPTUNE
10. PLUTO

54.

Brushy Peaks–Gray Pine Loop
including the Planet Walk
SUGARLOAF RIDGE STATE PARK

leaf maple, California bay laurel, and California buckeye. Along the open meadows are oak and fir woodlands. Atop the dry exposed ridges are chaparral varieties, including manzanita, toyon, coyote brush, and chamise. This loop hike explores all three habitats. The first half of the hike follows the Planet Walk. This interpretive trail illustrates the size of our solar system by reducing its size over two billion times to fit within the park boundaries. Interpretive panels represent the sun and each of the nine planets: Mercury, Venus, Earth, Mars, Jupiter, Saturn, Uranus, Neptune, and Pluto. The Planet Walk begins at the gated road by the Robert Ferguson Observatory and ends on the ridge straddling Napa and Sonoma counties.

Driving directions: NORTH SONOMA VALLEY: From Highway 12 and Calistoga Road on the north end of Sonoma Valley, drive 6 miles southeast on Highway 12 (Sonoma Highway) to Adobe Canyon Road. Turn left and continue 3.8 miles up the winding mountain road to the end of the road. It is located 0.4 miles past the park entrance station. Park in the posted area on the right. A parking fee is required.

KENWOOD: From the town of Kenwood in Sonoma Valley, drive 0.9 miles north on Highway 12 (Sonoma Highway) to Adobe Canyon Road on the right. Turn right and continue with the directions above.

Hiking directions: Walk past the vehicle gate and observatory sign, following the wide gravel road along a stream. Pass the Robert Ferguson Observatory on its right side, and walk through the trail gate. Cross over the stream and pass the Hillside Trail. Skirt the north edge of the large meadow to Sonoma Creek at a half mile. En route, interpretive signs about the planets line the trail. Follow the creek upstream through towering oaks and bay laurel. At 0.9 miles, pass a sprawling big-leaf maple called the Heritage Tree in a picnic area on the banks of Sonoma Creek. Cross the wood bridge over the creek to a junction with the Gray Pine Trail on the left—our return route.

Begin the loop straight ahead, and walk sixty yards to a posted junction. The Hillside Trail (Hike 53) is straight ahead. Bear left on the Brushy Peaks Trail, and traverse the forested hillside under a canopy of oak, manzanita, and toyon. Parallel the Malm Fork of Sonoma Creek, gradually gaining elevation. Cross a small branch of the Malm Fork, and climb the east wall of the canyon on a series of switchbacks. The climb levels out and curves left to a clearing overlooking Sugarloaf Ridge, Sonoma Valley, and the coastal range. En route are more interpretive panels about Uranus, Neptune, and Pluto. Continue uphill to a grassy meadow dotted with oaks and the ridge. Follow the rolling ridge for a half mile over four peaks, with views of Red Mountain, Bald Mountain, and sweeping vistas across Napa County and Sonoma County. After the fourth peak, curve left, straddling the county line. The views extend to the Mayacamas Mountains; the vineyards of Napa Valley; Lake Hennessey and Rector Reservoir in the lower foothills; and the towns of Mount St. Helena and Yountville. Continue along the rolling ridge on a rocky fire road over a series of dips and peaks. On top of the sixth peak, cross under power lines. After the seventh rise, descend to the posted Gray Pine Trail on the left at 4 miles.

Bear left on the Gray Pine Trail, and steadily descend on the wide dirt trail. At 4.8 miles, curve left and follow a branch of Sonoma Creek in an oak grove. Make an S-bend and cross another feeder creek. Parallel and hop over Sonoma Creek to a junction with the Vista Trail at 5.3 miles. Ford the creek again, reaching a T-junction with the Meadow Trail, which completes the loop. Bear right and cross a wood bridge over Sonoma Creek to the Heritage Tree. Return along the same trail back to the Ferguson Observatory and the trailhead. ■

55. Bald Mountain—Headwaters—Vista Loop

SUGARLOAF RIDGE STATE PARK

2605 Adobe Canyon Road · Kenwood

Hiking distance: 5.2-mile loop
Hiking time: 2.5 hours
Elevation gain: 1,000 feet
Dogs: not allowed
Maps: U.S.G.S. Kenwood and Rutherford
  Sugarloaf Ridge State Park

Summary of hike: Sonoma Creek forms from three ephemeral forks on the east slope of Bald Mountain and Red Mountain. The Headwaters Trail is a scenic half-mile trail that skirts the western fork of Sonoma Creek in a fern-filled oasis, connecting the Red Mountain Trail with the Vista Trail. The Vista Trail leads through a lush forested corridor, crossing a couple of ravines with small streams, and traverses a grassy hillside. This hike begins on the Bald Mountain Trail and forms a loop on the Headwaters and Vista Trails, returning through the park meadow along the banks of Sonoma Creek.

Driving directions: NORTH SONOMA VALLEY: From Highway 12 and Calistoga Road on the north end of Sonoma Valley, drive 6 miles southeast on Highway 12 (Sonoma Highway) to Adobe Canyon Road. Turn left and continue 3.5 miles up the winding mountain road to the large trailhead parking area on the left. It is located 0.1 miles past the park entrance station. A parking fee is required.

KENWOOD: From the town of Kenwood in Sonoma Valley, drive 0.9 miles north on Highway 12 (Sonoma Highway) to Adobe Canyon Road on the right. Turn right and continue with the directions above.

Hiking directions: Walk past the trailhead map and head up the grassy slope. Weave through an oak grove to a meadow and a triangle junction. The right fork leads to the observatory on the

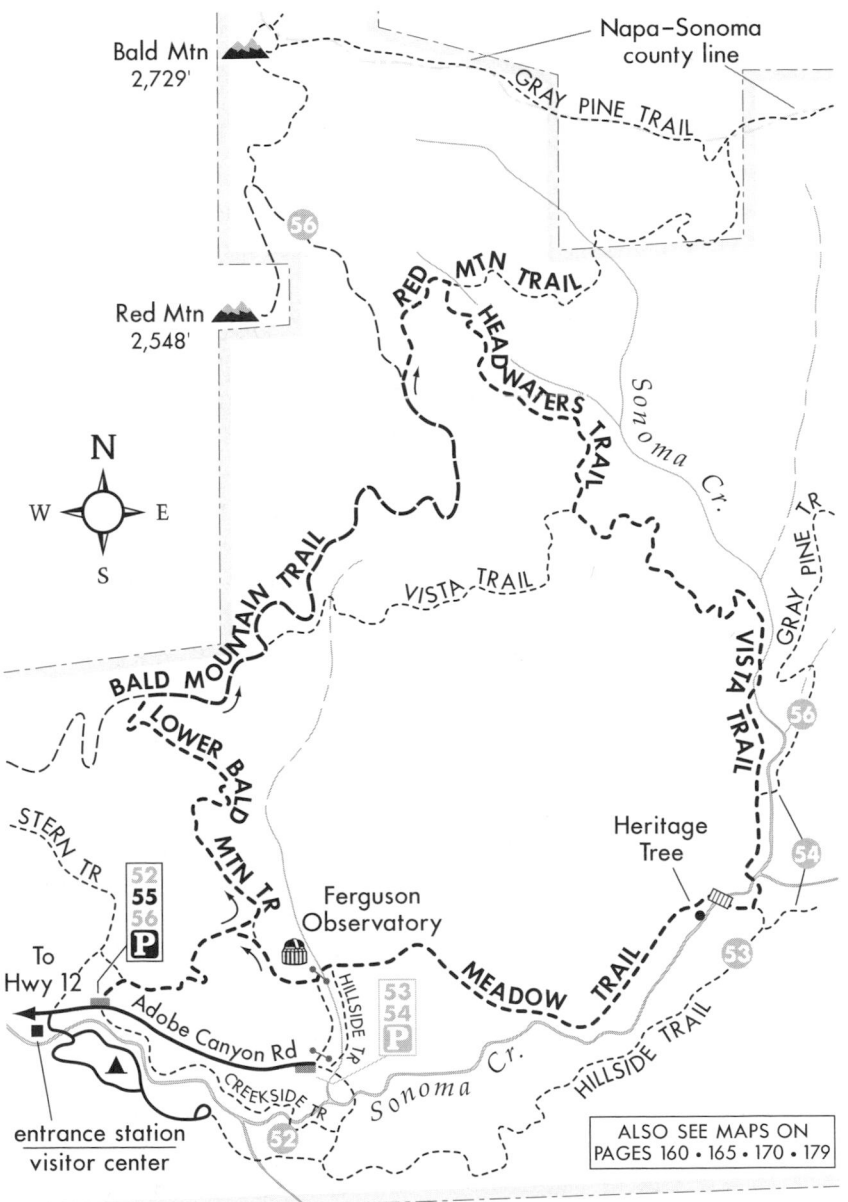

Bald Mtn
2,729'

Napa–Sonoma
county line

GRAY PINE TRAIL

Red Mtn
2,548'

RED MTN TRAIL

HEADWATERS TRAIL

Sonoma Cr.

N
W · E
S

BALD MOUNTAIN TRAIL

VISTA TRAIL

VISTA TRAIL

GRAY PINE TR

56

BALD MOUNTAIN

LOWER BALD MTN TR

STERN TR

52
55
56
P

To
Hwy 12

Ferguson
Observatory

Heritage
Tree

54

53

MEADOW TRAIL

Adobe Canyon Rd

HILLSIDE TR

53
54
P

HILLSIDE TRAIL

Sonoma Cr.

CREEKSIDE TR

52

entrance station
visitor center

ALSO SEE MAPS ON
PAGES 160 · 165 · 170 · 179

55. **Bald Mountain–**
Headwaters–Vista Loop
SUGARLOAF RIDGE STATE PARK

Meadow Trail—the return route. Go to the left on the Lower Bald Mountain Trail, beginning the loop. Climb to the upper end of the meadow, and enter an oak grove with manzanita and madrone. At one mile the trail reaches the Bald Mountain Trail, a paved fire road. Bear right and head up the narrow road to sweeping views of Sonoma Valley and the surrounding mountains. Pass the Vista Trail at 1.2 miles on a U-shaped bend. For a shorter 4.4-mile loop, take the Vista Trail to the right. For this hike, continue straight, weaving up the contours of the forested mountain. Pass a couple of stream-fed gullies and overlooks to the Red Mountain Trail at 2 miles. The Bald Mountain Trail continues straight ahead to the summit (Hike 56).

For this hike, leave the road and bear right on the Red Mountain Trail along the southeast flank of Red Mountain. Weave through the forest on the footpath, and descend 0.2 miles to a signed junction with the Headwaters Trail. The Red Mountain Trail crosses the upper reaches of Sonoma Creek in a moss-filled rocky grotto and climbs to the ridge straddling the county line. For this hike, take the Headwaters Trail to the right, and follow a seasonal fork of Sonoma Creek. Descend through the shaded forest along the west side of the creek, passing lush rock walls, ferns, moss-covered trees, and pools of water. The half-mile trail ends in an oak grove at a T-junction with the Vista Trail. Bear left on the Vista Trail, and traverse the hillside overlooking the park valley, Brushy Peaks, and Sugarloaf Ridge. The serpentine path steadily loses elevation through a mixed forest with big-leaf maples, oaks, and ferns. Continue along the watercourse of Sonoma Creek to the valley floor at the Gray Pine Trail at 3.6 miles.

Veer to the right on the old dirt road, and cross Sonoma Creek to the Meadow Trail. Bear right and cross a wood bridge over Sonoma Creek to Heritage Tree, a massive big-leaf maple on the banks of the creek. Stroll through the open meadow along Sonoma Creek to the Ferguson Observatory at 4.5 miles. Leave the road and continue on the Meadow Trail to the right. Walk up the slope and veer left at the triangle junction, completing the loop. Retrace your steps 0.4 miles to the left. ■

56. Bald Mountain—Gray Pine Loop

SUGARLOAF RIDGE STATE PARK

2605 Adobe Canyon Road · Kenwood

Hiking distance: 7-mile loop
Hiking time: 4 hours
Elevation gain: 1,600 feet
Dogs: not allowed
Maps: U.S.G.S. Kenwood and Rutherford
      Sugarloaf Ridge State Park

**map
page 179**

Summary of hike: Sugarloaf Ridge State Park is located in the heart of the Mayacamas Mountains high above the town of Kenwood. Towering Bald Mountain, the park's highest peak at 2,729 feet, straddles the county line between Sonoma and Napa Counties. This hike forms a loop from the lower sloping meadow to the Bald Mountain summit. At the summit are 360-degree views, from the Sierra Nevada Range to the San Francisco skyline and the Golden Gate Bridge. Two illustrated panels point out more than 30 of the surrounding peaks, towns, and valleys. The Gray Pine Trail, the return route, follows the isolated Sugarloaf Ridge for over a mile along the county border, then descends along the headwaters of Sonoma Creek.

Driving directions: Same as Hike 55.

Hiking directions: Walk past the trailhead map and head up the grassy slope. Weave through an oak grove to a meadow and a triangle junction. The right fork leads to the observatory on the Meadow Trail. Go to the left on the Lower Bald Mountain Trail, beginning the loop. Climb to the upper end of the meadow, and enter an oak grove with manzanita and madrone. At one mile the trail reaches the Bald Mountain Trail, a paved fire road. Bear right and head up the narrow road to sweeping views of Sonoma Valley and the surrounding mountains. Pass the Vista Trail at 1.2 miles on a U-shaped bend. Continue straight, weaving up the contours of the forested mountain. Pass a couple of stream-fed gullies and overlooks. At 2 miles, the Red Mountain Trail cut-across breaks off to the right (Hike 55). Continue 0.4 miles to a road on the left that leads up to the top of Red Mountain. This short quarter-mile paved road heads up to the microwave tower at the 2,548-foot summit. The road ends at a gate before reaching the tower.

Back on the main trail, weave up the dirt road on the upper mountain slope to amazing vistas. The final ascent curves clockwise to a junction with the High Ridge Trail. Bear right and walk 80 yards to the Gray Pine Trail on the left, just shy of the summit. Detour right to the 2,729-foot bald summit with 360-degree vistas, a bench, and two interpretive maps.

After resting and savoring the views, return 20 yards to the Gray Pine Trail. Descend along the rolling ridge, which follows the Napa–Sonoma county line. The views extend down both valleys from the ridge. Enter a mixed forest and continue east, staying on the ridge to the east end of Red Mountain Trail and a picnic bench at 3.6 miles. At just under 4 miles, curve right, leaving the ridge, and head south to a signed junction with the Brushy Peaks Trail. Bend right, staying on the Gray Pine Trail, and steadily descend on the wide dirt trail. At 4.8 miles, curve left and follow a branch of Sonoma Creek in an oak grove. Make an S-bend and cross another feeder creek. Parallel and hop over Sonoma Creek to a junction with the Vista Trail at 5.3 miles (Hike 55).

Ford the creek again, reaching a T-junction with the Meadow Trail. Bear right and cross a wood bridge over Sonoma Creek to Heritage Tree, a massive big-leaf maple tree on the banks of Sonoma Creek. Stroll through the open meadow along Sonoma Creek to the Ferguson Observatory at 6.4 miles. Leave the road and continue on the Meadow Trail to the right. Walk up the slope and veer left at the triangle junction, completing the loop at 6.6 miles. Retrace your steps 0.4 miles to the left.■

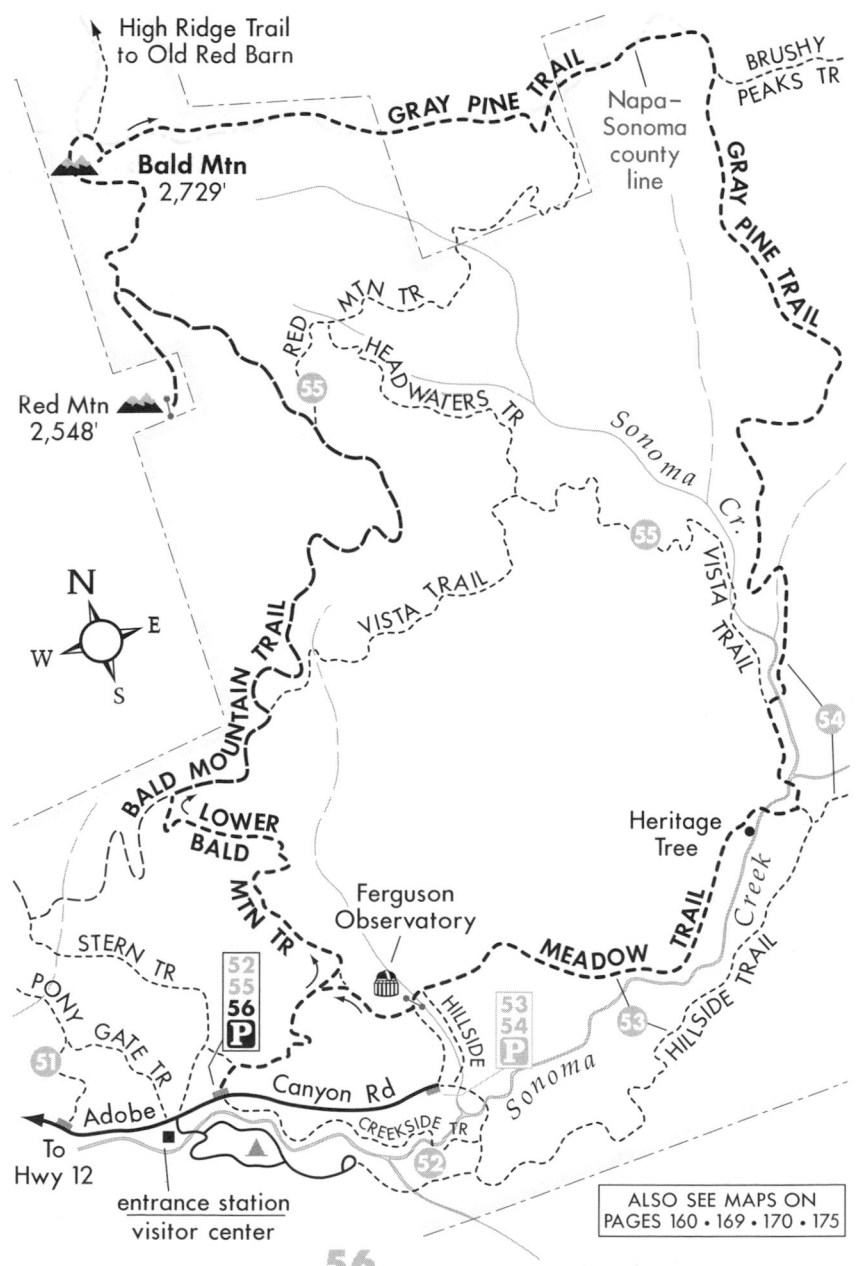

High Ridge Trail to Old Red Barn

GRAY PINE TRAIL

BRUSHY PEAKS TR

Napa-Sonoma county line

GRAY PINE TRAIL

Bald Mtn 2,729'

RED MTN TR

HEADWATERS TR

55

Red Mtn 2,548'

Sonoma Cr.

55

VISTA TRAIL

VISTA TRAIL

N
W E
S

BALD MOUNTAIN TRAIL

VISTA TRAIL

54

LOWER BALD MTN TR

STERN TR

Ferguson Observatory

MEADOW TRAIL

Heritage Tree

Creek

PONY GATE TR

51

52
55
56
P

HILLSIDE

53
54
P

53

HILLSIDE TRAIL

Canyon Rd

Adobe

CREEKSIDE TR

Sonoma

To Hwy 12

52

entrance station
visitor center

ALSO SEE MAPS ON
PAGES 160 • 169 • 170 • 175

56.

Bald Mountain–Gray Pine Loop
SUGARLOAF RIDGE STATE PARK

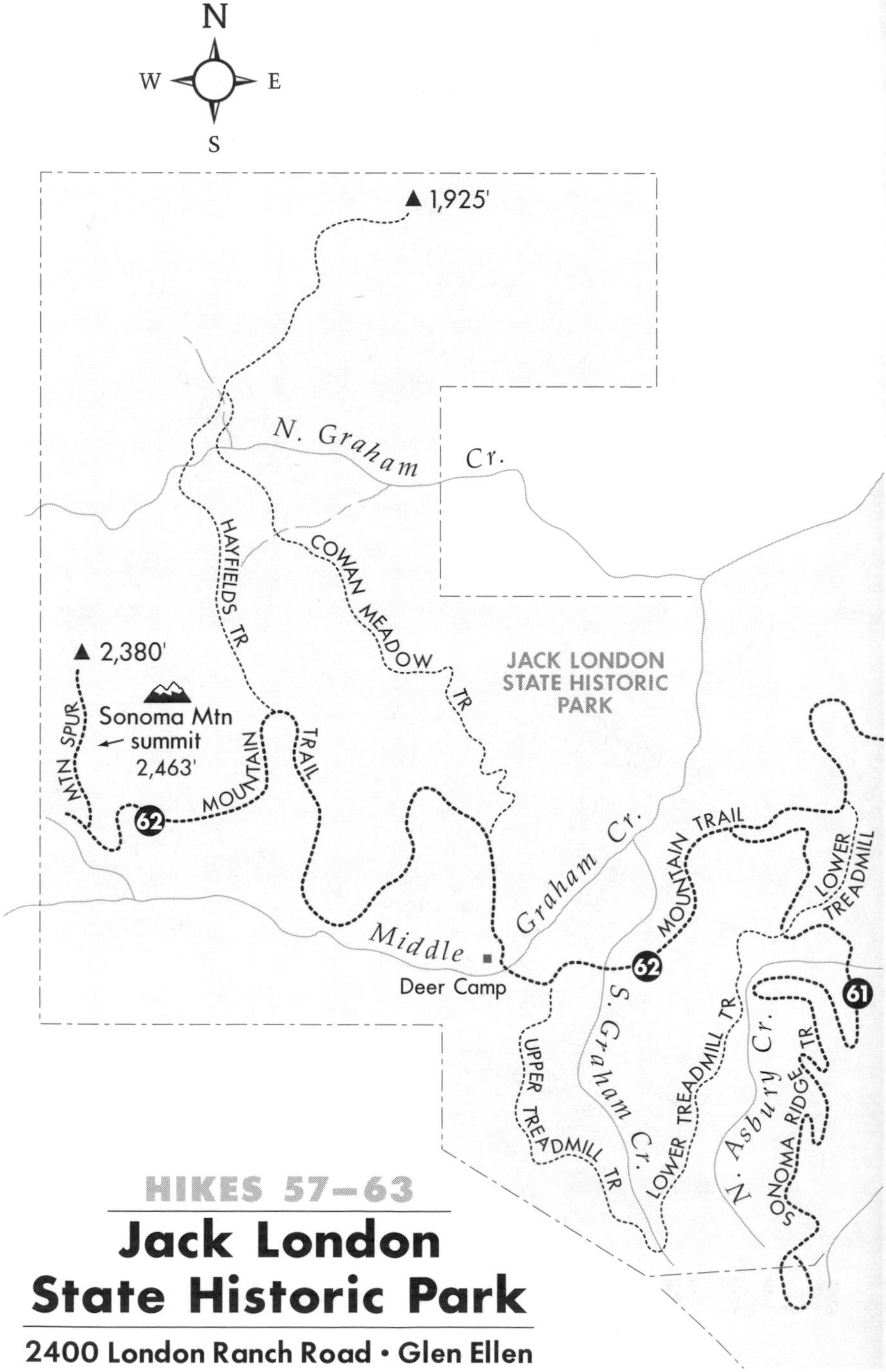

N
W E
S

▲ 1,925'

N. Graham Cr.

HAYFIELDS TR

COWAN MEADOW TR

JACK LONDON
STATE HISTORIC
PARK

▲ 2,380'

Sonoma Mtn
← summit
2,463'

MTN SPUR

MOUNTAIN TRAIL

62

Graham Cr.

MOUNTAIN TRAIL

LOWER TREADMILL

62

61

Middle
Deer Camp

S. Graham Cr.

UPPER TREADMILL TR.

LOWER TREADMILL TR.

N. Asbury Cr.

SONOMA RIDGE TR.

HIKES 57–63
Jack London
State Historic Park
2400 London Ranch Road · Glen Ellen

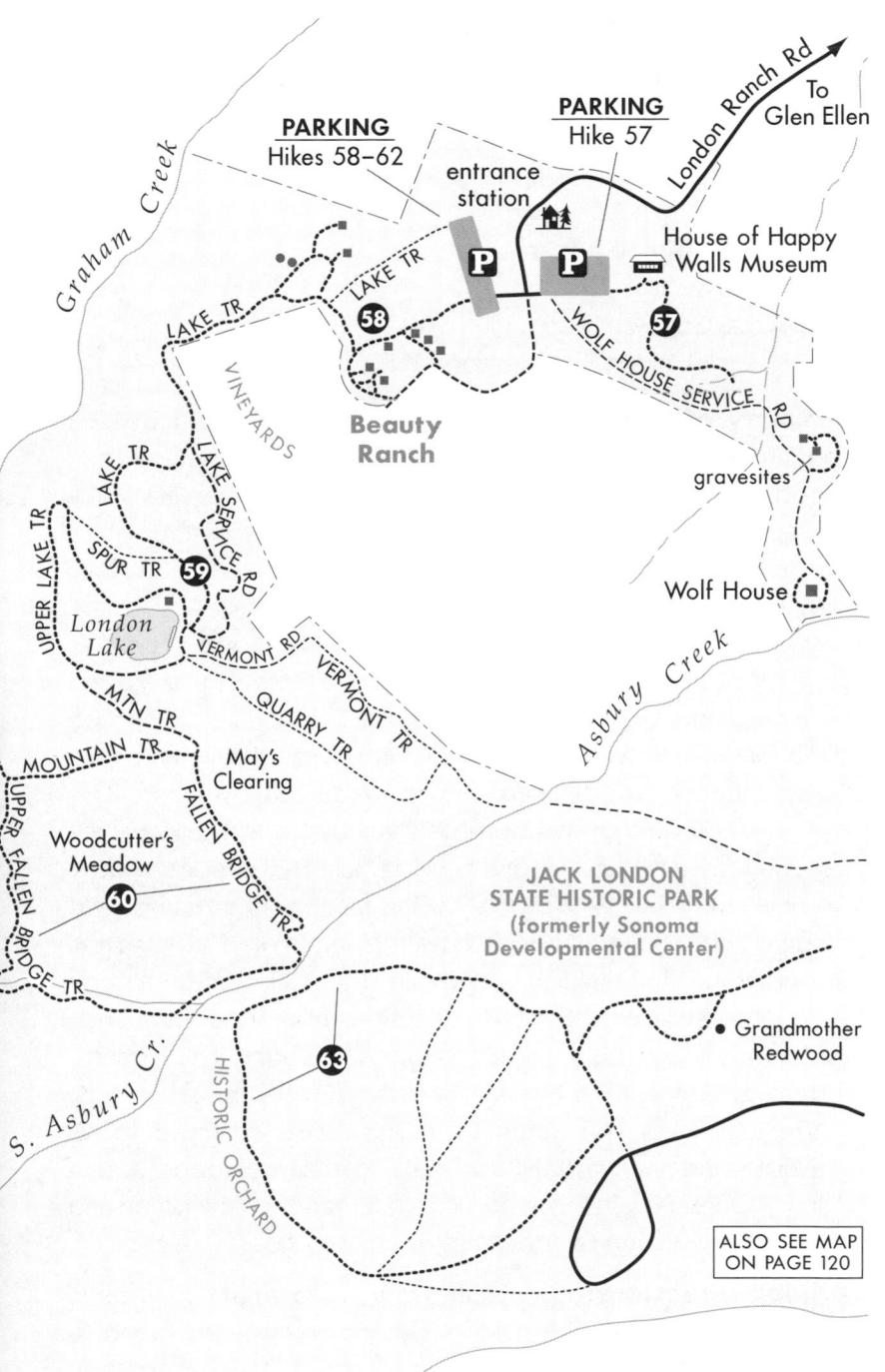

PARKING
Hikes 58–62

PARKING
Hike 57

London Ranch Rd

To
Glen Ellen

entrance
station

House of Happy
Walls Museum

Graham Creek

LAKE TR

LAKE TR

58

WOLF HOUSE SERVICE RD

57

Beauty
Ranch

VINEYARDS

gravesites

LAKE TR

LAKE SERVICE RD

SPUR TR

UPPER LAKE TR

59

Wolf House

London
Lake

VERMONT RD

VERMONT TR

QUARRY TR

Asbury Creek

MTN TR

MOUNTAIN TR

May's
Clearing

UPPER FALLEN BRIDGE TR

FALLEN BRIDGE TR

Woodcutter's
Meadow

60

JACK LONDON
STATE HISTORIC PARK
(formerly Sonoma
Developmental Center)

S. Asbury Cr.

HISTORIC ORCHARD

63

Grandmother
Redwood

ALSO SEE MAP
ON PAGE 120

57. Wolf House Ruins and Jack London's Grave
JACK LONDON STATE HISTORIC PARK

Hiking distance: 1.5 miles round trip
Hiking time: 1 hour
Elevation gain: 150 feet
Dogs: allowed
Maps: U.S.G.S. Glen Ellen
Jack London State Historic Park

Summary of hike: The Wolf House was Jack London's 26-room mansion built from locally quarried stone, unpeeled redwood logs, and Spanish tiles. The massive four-level, lava-rock house encompassed 15,000 square feet and had nine fireplaces. His dream house burned down in 1913, days before the Londons planned to move in. The stonework and walls remain.

Jack London's grave sits on a quiet knoll in a grove of oaks. A large block of red lava from the Wolf House rests atop Jack's and his wife Charmian's ashes. Adjacent to the boulder are the marked older graves of two pioneer children named David and Lillie Greenlaw. Their wooden headstones are dated November 1876, the year Jack London was born. The trail begins at The House of Happy Walls, a beautiful stone building built by London's widow Charmian between 1919 and 1922. The two-story structure was modeled after the Wolf House. It now functions as a museum and visitor center. The building is dedicated to Jack London and his work. It houses mementos and collections from London's world-wide travels and personal possessions, including his writings, letters, photographs, art, home furnishings, and clothes.

This trail takes you through a mixed forest en route to his gravesite and the Wolf House ruins in the redwoods above Asbury Creek. A path loops around the exterior of the house and climbs to a platform overlooking the second floor.

Driving directions: KENWOOD: From the town of Kenwood in Sonoma Valley, drive 3.6 miles south on Highway 12 (Sonoma Highway) to Arnold Drive. Turn right and drive 0.9 miles, passing

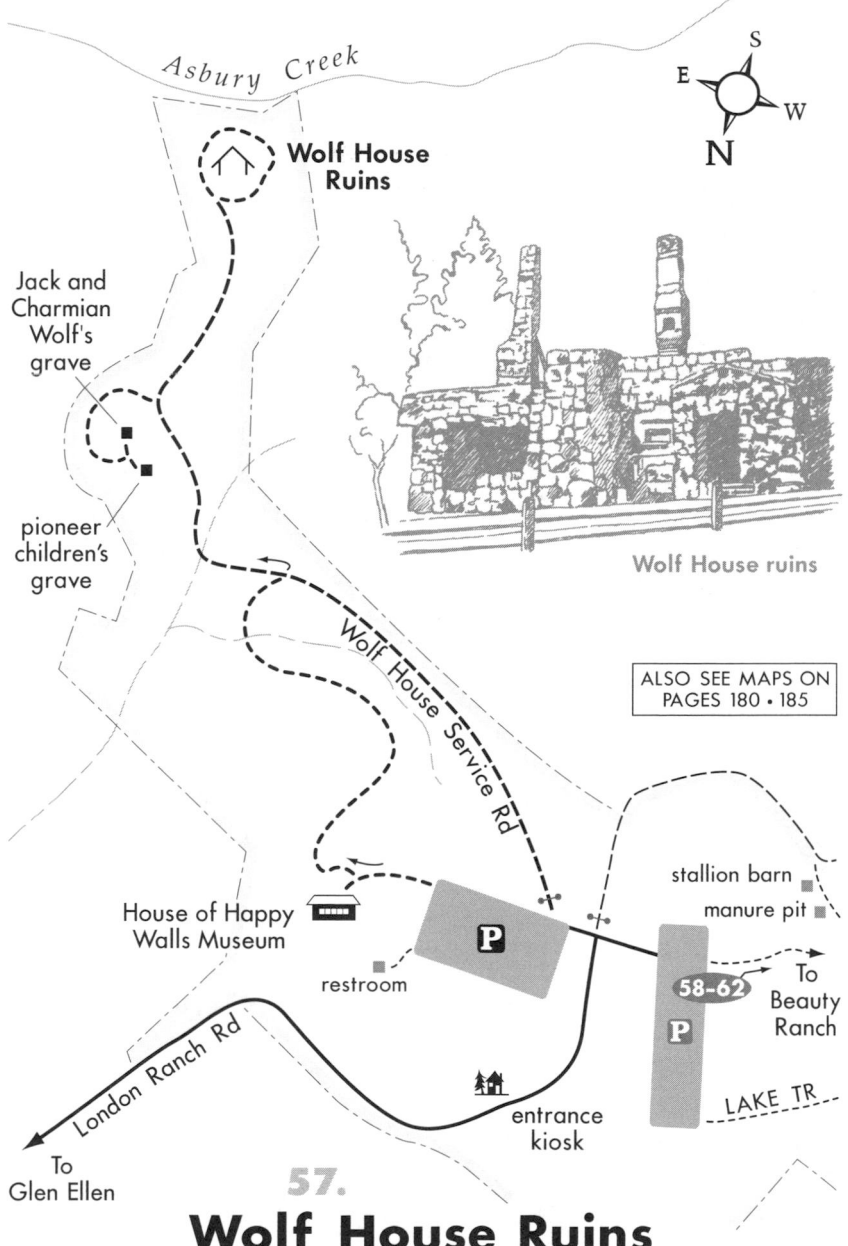

Wolf House ruins

ALSO SEE MAPS ON PAGES 180 · 185

Wolf House Ruins
Jack and Charmian Wolf's grave
pioneer children's grave
Asbury Creek
Wolf House Service Rd
House of Happy Walls Museum
restroom
stallion barn
manure pit
58-62
To Beauty Ranch
London Ranch Rd
entrance kiosk
LAKE TR
To Glen Ellen

57.
Wolf House Ruins
Jack London's grave
JACK LONDON STATE HISTORIC PARK

through the town of Glen Ellen, to London Ranch Road. Turn right and continue 1.3 miles up the hill to the park entrance station. From the kiosk, turn left and drive 0.1 mile to the museum parking lot. A parking fee is required.

SONOMA: From West Napa Street in Sonoma, drive 5.9 miles north on Highway 12 (Sonoma Highway) to Arnold Drive and turn left. Continue with the directions above.

Hiking directions: From the far end of the parking lot, walk up the paved path to the House of Happy Walls Museum, a field-stone structure with Spanish roof tiles. After visiting the museum and the exhibits, take the signed trail from the southeast corner of the building. Gently descend on the forested dirt path through bay laurel, madrone, and oaks. Cross a stream, reaching the Wolf House Service Road at 0.3 miles. Bear left on the narrow road, parallel to the creek on the left. Cross over the creek and head uphill to a road fork. Detour left and wind around about 110 yards to Jack London's gravesite on a knoll. On the left are the graves of Jack and his wife Charmian, dated 11-26-16. A lava boulder from the house ruins sits atop their ashes. To the right are the graves of the two pioneer children. Return to the main trail and continue 0.15 miles to the Wolf House in a redwood grove. A path circle the ruins, with views of the gorgeous lava rock arches and fireplaces. A raised platform overlooks the pool and the house. Return on the same trail.■

58. Beauty Ranch
JACK LONDON STATE HISTORIC PARK

Hiking distance: 0.75 miles round trip
Hiking time: 1 hour
Elevation gain: 50 feet
Dogs: allowed
Maps: U.S.G.S. Glen Ellen
       Jack London State Historic Park

Summary of hike: Jack London's Beauty Ranch is tucked into the foothills of Sonoma Mountain above the town of Glen Ellen.

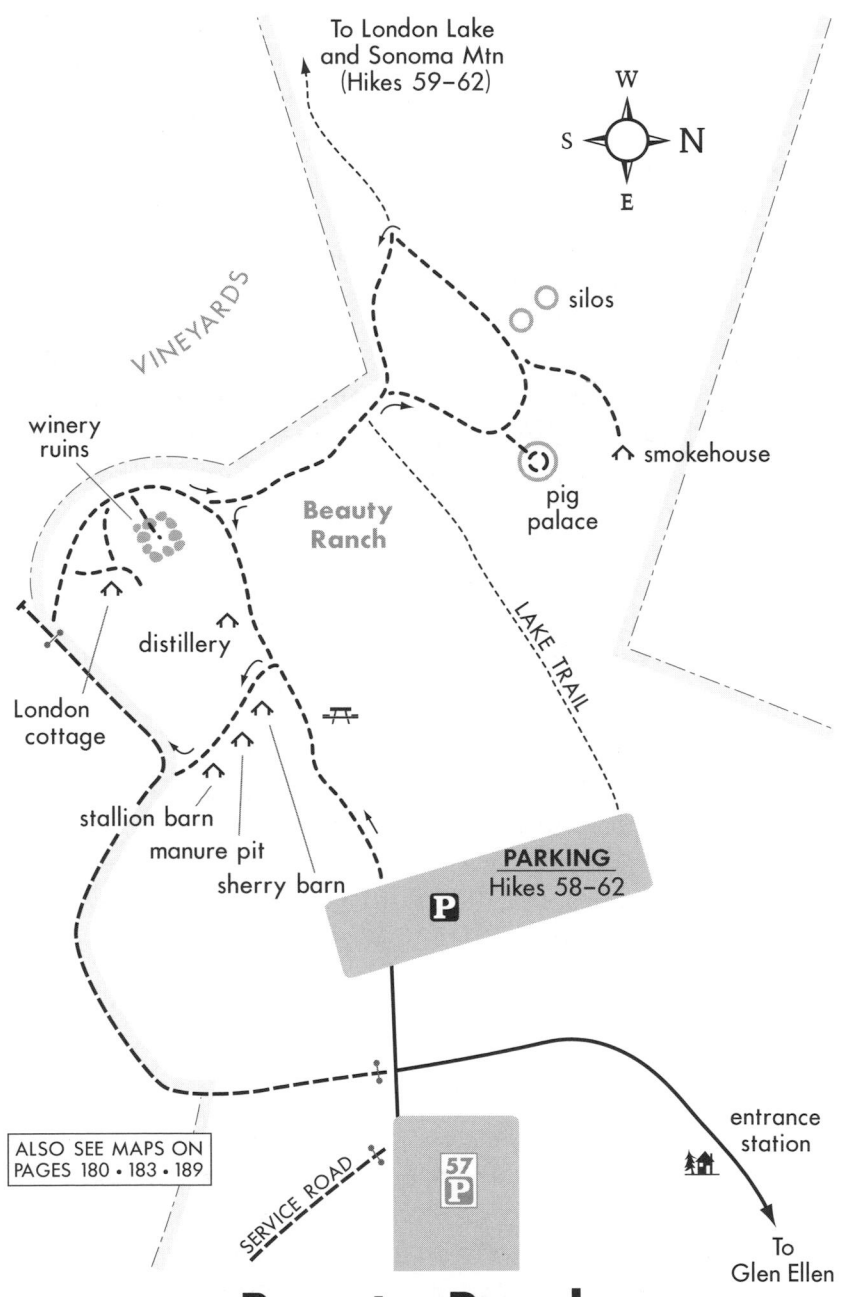

To London Lake and Sonoma Mtn (Hikes 59-62)

W N S E

VINEYARDS

silos

winery ruins

smokehouse

Beauty Ranch

pig palace

LAKE TRAIL

distillery

London cottage

stallion barn

manure pit

sherry barn

PARKING
Hikes 58-62

P

ALSO SEE MAPS ON PAGES 180 • 183 • 189

SERVICE ROAD

57 P

entrance station

To Glen Ellen

58. **Beauty Ranch**
JACK LONDON STATE HISTORIC PARK

The experimental ranch, part of the state historic park, still contains the original structures. The wood-framed cottage is where London lived and wrote many of his books from 1905 until his death in 1916. Over the course of 16 prolific years, Jack London wrote 51 books and nearly 200 short stories, including *Call of the Wild* and *The Sea Wolf*. Sonoma Valley became known as *Valley of the Moon*, from London's 1913 novel by the same name. There are several unique structures included amongst the ranch buildings. The innovative Pig Palace is a circular piggery with a central feeding and round storage tower designed by London. Two 40-foot-high silos were built in 1914, the first cement silos in California. A rock sherry barn, part of the old Kohler–Frohling winery, was built by Chinese laborers in 1884, then converted into a stable for London's English shire horses. London hired Italian masons to build an additional stallion barn and a rock manure pit. A distillery building from the old winery still exists, as well as other ruins from the 1880s winery damaged by the 1906 earthquake. This interpretive hike loops through the grounds of the historic former ranch.

Driving directions: KENWOOD: From the town of Kenwood in Sonoma Valley, drive 3.6 miles south on Highway 12 (Sonoma Highway) to Arnold Drive. Turn right and drive 0.9 miles, passing through the town of Glen Ellen, to London Ranch Road. Turn right and continue 1.3 miles up the hill to the park entrance station. From the kiosk, turn right and drive 0.1 mile to the trailhead parking lot. A parking fee is required.

SONOMA: From West Napa Street in Sonoma, drive 5.9 miles north on Highway 12 (Sonoma Highway) to Arnold Drive and turn left. Continue with the directions above.

Hiking directions: At the trailhead, directly across from the road to the parking lot, take the posted Beauty Ranch–Mountain Trails path. Walk through a eucalyptus grove and picnic area to a T-junction by the sherry barn on the left. Bear left past the barn to the rock-walled manure pit and stallion barn. Curve right on the paved service road. Continue along the edge of a vineyard on the left to the Jack London Cottage on the right and a view of the terraced hillside. Curve right, passing the cottage to the rock-wall ruins of the historic winery. Stroll past the rock walls or enter the open structure. Curve left, staying on the edge of the vineyard toward the two 40-foot silos erected between 1912 and 1915. As the gravel road curves left (before reaching the silos) veer to the right on the grassy path. Climb to the circular rock-walled Pig Palace in an oak grove. Loop around the central feed tower and the ring of 17 pig pens. Continue to the cement-block silos and a junction. A side path goes right to a rock smokehouse behind the Pig Palace. Return to the main road. The right fork on the Lake Trail leads to the lake and bathhouse (Hike 59). Instead, bear left and return to the trail split by the winery ruins. Curve left, passing the distillery building constructed in 1888. Complete the loop at the sherry barn. Return to the left. ■

59. Lake Trail Loop
JACK LONDON STATE HISTORIC PARK

Hiking distance: 2.5-mile double loop
Hiking time: 1.5 hours
Elevation gain: 400 feet

map
page 189

Dogs: not allowed
Maps: U.S.G.S. Glen Ellen
        Jack London State Historic Park

Summary of hike: London Lake sits at the foot of Sonoma Mountain surrounded by redwood groves. Jack London originally built the lake in 1915 as a five-acre irrigation reservoir. It quickly became a swimming hole and entertainment area for the Londons and their guests. The redwood bathhouse on the northeast shore and the curved stone dam to the south were also built by London. Encroaching vegetation and sediment have reduced the lake's size in half. Cattails rim the shore and redwoods cover the mountain slope. This trail strolls through Beauty Ranch (Hike 58), then loops around the lake to vista points and overlooks.

Driving directions: KENWOOD: From the town of Kenwood in Sonoma Valley, drive 3.6 miles south on Highway 12 (Sonoma

Highway) to Arnold Drive. Turn right and drive 0.9 miles, passing through the town of Glen Ellen, to London Ranch Road. Turn right and continue 1.3 miles up the hill to the park entrance station. From the kiosk, turn right and drive 0.1 mile to the trailhead parking lot. A parking fee is required.

SONOMA: From West Napa Street in Sonoma, drive 5.9 miles north on Highway 12 (Sonoma Highway) to Arnold Drive and turn left. Continue with the directions above.

Hiking directions: At the trailhead, directly across from the road to the parking lot, take the posted Beauty Ranch–Mountain Trails path. Walk through a eucalyptus grove and picnic area to a T-junction by the sherry barn on the left. Go to the right, passing the distillery and winery ruins to a trail split. Veer to the right, skirting the Jack London Vineyard, and curve left, passing the 40-foot silos on the right. Leave Beauty Ranch on the Lake Trail, with close-up views of Sonoma Mountain. Follow the dirt road through oak groves, pines, and madrones to a posted junction with a pipe gate across the road. Leave the road and begin the loop on the Lake Trail to the right, a hiking-only trail. Walk through the dense forest with redwoods and bay laurel, and rejoin the Lake Service Road at one mile. Continue 20 yards to the right, and veer right on the footpath, located to the east side of London Lake by the redwood bathhouse and the stone dam. Take the Upper Lake Trail, passing the old log bathhouse, and follow the north side of the lake. Pass the Lake Spur Trail on the right. Make a U-shaped left bend, and traverse the hillside to an overlook of the lake. Descend to the Mountain Trail Road on a horseshoe bend. The right fork heads up to Sonoma Ridge and the summit of Sonoma Mountain (Hike 62). For this hike, go to the left and cross the lake's inlet stream. Follow the south side of London Lake to a T-junction. To the right is the Vineyard Trail. Bear left along the rock dam, completing the loop. Follow the winding dirt service road downhill back to Jack London's Vineyard, completing the second loop. Return to Beauty Ranch and the trailhead. ■

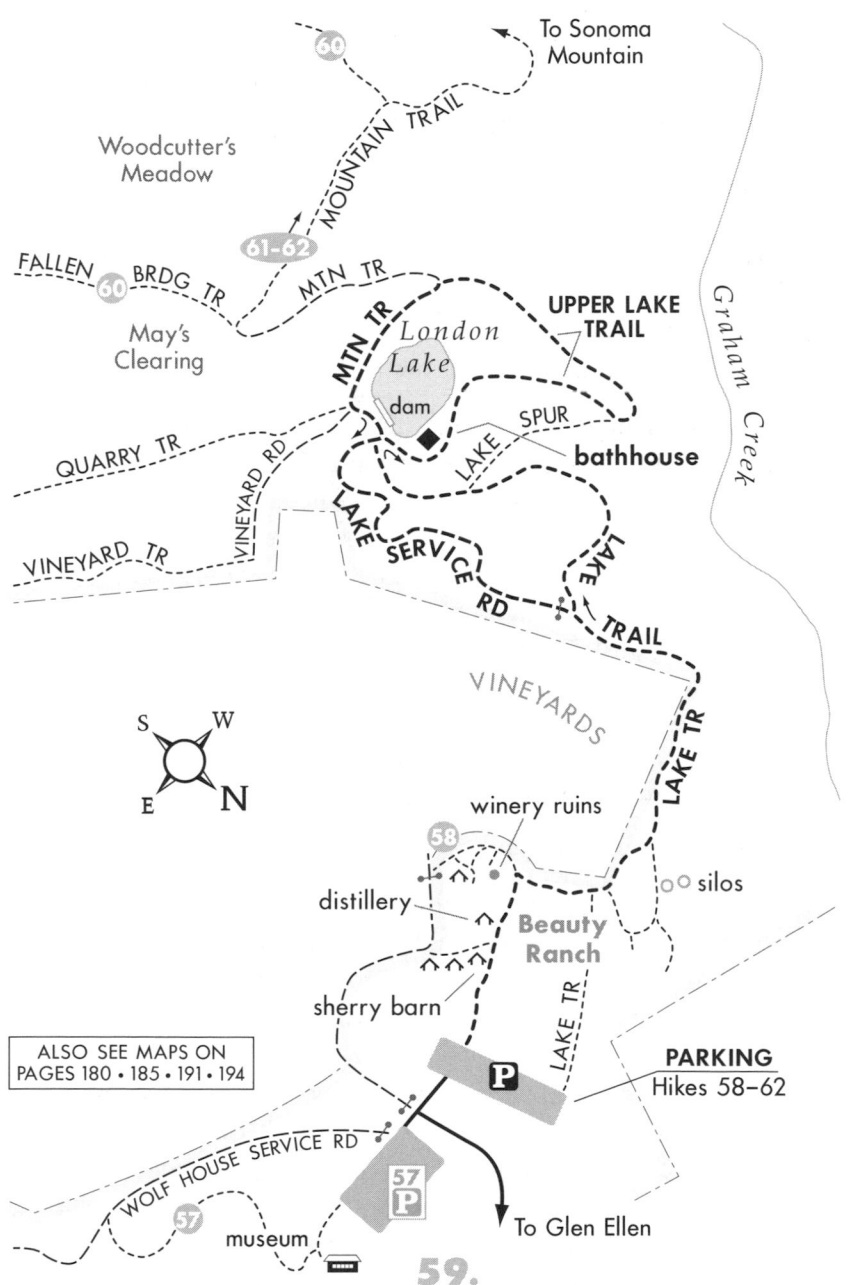

To Sonoma Mountain

60

MOUNTAIN TRAIL

Woodcutter's Meadow

61-62

MTN TR

FALLEN 60 BRDG TR

May's Clearing

MTN TR

UPPER LAKE TRAIL

London Lake

dam

LAKE SPUR

Graham Creek

bathhouse

QUARRY TR

VINEYARD RD

LAKE SERVICE RD

LAKE TRAIL

VINEYARD TR

VINEYARDS

LAKE TR

S W

N E

winery ruins

58

distillery

silos

Beauty Ranch

LAKE TR

sherry barn

ALSO SEE MAPS ON PAGES 180 • 185 • 191 • 194

P

PARKING Hikes 58–62

WOLF HOUSE SERVICE RD

57 P

57

museum

To Glen Ellen

59.

Lake Trail Loop
JACK LONDON STATE HISTORIC PARK

60. Woodcutter's Meadow
Fallen Bridge—Upper Fallen Bridge Loop
JACK LONDON STATE HISTORIC PARK

Hiking distance: 4.5 miles round trip with a loop
Hiking time: 3 hours
Elevation gain: 700 feet
Dogs: not allowed
Maps: U.S.G.S. Glen Ellen
Jack London State Historic Park

Summary of hike: The Fallen Bridge Trail begins at May's Clearing, an open grassy slope above London Lake at the north end of Woodcutter's Meadow. At the meadow is a vista point with views down Sonoma Valley to San Pablo Bay and across the valley to the Mayacamas Mountains. The Upper Fallen Bridge Trail loops around Woodcutter's Meadow on the forested slope of Sonoma Mountain. The two trails form a loop through a dense forest of redwoods, crossing two bridges over cascading North Asbury Creek. Access to the loop is from the Lake Trail and Mountain Trail (Hike 59). En route, the trail weaves through the historic buildings of Beauty Ranch and passes London Lake.

Driving directions: Same as Hike 59.

Hiking directions: At the trailhead, directly across from the road to the parking lot, take the posted Beauty Ranch–Mountain Trails path. Walk through a eucalyptus grove and picnic area to a T-junction by the sherry barn on the left. Go to the right, passing the distillery and winery ruins to a trail split. Veer to the right, skirting the Jack London Vineyard, and curve left, passing the 40-foot silos on the right. Leave Beauty Ranch on the Lake Trail. Follow the dirt road through oak groves, pines, and madrones to a posted junction. Continue straight, passing through the vehicle gate on the dirt road. Follow the edge of the Jack London Vineyard on the left. Weave up the road to the southeast corner of London Lake. Walk along the base of the rock-walled dam to a signed junction. Go to the right on the Mountain Trail, and fol-

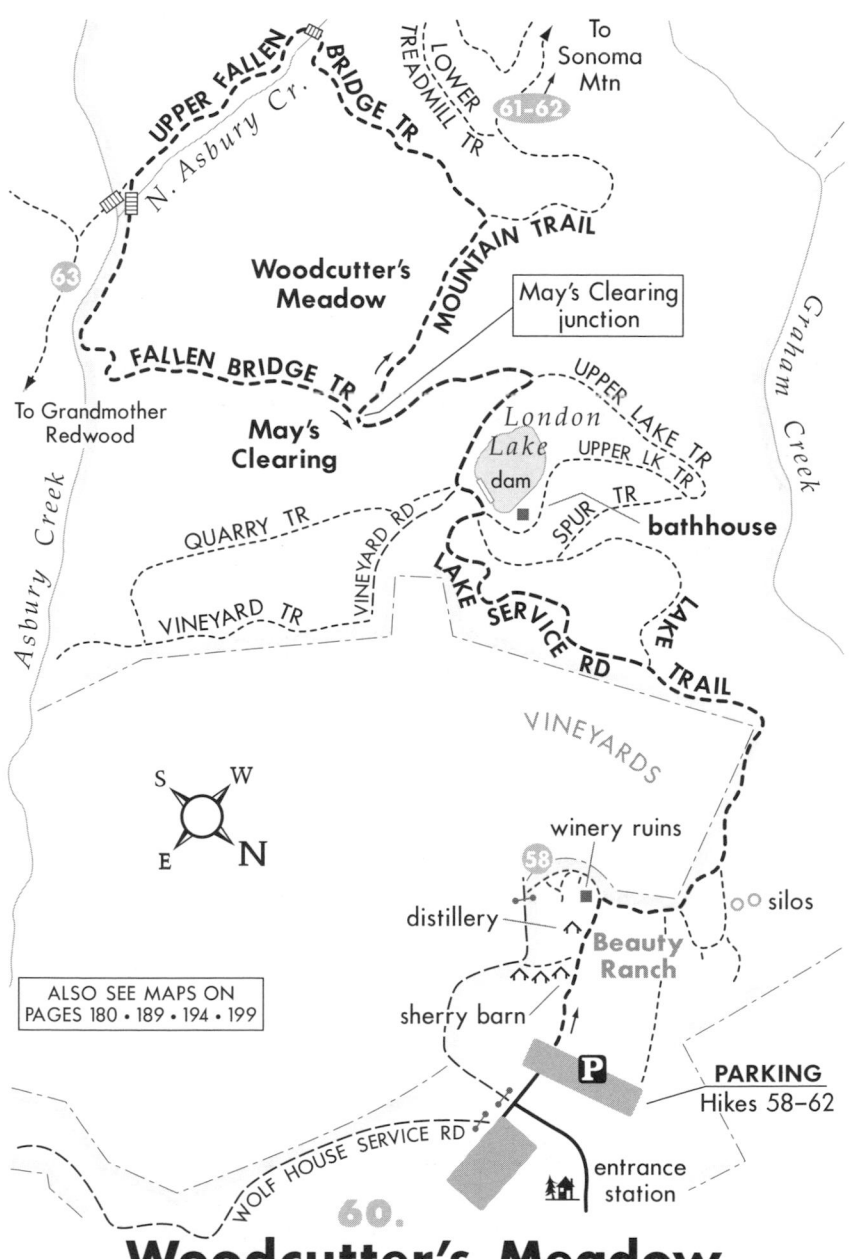

Woodcutter's Meadow
Fallen Bridge—Upper Fallen Bridge
JACK LONDON STATE HISTORIC PARK

low the south side of London Lake to a horseshoe left bend and a junction. The Upper Lake Trail (Hike 59) goes to the right. Stay on the road to the left, and climb to a clearing with a bench and junction. This point overlooks May's Clearing, a large grassy meadow.

The Fallen Bridge Trail, our return route, goes to the left. Begin the loop to the right, staying on the Mountain Trail. Enter a lush forest with redwoods, madrones, bay laurel, and ferns. Climb 0.2 miles to a signed junction with the Upper Fallen Bridge Trail. Leave the road and head 0.3 miles south through Woodcutter's Meadow to North Asbury Creek. Cross a bridge over the cascading creek and curve left. Descend along the stair-stepping creek under the shade of towering redwoods to the lower bridge and junction. The trail straight ahead enters the newly acquired land of Jack London State Historic Park, leading to a historic orchard and Grandmother Redwood (Hike 63). Bear left and cross the bridge over North Asbury Creek. Curve away from the creek on the cliffside path. Cross a tributary stream and head up to May's Clearing on the right. Complete the loop at the vista point. Return 1.4 miles to the right, retracing your route.■

61. Sonoma Ridge Trail
JACK LONDON STATE HISTORIC PARK

Hiking distance: 9.5 miles round trip
Hiking time: 6 hours
Elevation gain: 1,300 feet
Dogs: not allowed
Maps: U.S.G.S. Glen Ellen
　　　　Jack London State Historic Park

map
page 194

Summary of hike: Sonoma Mountain has a long forested ridge running north and south that forms the backbone of Jack London State Historic Park. The Sonoma Ridge Trail follows the east side of the ridge through the 1,400-acre state park, climbing steadily south. The hike begins at Beauty Ranch and climbs up the forested slope beyond London Lake. The trail passes through deep woods, redwood groves, and open meadows, offering sweeping vistas down Sonoma Valley to San Pablo Bay and across to the Mayacamas Mountains.

Driving directions: KENWOOD: From the town of Kenwood in Sonoma Valley, drive 3.6 miles south on Highway 12 (Sonoma Highway) to Arnold Drive. Turn right and drive 0.9 miles, passing through the town of Glen Ellen, to London Ranch Road. Turn right and continue 1.3 miles up the hill to the park entrance station. From the kiosk, turn right and drive 0.1 mile to the trailhead parking lot. A parking fee is required.

SONOMA: From West Napa Street in Sonoma, drive 5.9 miles north on Highway 12 (Sonoma Highway) to Arnold Drive and turn left. Continue with the directions above.

Hiking directions: Follow the hiking directions for Hike 60 to the junction at May's Clearing. The Fallen Bridge Trail veers off to the left (south) to North Asbury Creek. Continue straight on the Mountain Trail. Enter a lush forest with redwoods, bay laurel, tanbark oaks, and ferns. Traverse Woodcutter's Meadow on the left, passing the Upper Fallen Bridge Trail. Pass Pine Tree Meadows, a small glade on the right, and make a horseshoe left bend to the Lower Treadmill Road on the right. A short distance ahead is the Sonoma Ridge Trail by a map kiosk at 2.2 miles.

Bear left on the Sonoma Ridge Trail, and angle up the side of the mountain. Cross the Lower Treadmill Trail through a forest of Douglas fir, madrone, and bay to rocky North Asbury Creek in a redwood grove. Cross over to the south side of the creek, and zigzag up switchbacks at an easy grade. The far-reaching vistas extend to a grassy slope below the ridgeline at 2,100 feet. At 5.3 miles is a road split, forming a 0.3-mile loop. Circle the loop at the park boundary and retrace your steps. ∎

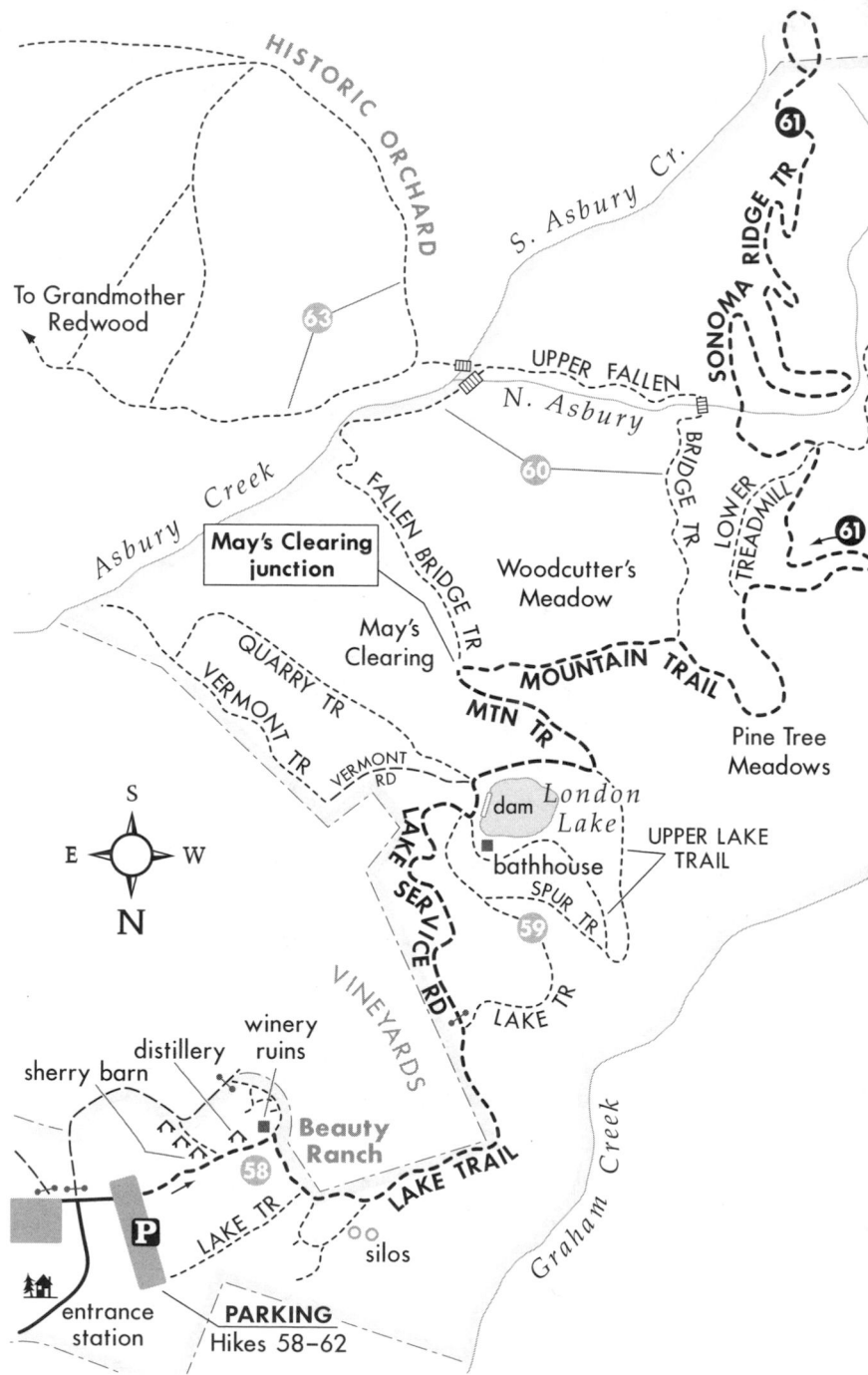

To Grandmother Redwood

HISTORIC ORCHARD

S. Asbury Cr.

SONOMA RIDGE TR

61

63

UPPER FALLEN

N. Asbury

60

Asbury Creek

FALLEN BRIDGE TR

BRIDGE TR

LOWER TREADMILL

61

May's Clearing junction

Woodcutter's Meadow

May's Clearing

MOUNTAIN TRAIL

MTN TR

Pine Tree Meadows

QUARRY TR

VERMONT TR

VERMONT RD

LAKE SERVICE RD

dam

London Lake

bathhouse

SPUR TR

UPPER LAKE TRAIL

59

S

E — W

N

VINEYARDS

LAKE TR

distillery

winery ruins

sherry barn

Beauty Ranch

58

LAKE TR

LAKE TRAIL

Graham Creek

P

silos

entrance station

PARKING
Hikes 58–62

Sonoma Ridge Trail

Sonoma Mountain Trail
to summit

JACK LONDON STATE HISTORIC PARK

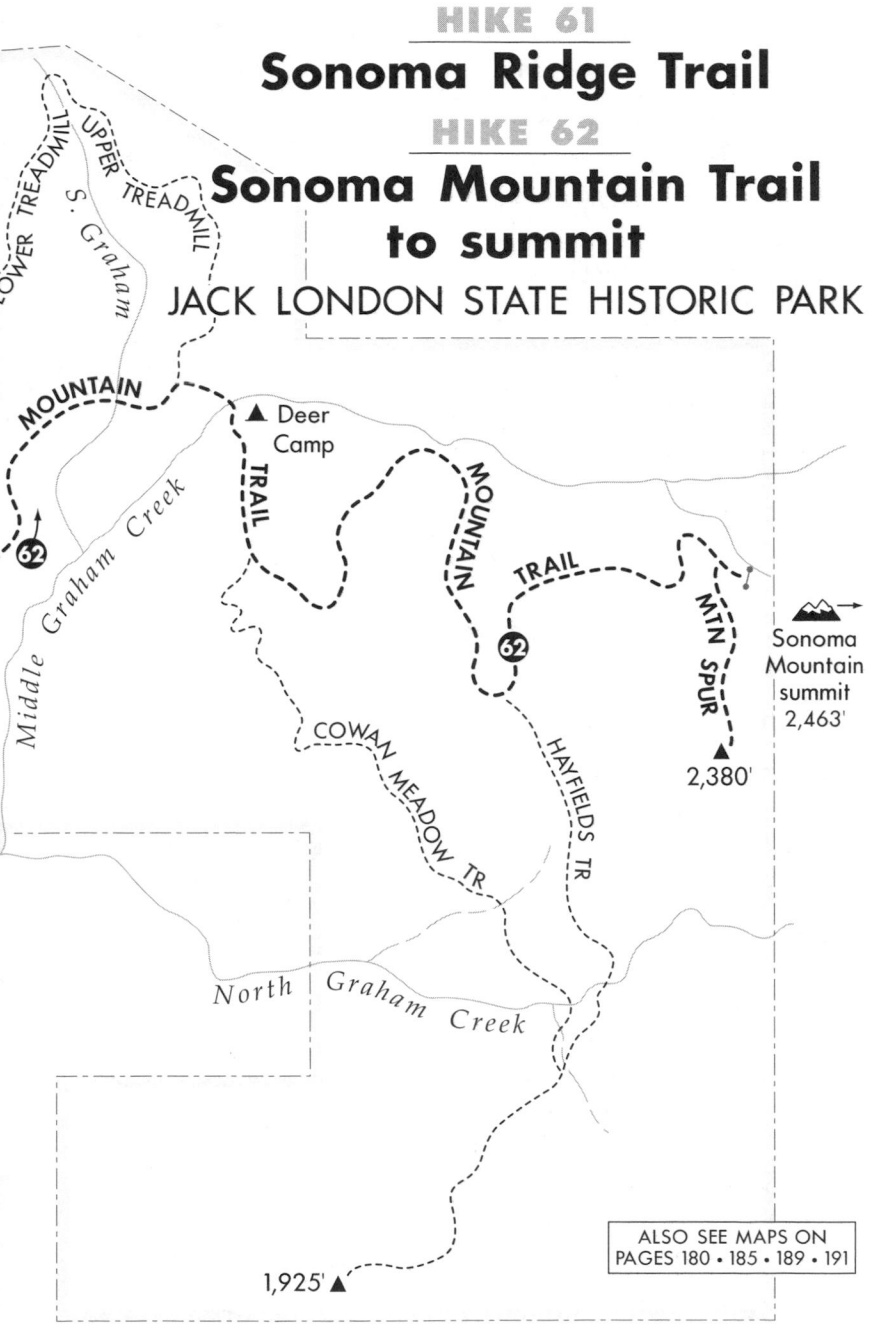

LOWER TREADMILL

UPPER TREADMILL

S. Graham

MOUNTAIN

▲ Deer Camp

TRAIL

Middle Graham Creek

MOUNTAIN

TRAIL

MTN SPUR

Sonoma Mountain summit 2,463'

▲ 2,380'

COWAN MEADOW TR

HAYFIELDS TR

North Graham Creek

ALSO SEE MAPS ON PAGES 180 • 185 • 189 • 191

1,925' ▲

62. Sonoma Mountain Trail to Summit
JACK LONDON STATE HISTORIC PARK

Hiking distance: 8 miles round trip
Hiking time: 5 hours
Elevation gain: 1,800 feet
Dogs: not allowed
Maps: U.S.G.S. Glen Ellen
       Jack London State Historic Park

map
page 194

Summary of hike: The Sonoma Mountains stretch from Santa Rosa to Sonoma. The volcanic range forms the western rim of 17-mile-long Sonoma Valley, known as the Valley of the Moon. The Mountain Trail, a fire road, climbs along Sonoma Mountain through Jack London State Historic Park. The trail leads through unspoiled forests with redwoods, big-leaf maple, redwood, black oak, buckeye, bay, and madrone to the park summit, a short distance east of the 2,463-foot summit of Sonoma Mountain. The actual summit sits just outside the park boundary on private land.

Driving directions: Same as Hike 61.

Hiking directions: Follow the hiking directions for Hike 60 to the junction at May's Clearing. The Fallen Bridge Trail veers off to the left (south) to North Asbury Creek. Continue straight on the Mountain Trail, and enter a lush forest with redwoods, bay laurel, tanbark oaks, and ferns. Traverse Woodcutter's Meadow on the left, passing the Upper Fallen Bridge Trail. Pass Pine Tree Meadows, a small glade on the right, and make a horseshoe left bend to the Lower Treadmill Road on the right. A short distance ahead is the Sonoma Ridge Trail by a map kiosk at 2.2 miles. Hike #81 heads left (south) on the Sonoma Ridge Trail.

For this hike, continue straight ahead through the forest, crossing South Graham Creek to Upper Treadmill Road on the left. Continue on the Mountain Trail. Cross Middle Graham Creek to the Deer Camp rest area in a redwood grove on the north side of the creek, once a camping site for Jack London and his guests. Climb through a meadow, with views of Sonoma Valley and the Mayacamas Mountains, to the Cowan Meadow Trail on the right.

Stay left, continually climbing to the north canyon wall above Middle Graham Creek. Climb through meadows and oak forests to the Hayfields Trail, breaking off to the right en route to the park's north boundary. Stay to the left, contouring through a large meadow to the north branch of the Middle Graham Creek headwaters. Climb along the creek to the west boundary of the park. Curve right and climb a quarter mile to the 2,380-foot park summit, a short distance from, and 80 feet lower than, the privately owned Sonoma Mountain summit. Return along the same route. ■

63. Fern Lake, Historic Orchard, and Grandmother Redwood
JACK LONDON STATE HISTORIC PARK

Hiking distance: 4.5 miles round trip
Hiking time: 2.5 hours
Elevation gain: 650 feet
Dogs: allowed
Maps: U.S.G.S. Glen Ellen

map
page 199

Summary of hike: In 1991, land was transferred from the Sonoma Developmental Center to Jack London State Historic Park. The Sonoma Developmental Center is a state-owned facility for the mentally and physically impaired. The 1,600-acre facility is part of the small town called Eldridge, with its own post office and fire department. The orchard was planted in the early 1900s as a way for the residents to have meaningful work growing and selling fruit. The historic orchard encompasses 400 acres, with apple, peach, plum, pear, prune, apricot, and cherry trees. Most of the original orchard remains today. Fern Lake was used for irrigating the orchard. An ancient redwood tree known as Grandmother Redwood is an enormous first growth redwood in a quiet grove along the trail to the orchard. The giant tree has a huge girth but the top of the tree is gone, either snapped off by the 1906 earthquake or from fire. Owls are frequently spotted in the tree. This hike begins from the small town of Eldridge, located just south of Glen Ellen. The hike leads to Fern Lake and

Grandmother Redwood, then circles the historic orchard. A side path crosses a bridge over Asbury Creek and enters the original section of Jack London State Historic Park. A trail system for the new tract of land is in the planning stage but has not yet been fully realized.

Driving directions: KENWOOD: From the town of Kenwood in Sonoma Valley, drive 3.6 miles south on Highway 12 (Sonoma Highway) to Arnold Drive. Turn right and drive 2.2 miles, passing through the town of Glen Ellen, to Holt Street. Turn right and continue a quarter mile to Manzanita at a T-intersection. Turn right and go 0.15 miles to a parking pullout on the left.

SONOMA: From West Napa Street in Sonoma, drive 5.9 miles north on Highway 12 (Sonoma Highway) to Arnold Drive and turn left. Continue with the directions above.

Hiking directions: Pass the chained entrance and head west on the grassy path. Walk through a grove of gnarled oaks with lace lichen draped from the branches. Cross two draws and continue through the rolling hills, gaining elevation. Merge with an old dirt road in a pocket of bay laurel trees. Stay left at an unsigned fork, where views open up of Sonoma Valley, Sugarloaf Ridge, and the towers atop Sonoma Mountain. At 0.8 miles, the trail reaches a road. The left fork returns to the town of Eldridge via Orchard Road. Cross the road and continue on the footpath straight ahead to an overlook of Fern Lake. Skirt the northeast side of the lake, and descend to the northern tip. Cross the outlet stream and climb the forested hillside. The path levels out and enters a redwood forest. Stroll through the shady grove, passing circular stands of redwoods. Watch on the left for a side path. Bear left 30 yards into a hollow. Grandmother Redwood stands on the left. After marveling at the details of the ancient tree, continue past the tree and loop back to the main trail. Bear left and walk a short distance to a trail split. The left fork leads to Camp Via. Begin the loop to the right, passing a couple of trail forks. Stay to the right, entering an open expanse. Circle the perimeter of the meadow above Asbury Creek to a trail fork. The right fork leads 30 yards to the creek and enters the original

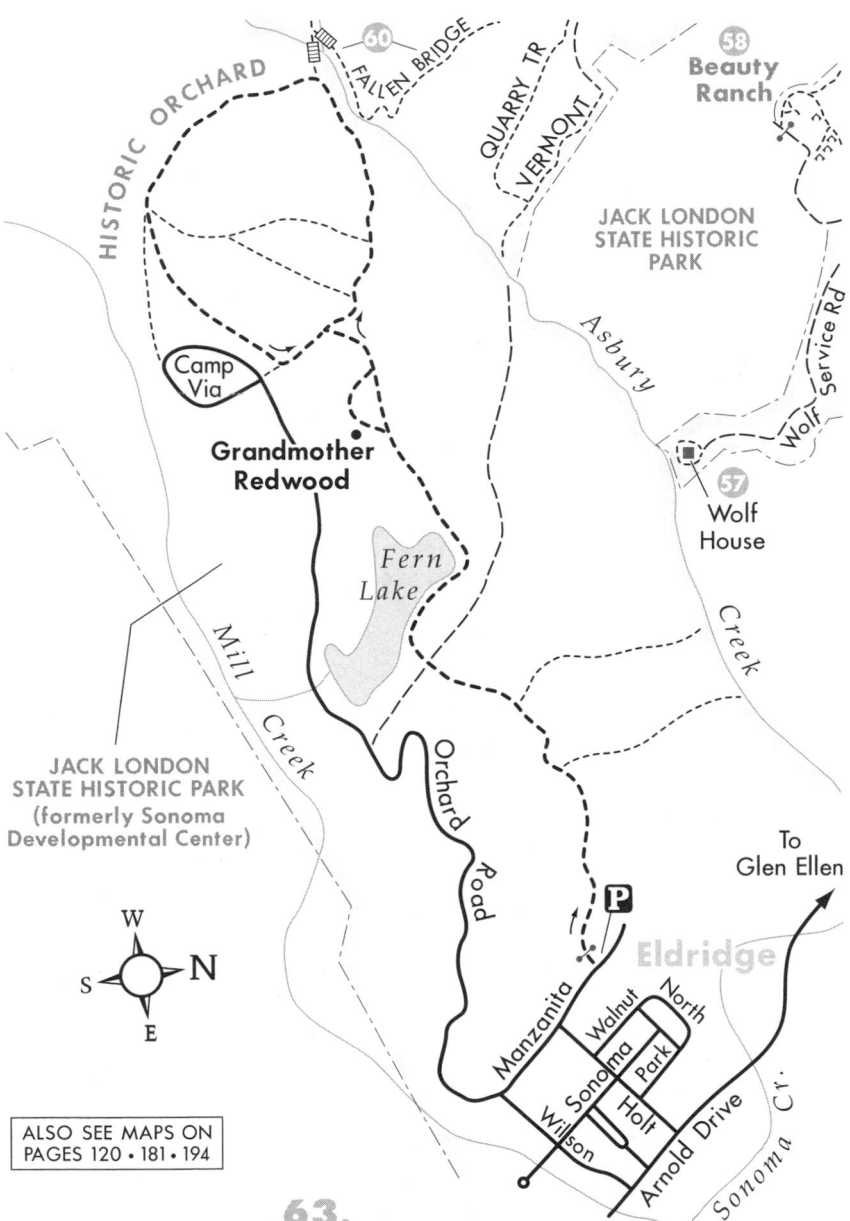

63.
Fern Lake · Historic Orchard
Grandmother Redwood
JACK LONDON STATE HISTORIC PARK

tract of Jack London State Historic Park. Curve left and walk to an overlook of Camp Via and the historic orchard. Traverse the hillside above the orchard to a T-junction by a wire fence. The right fork enters the camp. Bear left 200 yards, completing the loop. Retrace your steps back to the trailhead.■

64. Sonoma Valley Regional Park

13630 Sonoma Highway 12 · Glen Ellen

Hiking distance: 2.5-mile loop
Hiking time: 1.5 hours
Elevation gain: 225 feet
Dogs: allowed
Maps: U.S.G.S. Glen Ellen
      Sonoma Valley Regional Park

Summary of hike: Sonoma Valley Regional Park is tucked into the base of the Sonoma Mountains along the verdant valley floor. The park sits on the west edge of the wide valley, just south of the creekside town of Glen Ellen and six miles north of Sonoma. The 162-acre park is filled with rolling oak woodlands and grassy meadows and is known for its beautiful displays of California poppies, wild irises, and lupine. The park has picnic areas and the Liz Perrone Dog Park, a one-acre fenced grassland for off-leash canines. Dirt and paved trails used for hiking, biking, and horseback riding weave through the streamside corridor. This hike stays on the wide main route, climbing the rolling hillside to the picturesque ridge and returning through the stream-fed meadow with gorgeous blue oaks.

Driving directions: KENWOOD: From the town of Kenwood In Sonoma Valley, drive 4 miles south on Highway 12 (Sonoma Highway) to the posted park entrance. (It is located 0.4 miles south of Arnold Drive.) Turn right and drive 0.2 miles to the trailhead parking lot. A parking fee is required.

SONOMA: From East Napa Street in Sonoma, drive 5.5 miles north on Highway 12 (Sonoma Highway) to the park entrance on

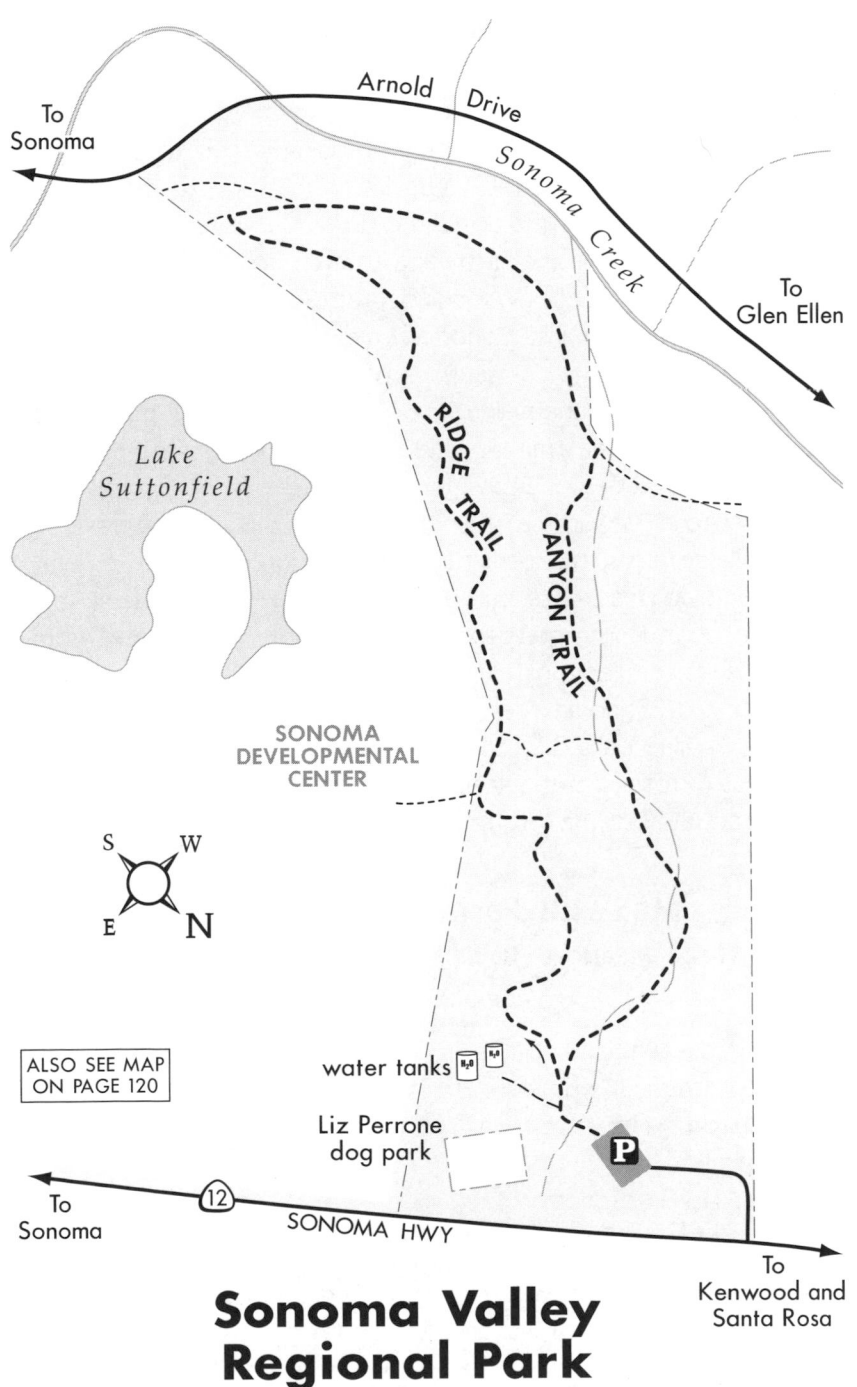

To Sonoma

Arnold Drive

Sonoma Creek

To Glen Ellen

Lake Suttonfield

RIDGE TRAIL

CANYON TRAIL

SONOMA DEVELOPMENTAL CENTER

S W
E N

ALSO SEE MAP ON PAGE 120

water tanks

Liz Perrone dog park

P

To Sonoma

(12) SONOMA HWY

To Kenwood and Santa Rosa

Sonoma Valley Regional Park

the left. (It is located 1.8 miles north of Madrone Road.) Turn left and drive 0.2 miles to the trailhead parking lot.

Hiking directions: From the far end of the parking lot, take the paved path. Curve to the right, passing a road to the water tanks, to a trail fork at 100 yards. Begin the loop to the left on the Ridge Trail, and climb up to the ridge. Curve to the right and follow the grassy ridge dotted with oaks to an overlook with sitting benches. The views include the Sonoma Mountains, the Mayacamas Mountains, Sonoma Valley, and Lake Suttonfield. Continue through the oak savanna, passing a series of side paths that veer off from the main route. Stay on the wider, main route to a fenceline. The trail beyond the fence enters the Sonoma Developmental Center. Bear right, keeping the fence to your left, and descend 40 yards to a junction. Go to the left and traverse the hillside along the park boundary through a forest of oak, madrone, and manzanita. Curve right and weave down the hillside to the open rolling grasslands on the valley floor near Arnold Drive. Take the Canyon Trail to the right, and parallel a seasonal tributary of Sonoma Creek. Meander through the stream-fed meadow. Blue oaks draped with strands of lace lichen dot the meadow. Cross over the seasonal creek seven times, completing the loop. Stay to the left, returning to the trailhead.■

65. Maxwell Farms Regional Park
Three Meadow—Back Meadow—Bay Tree Loop
100 Verano Avenue · Sonoma

Hiking distance: 1-mile loop
Hiking time: 35 minutes
Elevation gain: Level
Dogs: allowed
Maps: U.S.G.S. Sonoma
       Maxwell Farms Regional Park

Summary of hike: Maxwell Farms Regional Park is located at the northwest end of Sonoma just south of Boyes Hot Springs. The 85-acre park borders Sonoma Creek in a lush riparian corridor. The park has two distinct personalities. The developed northeast portion of the park includes picnic areas, athletic fields, a playground, and a Boys and Girls Club. The southwest half of the park is a natural 40-acre oasis with woodlands that are dominated by immense California bays and lush grassland meadows. The Maxwell family lived on this land from 1859 to 1968. They planted plum and apricot orchards in the late 1800s, which are still productive. This hike loops around the natural area and follows the watercourse of Sonoma Creek.

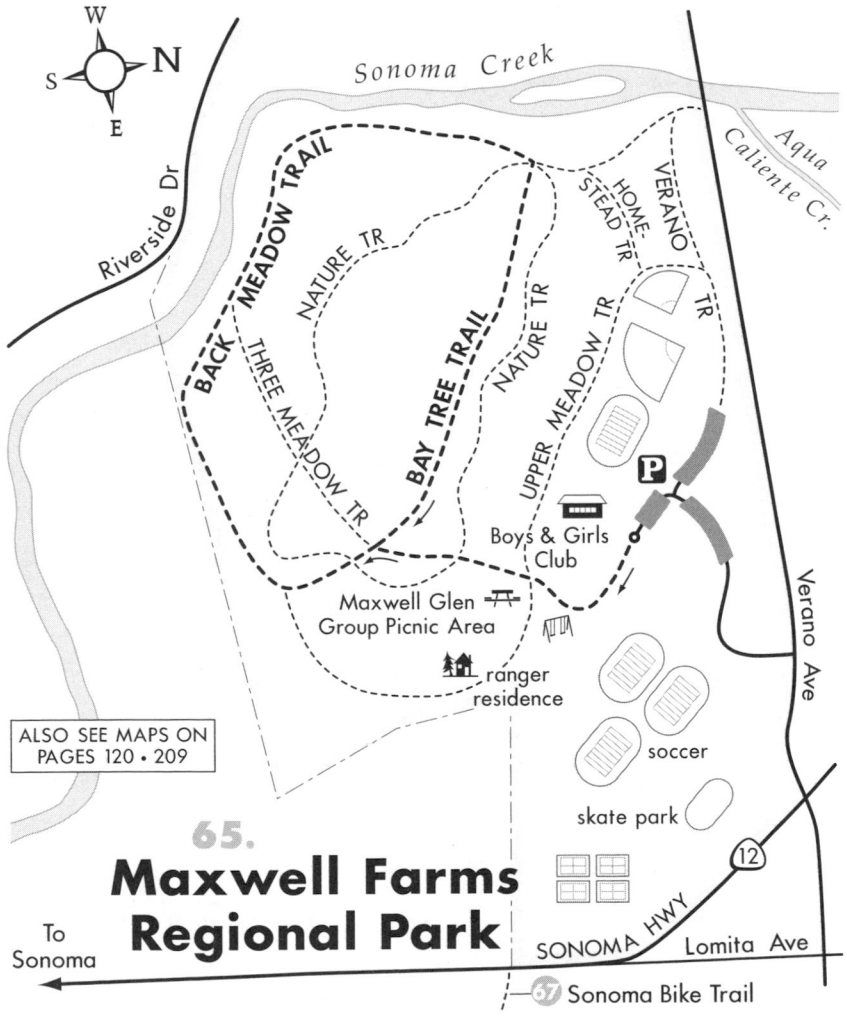

Driving directions: SONOMA: From Sonoma Plaza in downtown Sonoma, drive 1 mile west on West Napa Street to Highway 12 (Sonoma Highway). Turn right and continue 0.6 miles to Verano Avenue. Turn left and go 0.1 mile to the posted park entrance on the left. Turn left and park in the lot. A parking fee is required.

KENWOOD: From the town of Kenwood in Sonoma Valley, drive 8 miles south on Highway 12 (Sonoma Highway) to Verano Avenue and turn right. Continue with the directions above.

Hiking directions: From the far, southeast end of the parking lot, walk down the service road past the Valley of the Moon Boys and Girls Club. Curve right to the group picnic area on the left and a posted junction. Continue straight ahead on the Three Meadow Trail—a dirt footpath—to a 4-way junction. Begin the loop to the left on the Bay Tree Trail through oaks, bay laurels, and blackberry bushes to the south park boundary and another junction. The left fork loops back to the ranger residence and returns to the group picnic area. Curve to right on the Back Meadow Trail, skirting the south end of the park. The trail merges with the Three Meadow Trail and continues along the park boundary 20 feet above Sonoma Creek. Follow the creek upstream, heading north to the west end of the Bay Tree Trail. Bear right on the Bay Tree Trail, and stroll through an amazing tunnel of massive bay laurels. Complete the loop at the junction with the Three Meadows Trail. Return left to the parking lot.■

66. Sonoma Overlook Trail

Hiking distance: 3 miles round trip
Hiking time: 1.5 hours
Elevation gain: 400 feet
Dogs: not allowed
Maps: U.S.G.S. Sonoma
      Sonoma Overlook trail map

Summary of hike: The Sonoma Overlook Trail is a gorgeous hike that is a short half mile from the Sonoma Plaza in downtown Sonoma. The trail traverses the hillside above the north end of

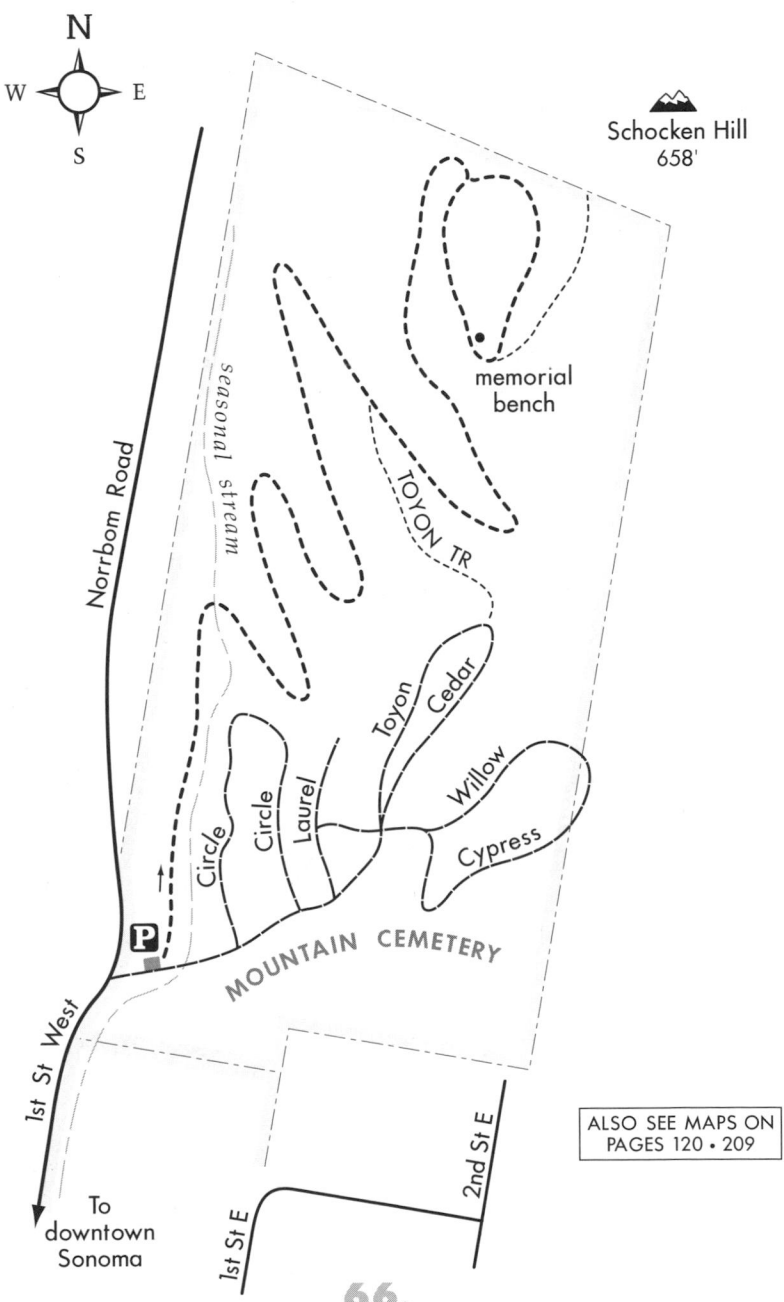

N
W E
S

Schocken Hill
658'

memorial
bench

TOYON TR

Norrbom Road

seasonal stream

Cedar

Toyon

Willow

Laurel

Cypress

Circle

Circle

P

MOUNTAIN CEMETERY

1st St West

2nd St E

1st St E

To
downtown
Sonoma

ALSO SEE MAPS ON
PAGES 120 • 209

66.

Sonoma Overlook Trail

town to a grassy plateau below the summit of Schocken Hill. The hike begins at Mountain Cemetery and leads to the plateau through a mixed woodland forest. A short trail loops around the plateau to a memorial bench with a bird's-eye view of Sonoma, the sloping ridge of Sonoma Mountain, and vistas across Sonoma Valley to San Pablo Bay.

Driving directions: From West Napa Street by the Sonoma Plaza in downtown Sonoma, drive 0.5 miles north on First Street West (along the west edge of the plaza) to the posted Mountain Cemetery on the right. It is across the street from Depot Park and just before the hill. Turn right and park by the signed trailhead.

Hiking directions: Pass the trailhead panel and walk up the grassy slope, skirting the west edge of the cemetery. Cross a seasonal stream in a small canyon, and zigzag up the hillside in a grove of oaks and California bays. Pass a moss-covered lava rock and an old rock wall. Emerge from the forest to a clearing in a sloping meadow and a Y-fork with a vista of Sonoma and the surrounding mountains. The Toyon Trail veers right and descends to Toyon Road at the upper end of Mountain Cemetery. This trail can be used on the return route by winding down the cemetery roads to the entrance and trailhead. For now, continue straight on the left fork. Steadily gain elevation through manzanita and majestic, twisted valley oaks. Switchback to the left, and gently climb to a junction at the Upper Meadow at 1.25 miles. Begin the loop around the meadow to the right. Pass basalt outcroppings en route to sweeping vistas, including the sloping ridge of Sonoma Mountain. At the south end of the loop is a memorial stone bench. Just beyond the bench is a trail split. The right fork curves to the upper end of the meadow and ends at the fenced boundary. The main trail stays on the plateau to the left and completes the loop. Return on the same trail, or use the alternative Toyon Trail. ▪

67. Sonoma Bike Path

Hiking distance: 3 miles round trip
Hiking time: 1.5 hours
Elevation gain: Level
Dogs: allowed
Maps: U.S.G.S. Sonoma
      Sonoma State Historic Park

**map
page 209**

Summary of hike: The Sonoma Bike Path is a hiking, biking, and jogging trail that crosses through the heart of Sonoma just north of Sonoma Plaza. The path stretches from Fourth Street East, by Sebastiani Vineyards and Winery, to the Sonoma Highway across from Maxwell Farms Regional Park (Hike 65). The dog friendly path passes through vineyards, Depot Park, the Sonoma Depot Museum (built as a replica of Sonoma's first train depot of 1880), Sonoma State Historic Park, and the open grasslands around General Vallejo's gothic Victorian home. The trail is popular with locals as well as visitors.

Driving directions: From East Napa Street by the Sonoma Plaza in downtown Sonoma, drive 0.5 miles east on East Napa Street to Fourth Street East. Turn left and continue a quarter mile to the posted trail across from Lovall Valley Road by the Sebastiani Vineyards. Park along either side of the street.

Hiking directions: From Fourth Street East at the west end of Lovall Valley Road, head west on the paved path through the Sebastiani Vineyards. Cross Second Street East, and continue through a landscaped greenbelt to First Street East at 0.35 miles. Cross the street and enter Depot Park, with a eucalyptus grove, historical museum, and train cars on the left. Athletic fields are on the right. A side path circles the museum and train cars. At a half mile is First Street West and the historic Depot Hotel, built in 1870 and closed in 1923. Cross through the vast grasslands of Sonoma State Historic Park to Third Street West. To the right, the forested road leads to General Mariano Vallejo's home, dating back to the 1850s. Continue straight ahead through the open meadow to Fourth Street West. Cross the street, leaving the state park, and pass through a greenbelt corridor between homes. Cross Fifth Street West at just over one mile, and continue through the corridor. Pass Olsen Park, Juaquin Drive, Junipero Serra Drive, and Robinson Road to the end of the trail at the Sonoma Highway (Highway 12). Across the highway is Maxwell Farms Regional Park (Hike 65). Return by retracing your steps.■

68. Bartholomew Memorial Park
Grape Stomp—You-Walk Miwok Trail Loop
1695 Castle Road · Closed from January 1 to April 1

Hiking distance: 2.4-mile loop
Hiking time: 1.5 hours
Elevation gain: 450 feet
Dogs: allowed
Maps: U.S.G.S. Sonoma
       Bartholomew Foundation trail map

map page 211

Summary of hike: Bartholomew Memorial Park is a little known gem tucked into the hills less than two miles northeast of Sonoma. The 375-acre park leases part of its diverse land to Bartholomew Winery. This hike is not a meandering stroll through a winery, it only begins and ends there. The trail is a backcountry hike winding through oak-covered mountain slopes and redwood groves. The hike follows sections of the Arroyo Seco to a pond, lake, cave, and two awesome overlooks.

Driving directions: From East Napa Street by the Sonoma Plaza in downtown Sonoma, drive one mile east on East Napa Street to 7th Street East. Turn left and continue 0.3 miles to Castle Road. Turn right and drive 0.4 miles to the Bartholomew Park Winery entrance. Enter the winery grounds and go a quarter mile to a road fork. The right fork leads to the tasting room. Veer left 0.1 mile to the trailhead parking lot.

A second trailhead is located off of Old Winery Road. From East Napa Street, just east of 8th Street East, turn north on Old Winery Road. Drive 0.75 miles to the posted trailhead parking area on the left.

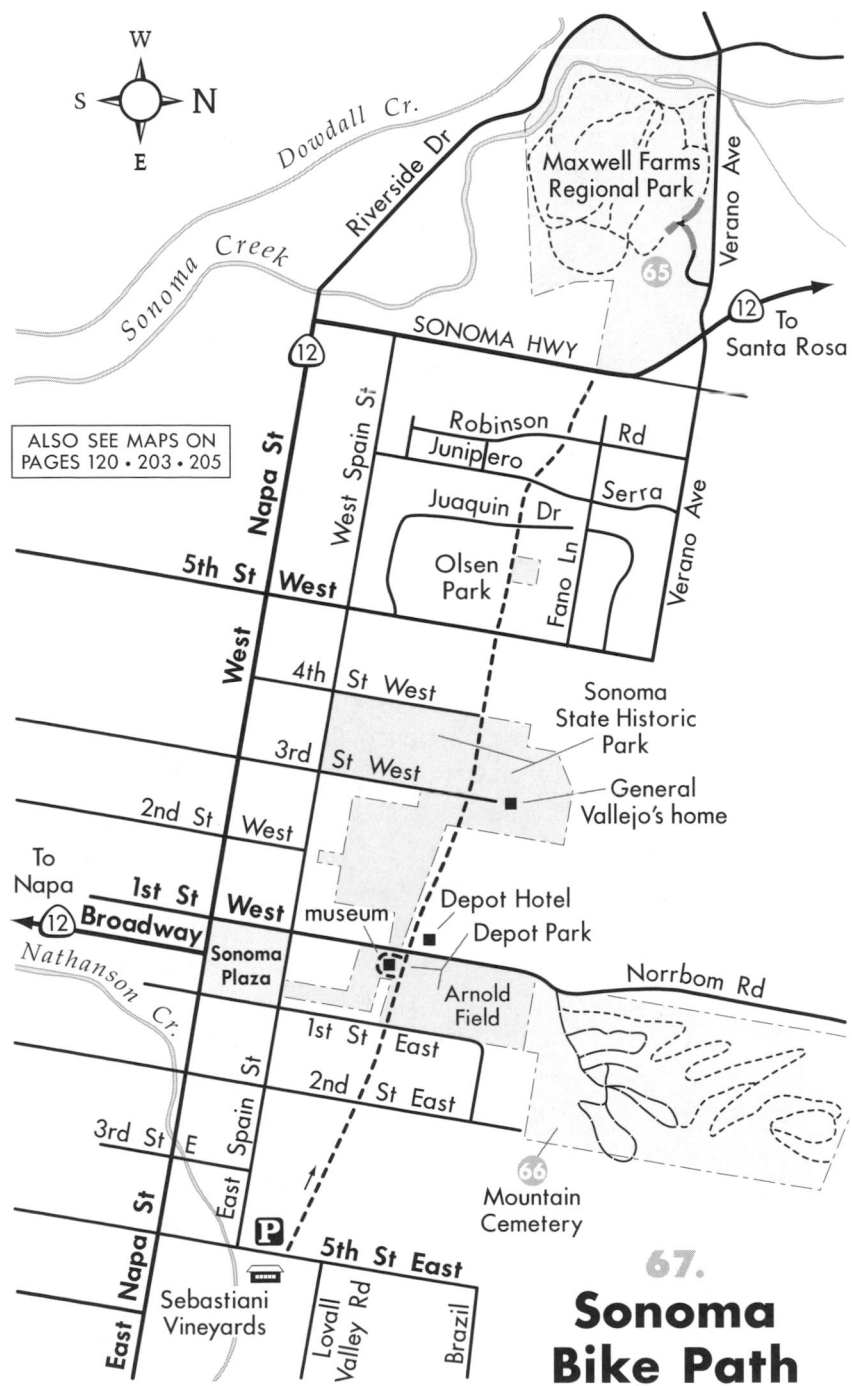

W · N · S · E

Dowdall Cr.

Riverside Dr

Sonoma Creek

Maxwell Farms Regional Park

Verano Ave

65

SONOMA HWY

12

12 To Santa Rosa

ALSO SEE MAPS ON PAGES 120 · 203 · 205

Napa St

West Spain St

Robinson Rd

Junipero

Juaquin Dr

Serra

Verano Ave

Olsen Park

Fano Ln

5th St West

West

4th St West

Sonoma State Historic Park

3rd St West

2nd St West

General Vallejo's home

To Napa

1st St West

12 Broadway

museum

Depot Hotel

Depot Park

Nathanson Cr.

Sonoma Plaza

Norrbom Rd

1st St East

Arnold Field

2nd St East

3rd St E

East Spain St

66

Mountain Cemetery

East Napa St

P

5th St East

Sebastiani Vineyards

Lovall Valley Rd

Brazil

67.

Sonoma Bike Path

Hiking directions: From the north end of the parking lot, follow the posted trail 40 yards to Duck Pond. Curve right along the east side of the pond to a trail gate. Pass through the gate and cross a stream in an oak, manzanita, and madrone forest. Climb the hill on the Grape Stomp Trail and traverse the slope, parallel to the stream. Head up the shaded draw and recross the stream. Climb steps and zigzag up the hill to Grape Stomp Bench and an overlook of Sonoma and San Pablo Bay. Weave along the contours of the hills with small dips and rises. Descend to a fork of Arroyo Seco Creek by a private road. Rock-hop over the creek and cross the road. Climb eight steps and head up the forested hillside. Follow the north side of Arroyo Seco Creek, passing above Benicia's Lake. Descend steps and hop over the creek upstream of the lake. Enter a redwood grove with Douglas fir and continue climbing. A side path on the right leads to the east shore of the lake. The main trail continues to a posted junction at one mile. Angel's Flight Trail descends to the right for a slightly shorter and easier loop.

Bear left on the You-Walk Miwok Trail, climbing to the 640-foot summit that is just past a bench. On clear days, the vistas extend as far as the Golden Gate Bridge. Descend from the upper slope with the aid of dirt and log steps to the Shortcut Trail on the right. Stay straight 20 yards to a side path on the right to Szeptaj Point Bench, with beautiful views of Sonoma from under a canopy of oaks. Continue downhill on the main trail to a posted junction. Detour to the left 80 yards. Follow the South Fork of Arroyo Seco upstream, passing small waterfalls. Continue over mossy boulders to Solano's Hideaway, a massive rock formation with caves. Solano was an Indian chief of the Suisun Tribe and a friend of General Vallejo.

Return to the junction and continue west, passing a junction with the lower south end of Angel's Flight Trail. Pass through a trail gate and skirt the backside of the Buena Vista Winery. Pass through a second gate to a narrow paved road by a gazebo on the left. Cross a rock bridge over Arroyo Seco Stream and follow the path on the right side of the road. Cross Castle Road and complete the loop at the trailhead parking lot. ∎

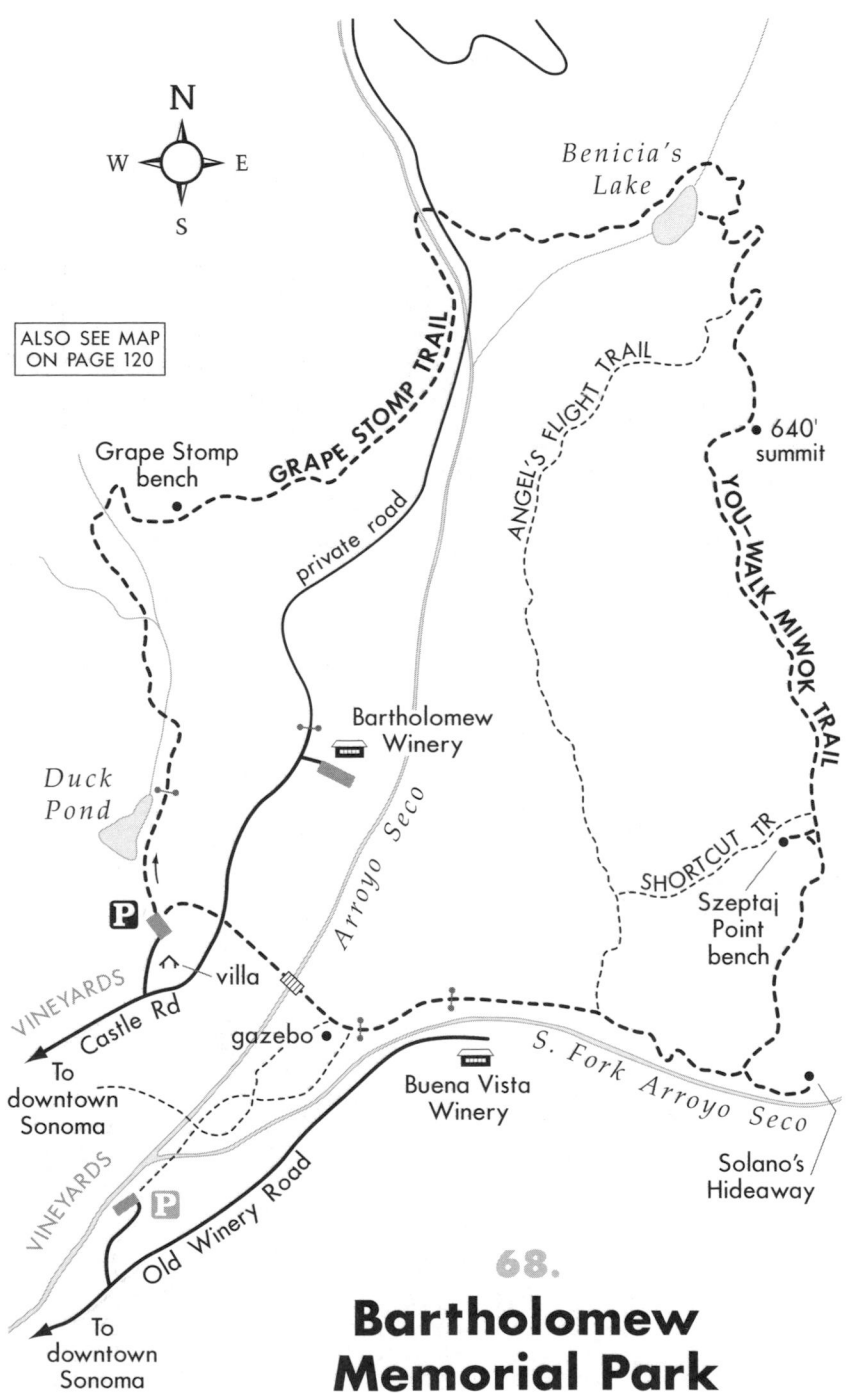

N
W E
S

ALSO SEE MAP
ON PAGE 120

Benicia's
Lake

GRAPE STOMP TRAIL

ANGEL'S FLIGHT TRAIL

YOU-WALK MIWOK TRAIL

640'
summit

Grape Stomp
bench

private road

Bartholomew
Winery

Duck
Pond

Arroyo Seco

SHORTCUT TR.

Szeptaj
Point
bench

P

villa

Castle Rd

VINEYARDS

gazebo

Buena Vista
Winery

S. Fork Arroyo Seco

To
downtown
Sonoma

Solano's
Hideaway

VINEYARDS

P

Old Winery Road

To
downtown
Sonoma

68.

Bartholomew
Memorial Park

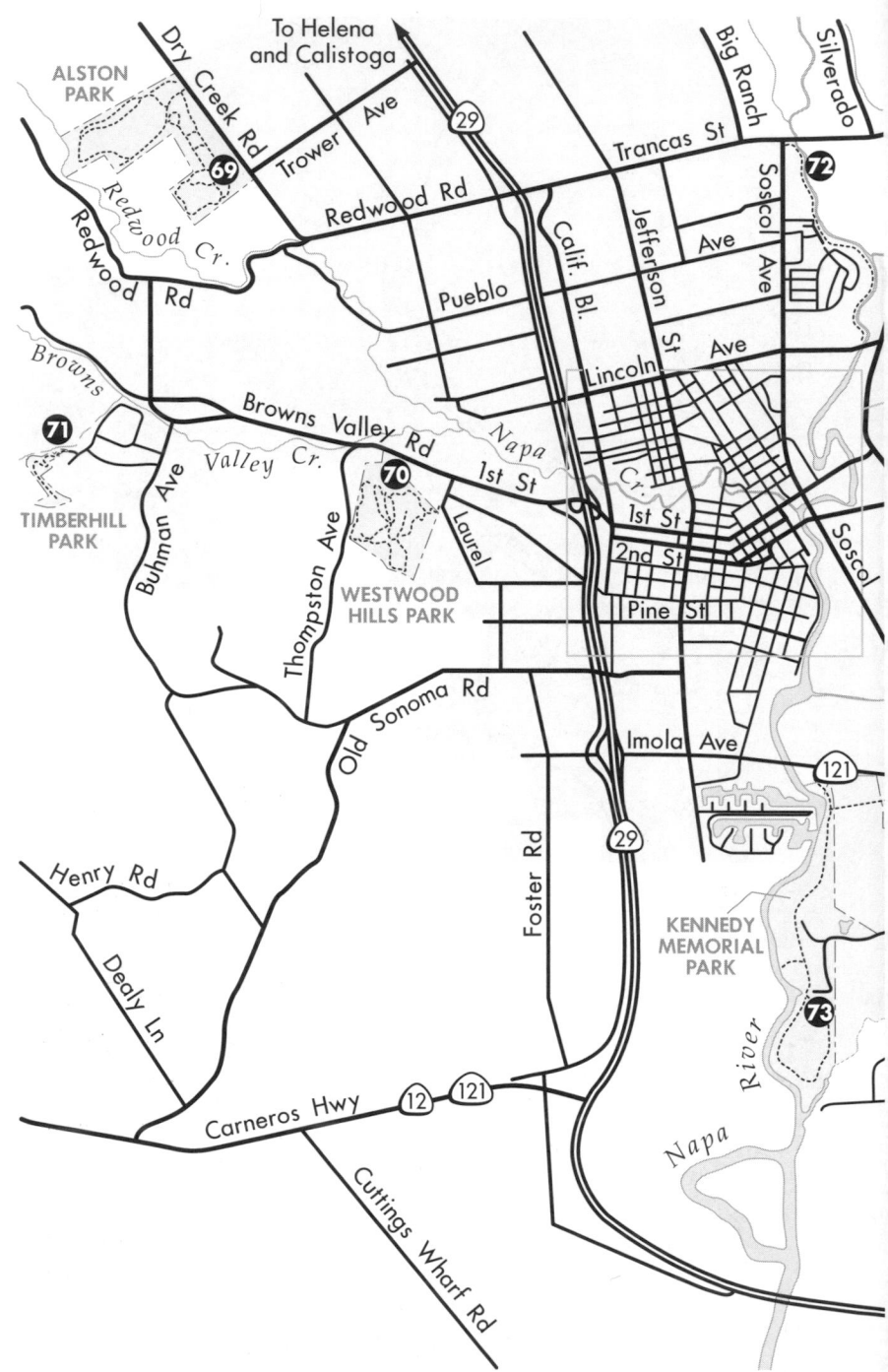

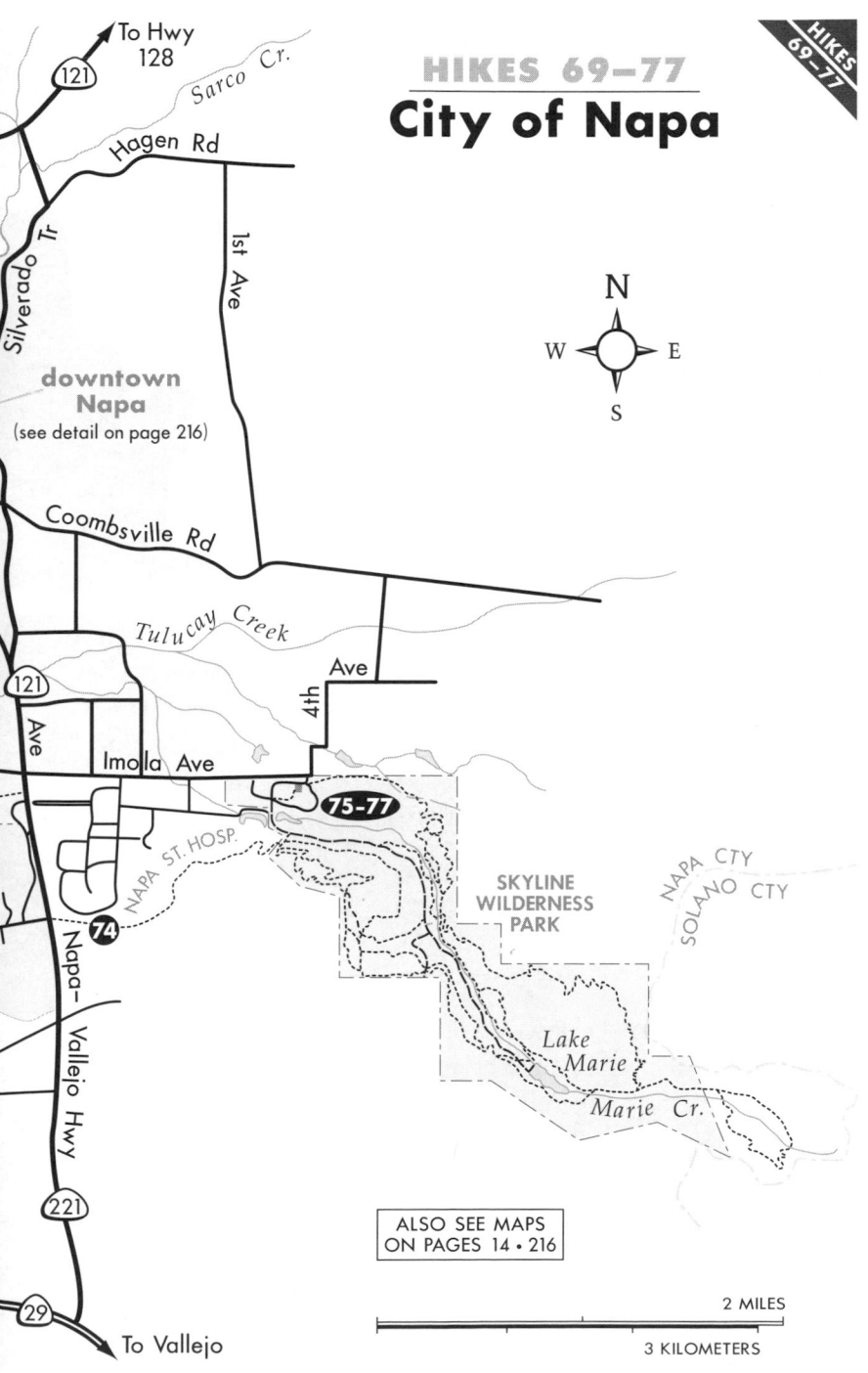

City of Napa

HIKES 69–77

To Hwy 128

121

Sarco Cr.

Hagen Rd

Silverado Tr

1st Ave

N
W — E
S

downtown Napa
(see detail on page 216)

Coombsville Rd

Tulucay Creek

121

Ave

4th Ave

Imola Ave

75-77

NAPA ST. HOSP.

74

SKYLINE WILDERNESS PARK

NAPA CTY
SOLANO CTY

Napa–Vallejo Hwy

Lake Marie

Marie Cr.

221

ALSO SEE MAPS ON PAGES 14 • 216

29

To Vallejo

2 MILES

3 KILOMETERS

69. Alston Park

Dry Creek Road · Napa

Hiking distance: 2.5-mile double loop
Hiking time: 1.5 hours
Elevation gain: 170 feet
Dogs: allowed
Maps: U.S.G.S. Napa
City of Napa—Alston Park

Summary of hike: Alston Park covers 157 acres in the unobstructed rolling hills of northwest Napa. The open-space park, owned by the city of Napa, was made public in 1991. Alston Park has three miles of meandering trails that are open to equestrians, mountain bikers, hikers, and dog walkers. Redwood Creek, a tributary of the Napa River, forms the park's western boundary. This hike climbs to the upper area known as Canine Commons, a popular off-leash dog area. The trail circles the oak-dotted grassland through an old plum orchard on the south and wildflower-covered meadows with oak and madrone groves to the north. The hike detours into the shaded canyon by Redwood Creek and leads to picnic areas and overlooks, offering sweeping vistas of the city of Napa and Napa Valley.

Driving directions: From Highway 29 in the city of Napa, drive one mile west on Trower Avenue to Dry Creek Road. Turn right, then quickly turn left into the Alston Park parking lot. A second parking lot is located 0.3 miles north on Dry Creek Road.

Hiking directions: Head west past the trailhead kiosk on the wide trail to the base of the hill and a junction. Continue straight, traversing the hill to the upper plateau and a major junction with the Valley View Trail. Bear left and loop around the south end of Alston Park on the Prune Picker Trail bordering a vineyard. Slowly curve right around the abandoned orchard, forming a one-mile loop back to the Valley View Trail. Bear left on the Valley View Trail to a Y-fork with views across Napa. Stay to the right and climb the slope to an overlook with a picnic bench atop a knoll.

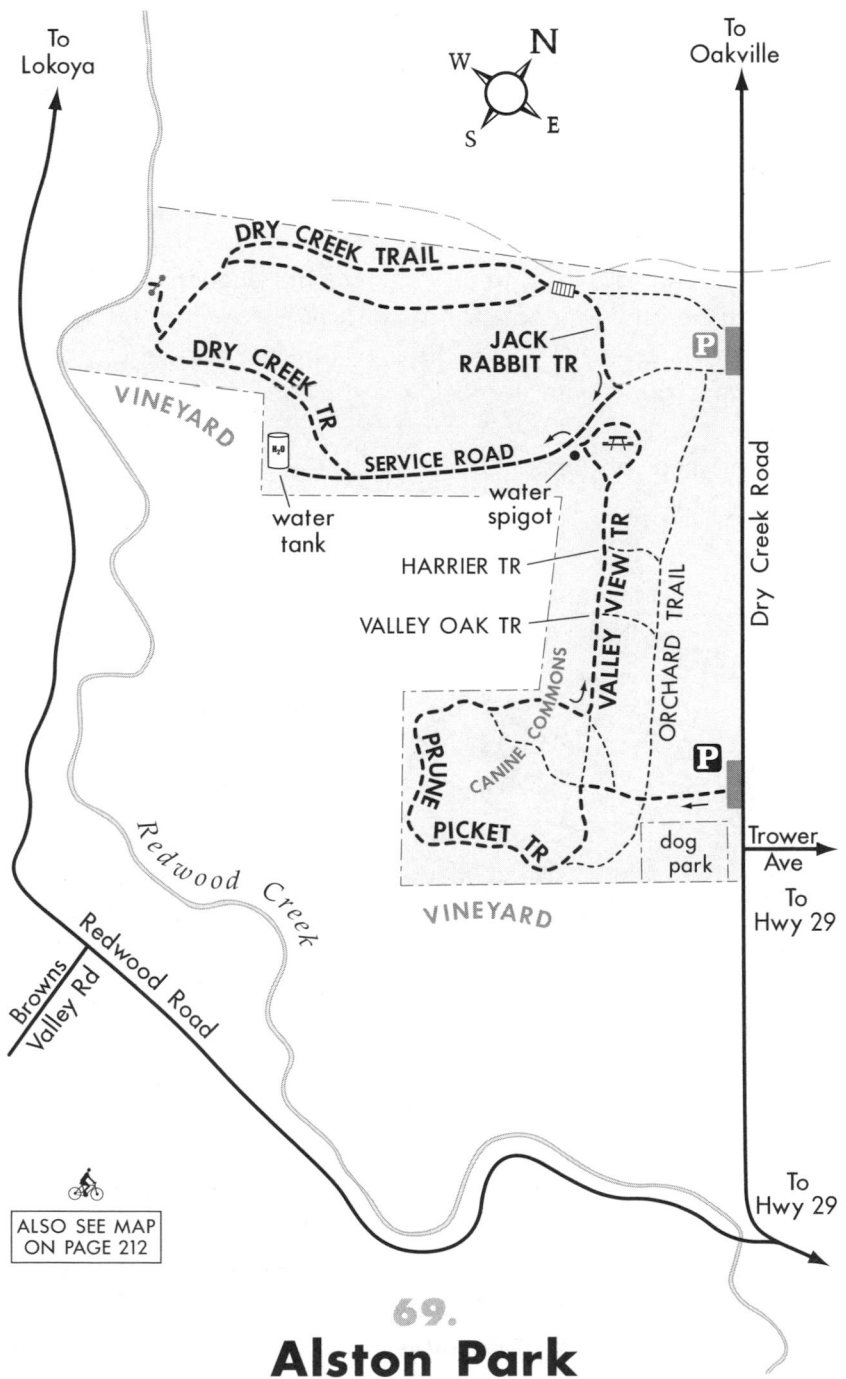

To Lokoya

To Oakville

DRY CREEK TRAIL

DRY CREEK TR

JACK RABBIT TR

VINEYARD

SERVICE ROAD

water tank

water spigot

HARRIER TR

VALLEY OAK TR

VALLEY VIEW TR

ORCHARD TRAIL

CANINE COMMONS

PRUNE PICKET TR

dog park

Dry Creek Road

Trower Ave

To Hwy 29

VINEYARD

Redwood Creek

Redwood Road

Browns Valley Rd

To Hwy 29

ALSO SEE MAP ON PAGE 212

69.

Alston Park

Continue uphill on the open grasslands to a junction by a water spigot. Take the right trail to the upper knoll and a gravel road by a water tank. Veer right on the road along the edge of the vineyard. Top the slope and descend west toward the forested hills. At the oak trees is a junction. Detour to the left and drop down through a shaded pocket of trees to an opening in a fence. Walk 20 yards to Redwood Creek under a lush riparian canopy of buckeye and valley oak trees. Return to the junction and continue to the northwest corner of Alston Park. Follow the north edge of the park on the Dry Creek Trail, or take the parallel footpath through a draw with live oak and madrone groves. The trails rejoin, cross a small footbridge, and continue east. Curve right on the unsigned Jack Rabbit Trail beneath the knoll with the picnic bench. Bear right on the service road a short distance, completing the loop at the water spigot. Go left and return to the trailhead. ■

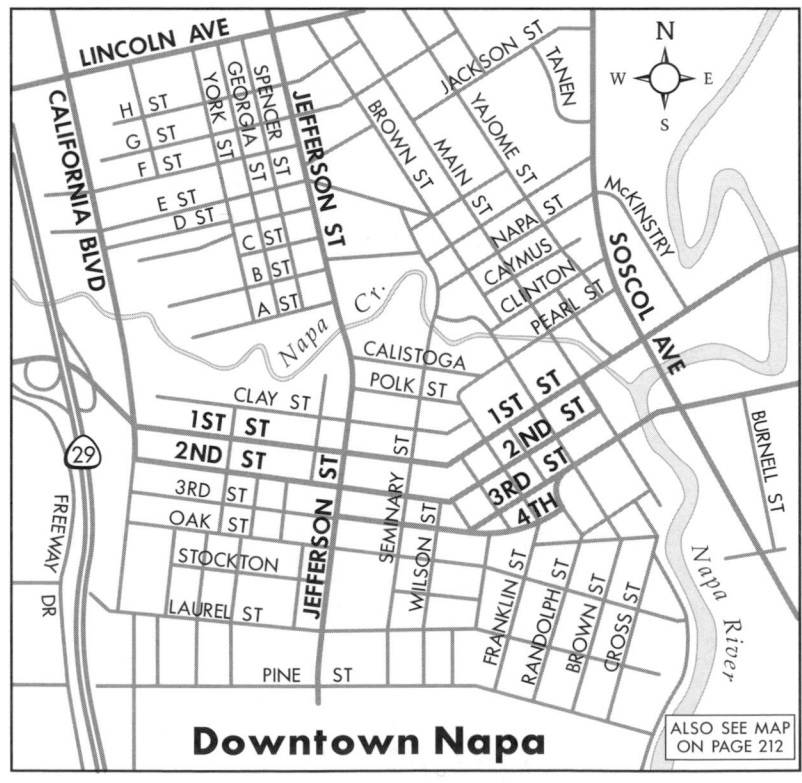

Downtown Napa

ALSO SEE MAP ON PAGE 212

70. Westwood Hills Park
Rocky Ridge—Meadow—Valley View Loop
Browns Valley Road · Napa

Hiking distance: 2-mile loop
Hiking time: 1 hour
Elevation gain: 350 feet
Dogs: not allowed on trails
Maps: U.S.G.S. Napa
　　　　City of Napa—Westwood Hills Park

**map
page 219**

Summary of hike: Westwood Hills Park covers 110 acres of heavily wooded hills in west Napa, less than one mile from Highway 29 and minutes from downtown Napa. The city park, opened to the public in 1976, provides three miles of inter-connecting fire roads and footpaths. Dirt trails wind through lush coast live oak groves, eucalyptus-filled canyons, and grassy meadows dotted with buckeye trees. The paths lead to ridges with mossy boulders, picnic sites, and expansive overlooks of the city of Napa, lower Napa Valley, the Mayacamas Range, and the Vaca Mountains. The vistas span from Mount St. Helena above Calistoga to Mount Diablo in the East Bay and Mount Tamalpais in Marin County.

The Carolyn Parr Nature Center, a non-profit museum, is locat-ed just west of the trailhead parking lot. The center is open on weekends from 1—4 p.m. year round. During the summer, it is open Tuesday through Sunday.

Dogs are not allowed on the trails, but many have been seen enjoying the park. Cows are permitted to graze in the park from April through October.

Driving directions: From Highway 29 in the city of Napa, drive one mile west on First Street (which becomes Browns Valley Road en route) to the trailhead parking lot and picnic area on the left.

Hiking directions: From the east end of the parking lot, head up the dirt road to the trailhead gate. Take the Valley View Trail under a towering eucalyptus forest, passing the old ranch house on the left. Walk through another trail gate, and continue uphill to a 4-way junction by a bench. Begin the loop on the footpath to the right. Pass through a wooden gate in a forest of oaks, bay laurel, and eucalyptus to a surreal garden of moss-covered boulders on the right. Go through a fourth gate to the Rocky Ridge Trail and a junction. The right fork descends into the canyon on the Red Hawk Trail. Go straight along the rocky ridge, and descend to a major 5-way junction with the Rocky Ridge, Valley View, Gum Canyon, and Meadow Trails. A sharp left returns to the trailhead on the Valley View Trail. The Gum Canyon Trail is the 90-degree left trail. The trail second to right continues south on the Valley View Trail, our return route.

For now, take a sharp right on the Meadow Trail. Gently descend through the rolling grassland rimmed with oaks and climb to a ridge. Detour 150 yards to the right to a picnic table on an oak-dotted knoll overlooking the rolling hillsides and vineyards. Return to the junction and head east on the Oak Knoll Trail. Veer right at an unsigned fork. Weave up the shaded drainage to the park boundary by a vineyard. Climb steps and walk up a sloping meadow to the summit with a spectacular view of the city of Napa, the Mayacamas Mountains, and the Vaca Mountains. Follow the summit ridge north (left), savoring the sweeping vistas on the Valley View Trail, to a junction at signpost 10. The right fork leads to another vista point on the North Knoll Trail. Curve left and descend, staying on the Valley View Trail. Return to the 5-way junction. The Gum Canyon Trail and Valley View Trail, the two right forks, return downhill through the forest and rejoin near the trailhead. ■

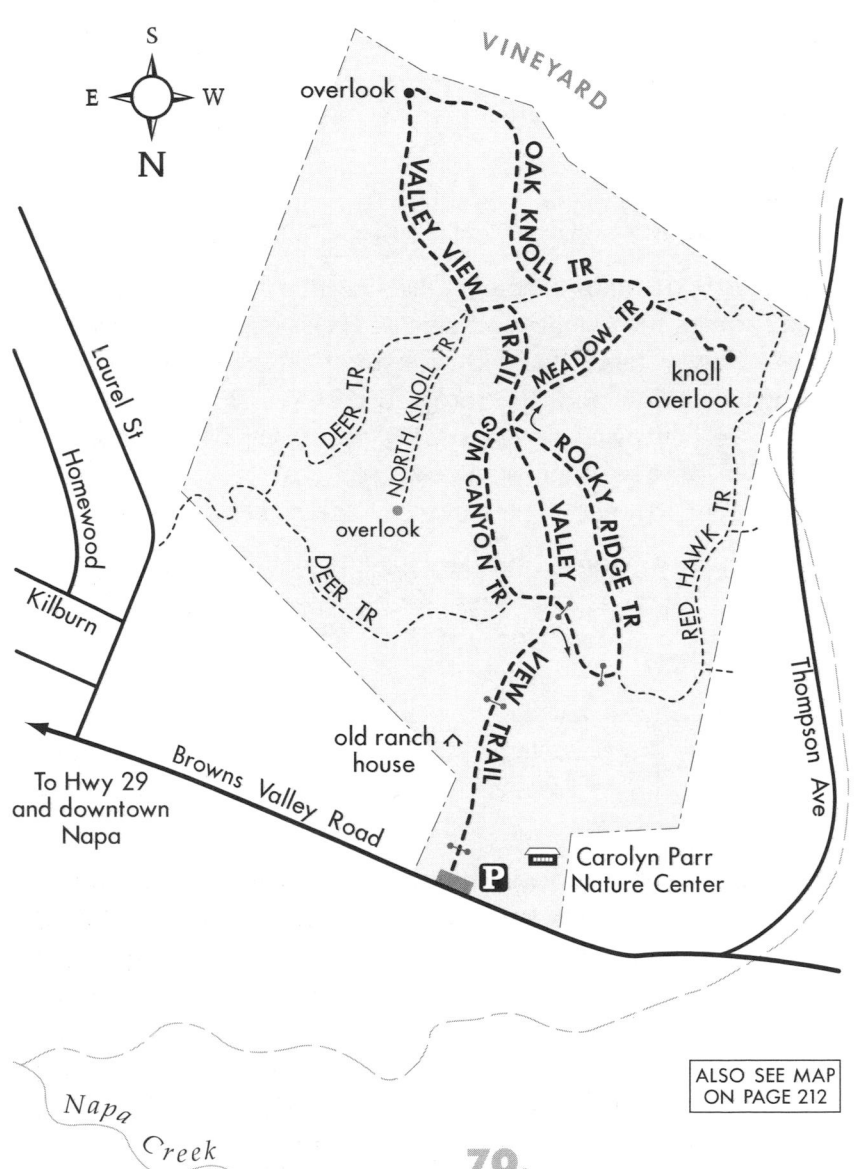

S E W N

VINEYARD

overlook

OAK KNOLL TR

VALLEY VIEW TRAIL

MEADOW TR

knoll overlook

DEER TR

NORTH KNOLL TR

GUM CANYON TR

ROCKY RIDGE TR

VALLEY

RED HAWK TR

overlook

DEER TR

Laurel St

Homewood

Kilburn

Browns Valley Road

VIEW TRAIL

old ranch house

To Hwy 29 and downtown Napa

P

Carolyn Parr Nature Center

Thompson Ave

Napa Creek

ALSO SEE MAP ON PAGE 212

70.

Westwood Hills Park
Rocky Ridge – Meadow – Valley View Loop

71. Timberhill Park

Hiking distance: 1.5 miles round trip
Hiking time: 1 hour
Elevation gain: 400 feet
Dogs: allowed
Maps: U.S.G.S. Napa
The Thomas Guide: Napa and Sonoma Counties

Summary of hike: Timberhill Park is an undeveloped park in the foothills framing the west side of Napa. The 10-acre park is a tucked-away gem at the end of a street on the edge of a residential neighborhood. The forested park has an unusual shape, not logical to any of the surrounding land forms. The trail leads to a 723-foot summit on a grassy knoll that is surrounded by pastureland, overlooking the city of Napa and Napa Valley.

Driving directions: From Highway 29 in the city of Napa, drive 1.8 miles west on First Street (which becomes Browns Valley Road en route) and veer left, staying on Browns Valley Road. Continue a quarter mile to Buhman Avenue and turn left. Go 0.1 miles to Meadowbrook Drive and turn right. Drive 0.3 miles to Stonybrook Drive and turn left. Continue 0.1 mile to Timberhill Lane and turn right. Proceed to the end of the block, and park along the curb near the posted park entrance.

Hiking directions: Pass through the metal gate at the end of Timberhill Lane. Follow the old asphalt road through a forest of oaks, bay laurel, and maple trees. Pass through a second gate and continue uphill to a washout in the road. Traverse the north-facing hillside on a footpath, and rejoin the old road ahead. Emerge from the forest to the open, rolling grasslands dotted with oaks. Steadily climb, with great views of the surrounding geography. Curve left to a ridge with views of Westwood Hills Park, Skyline Wilderness Park, and the Napa–Sonoma marshes. Follow the ridge to the end of the road. Cross the grassy ridge above the pastureland with grazing horses and cattle to the 723-foot summit. At the summit are two benches and 360-degree vistas, with a full view of Napa and the surrounding mountains. ■

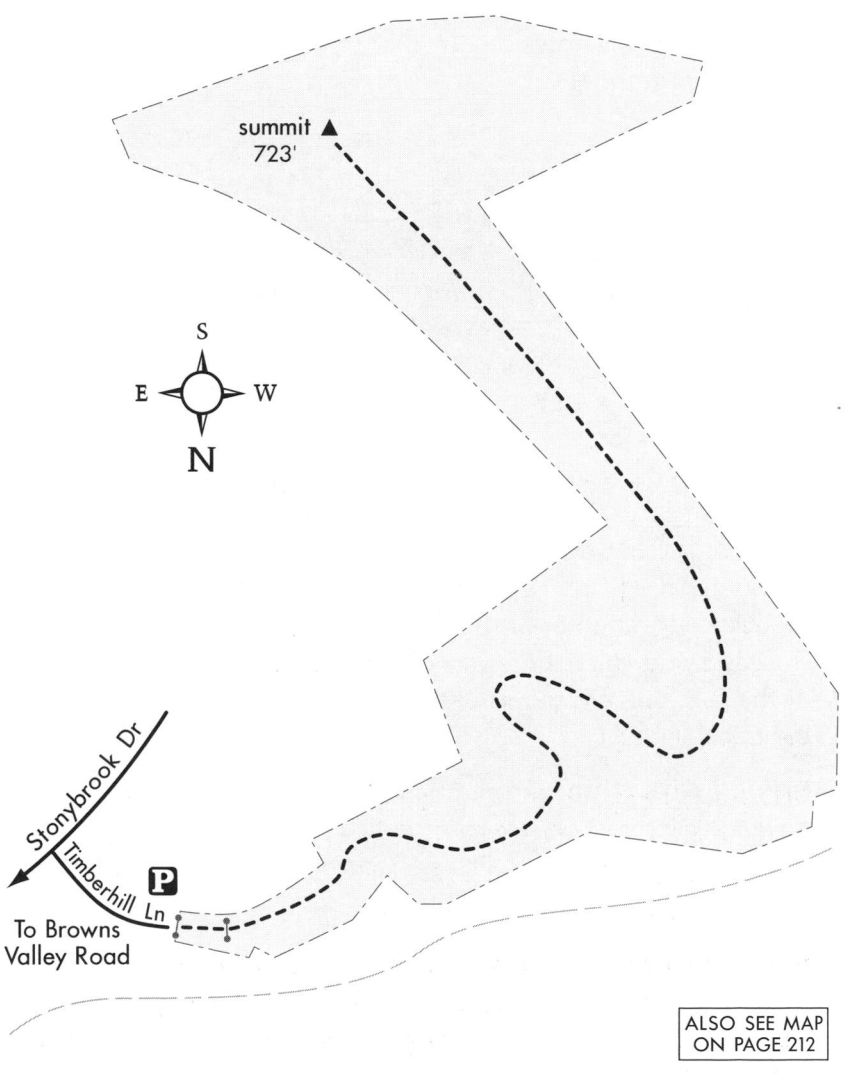

summit ▲
723'

S
E ─○─ W
N

Stonybrook Dr

Timberhill Ln

P

To Browns
Valley Road

ALSO SEE MAP
ON PAGE 212

71.

Timberhill Park

72. Napa River Trail
from Trancas Street to Lincoln Avenue

Hiking distance: 2.4 miles round trip
Hiking time: 1.5 hours
Elevation gain: Level
Dogs: allowed
Maps: U.S.G.S. Napa
        AAA Napa Valley City Series

Summary of hike: The Napa River flows 50 miles from the headwaters on the slopes of Mount St. Helena into San Pablo Bay. The river, among the largest in the Central Coast Range, runs through the heart of Napa Valley. The river drains 426 square miles (270,000 acres) of land with 47 tributaries (250 miles of streams) on its journey south. Along the lower 17 miles, the freshwater from the streams mingles with salty tidal waters from the bay (from San Pablo Bay in Vallejo to Trancas Street in Napa). Below Napa, the river spreads out into the productive marshes and wetlands of the Napa–Sonoma Estuary. This hike follows a 1.2-mile-long stretch of the river in downtown Napa, from Trancas Street to Lincoln Avenue. The trail parallels the west bank of the river. It is a wonderful spot for viewing birds and enjoying the tranquil beauty.

Driving directions: From Highway 29 in the city of Napa, drive 1.2 miles east on Trancas Street to Soscol Avenue. Turn right and park in the Silverado Plaza Shopping Center parking lot on the southwest corner of the intersection.

Hiking directions: Cross Soscol Avenue and walk 40 yards to the posted Napa River Trail on the right. It is located just before crossing the Trancas Street Bridge over the Napa River. Curve right on the paved, fenced, and landscaped corridor. Descend past the fence into the forest on the west bank of the river. Continue downstream through live oak and bay trees. Curve around a grassy picnic area on the left. A side path leads through the picnic area and follows the riverbank to trail's end at the edge of the river. From the main trail, parallel the flow of the river, and pass through a grassland with a sitting bench. Skirt the River Pointe Vacation Cottages, and emerge at Lincoln Avenue at 1.2 miles. Return by retracing your steps. ■

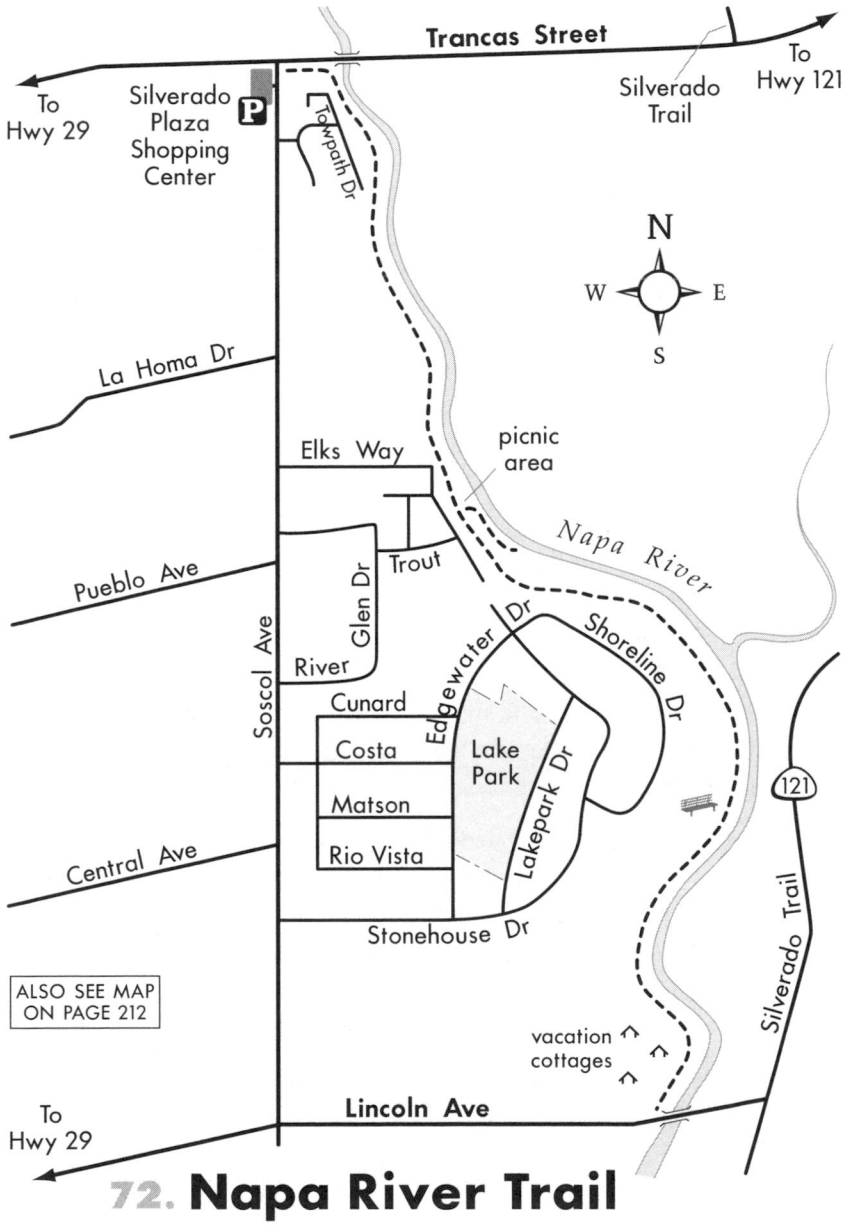

72. Napa River Trail
Trancas Street to Lincoln Avenue

73. Napa River Trail
JOHN F. KENNEDY MEMORIAL PARK
2295 Streblow Drive · Napa

Hiking distance: Up to 3.4 miles round trip
Hiking time: 1.5 hours
Elevation gain: Level
Dogs: allowed
Maps: U.S.G.S. Napa
AAA Napa Valley

map next page

Summary of hike: Kennedy Memorial Park runs along the Napa River south of downtown Napa. The diverse 350-acre park has picnic areas, ball fields, a boat launch, an 18-hole golf course, the River to Ridge Trail to Skyline Wilderness Park (Hike 73), and this hike—a section of the Napa River Trail. The trail follows a 1.6-mile stretch of the river from the south end of the park to the bridge at Imola Avenue. The river trail is being constructed in sections. When complete, it will provide river-front recreational opportunities for hikers, fishermen, joggers, and bicyclists for seven contiguous miles, from Kennedy Park to Trancas Street in downtown Napa (Hike 72). This hike follows the level, scenic trail overlooking the Napa River and the massive marshland and tidal wetlands that stretch to San Pablo Bay. The bountiful bird population includes egrets, herons, hawks, grebes, and woodpeckers.

Driving directions: From Highway 29 in the city of Napa, drive 1.4 miles east on Imola Avenue to the Napa–Vallejo Highway at the junction of Highway 121 and Highway 221. Turn right and continue 0.7 miles to Streblow Drive, just past the Napa Valley Community College. Turn right and drive 0.9 miles, passing the golf course and veering left, to the boat launch parking lot.

Hiking directions: Bear left on the paved path and parallel the Napa River downstream. Curve left, following the curvature of the river on the levee. A baseball diamond lies below on the left. Beyond left field, the path curves left away from the river and forms a loop. The loop route returns just south of the trailhead parking lot. This route is not as appealing as retracing your steps along the river. Back at the trailhead, by the boat launch and map kiosk, follow the paved path north. Skirt the grassy picnic area on the paved path to a trail fork. The left branch leads 70 yards to a river access. The main path continues between the natural wetlands on the left and the manicured parkland on the right. Pass a baseball field and the Napa Valley Community College sports fields, continuing along the edge of the reed-filled wetland. Two hundred yards before the Imola Avenue bridge is a 4-way junction. Straight ahead, the path leads to a bridge crossing over a water channel just shy of the Imola Avenue bridge. The left fork follows a dirt path to the boat marina; the right fork leads 0.2 miles to Highway 221, south of Imola Avenue. Return to Kennedy Memorial Park on the same path.■

74. River to Ridge Trail
JOHN F. KENNEDY MEMORIAL PARK
to SKYLINE WILDERNESS PARK
2295 Streblow Drive · Napa

Hiking distance: 5 miles round trip
Hiking time: 2.5 hours
Elevation gain: 350 feet
Dogs: not allowed
Maps: U.S.G.S. Napa and Mt. George
      AAA Napa Valley

map next page

Summary of hike: The River to Ridge Trail, part of the Bay Area Ridge Trail, connects Kennedy Memorial Park at the Napa River to Skyline Wilderness Park in the forested mountains. The trail begins in a corridor between the Napa State Hospital and the privately owned Syar quarries. It soon opens up to an oak savannah and manzanita woodland with views of Napa Valley and the Mayacamas Mountains.

Driving directions: From Highway 29 in the city of Napa, drive 1.4 miles east on Imola Avenue to the Napa–Vallejo Highway at the junction of Highway 121 and Highway 221. Turn

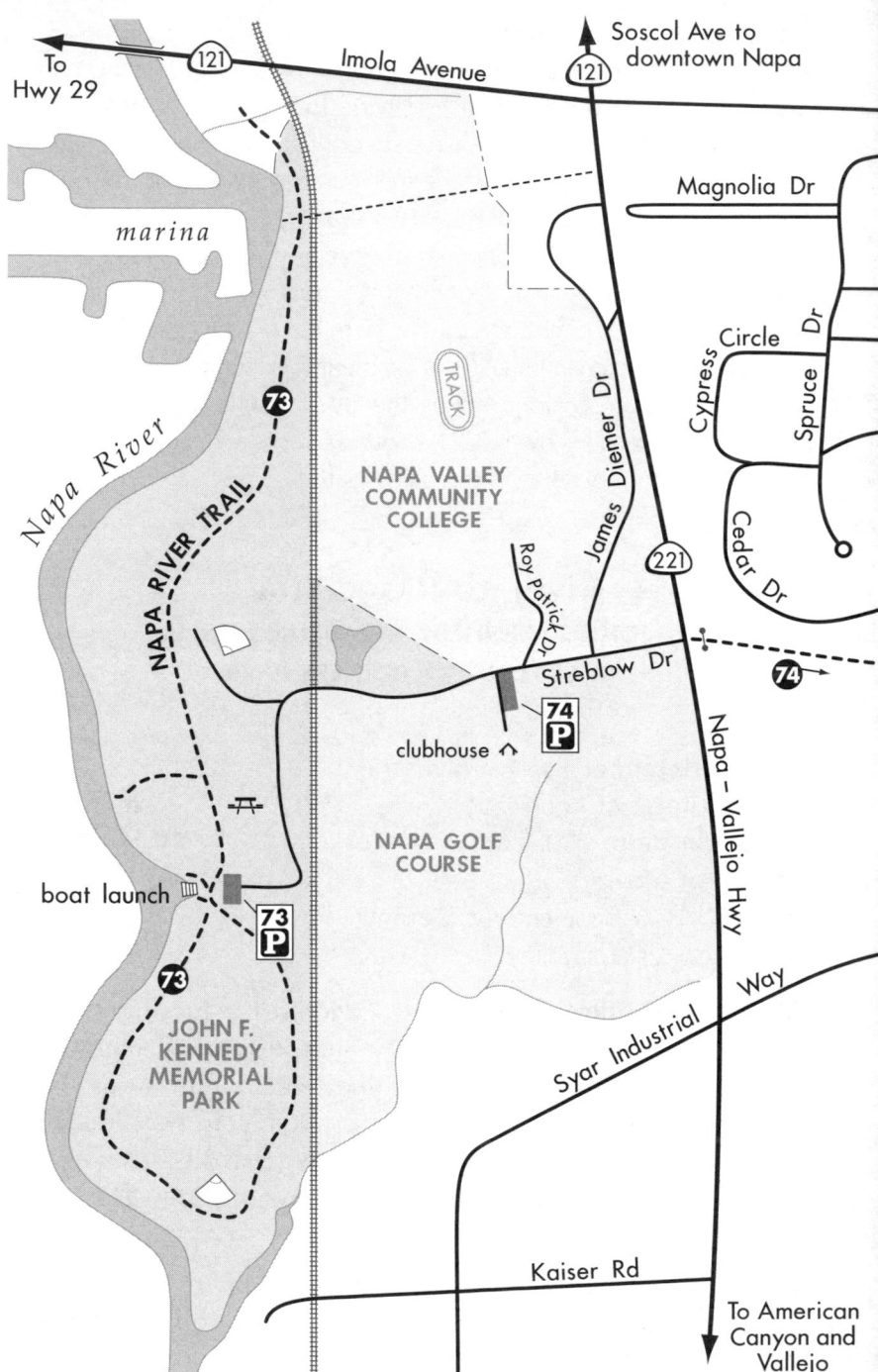

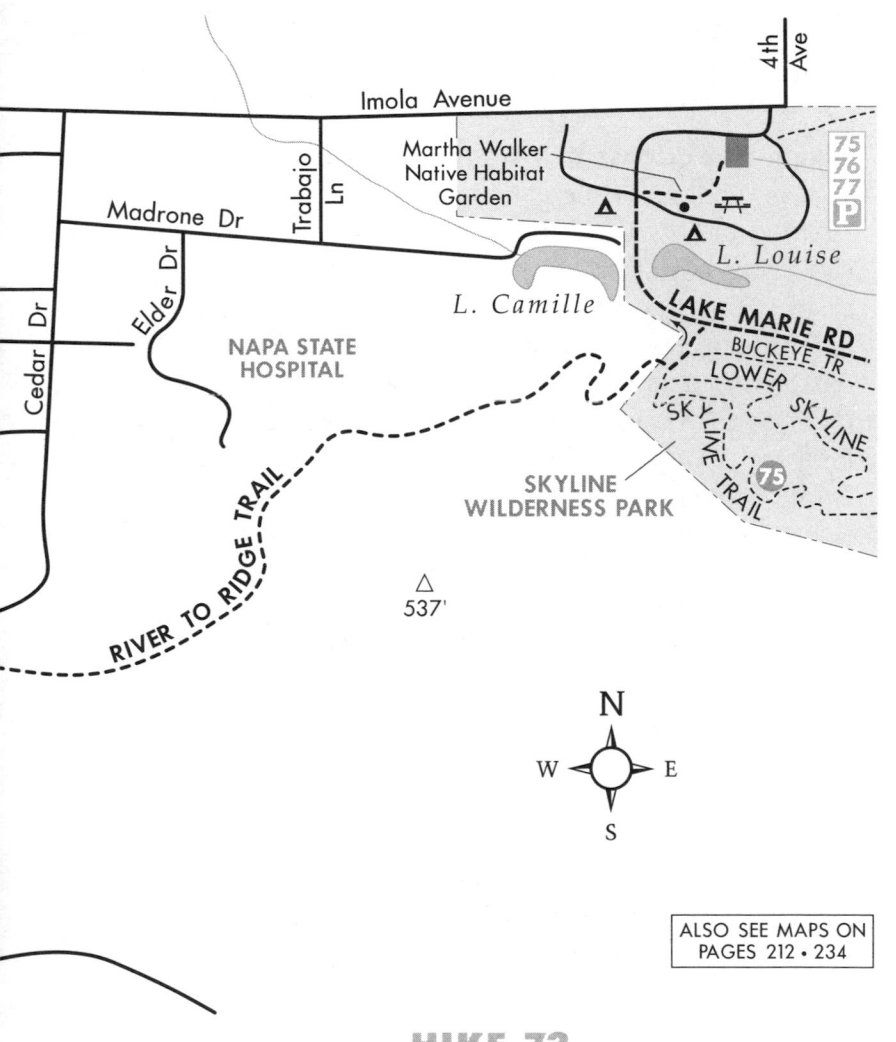

ALSO SEE MAPS ON
PAGES 212 • 234

HIKE 73

Napa River Trail
JOHN F. KENNEDY MEMORIAL PARK

HIKE 74

River to Ridge Trail
JOHN F. KENNEDY MEMORIAL PARK
to SKYLINE WILDERNESS PARK

right and continue 0.7 miles to Streblow Drive, just past the Napa Valley Community College. Turn right and drive 0.2 miles to the graveled formal garden parking lot on the left.

Hiking directions: Walk 0.2 miles back on Streblow Drive to Highway 221. Cross the highway and pass through the posted trailhead gate. Walk through the fence-lined corridor towards the hills among bays, oaks, and blackberry bushes while skirting the edge of the Napa State Hospital. Curve away from the hospital as the fence ends. Slowly gain elevation through chaparral into an oak and manzanita forest with moss-covered trees and rocks. Emerge into a clearing with a view across Napa to the Mayacamas Mountains. Weave up the foothills and curve left around a gully. Traverse the north-facing slope, passing a water tank on the right. Gently descend and cross the paved hospital road. Join the Skyline Trail access, a gravel road in Skyline Wilderness Park. Veer left fifty yards to a junction with the dirt Lake Marie Road. The right fork leads to Lake Marie (Hike 75). Go to the left through the fenced trail corridor between Lake Camille on the left and Lake Louise on the right. Curve right to the Martha Walker Native Habitat Garden and the Skyline Park picnic area and campground. Return by retracing your steps. ■

75. South Canyon Wall: Skyline—Lake Marie Loop
SKYLINE WILDERNESS PARK
2201 Imola Avenue · Napa

Hiking distance: 5.7-mile loop
Hiking time: 3 hours
Elevation gain: 800 feet
Dogs: not allowed
Maps: U.S.G.S. Napa and Mt. George
Skyline Wilderness Park

map
page 231

Summary of hike: Skyline Wilderness Park is an 850-acre park on the southeast edge of the city of Napa. The park, managed by volunteers, has an RV park; tent camping sites; picnic and barbecue areas; an archery range; a disc golf course; a 2.5-acre native garden; three man-made lakes; and more than 20 miles of hiking, biking, and equestrian trails. Six scenic, parallel routes follow Marie Creek Canyon to Lake Marie. Two routes traverse the south canyon wall, two follow the north canyon wall, and two lead along the lush canyon floor.

This hike follows the Skyline Trail along the south canyon wall. The route is part of the Bay Area Ridge Trail, a 400-mile trail connecting parks, preserves, and open spaces along the ridgelines surrounding San Francisco Bay. The Skyline Trail climbs to the south rim of Marie Creek Canyon in an oak and buckeye woodland, follows the ridge, and drops down to Lake Marie. Lake Marie lies in a bowl surrounded by forested hills at the southern foot of Sugarloaf Peak. An earthen dam built on Marie Creek in 1908 formed the lake and provided water for the state hospital. The hike returns 2.5 miles down the canyon floor on shaded Lake Marie Road, a scenic dirt road under a forest of towering oaks, bay laurels, and madrones.

Driving directions: Same as Hike 76.

Hiking directions: From the southwest corner of the parking lot, take the signed trail down steps and curve to the right. Walk past the Martha Walker Native Habitat Garden on the left, and cross a small bridge. Pass a picnic area and campground, staying to the right. Follow the signs through a trail corridor between Lake Camille on the right and Lake Louise on the left to a posted junction. The Lake Marie Road, our return route, continues straight ahead. Begin the loop to the right, and head south on the Skyline Trail. Stroll through the oak-dotted grassland. Pass the River to Ridge Trail (Hike 74) on the right and the Buckeye Trail and Lower Skyline Trail on the left to the Skyline Trail sign. Bear left and head up the hillside that overlooks the entire city of Napa, lower Napa Valley, endless vineyards, and the ridges that encircle Lake Berryessa. Weave up the hill, skirting an old hand-built stone wall on the park boundary. Pass the upper end of the Lower Skyline Trail and continue straight. Descend into a side canyon, passing the posted Bayleaf Trail on the left. Head downhill, parallel to the lichen-covered rock wall. En route, the trail overlooks the Napa–Sonoma Marshes Wildlife Area and San Pablo Bay. Meander through an open meadow with views of Mount George, West Sugarloaf Peak, and Mount Veeder. Enter a beautiful oak grove and drop down to a junction at Passini Road. The narrow dirt road leads to Lake Marie Road on the canyon floor. Instead, continue straight, staying on the forested Skyline Trail. Emerge from the oak forest into the grasslands with sweeping vistas of Marie Creek Canyon. Follow the serpentine path and watch for an unsigned path on the right that leads 70 yards to an overlook atop the east-west ridge. Return to the Skyline Trail and drop down, passing the Buckeye Trail to a Y-fork. For a slightly shorter hike, take the left fork and descend to Lake Marie Road, 120 yards shy of Lake Marie and the dam at the north end of the lake.

For the longer hike, stay to the right, passing a rock foundation and a chimney, remains from an old retreat. Follow the hillside above the southwest side of Lake Marie, and descend to Marie Creek above the lake. Cross the creek and walk 40 yards under giant alders and bay laurel to the signed Chaparral Trail on the left. The Skyline Trail continues straight ahead to the Tuteur Loop (Hike 76).

For this hike, switchback left on the Chaparral Trail and traverse the south-facing slope. Climb to a perch overlooking Lake Marie and the gorgeous canyon. Continue northwest and slowly descend to a junction past the lake, where the Chaparral Trail ends. The right fork continues on the Marie Creek Trail (Hike 77).

Bear left and walk a short distance to the Lake Marie Dam, built in 1908. Cross the dam and go to the right on the Lake Marie Road. Walk down the dirt road in the shade of the oak, bay laurel, and madrone forest on the south canyon wall above Marie Creek. Pass a massive rock structure and foundation to the lower end of Passini Road on a small rise. To the right is a picnic area that connects on the east to the Rim Rock Trail, Marie Creek Trail, and Manzanita Trail. Follow the undulating road while enjoying the views across Napa Valley, completing the loop at the Skyline Trailhead. Walk through the fence-lined causeway between Lake Camille and Lake Louise to the parking lot. ■

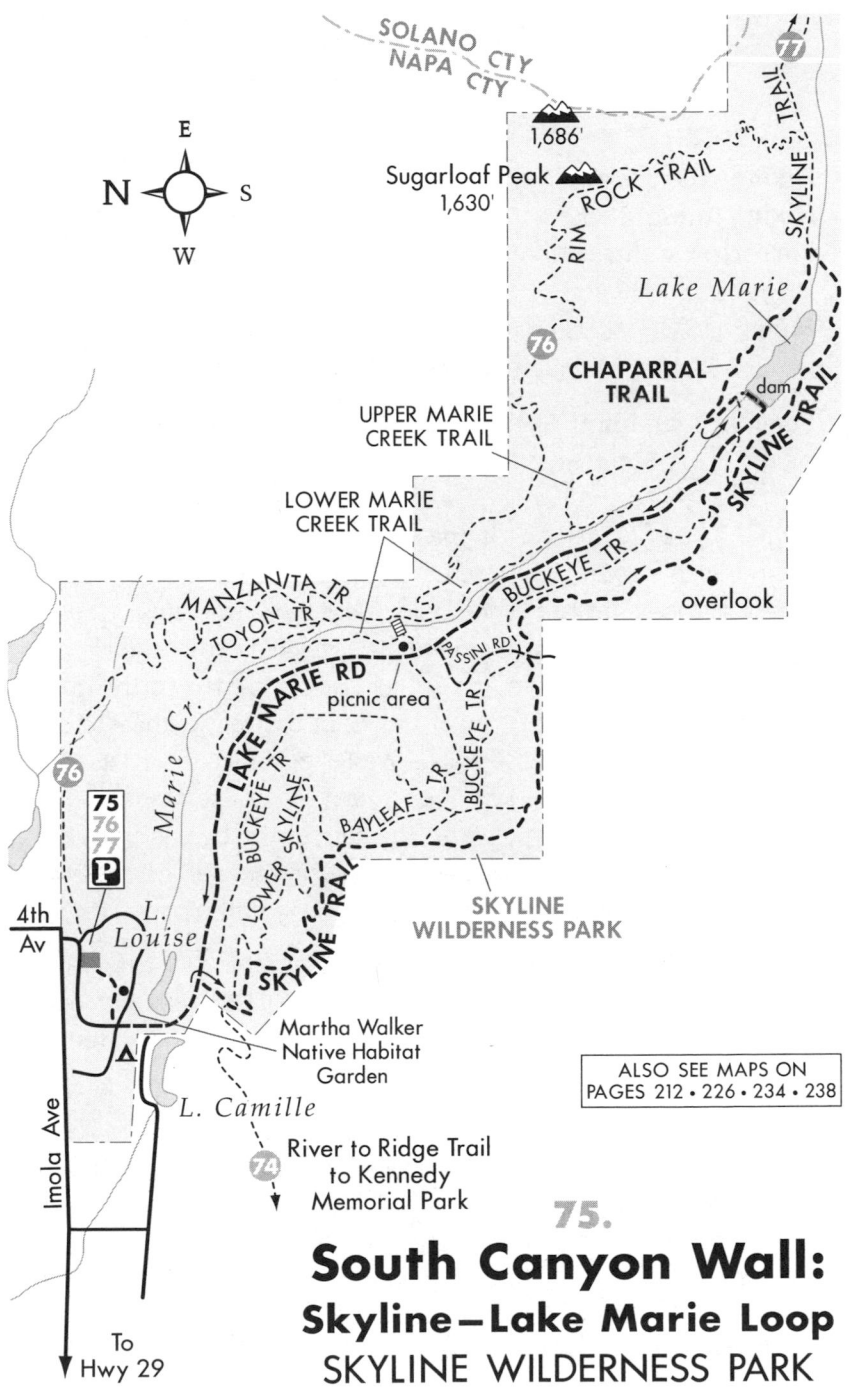

SOLANO CTY
NAPA CTY

N — E / S / W (compass)

1,686'

Sugarloaf Peak
1,630'

RIM ROCK TRAIL

SKYLINE TRAIL

Lake Marie

76

CHAPARRAL
TRAIL

dam

UPPER MARIE
CREEK TRAIL

SKYLINE TRAIL

LOWER MARIE
CREEK TRAIL

BUCKEYE TR.

overlook

MANZANITA TR.

TOYON TR.

PASSINI RD.

LAKE MARIE RD

picnic area

BUCKEYE TR.

Marie Cr.

76

75
76
77
P

BUCKEYE TR

BAYLEAF TR.

4th
Av

L.
Louise

LOWER SKYLINE TR.

SKYLINE TRAIL

SKYLINE
WILDERNESS PARK

Martha Walker
Native Habitat
Garden

Imola Ave

L. Camille

74

River to Ridge Trail
to Kennedy
Memorial Park

ALSO SEE MAPS ON
PAGES 212 · 226 · 234 · 238

To
Hwy 29

75.

South Canyon Wall:
Skyline–Lake Marie Loop
SKYLINE WILDERNESS PARK

76. Tuteur Loop
SKYLINE WILDERNESS PARK
2201 Imola Avenue · Napa

Hiking distance: 7.6-mile loop
Hiking time: 4.5 hours
Elevation gain: 900 feet
Dogs: not allowed
Maps: U.S.G.S. Napa and Mt. George
      Skyline Wilderness Park

**map
next page**

Summary of hike: Skyline Wilderness Park was formerly part of the Napa State Hospital, dating back to the 1870s. The park was opened to the public in 1980. John Tuteur was very instrumental in the formation of the volunteer-run park. The Tuteur family ranch covers 1,300 acres of open grasslands and scenic ridgetops adjacent to Skyline Wilderness Park. The family donated a trail easement through their cattle ranch, part of the Napa–Solano Ridge Trail System. The Tuteur Loop, opened to the public in 2005, is a 1.3-mile trail that begins at the far southeast corner of Skyline Wilderness Park above Lake Marie. This hike continues from the end of Hike 75, upstream from Lake Marie on the southern base of Sugarloaf Peak. The gate at the beginning of the Tuteur Loop is just past the park boundary. The trail follows the lush creekside corridor under oak trees hung with Spanish moss.

Driving directions: From Highway 29 in the city of Napa, drive 2.8 miles east on Imola Avenue to the posted park entrance. Turn right and park in the lot on the right. A parking fee is required.

Hiking directions: Follow the hiking directions for Hike 75 to the junction with the Chaparral Trail at 3.4 miles. The junction is upstream from Lake Marie, located 40 yards beyond crossing Marie Creek. Continue straight ahead (east) on the Skyline Trail. The trail follows along the north side of Marie Creek through a bay and alder forest to the posted Rim Rock Trail on the left. The Rim Rock Trail climbs to the summit of Sugarloaf Peak (Hike 77).

For this hike, follow the creek upstream. Skirt the forest along a grassy slope to a Y-fork with the Tuteur Loop Trail, a section of the future Napa–Solano Ridge Trail. Begin the 1.3-mile loop to the right, and cross a metal bridge over Marie Creek. Weave up the forested hillside and pass through a trail gate. Continue up the canyon to a fence at the east end of the loop. Zigzag down the slope on four switchbacks to a bridge at Marie Creek. Cross the bridge and curve west. Traverse the grassy slope bordered by an oak woodland. Pass through the Tuteur land gate and complete the loop. Return via Lake Marie Road (following the hiking directions of Hike 75), or via the Chaparral Trail and Marie Creek Trail (following the hiking directions of Hike 77).

The hike can be extended to include a climb to the 1,630-foot summit of Sugarloaf Peak. This trail is steep and the return is not recommended for the light hearted. To ascend the peak, take the Rim Rock Trail north and head up the hill, leaving the shade of the canyon to the exposed south-facing slope of Sugarloaf Peak. Zipper up the mountain at a steep grade, overlooking forested Marie Creek Canyon. The far-reaching vistas extend across the Napa–Sonoma Marshes and San Pablo Bay. Continue up a side canyon with a view of the communication towers of the mountain's east peak. Enter an oak and manzanita forest, climbing to the large rounded summit at one mile. Several paths loop around the summit. The paths were formed by animals and those in search of finding the best views through the oaks. The trail continues northwest and eventually joins the Manzanita Trail near Lake Marie Road. Or, retrace your steps back to the Skyline Trail in Marie Creek Canyon. ▪

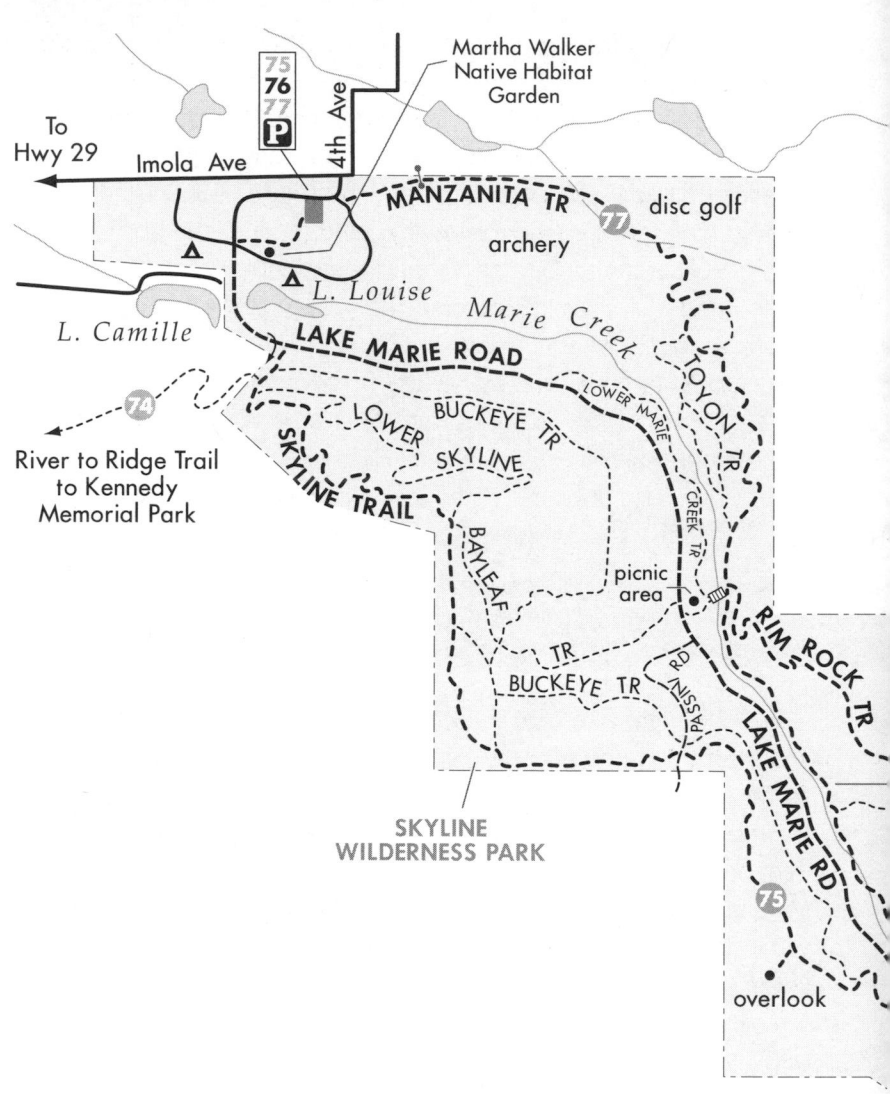

To Hwy 29

Imola Ave

4th Ave

75
76
77
P

Martha Walker Native Habitat Garden

MANZANITA TR

77 disc golf

archery

L. Louise

L. Camille

Marie Creek

LAKE MARIE ROAD

74

River to Ridge Trail to Kennedy Memorial Park

LOWER MARIE

TOYON TR

BUCKEYE TR

LOWER SKYLINE

SKYLINE TRAIL

BAYLEAF

CREEK TR

picnic area

RIM ROCK TR

TR

BUCKEYE TR

PASS IN

RD

LAKE MARIE RD

SKYLINE WILDERNESS PARK

75

overlook

ALSO SEE MAPS ON PAGES 212 • 231 • 238

76.
Tuteur Loop
SKYLINE WILDERNESS PARK

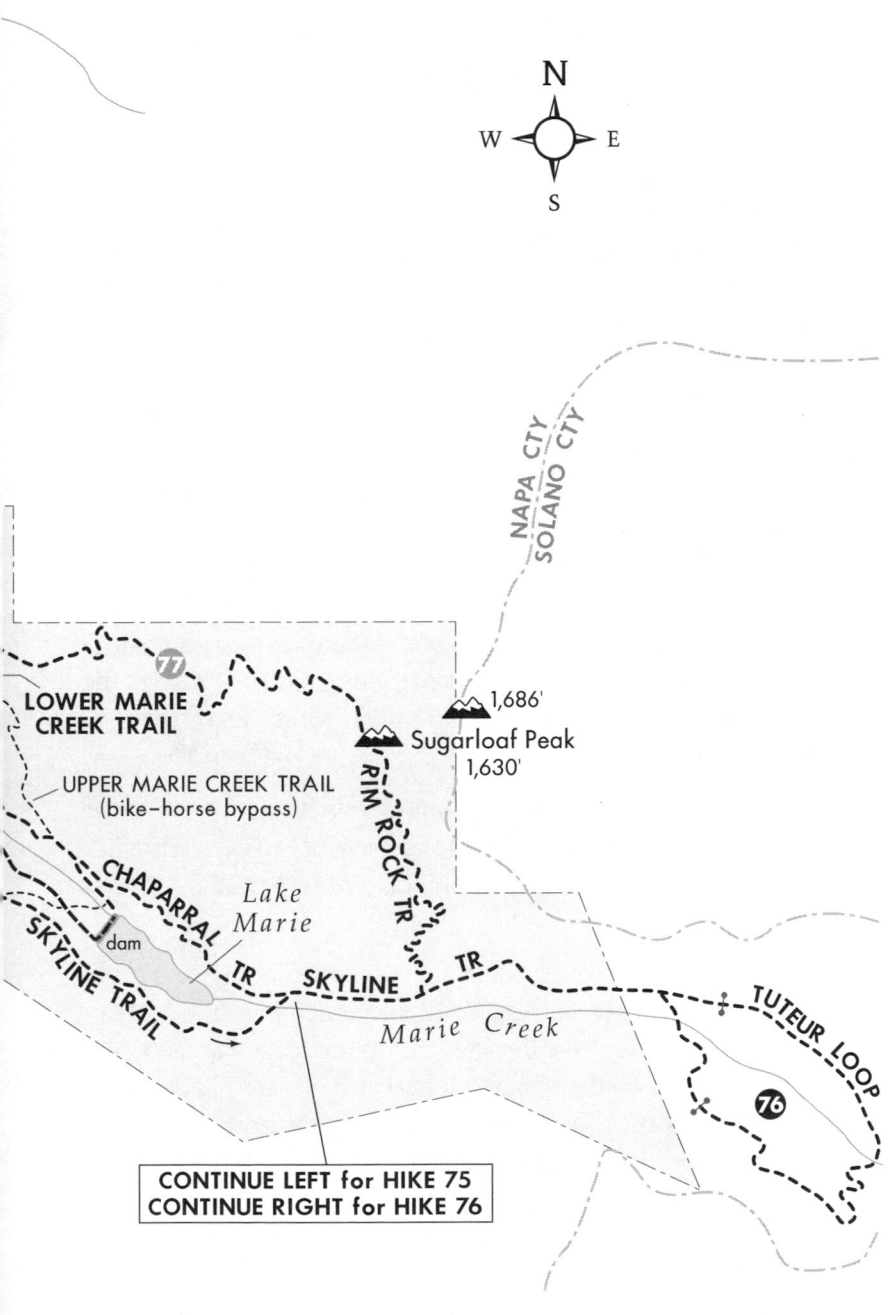

N
W · E
S

NAPA CTY
SOLANO CTY

LOWER MARIE CREEK TRAIL

1,686'

Sugarloaf Peak
1,630'

UPPER MARIE CREEK TRAIL
(bike–horse bypass)

RIM ROCK TR

CHAPARRAL TR

Lake Marie

SKYLINE TRAIL

dam

SKYLINE TR

Marie Creek

TUTEUR LOOP

76

**CONTINUE LEFT for HIKE 75
CONTINUE RIGHT for HIKE 76**

77. North Canyon Wall to Sugarloaf Peak: Manzanita—Rim Rock—Marie Creek Loop

SKYLINE WILDERNESS PARK

2201 Imola Avenue · Napa

Hiking distance: 7-mile loop
Hiking time: 4 hours
Elevation gain: 1,500 feet
Dogs: not allowed
Maps: U.S.G.S. Napa and Mt. George
Skyline Wilderness Park

map next page

Summary of hike: The Rim Rock Trail is the most scenic but also the most difficult trail in Skyline Wilderness Park. The trail follows the sinuous north ridge of Marie Creek Canyon to the 1,630-foot summit of Sugarloaf Peak, the park's highest peak. On clear days, the views extend to San Francisco Bay, Mount Tamalpais, and Mount Diablo. This hike utilizes the Rim Rock Trail to Sugarloaf Peak, then returns through the canyon on the exposed south-facing slope. Along the trail are the best views of Lake Marie. The return loop continues under a lush riparian forest with towering alder and bay trees.

Driving directions: From Highway 29 in the city of Napa, drive 2.8 miles east on Imola Avenue to the posted park entrance. Turn right and park in the lot on the right. A parking fee is required.

Hiking directions: Head back to the entrance kiosk, and cross the open grassland to the posted Manzanita Trail at the archery range and fenceline. Walk through the gated opening, and skirt the archery range on the right. Descend into an oak-filled canyon to a picnic area by a seasonal stream. Cross a bridge over the drainage and head upstream on the north side of the waterway. Pass a disc-golf course on the left and stroll through the rolling terrain. Cross a bridge over a rock-walled drainage, and head up the foothills on a series of switchbacks to a Y-fork. The two routes form a loop, with the bikers' bypass route to the left and the hikers-only route to the right. The hikers-only route leads to an overlook with views across the city of Napa, then to a posted junction with the Toyon Trail. Stay left on the Manzanita Trail, passing old man-made rock walls. Descend past a second junction with the Toyon Trail to a 4-way junction at a bridge crossing over Marie Creek. Across the bridge is a picnic area with a large fig tree and Lake Marie Road. The Marie Creek Trail continues straight ahead.

Begin the loop and bear left on the Rim Rock Trail. Walk through groves of manzanita and oak trees. Traverse the hillside on a gradual uphill grade. Zigzag up the hill as the grade steepens and offers views into forested Marie Creek Canyon. Follow the contours of the north canyon wall, and curve left into a shaded side canyon. Climb a series of ten switchbacks to the ridge with vistas stretching across Napa Valley, from Calistoga and Mount St. Helena to San Pablo Bay and Mount Tamalpais. Follow the ridge among the oaks, with a view of the communication towers on the east peak of Sugarloaf Peak. The trail levels out on the grassy, oak-covered knoll atop the west summit of Sugarloaf Peak. After resting, continue across the knoll and begin the descent. Some very steep sections contain loose gravel. Use caution! Zipper down the mountain on 23 switchbacks amid reddish volcanic rock. The trail ends at a T-junction with the Skyline Trail in the lush canyon bottom at Marie Creek. The left fork leads to the Tuteur Loop (Hike 76)

Bear right and follow the north side of the creek downstream in the mossy, tree-shaded canyon. Forty yards shy of the Marie Creek crossing, leave the Skyline Trail and veer right on the signed Chaparral Trail. Traverse the south-facing slope, and climb to a perch overlooking Lake Marie. Continue northwest and slowly descend to a junction past the lake, where the Chaparral Trail ends. The left fork leads a short distance to the Lake Marie Dam, built in 1908, and Lake Marie Road. Stay to the right on the Marie Creek Trail to a signed junction with the Upper and Lower Marie Creek Trails. The upper trail allows horses and bikes. The Lower trail is for hikers only. Both routes merge up ahead. Bear left on

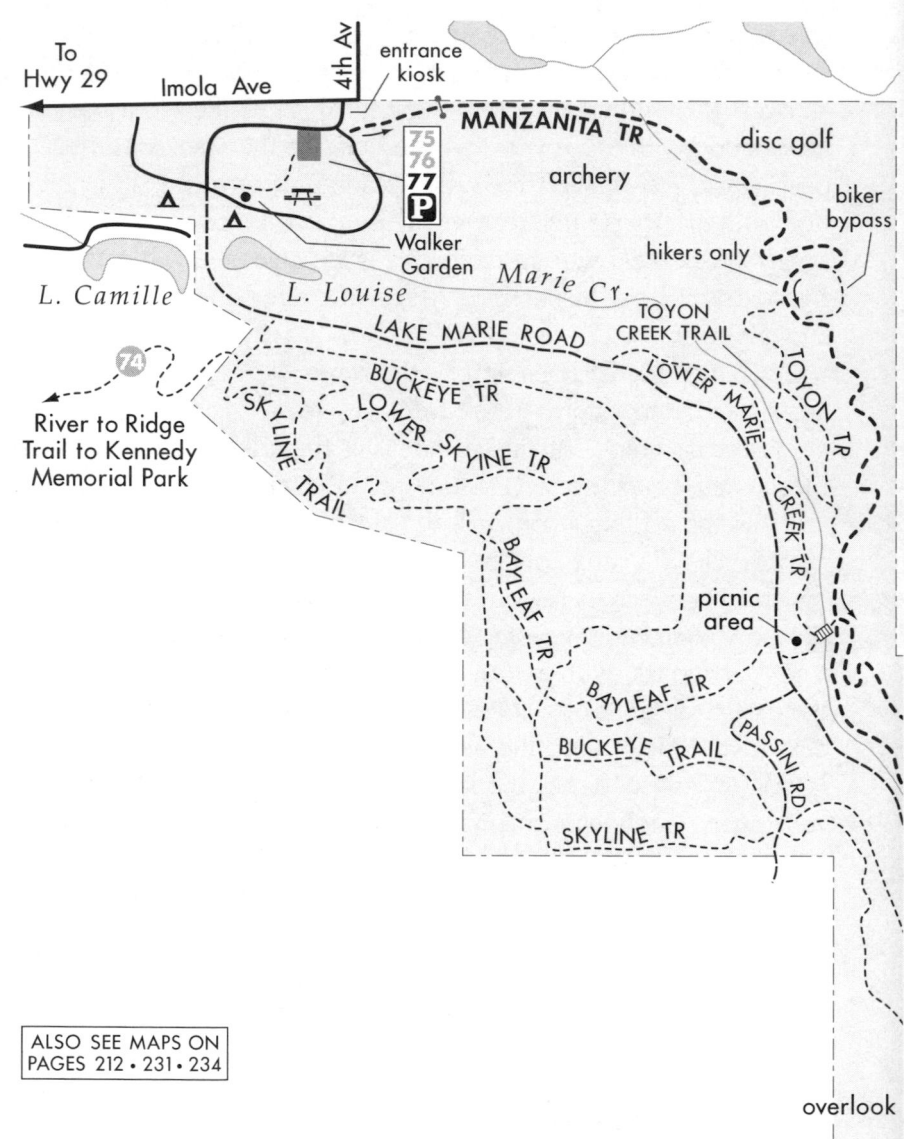

To
Hwy 29 Imola Ave 4th Av entrance kiosk

MANZANITA TR disc golf

archery

biker bypass

75
76
77
P

Walker Garden Marie Cr. hikers only

L. Camille L. Louise LAKE MARIE ROAD TOYON CREEK TRAIL

River to Ridge Trail to Kennedy Memorial Park

BUCKEYE TR LOWER MARIE

SKYLINE TRAIL LOWER SKYLINE TR TOYON TR

CREEK TR

BAYLEAF TR picnic area

BAYLEAF TR

BUCKEYE TRAIL PASSINI RD

SKYLINE TR

ALSO SEE MAPS ON
PAGES 212 · 231 · 234

overlook

77.
North Canyon Wall:
Manzanita—Rim Rock—Marie Creek Loop
to Sugarloaf Peak
SKYLINE WILDERNESS PARK

the Lower Marie Creek Trail, and descend through the lush forest with 100-foot alder trees to the banks of the creek. Rock-hop over the creek, and continue downstream among ferns and mossy rocks. Recross Marie Creek and merge with the Upper Trail. Cross the creek two more times, and complete the loop at the bridge by the Rim Rock—Manzanita Trail junction. To return, either cross the wooden footbridge over Marie Creek to Lake Marie Road and return to the right, or retrace your steps on the Manzanita Trail.■

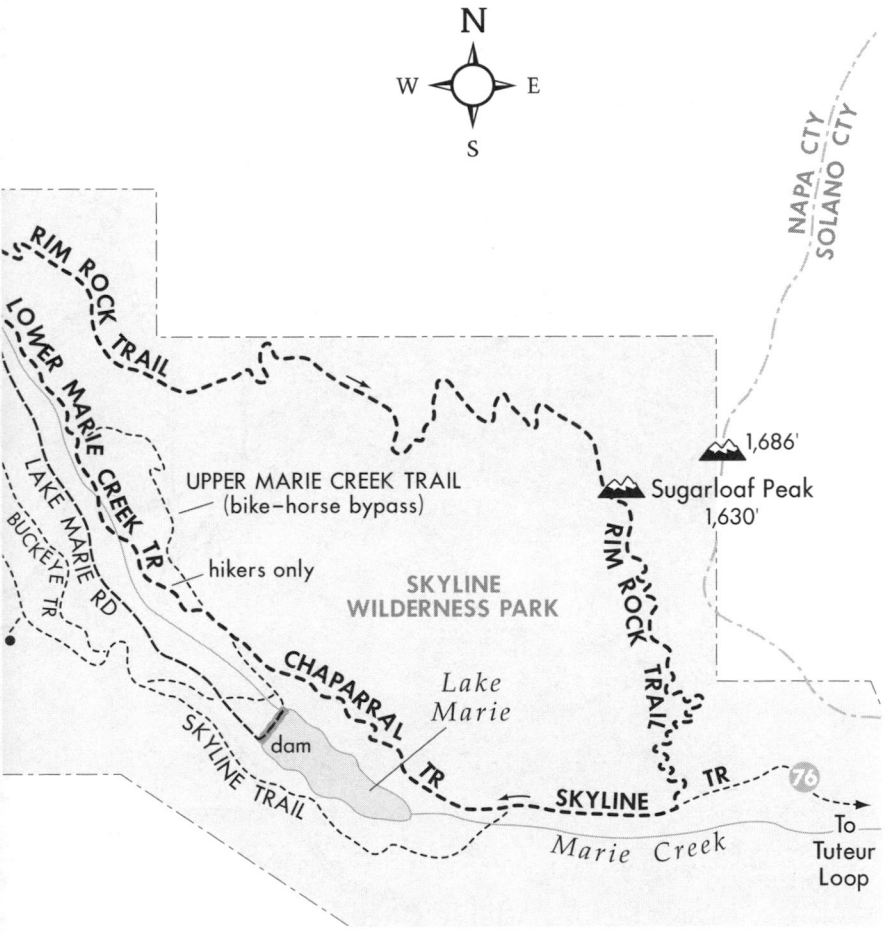

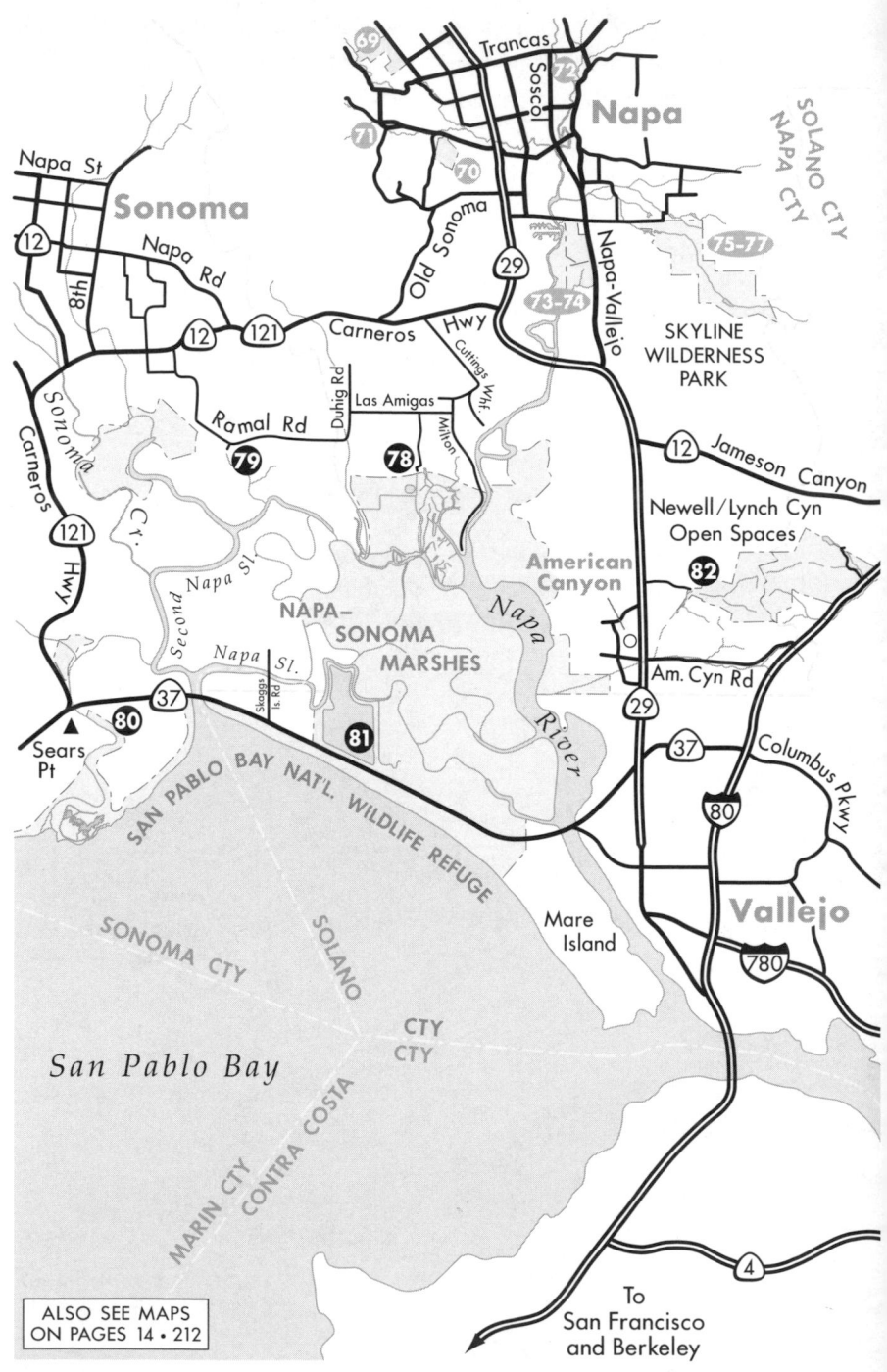

ALSO SEE MAPS
ON PAGES 14 • 212

HIKES 78–88

South of Napa Valley

NAPA–SONOMA MARSHES to SUISUN BAY

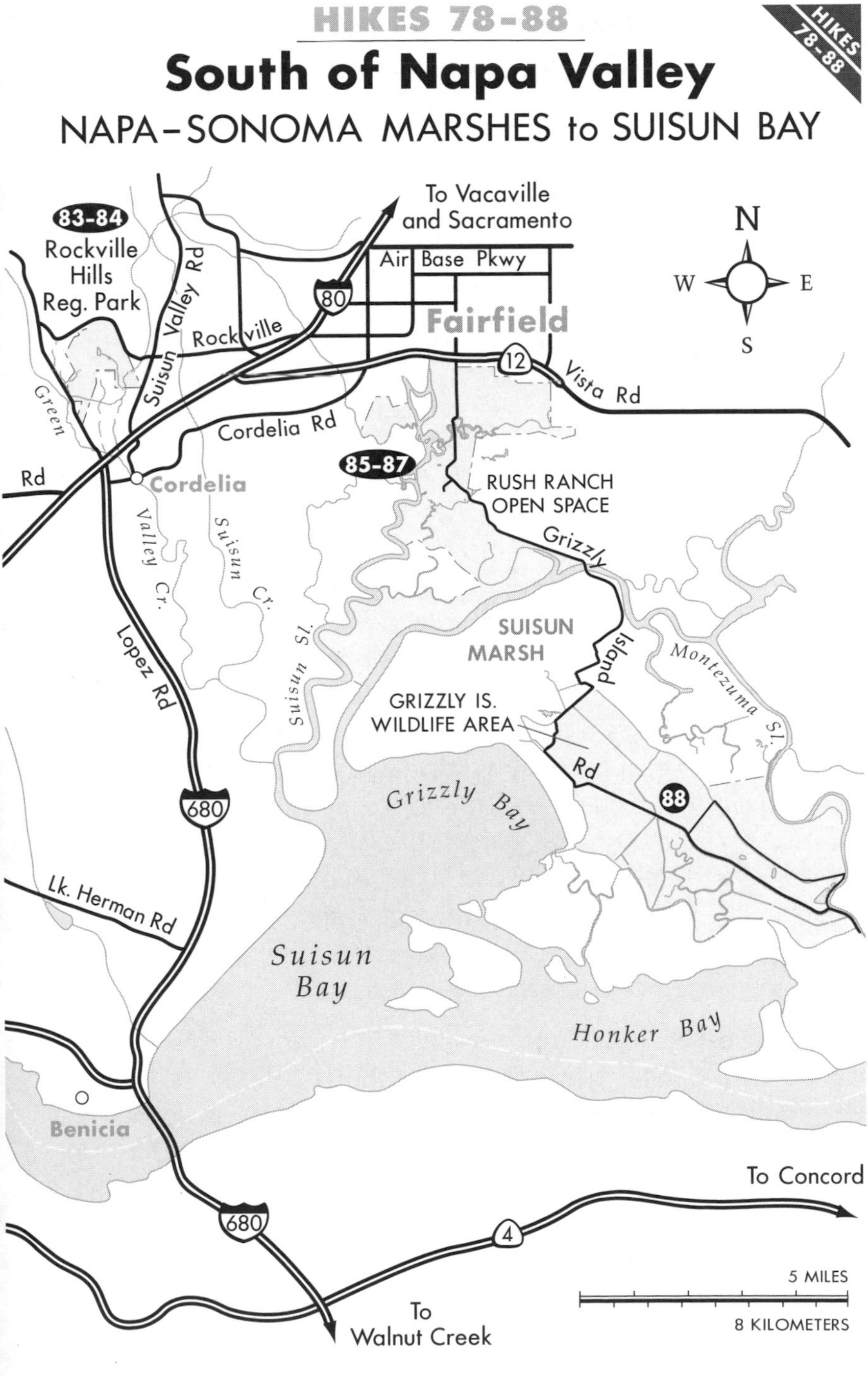
HIKES 78-88
To Vacaville and Sacramento
N
W
E
S
83-84
Rockville Hills Reg. Park
Suisun Valley Rd
Air Base Pkwy
80
Fairfield
Rockville
12
Vista Rd
Green
Cordelia Rd
85-87
Rd
Cordelia
RUSH RANCH OPEN SPACE
Valley Cr.
Suisun Cr.
Grizzly
Lopez Rd
SUISUN MARSH
Island
Montezuma Sl.
Suisun Sl.
GRIZZLY IS. WILDLIFE AREA
Rd
88
680
Grizzly Bay
Lk. Herman Rd
Suisun Bay
Honker Bay
Benicia
To Concord
680
4
5 MILES
8 KILOMETERS
To Walnut Creek

78. Huichica Creek Unit
NAPA—SONOMA MARSHES WILDLIFE AREA

Hiking distance: Hike 1: 1—3 miles round trip
Hike 2: 1.3-mile loop
Hiking time: 1—2 hours
Elevation gain: Level
Dogs: allowed
Maps: U.S.G.S. Cuttings Wharf
Napa-Sonoma Marshes Wildlife Area map

Summary of hike: The Napa—Sonoma Marsh covers 48,000 acres on the north edge of San Pablo Bay. The marsh lies between Highway 12 on the north and Highway 37 on the south, straddling Napa, Sonoma, and Solano counties. Within the marsh are saltwater ponds, tidal marshes, seasonally flooded wetlands, agricultural fields, sloughs, and rivers. The rich wetland is fed by the Napa River, which drains Napa Valley, and Sonoma Creek, which drains Sonoma Valley. It is an important habitat for fish, shorebirds, and waterfowl and is a premier place to observe wildlife. The tidal marsh was diked for agricultural uses in the late 1800s and early 1900s. In the early 1950s the Leslie Salt Company purchased much of the land and developed it for salt production.

Hikes 76 through 78 access the Napa—Sonoma Marshes Wildlife Area from northern and southern points. This hike leads through the north end of the wetlands in the 808-acre Huichica Creek area. Two paths follow the levees above mudflats, a 300-acre salt pond, water channels, and grasslands.

Driving directions: From Highway 29, two miles south of Napa, drive 2.4 miles west on Highway 12/121 (Carneros Highway) toward Sonoma to Duhig Road. Turn left and continue 2.2 miles to Las Amigas Road. Turn left on Duhig Road, and go 1.3 miles to Buchli Station Road. Turn right and drive 1.2 miles to the trailhead parking lot at the end of the road, just south of the railroad tracks.

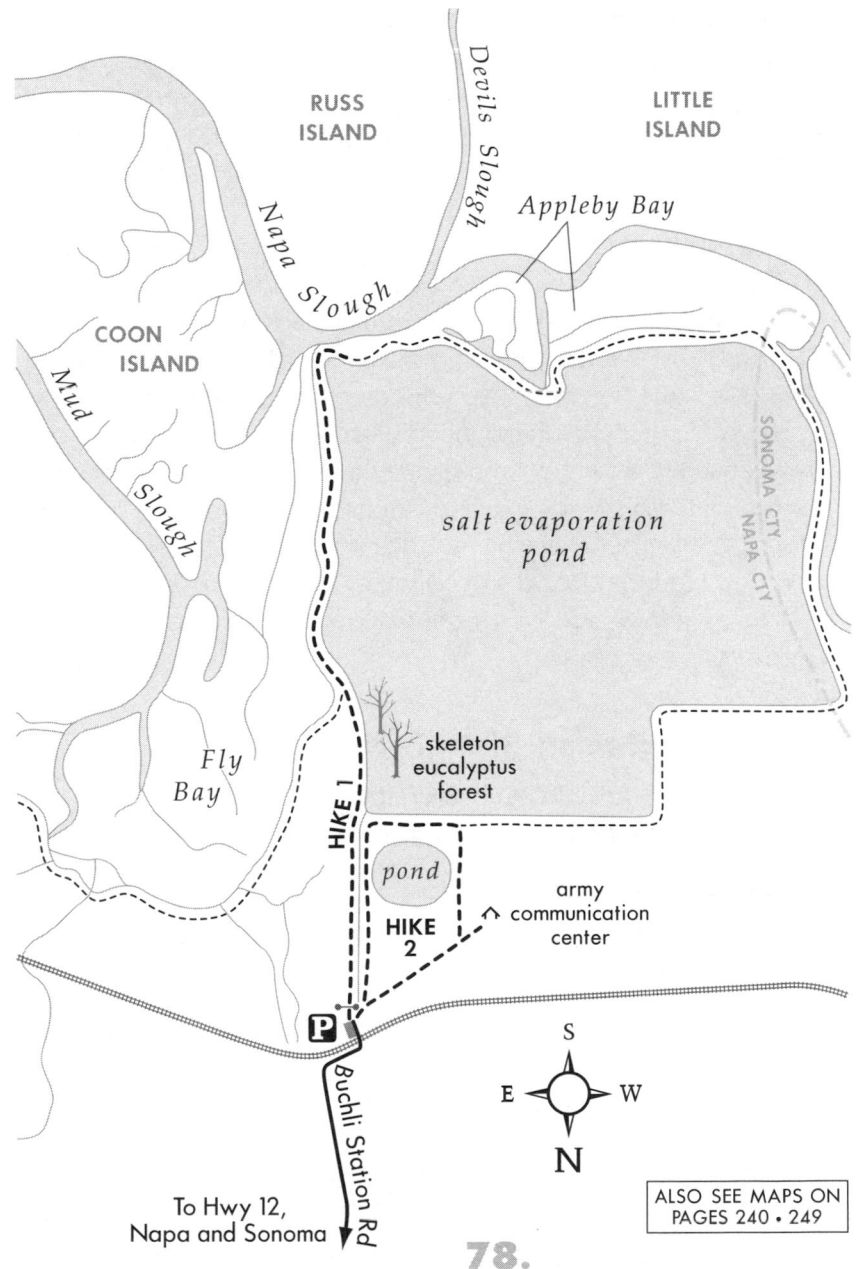

RUSS ISLAND

LITTLE ISLAND

Devils Slough

Appleby Bay

Napa Slough

COON ISLAND

Mud Slough

SONOMA CTY
NAPA CTY

salt evaporation pond

Fly Bay

HIKE 1

skeleton eucalyptus forest

pond

HIKE 2

army communication center

P

Buchli Station Rd

To Hwy 12, Napa and Sonoma

S
E — W
N

ALSO SEE MAPS ON PAGES 240 • 249

78.
Huichica Creek Unit
NAPA–SONOMA MARSHES WILDLIFE AREA

Hiking directions: HIKE 1. Walk south past the yellow gate on the wide gravel levee. Stroll through the wetlands, passing water channels, mudflats, and ponds. At a half mile, follow the east edge of a 300-acre pond with a row of dead eucalyptus trees along the eastern edge of the pond. Once used as salt evaporation ponds, the grove of bare tree trunks are the result of the high saltwater content. This area forms the upper ponds of the Napa River Unit at the southern end of the Napa—Sonoma Marsh. The levee passes Fly Bay on the east and leads to Napa Slough at 1.5 miles. The views extend across the flatlands to Mount Tamalpais in the west. Choose your own turn around point

HIKE 2. From the trailhead, head west along the north edge of the wetland to a junction at a quarter mile. Detour straight ahead to the old bunker, an old army communication center during World War II. After checking out the structure, return to the junction. Head south and loop around the reed-filled pond. Curve left and follow the west edge of the water channel, returning to the trailhead.■

79. Hudeman Slough Nature Trail
RINGSTROM BAY UNIT of the
NAPA—SONOMA MARSHES WILDLIFE AREA

Hiking distance: 2.5-mile loop
Hiking time: 1.5 hours
Elevation gain: Level
Dogs: allowed
Maps: U.S.G.S. Sears Point
Napa-Sonoma Marshes Wildlife Area map

Summary of hike: The Napa—Sonoma Marshes Wildlife Area encompasses over 13,000 acres of mainly abandoned salt evaporation ponds. The high salt content in the ponds killed the trees, leaving visible skeleton forests. The ponds are part of an extensive restoration program that is in the early stages of development. The goal of the restoration effort is to reclaim former tidal marshes that were diked many years ago.

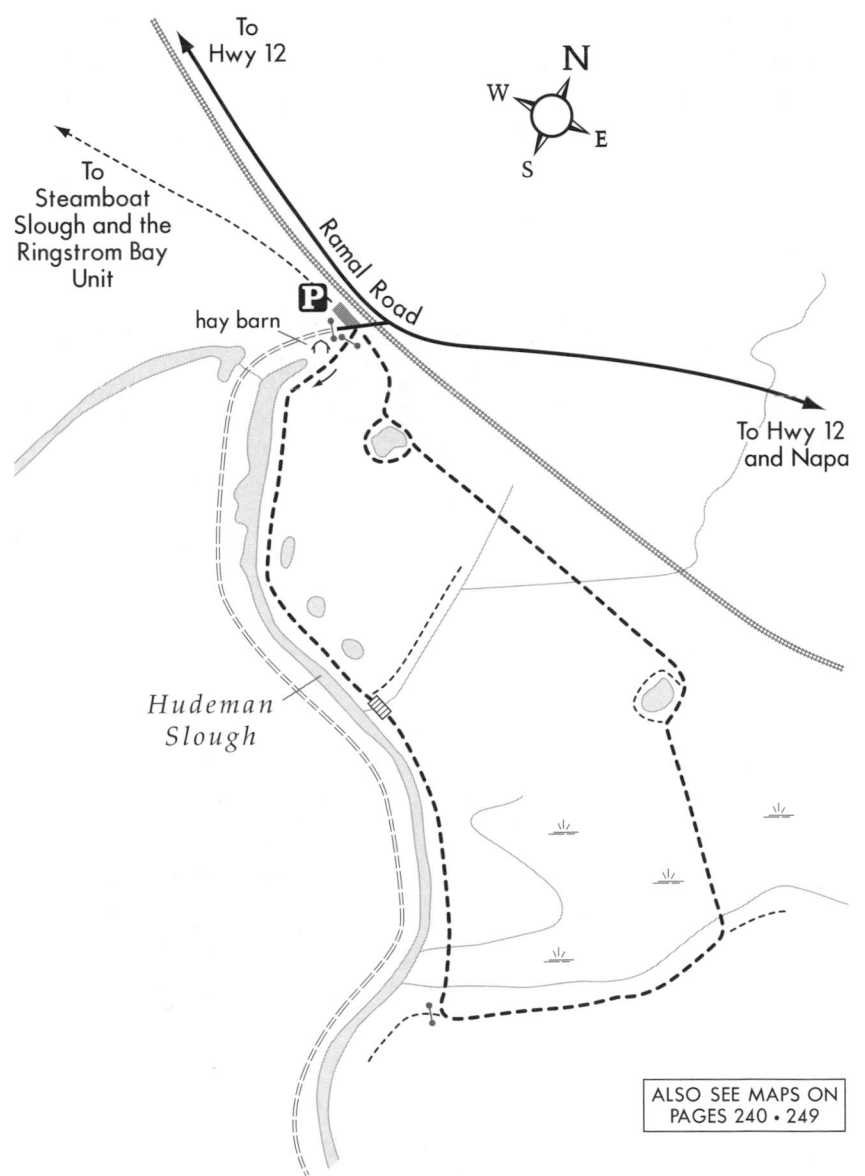

To Hwy 12

N
W · E
S

To Steamboat Slough and the Ringstrom Bay Unit

Ramal Road

P

hay barn

To Hwy 12 and Napa

Hudeman Slough

ALSO SEE MAPS ON
PAGES 240 · 249

79.
Hudeman Slough Nature Trail
RINGSTROM BAY UNIT of the
NAPA–SONOMA MARSHES WILDLIFE AREA

The sizeable expanse of marshland is a productive estuarine ecosystem, providing habitat for millions of birds. It is an important wintering habitat for Pacific Flyway waterfowl. Most of the wildlife area is accessible only by boat or footpaths. Levees offer foot access and are regularly used by fisherman, hunters, photographers, bird watchers, bikers, boaters, and hikers. This hike loops through Hudeman Slough on the north end of the wildlife area.

Driving directions: From Highway 29, two miles south of Napa, drive 2.4 miles west on Highway 12 (Carneros Highway) toward Sonoma to Duhig Road. Turn left on Duhig Road, and continue 5 miles to the large metal hay barn on the left. (En route, Duhig Road becomes Ramal Road.) Turn left and park in the lot on the right.

Hiking directions: From the access gate at the east end of the parking lot, follow the grassy berm on the edge of Hudeman Slough. Gradually curve left following the curvature of the slough. Pass a series of ponds on the left to a footbridge at a half mile. Cross the bridge and curve right on the levee, savoring the expansive vistas. At a 90-degree bend, bear left and leave the banks of Hudeman Slough. Parallel a wide water channel on the left and agricultural fields on the right to a junction. Bear left and follow the levee between the wetlands. Walk up the grassy slope to a pond in a berm-lined basin. Go to the right and circle the pond counter clockwise to its north end. Descend to the dirt road and continue west. Climb a small rise to another pond and a Y-fork that circles the pond. Take either route, circling the pond to the northwest corner. Descend and parallel the railroad tracks 200 yards to the trailhead.

To extend the hike, from the west end of the parking lot, a trail leads 3 miles to Sonoma Creek and the 408-acre Ringstrom Bay Unit of the Napa–Sonoma Marshes Wildlife Area. The path leads 0.8 miles to a levee on the edge of the Steamboat Slough wetlands, passing an information kiosk and following a grassy path west past ponds and a major water channel from Steamboat Slough. The levees continue to Railroad Slough and Sonoma Creek. ■

80. Napa River Unit
NAPA—SONOMA MARSHES WILDLIFE AREA

Hiking distance: 2.4 miles round trip
Hiking time: 1 hour
Elevation gain: Level
Dogs: not allowed between March 2—June 30
Maps: U.S.G.S. Cuttings Wharf
Napa-Sonoma Marshes Wildlife Area map

map
next page

Summary of hike: This hike begins at the north edge of San Pablo Bay—the northern arm of San Francisco Bay—in the expansive Napa—Sonoma Marsh. The wetland habitat is located primarily between the Napa River and Sonoma Creek where they drain into San Pablo Bay. The trail follows a levee from the south end of the wildlife area through seasonal freshwater marshes and tidal salt marshes. This land was originally diked for hay and grain production. The area is now part of the former salt pond system. The Leslie Salt Company flooded the diked islands in the early 1950s for salt production.

The hike offers easy waterfowl and shorebird observation, a wide diversity of flora and fauna, and unobstructed vistas of the surrounding mountains.

Driving directions: From Highway 29 in Napa, drive 11 miles south on Highway 29 to Highway 37 (Sears Point Road). Curve right onto Highway 37, and drive 6 miles west to the large pull-out on the right by an 8-foot-high chain link fence. The pullout is located 3.6 miles west of the bridge over the Napa River.

Hiking directions: Walk through the trailhead gate, and head north on the gravel levee. Follow a water channel on the right and a massive pond on the left. The 360-degree vistas include the Mayacamas Range in Napa County, the Sonoma Mountain Range in Sonoma County, Mount Tamalpais in Marin County, and Mount Diablo in Contra Costa County. At 1.2 miles, the trail crosses under power lines, just before reaching South Slough. The trail north of the towers is closed to hunting, fishing, and hiking. ■

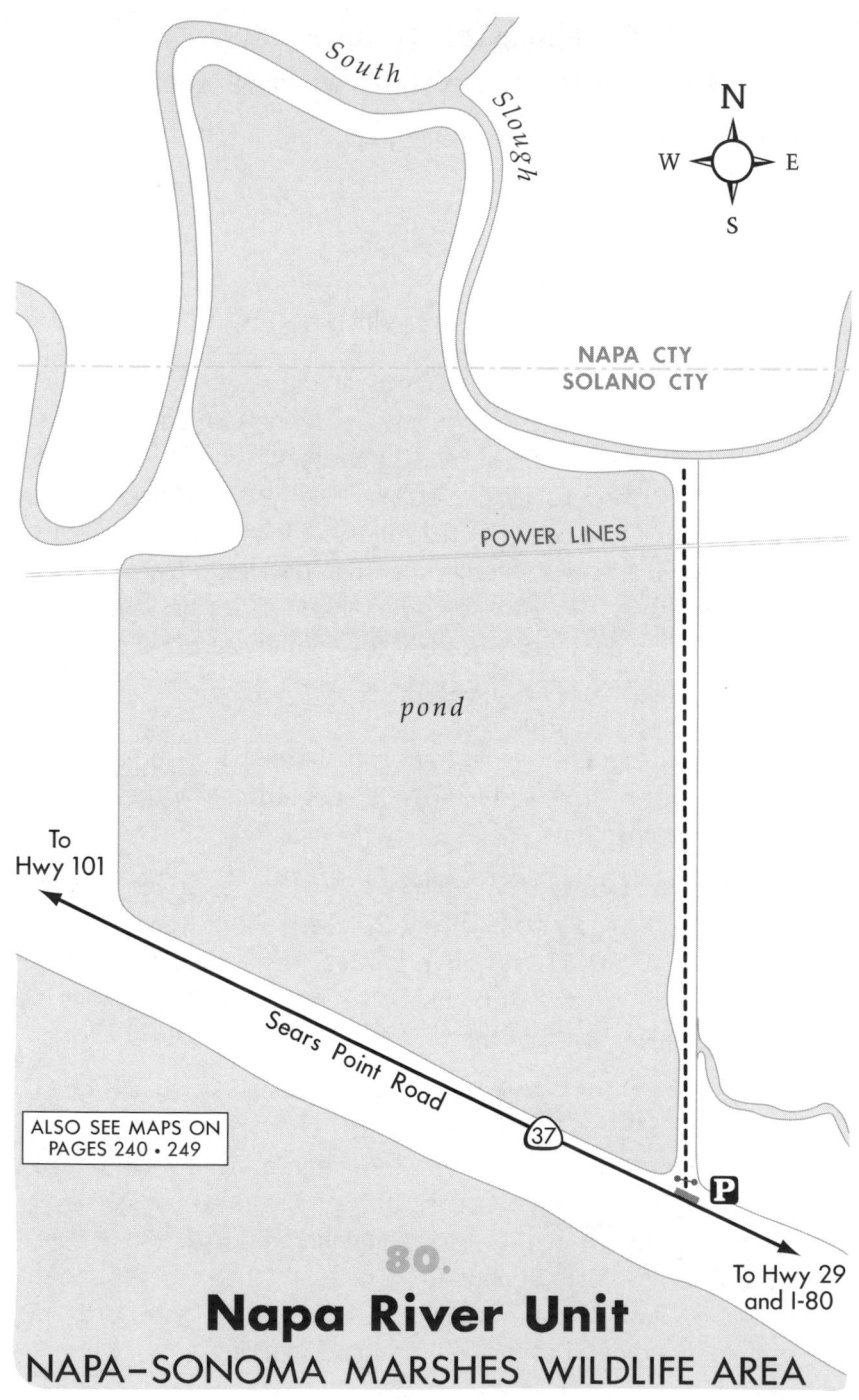

South Slough

N
W E
S

NAPA CTY
SOLANO CTY

POWER LINES

pond

To
Hwy 101

Sears Point Road

37

ALSO SEE MAPS ON
PAGES 240 • 249

P

To Hwy 29
and I-80

80.
Napa River Unit
NAPA–SONOMA MARSHES WILDLIFE AREA

Additional Trailheads
NAPA–SONOMA MARSHES WILDLIFE AREA

TOLAY CREEK UNIT (WEST ACCESS): The 350-acre Tolay Creek Unit of the Napa–Sonoma Marshes Wildlife Area is located off of Highway 121 (Carneros Highway) between Highway 12 and Highway 37. The turnoff is on the east side of the road. It is located 5.6 miles south of the Highway 12/Highway 116 junction and 0.9 miles north of Highway 37. From the turnoff, drive 0.4 miles east on the dirt road to the parking lot and grassland on the right.

WINGO UNIT (NORTHWEST ACCESS): The 782-acre Wingo Unit of the Napa–Sonoma Marshes Wildlife Area is located off of Highway 12/121 (Carneros Highway). From the junction of Highway 116 and Highway 12/121, drive 0.8 miles east on Highway 12/121 to Millerick Road and turn south. Continue 1.7 miles, passing through a winery, to the trailhead parking lot. The road follows the contours of Sonoma Creek. During the winter and spring months, this access road contains pools of water. Driving to the trailhead during this time is not advised. ∎

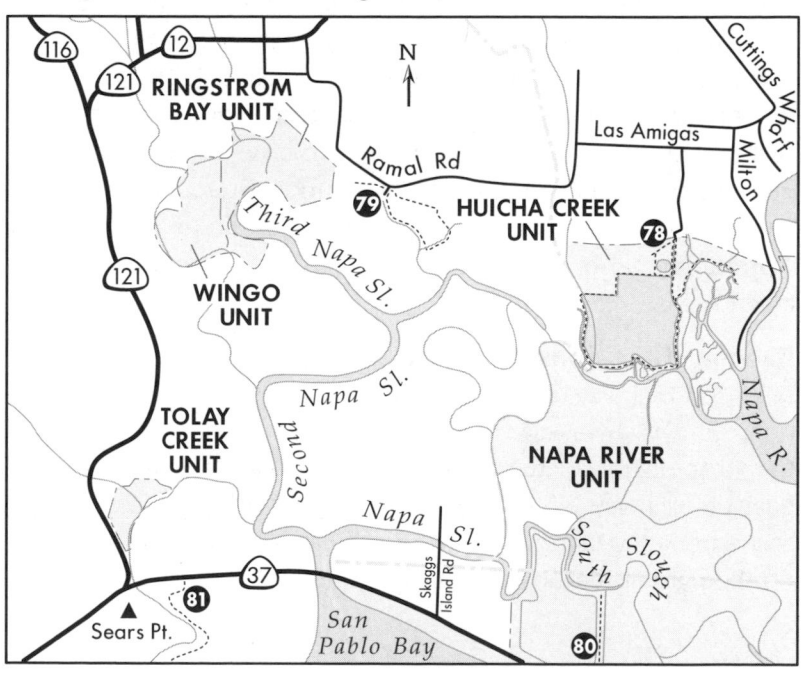

81. San Pablo Bay National Wildlife Refuge
Lower Tubbs Island • Tolay Creek

Hiking distance: 5.5—8 miles round trip
Hiking time: 3—5 hours
Elevation gain: Level
Dogs: not allowed past picnic area
Maps: U.S.G.S. Sears Point and Petaluma Point

Summary of hike: San Pablo Bay National Wildlife Refuge lies along San Pablo Bay at the northern reaches of San Francisco Bay. The wildlife refuge encompasses 13,000 acres between the mouth of the Petaluma River and Mare Island by Vallejo. The refuge includes tidal wetlands, mud flats, salt marshes, and open water. Numerous waterways drain through the surrounding terrain, including the Napa River, Petaluma River, Sonoma Creek, Tolay Creek, and many sloughs. The waterways are interspersed with grasslands, oak woodlands, and agricultural fields. Lower Tubbs Island, near Tolay Creek, is the most accessible portion of the national wildlife refuge, luring bird watchers, wildlife photographers, and hikers. Lower Tubbs Island Bird Sanctuary is a 332-acre preserve within the refuge. It is a sanctuary for migrating birds, waterfowl, and shorebirds. This trail follows a dirt levee 2.75 miles to the bird sanctuary on Lower Tubbs Island, then continues another 1.5 miles to Midshipman Point at the tip of the open waters. The terrain is flat, exposed, and windswept with wide open vistas.

Driving directions: From Highway 29 in Napa, drive 11 miles south on Highway 29 to Highway 37 (Sears Point Road). Curve right onto Highway 37, and drive 12 miles to Highway 121 (the Carneros Highway). Turn around and return to the left, heading east on Highway 37. Drive 0.7 miles, crossing over Tolay Creek and skirting the lagoon, to the first right turn. Turn right and park on the right at the posted trailhead.

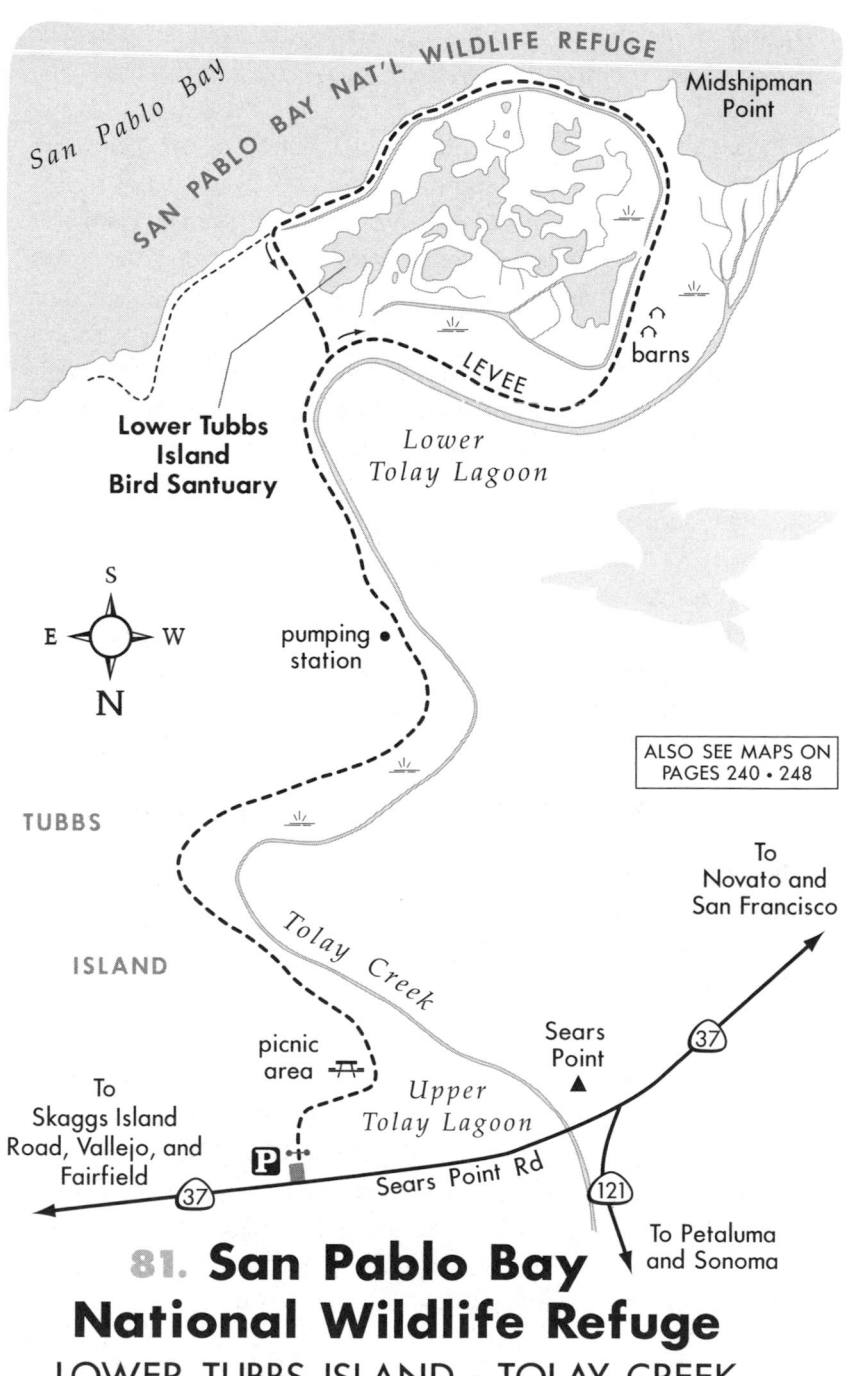

San Pablo Bay

San Pablo Bay Nat'l Wildlife Refuge

SAN PABLO BAY NAT'L WILDLIFE REFUGE

Midshipman Point

LEVEE

barns

Lower Tubbs Island Bird Santuary

Lower Tolay Lagoon

S
E ← → W
N

pumping station

ALSO SEE MAPS ON PAGES 240 • 248

TUBBS

ISLAND

Tolay Creek

To Novato and San Francisco

37

Sears Point

picnic area

Upper Tolay Lagoon

To Skaggs Island Road, Vallejo, and Fairfield

P

37

Sears Point Rd

121

To Petaluma and Sonoma

81. **San Pablo Bay National Wildlife Refuge**
LOWER TUBBS ISLAND • TOLAY CREEK

Hiking directions: Pass the trailhead gate and map panel on the dirt road. Follow the levee of Tolay Creek south along the edge of the wetlands and agricultural fields. At 0.4 miles curve left, passing a picnic area with an information map on the left. Continue southeast and bend right, with views of Mount Tamalpais and Mount Diablo in the distance. A parallel path follows the top of the levee on the right overlooking the Tolay Creek Lagoon. At 1.6 miles, veer left and pass a metal pumping station on the left. Continue southeast to a trail split at 2.3 miles by an information kiosk, the viewing area, and the entrance into the Lower Tubbs Island Bird Sanctuary. Begin the loop to the right between Lower Tolay Lagoon and Lower Tubbs Island, surrounded by tidal sloughs and salt marshes. Pass a group of red barns on the right, and curve left to the mouth of Tolay Creek. Follow the edge of San Pablo Bay on the levee road, where there is a view of Midshipman Point (the obvious promontory) and the mouth of the Petaluma River. At the east end of Lower Tubbs Island is a road split. Stay to the left along the Tubbs Island setback and complete the loop. Return to the right.■

82. Newell Open Space Preserve

Hiking distance: 5-mile loop
Hiking time: 2.5 hours
Elevation gain: 700 feet
Dogs: allowed
Maps: U.S.G.S. Cordelia

> map
> next page

Summary of hike: Newell Open Space Preserve encompasses 640 acres in the eastern hills above the city of American Canyon. The land stretches from American Canyon to the Solano County line, connecting with Lynch Canyon Open Space in Solano County. In 1999, Jack and Bernice Newell donated the ranchland to the city to preserve the hillsides, protect wildlife, and offer outdoor recreation to the public. The land is a raptor migration resting area and forms a protected wildlife corridor of 10,000 acres, extending eastward to Suisun Marsh. The preserve contains rolling grasslands, coast live oak, and bay laurel woodlands. Cattle still graze on the property. Dirt roads and footpaths, open to hikers, bikers, and equestrians, weave through the hills.

To access the property, a key to two entrance gates is needed. The key, along with a trail map, can be picked up at the American Canyon Community Services Department (address and driving directions below).

Driving directions: TO OBTAIN THE ACCESS KEY TO THE PRESERVE: From Highway 29 and American Canyon Road in American Canyon, drive 0.5 miles west on American Canyon Road to Elliott Drive. Turn right and go 0.3 miles to Benton Way. Turn left and continue a short distance to the American Canyon Community Services Department in the Aquatic Center building on the right at 100 Benton Way. The department's phone number is (707) 648-7275. See map on page 255.

TO THE TRAILHEAD: After getting the key, return to American Canyon Road and Highway 29. Turn left on Highway 29, and drive 1.3 miles north to Napa Junction Road. Turn right and drive 0.5 miles on a narrow dirt road (crossing over railroad tracks en route) to the entrance gate. Unlock the gate, drive through, and relock the gate. Continue up the slope, passing old barns, and veer to the right at a Y-fork, reaching the trailhead gate 0.4 miles ahead. Park to the side of the road.

Hiking directions: Unlock the gate and walk up through the open, rolling grassland. The wide, grassy path passes an old barn and skirts the south edge of the grasslands. Parallel an oak forest and a seasonal stream on the right to a junction at 0.6 miles. Begin the loop to the right, and cross over the seasonal drainage. Climb a slope and pass through another gate. The trail continues ascending, completely surrounded by the rolling hills. Pass a small pond on the left side of the trail to a Y-fork at 1.3 miles. For a shorter 4.1-mile hike, bear left, staying on the Newell Loop. For this hike, stay to the right. Climb to the ridge and the signed Prairie Ridge Trail. The ridge is on the boundary of Lynch Canyon

82.
Newell Open Space Preserve

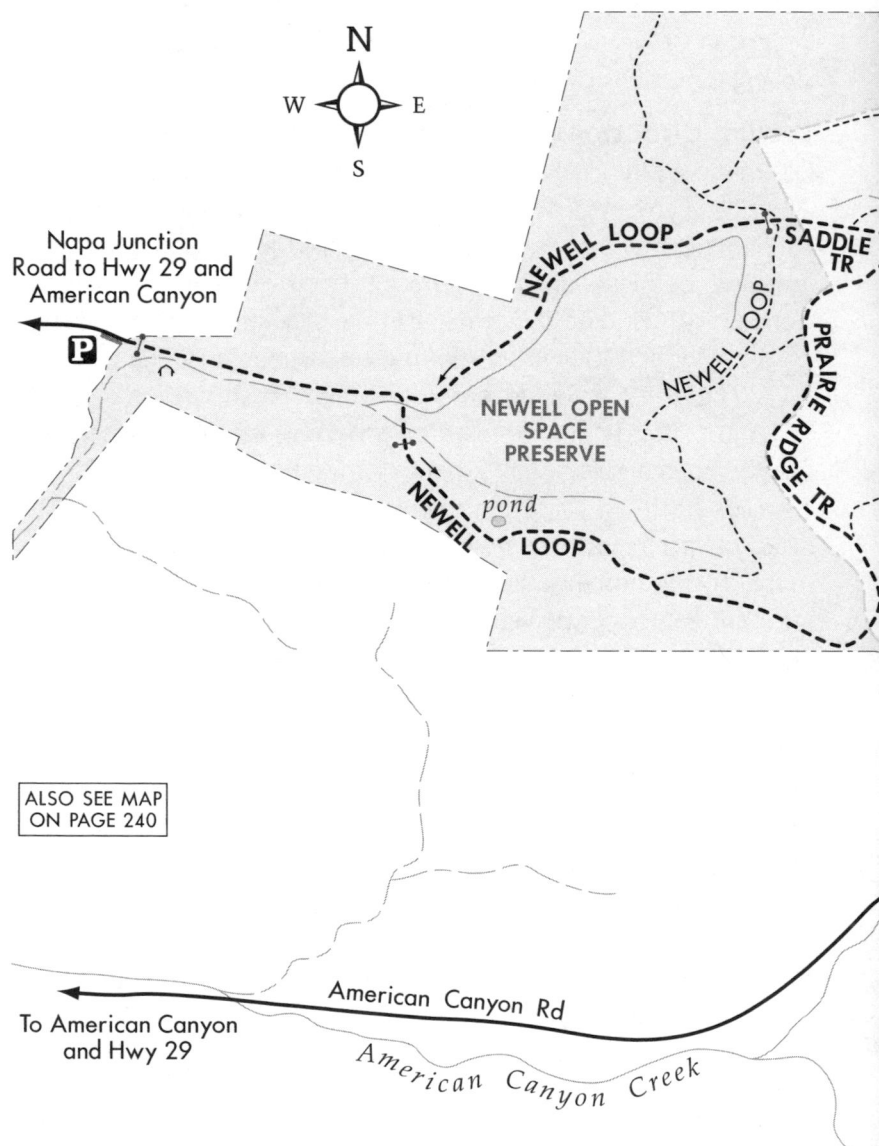

Napa Junction Road to Hwy 29 and American Canyon

NEWELL LOOP

SADDLE TR

NEWELL LOOP

PRAIRIE RIDGE TR

NEWELL OPEN SPACE PRESERVE

pond

NEWELL LOOP

ALSO SEE MAP ON PAGE 240

American Canyon Rd

To American Canyon and Hwy 29

American Canyon Creek

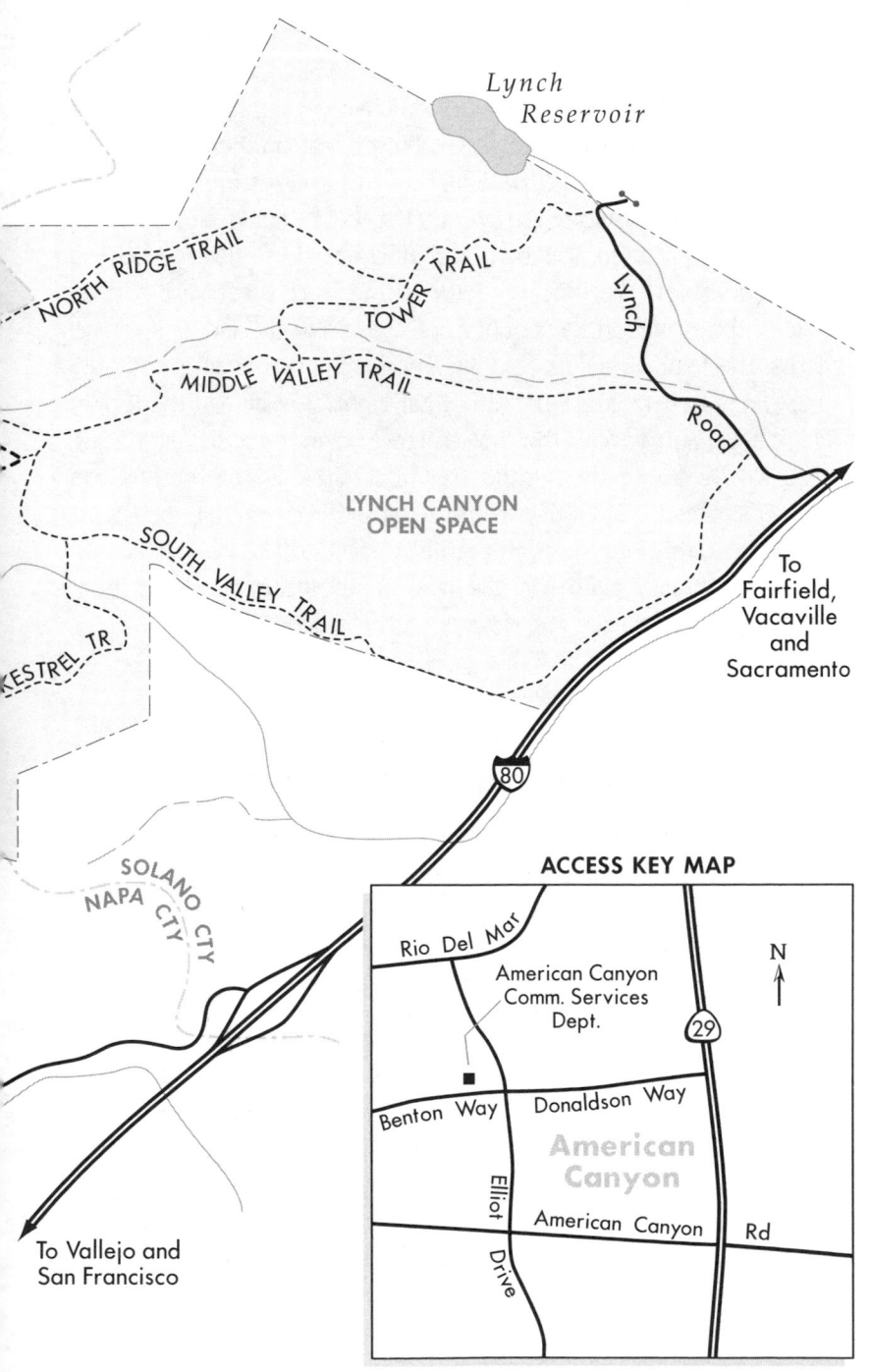

Lynch *Reservoir*

NORTH RIDGE TRAIL

TOWER TRAIL

MIDDLE VALLEY TRAIL

Lynch Road

LYNCH CANYON
OPEN SPACE

SOUTH VALLEY TRAIL

KESTREL TR

To
Fairfield,
Vacaville
and
Sacramento

80

SOLANO CTY
NAPA CTY

To Vallejo and
San Francisco

ACCESS KEY MAP

Rio Del Mar

American Canyon
Comm. Services
Dept.

N

29

Benton Way

Donaldson Way

**American
Canyon**

Elliot Drive

American Canyon Rd

Open Space and Solano County. The 360-degree vistas include San Pablo Bay, the Benicia Bridge, San Francisco Bay, the Golden Gate Bridge, Mount Tamalpais, Sonoma Mountain, the Mayacamas Range, and the Vaca Mountains. Go to the left on the Prairie Ridge Trail and follow the ridge, passing bay trees, oak trees, and beautiful sandstone boulders. Traverse the east-facing slope within Lynch Canyon Open Space to a signed junction with the Kestrel Trail. Curve left, returning to the ridge and westward views. Follow the ridge on the county line, savoring the landscape and vistas. The faint path cuts through an opening in the trees and outcroppings to a posted junction. Bear right, staying on the Prairie Ridge Trail, and follow the oak-dotted ridge. Descend along the spine of the hill to the Saddle Trail at 3 miles. Go to the left and walk 0.3 miles to a junction with the Newell Loop Trail, the lower cut-across trail. Pass through the gate and head down canyon on the wide, grassy path for one mile, completing the loop. Bear right and retrace your steps back to the trailhead. ■

83. Upper Lake
ROCKVILLE HILLS REGIONAL PARK

Hiking distance: 1.8-mile loop·
Hiking time: 1 hour
Elevation gain: 300 feet
Dogs: allowed
Maps: U.S.G.S. Cordelia and Mt. George
Rockville Hills Community Park map

Summary of hike: Rockville Hills Regional Park stretches across 610 acres of rolling hills on the northwest end of Fairfield. In 1966, the city of Fairfield acquired the open space park. The diverse park includes dense chaparral, grasslands, ridges, slopes, pockmarked volcanic formations, sedimentary cliffs, vista overlooks, a couple of valleys, two lakes, and foothill woodlands dominated by blue oak and buckeye trees. A mosaic of roads and trails, open to bikes and dogs, weaves through the park and

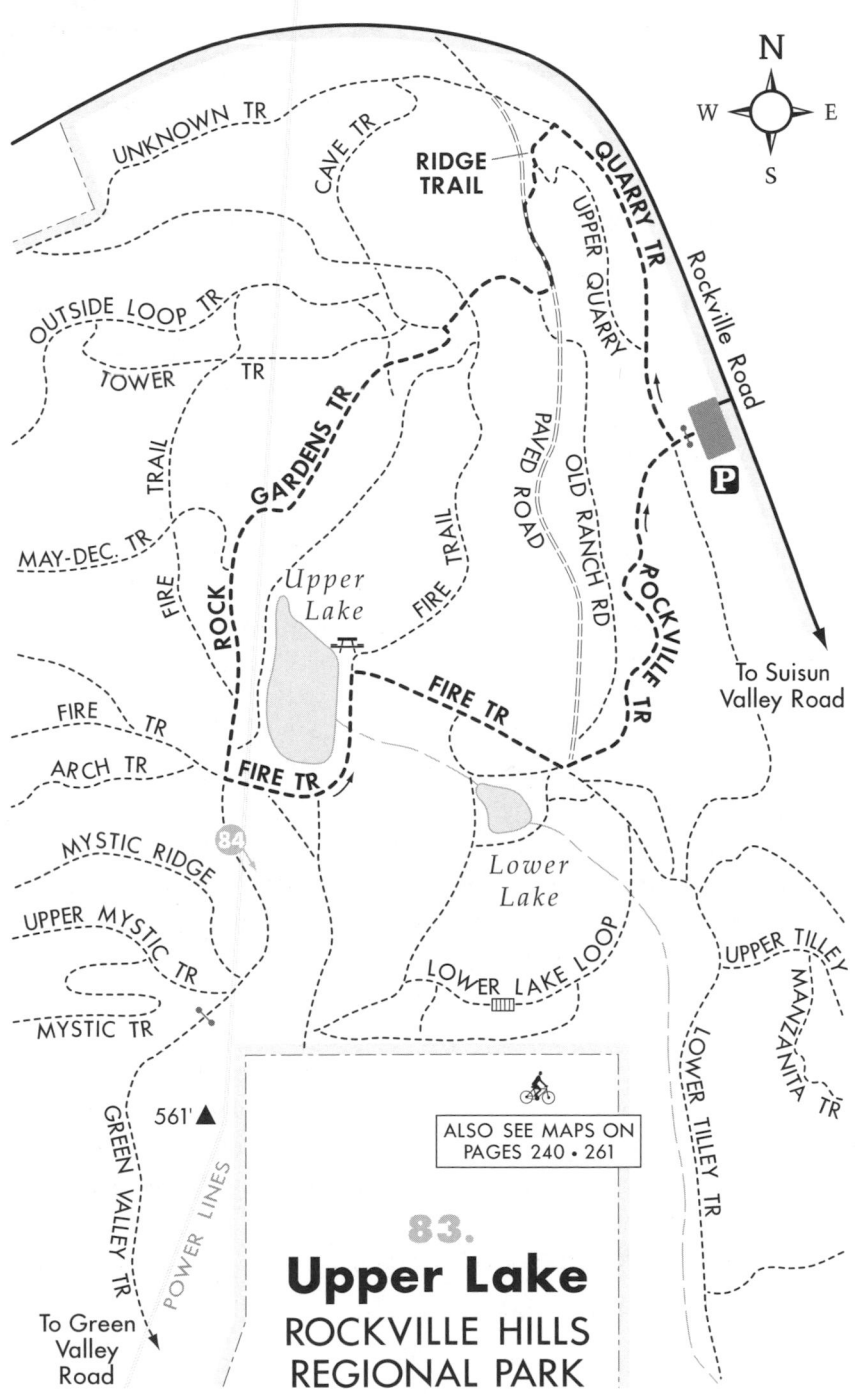

83.
Upper Lake
ROCKVILLE HILLS
REGIONAL PARK

ALSO SEE MAPS ON
PAGES 240 • 261

the gorgeous terrain. This loop hike visits Upper Lake (which sits in the center of the park) and explores rock outcroppings and caves. The trails meander through oak savannah, grasslands, and chaparral-covered hillsides. Most of the trails are unmarked, and numerous other trails are not shown on the park maps. However, the paths lead back to Upper Lake and/or to the main junctions, making it difficult to get lost.

Driving directions: From Interstate 80 in Fairfield, exit on Suisun Valley Road. Drive 1.5 miles north to Rockville Road at a light signal. Turn left and continue 0.7 miles to the posted park entrance on the left. Turn left and park in the lot. A day-use fee is required.

Hiking directions: Walk past the trailhead gate and bear right on the Quarry Trail. Head north along the base of the rocky, oak-covered hills. Follow the fenced park boundary among stands of oaks, manzanita, and toyon. Climb to a ridge and a junction. Bear left on the Ridge Trail, and traverse the hillside to a paved road. Bear left on the road and walk 150 yards to a fork. Veer right and quickly go right again. Weave down the hill to the end of a sweeping left bend and a junction. Climb 100 yards on the right fork to a slab-rock ridge. Bear left on the Rock Garden Trail through oaks and manzanita to a saddle. Side paths on the left lead through the wall-like rock formations to overlooks of the parkland. Gradually descend through the oak-studded grassland to the southwest corner of Upper Lake and a major junction.

To extend the hike into Green Valley, continue with Hike 84. For this shorter loop hike, go left on the trail signed for Lower Lake and the parking area. Skirt the perimeter of Upper Lake to the east shore by a picnic area. Bear right, leaving the lakeshore on the Fire Trail (a segment of the Bay Area Ridge Trail). Climb to a flat, grassy meadow and a 5-way junction by an information kiosk. Go straight through on the Rockville Trail, and traverse the oak-filled hillside, slowly descending to the trailhead parking lot. ■

84. Green Valley
ROCKVILLE HILLS REGIONAL PARK

Hiking distance: 4-mile loop
Hiking time: 2 hours
Elevation gain: 450 feet
Dogs: allowed
Maps: U.S.G.S. Cordelia
Rockville Hills Community Park map

map
next page

Summary of hike: Rockville Hills Regional Park sits on the rolling, oak-studded hills in Solano County between Green Valley and Suisun Valley. Green Valley, originally a wheat-growing region, is now a fruit producing area due to its flat terrain and ease of irrigation. Twenty miles of rolling fire roads and twisting single-track trails wind through this beautiful park. A short climb from the trailhead brings you to a grassy plateau that overlooks Upper Lake, the oak-dotted valley, volcanic outcroppings, and the small surrounding peaks. This hike visits Upper Lake and descends on the southwest slope of Rockville Hills Park into Green Valley. The trails weave through groves of blue oak, coast live oak, valley oak, buckeye, and maple.

Driving directions: From Interstate 80 in Fairfield, exit on Suisun Valley Road. Drive 1.5 miles north to Rockville Road at a light signal. Turn left and continue 0.7 miles to the posted park entrance on the left. Turn left and park in the lot. A day-use fee is required.

Hiking directions: Walk past the entrance gate and map kiosk. Head uphill on the Rockville Trail, a broad fire road that is part of the 400-mile Bay Area Ridge Trail. Traverse the rolling terrain along the oak-filled hillside to a flat grassland plateau and a 5-way junction by an information kiosk. Pass straight through the junction to Lower Lake, fifty yards ahead. From Lower Lake, veer right and merge with the dirt fire road, with views of the palisade rock formations. Continue to a T-junction on the east shore of

Upper Lake. Curve left, circling the edge of the lake to a major 4-way junction.

Take the posted Green Valley Trail, and climb the hillside on an old dirt road. Crest a ridge and descend straight ahead to a trail gate. Continue past the gate to an overlook of Fairfield and Suisun Bay. Curve right and descend towards the bottom of Green Valley, overlooking ranch and farm land. Just before reaching the valley floor, bear right on the distinct but unsigned Black Oak Trail. Cross the oak-covered hillside, and pass through a trail gate to a junction by a small bridge. Cross the bridge and traverse the hill on the Middle Mystic Trail to Jockey Junction. Stay on the main trail (the Fire Trail) and weave downhill, completing the loop at the 4-way junction above Upper Lake. Walk down to the lake and retrace your steps. ■

84.

Green Valley
ROCKVILLE HILLS
REGIONAL PARK

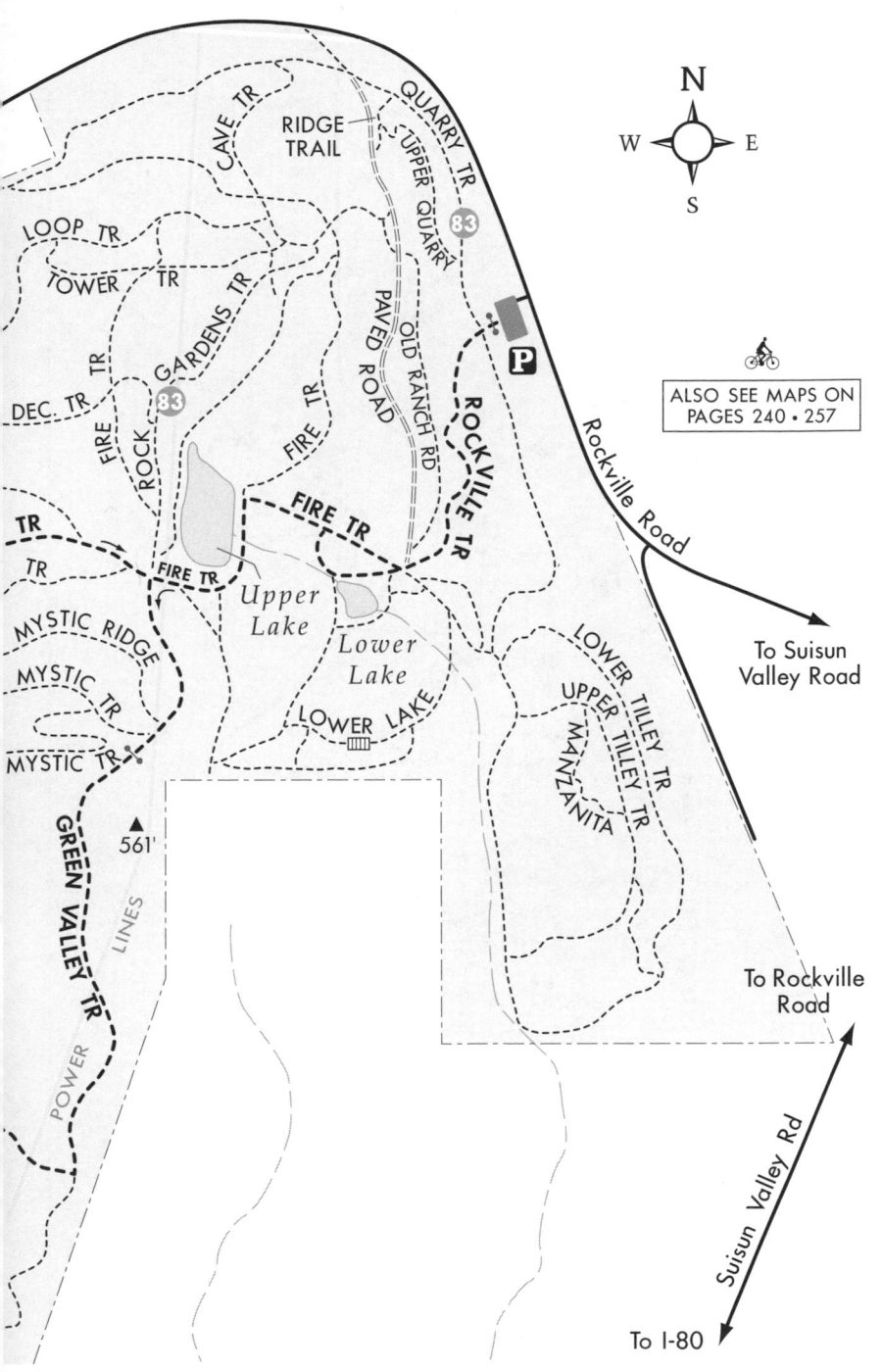

N
W   E
S

ALSO SEE MAPS ON
PAGES 240 • 257

CAVE TR
RIDGE TRAIL
QUARRY TR
UPPER QUARRY
83

LOOP TR
TOWER TR
DEC. TR
FIRE TR
ROCK GARDENS TR
83
FIRE TR
PAVED ROAD
OLD RANCH RD
ROCKVILLE TR

P

Rockville Road

To Suisun
Valley Road

TR
TR
FIRE TR
FIRE TR
Upper Lake
Lower Lake
FIRE TR
MYSTIC RIDGE
MYSTIC TR
MYSTIC TR
LOWER LAKE
LOWER TILLEY TR
UPPER TILLEY TR
MANZANITA

GREEN VALLEY TR
561'
POWER LINES

To Rockville
Road

Suisun Valley Rd

To I-80

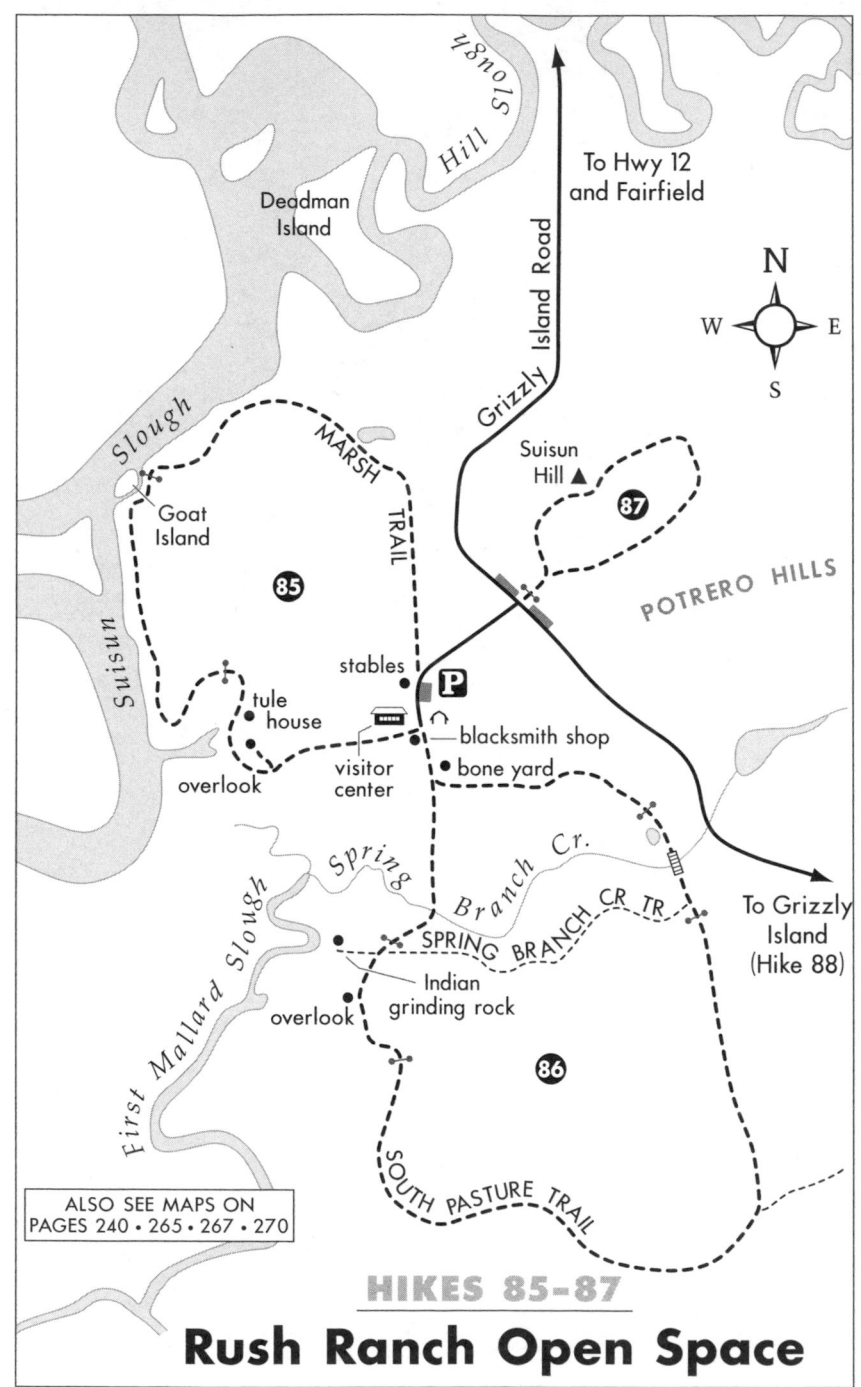

Deadman
Island

Hill Slough

To Hwy 12
and Fairfield

Grizzly Island Road

N
W E
S

Slough

MARSH TRAIL

Goat
Island

Suisun
Hill ▲

87

85

POTRERO HILLS

Suisun

stables

P

tule
house

blacksmith shop

visitor
center

bone yard

overlook

Spring Branch Cr.

SPRING BRANCH CR. TR.

To Grizzly
Island
(Hike 88)

First Mallard Slough

Indian
grinding rock

overlook

86

SOUTH PASTURE TRAIL

ALSO SEE MAPS ON
PAGES 240 • 265 • 267 • 270

HIKES 85-87

Rush Ranch Open Space

85. Marsh Trail
RUSH RANCH OPEN SPACE
Open Tuesday to Saturday · 8 a.m.—4:30 p.m.

Hiking distance: 2.2-mile loop
Hiking time: 1 hour
Elevation gain: Level
Dogs: not allowed
Maps: U.S.G.S. Fairfield South
Rush Ranch Marsh Trail Guide

**map
next page**

Summary of hike: Rush Ranch is a 2,070-acre open space cupped between Suisun Bay and the rolling Potrero Hills. It lies within Suisun Marsh, south of Fairfield and the city of Suisun. Suisun Marsh is the largest estuarial (part freshwater and part saltwater) marsh in the continental United States and the largest coastal wetland in California. The 100,000-acre estuary is located where the freshwater from the Sacramento River and San Joaquin River mixes with the saltwater from the ocean. Suisun Marsh is a critical stop-over on the Pacific Flyway, a freeway for millions of migrating waterfowl and shorebirds. It is a haven to more than 230 bird species and an incredible location for bird watching.

Rush Ranch consists of pasturelands, rolling native grasslands, and wetlands, of which 1,000 acres still remain in their natural state. Three trails loop through the ranch, exploring the different ecosystems. This hike, the Marsh Trail, is a 2.2-mile interpretive loop with numbered posts that correspond with a trail guide (available at the visitor center). The trail overlooks Suisun Slough and an 80-acre tidal marsh along a levee near the mouth of the Sacramento–San Joaquin River delta. Blackberry bushes, tule plants, sedges, and cattails surround the trail. From the open marshland and Suisun Slough, the hike finishes in an upland pasture planted with Harding grass.

Driving directions: From Interstate 80 in Fairfield, take the Suisun City exit (Highway 12). Drive 4.2 miles east to Grizzly Island Road. Turn right and continue 2.4 miles to the posted ranch. Turn right and drive 0.2 miles to the parking area by the ranch buildings.

Hiking directions: Walk past the 100-year-old barn to the blacksmith shop, and bear right to the visitor center. After visiting the center, pass through a eucalyptus grove planted long ago as a windbreak. Stroll through the open grasslands to a small hill. A side path on the right climbs the hill to an overlook with benches of Suisun Marsh and the Vaca Mountains. Loop clockwise around a hill between the grasslands and the salt marsh. Pass a reconstructed tule house on the right. It is a replica of a Patwin Indian home formed from willow branches and covered with grass or bark. Bear left through an old fence, and enter the salt marsh on a manmade levee dating back to the late 1800s. Pass tidal gates used to regulate water levels. Parallel Suisun Slough among the tall blackberry vines, cattails, and tules. Cross Goat Island, a natural island in the marsh, while enjoying the vistas of Mount Diablo, Mount Vaca, and the Potrero Hills. Pass through a trail gate by signpost 14 and bear left. Stroll between the tidal marsh and lush vegetation on the left and the upland grassland on the right. Curve away from the marsh towards Hill Slough. Rush Landing, a small cove where boats from Sacramento and San Francisco deliver goods, can be seen at the shoreline. Pass an alkaline pond on the left formed by drainage off of Suisun Hill. Continue through the Harding grass pasture, completing the loop at the stables and barn.■

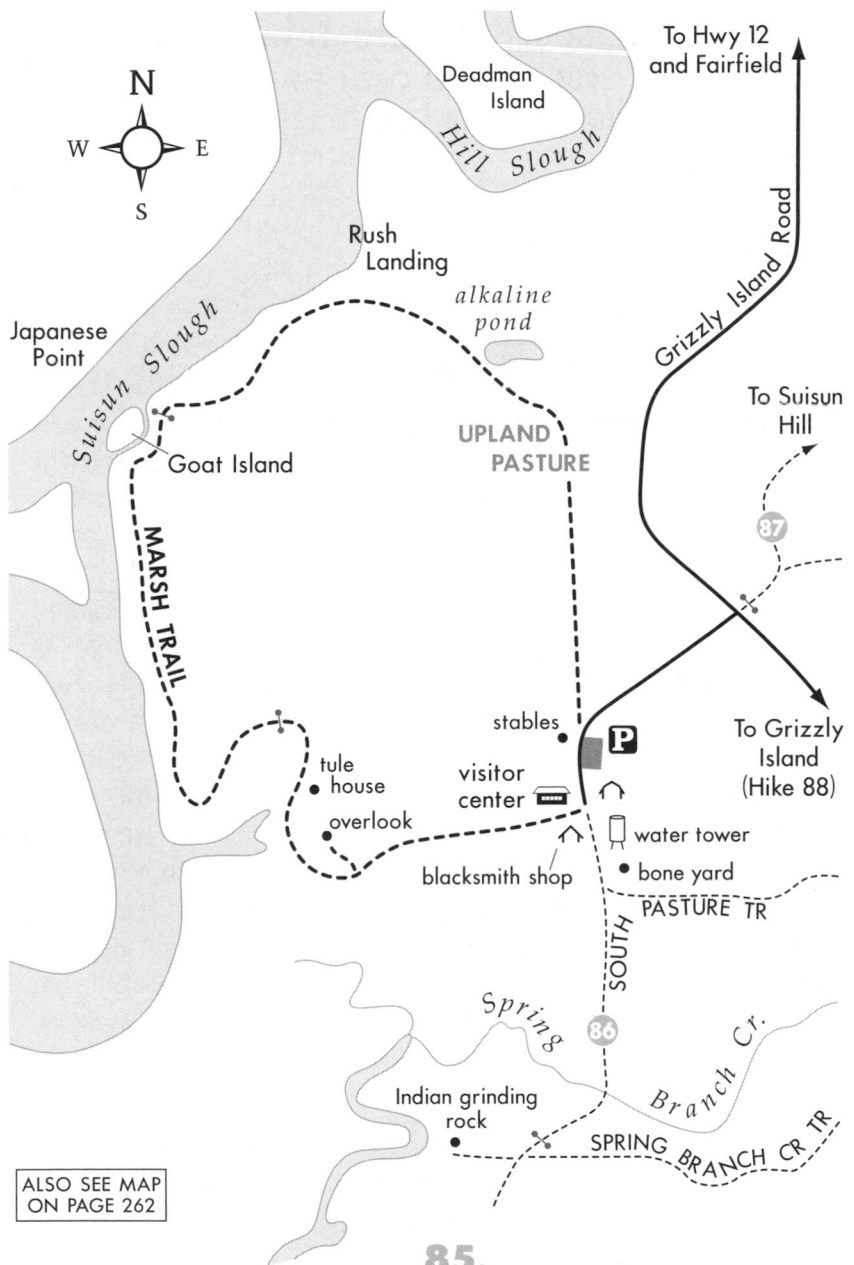

To Hwy 12 and Fairfield

Deadman Island

Hill Slough

Grizzly Island Road

Rush Landing

alkaline pond

To Suisun Hill

Japanese Point

Suisun Slough

87

UPLAND PASTURE

Goat Island

MARSH TRAIL

To Grizzly Island (Hike 88)

stables

P

visitor center

tule house

water tower

overlook

bone yard

blacksmith shop

PASTURE TR

SOUTH

Spring

86

Branch Cr.

Indian grinding rock

SPRING BRANCH CR TR

ALSO SEE MAP ON PAGE 262

85.
Marsh Trail
RUSH RANCH OPEN SPACE

86. South Pasture Trail
RUSH RANCH OPEN SPACE

Open Tuesday to Saturday · 8 a.m. — 4:30 p.m.

Hiking distance: 2.4-mile loop
Hiking time: 1 hour
Elevation gain: Level
Dogs: not allowed
Maps: U.S.G.S. Fairfield South
Rush Ranch South Pasture Trail Guide

Summary of hike: Suisun Marsh covers 10 square miles of tidal marsh. Historic Rush Ranch sits on 1.6 square miles of that land. For hundreds of years, the Patwin Indians lived in small seasonal villages on the land that is now Rush Ranch. They lived in huts made from tules gathered from the marsh. The evidence of their presence remains in rock formations, where grinding holes formed from processing seeds, dried fish and dried meat, still remain. In 1864, Hiram and Sarah Rush acquired the land and raised sheep, cattle, and horses. Rush Ranch was acquired for public access in 1988 and still operates as a working cattle and sheep ranch. The ranch has a visitor center, blacksmith shop, a restored 100-year-old barn, historical ranching equipment, and picnic areas. The South Pasture Trail is a 2.4-mile interpretive loop with numbered posts that correspond with a trail guide (available at the visitor center). The trail meanders through open grasslands with vistas of the surrounding hills and mountains, including Mount Diablo. The hike visits an overlook of Suisun Marsh, leads to a Patwin Indian grinding rock site, and continues through South Pasture, passing Spring Branch Creek and First Mallard Slough.

Driving directions: From Interstate 80 in Fairfield, take the Suisun City exit (Highway 12). Drive 4.2 miles east to Grizzly Island Road. Turn right and continue 2.4 miles to the posted ranch. Turn right and drive 0.2 miles to the parking area by the ranch buildings.

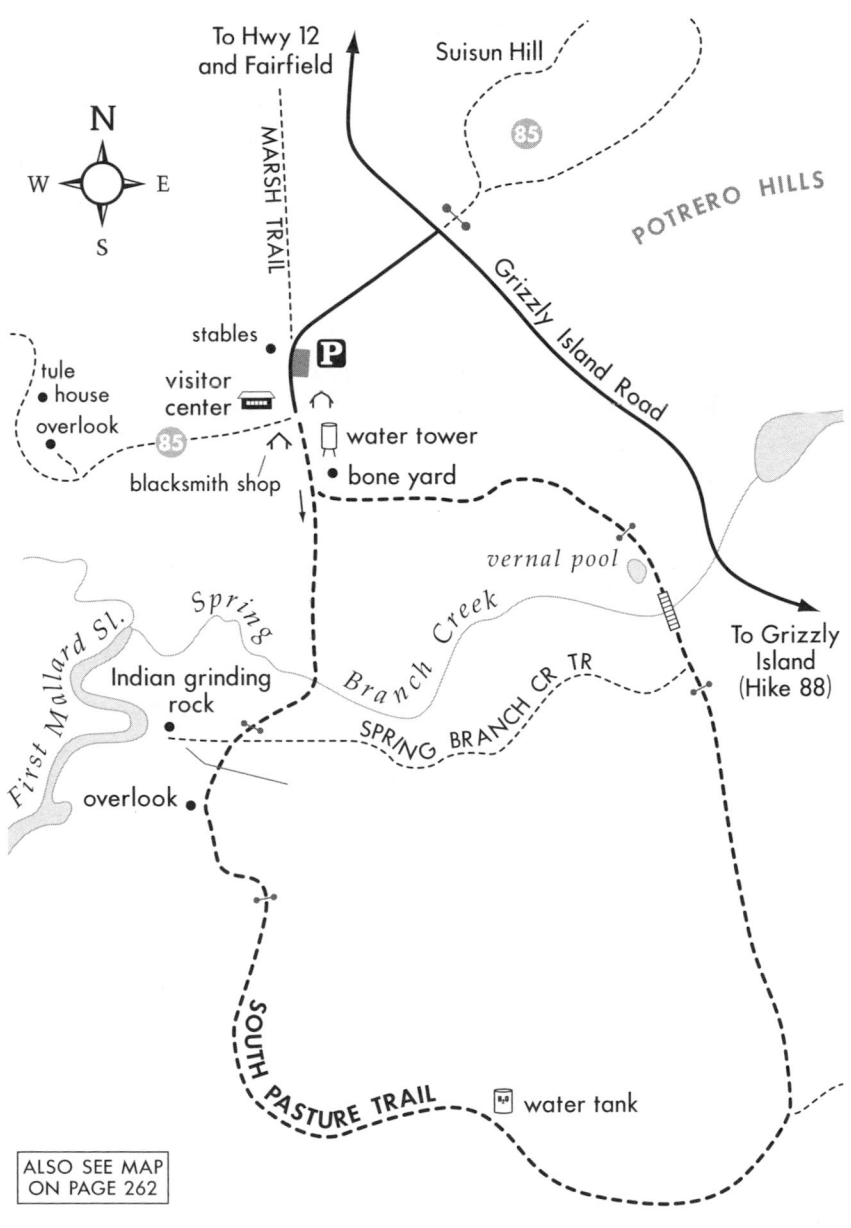

ALSO SEE MAP
ON PAGE 262

86.
South Pasture Trail
RUSH RANCH OPEN SPACE

Hiking directions: Walk past the barn and continue straight past the south side of the blacksmith shop to the wooden water tower. Head south through the bone yard, rich with discarded ranching equipment left to deteriorate in the weather. Begin the loop at the information kiosk on the right fork. Walk through the grasslands to the edge of Suisun Marsh to a gate and 4-way junction. To the left, the Spring Branch Creek Trail heads west, parallel to the creek. Detour one hundred yards to the right to the Indian grinding rock, a bedrock mortar on the right. Return to the South Pasture Trail, and ascend the knoll south to an overlook of the 2,000-acre tidal marsh. Pass through a cattle gate, and stroll through a Harding grass pastureland with a view of Mount Diablo straight ahead. Curve east (left) and walk towards the water tank and cattle trough, with a view of the Potrero Hills in the east and the bridge over Montezuma Slough to the southeast. At 1.4 miles, sixty yards past signpost 13, veer left at a fork. Descend into the Spring Branch Creek basin towards the Rush Ranch buildings, with a view of the Vaca Mountains and Blue Ridge. At the base of the slope, pass through a trail gate to a junction with the east end of the Spring Branch Creek Trail. Stay straight on the South Pasture Trail, and cross a boardwalk over Spring Branch Creek. Pass a vernal pool on the left, a natural depression that holds water for a short time during the rainy season. Pass through another gate and complete the loop at the bone yard. Return to the right. ■

87. Suisun Hill Trail
RUSH RANCH OPEN SPACE

Hiking distance: 1-mile loop
Hiking time: 40 minutes
Elevation gain: 200 feet
Dogs: allowed
Maps: U.S.G.S. Fairfield South
Rush Ranch trail map

map
next page

Summary of hike: The Potrero Hills are long, narrow, low rolling hills surrounded by the massive Suisun Marsh. The oblong hills stretch six miles east from historic Rush Ranch. Suisun Hill is the westernmost hill, rising 212 feet. The 1.5-mile Suisun Hill Trail begins east of the 2,000-acre ranch and climbs into the Potrero Hills. The loop trail meanders through the open grassland to the Suisun Hill summit. From the top are 360-degree vistas of the surrounding area. This trail is open seven days a week. (The ranch is open Tuesday—Saturday.)

Driving directions: From Interstate 80 in Fairfield, take the Suisun City exit (Highway 12). Drive 4.2 miles east to Grizzly Island Road. Turn right and continue 2.4 miles to the posted ranch. Park in the pullouts on the sides of the road, or turn right and drive 0.2 miles into Rush Ranch to the parking area by the ranch buildings.

Hiking directions: From the Rush Ranch parking area, walk back down the entrance road to Grizzly Island Road. Cross the road and go through the trailhead gate to the base of Suisun Hill and a junction. Begin the loop on the left fork, hiking clockwise. Traverse the slope to the ridge overlooking Suisun Slough, Hill Slough, and Rush Landing. Follow the ridge to the 212-foot summit, where there are benches for taking in the 360-degree views. In the distance is Mount Diablo in the south, Mount Vaca in the north, Twin Sisters in the northwest, Mount Tamalpais in the west, and the Potrero Hills in the east. Continue east along the ridge, descending to the base of Suisun Hill. Bear right and parallel the southern base of the hill, completing the loop near the trailhead. ■

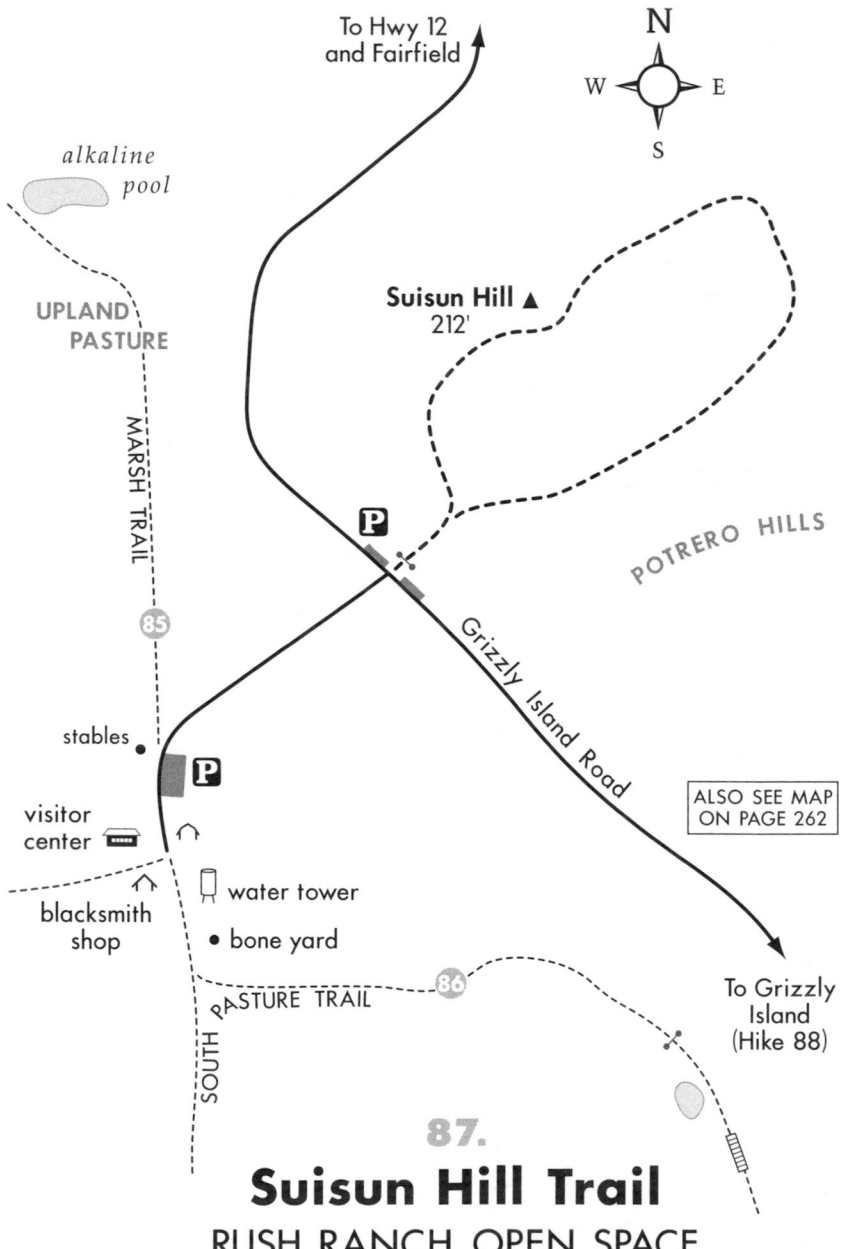

To Hwy 12 and Fairfield

N
W E
S

alkaline pool

UPLAND PASTURE

Suisun Hill ▲ 212'

MARSH TRAIL

85

POTRERO HILLS

P

Grizzly Island Road

stables

visitor center

P

ALSO SEE MAP ON PAGE 262

blacksmith shop

water tower

bone yard

86

SOUTH PASTURE TRAIL

To Grizzly Island (Hike 88)

87.
Suisun Hill Trail
RUSH RANCH OPEN SPACE

88. Grizzly Island Wildlife Area

2548 Grizzly Island Road · Suisun: (707) 425-3828
Open to hiking February — July

Hiking distance: Variable
Hiking time: Variable (include time for wildlife observation)
Elevation gain: Level
Dogs: not allowed
Maps: U.S.G.S. Denverton and Honker Bay
Grizzly Island Wildlife Area map

map page 274

Summary of hike: Grizzly Island Wildlife Area lies in the heart of Suisun Marsh south of Fairfield and Suisun City. The larger Grizzly Island complex, managed by the California Department of Fish and Game, encompasses 15,300 acres, of which 8,600 acres are the wildlife area.

The 100,000-acre Suisun Marsh is located where the Sacramento and San Joaquin Rivers blend with the ocean tides. It is the largest estuarine marsh in the continental United States. The area is comprised of tidal flats, salt marshes, managed wetlands, sloughs, seasonal ponds, and upland fields. The wetlands shelter thousands of shorebirds and more than 100,000 wintering waterfowl, including over 230 bird species. The sloughs contain large populations of river otters, while native tule elk are frequently spotted in the upland fields. The recreational opportunities include fishing, hunting, wildlife viewing, bird watching, nature study, and 75 miles of hiking roads and trails.

An unpaved, but well-maintained, 8-mile road runs through the middle of the Grizzly Island Wildlife Area, leading to eight different parking areas and trailheads. You may view wildlife from the car, or walk on the paths that meander along the natural and manmade water channels. A self-guided tour map is available at the Fish and Game office, located at the entrance to the wildlife area.

Driving directions: From Interstate 80 in Fairfield, take the Suisun City exit (Highway 12). Drive 4.2 miles east to Grizzly Island Road. Turn right and continue 9.1 miles to the California Department of Fish and Game Ranger Station on the left. From the ranger station (after signing in, paying an entrance fee, and getting a self-guided tour map), continue to the trailhead parking areas on the unpaved road:

LOT 1: 2.5 miles (on the right)

LOT 1A: 3.4 miles (on the left)

LOT 2: 4.1 miles (on the right)

Turn right by the metal barns and stay right into the parking area.

REDHOUSE ROAD: 4.8 miles (on the left)

LOT 3: 5.3 miles (on the left by an isolated stand of three eucalyptus trees)

LOT 4: 5.9 miles (on the left by a single eucalyptus tree)

LOT 4A: 6.6 miles (on the left)

LOT 5: 6.9 miles (on the left in a eucalyptus grove)

LOT 6: 7.9 miles (on the left at a right bend in road)

Hiking directions:

LOT 1: The trail passes through a gate and heads south through grasslands towards Grizzly Bay to Roaring River Slough, 0.25 miles ahead. The trail follows the slough 1.5 miles, connecting with the trail from Lot 2.

LOT 1A. At the trailhead is a wooden viewing platform overlooking the wetlands to observe waterfowl. Tule elk are often spotted in the uplands. The trail follows a levee 0.3 miles northeast to a large stand of eucalyptus on the banks of North Solano Cut. The path curves right and follows the water channel east along the treeline, continuing another 0.6 miles to parking lot 2.

LOT 2. Walk up to the yellow gate, located across South Solano Cut from the barns. Head southwest on the wide levee road, reaching a dirt road at Roaring River Slough in a little over one mile.

LOT 3. Cross the road to a wooden footbridge over Grizzly Ditch. Cross the ditch to a 3-way junction. To the left and right, the trail parallels Grizzly Ditch, offering a good opportunity to see river otters. Straight ahead, the path heads southwest through the grassy wetlands 0.2 miles to Howard Slough. This is a great bird observation route.

LOT 4. Across the road, pass a yellow gate and continue 0.2 miles south, paralleling a waterway to Howard Slough. Look for turtles sunbathing on the cliffs of the water channel. At Howard Slough, curve left, following the slough 300 yards to a levee that crosses the slough. The trail follows the opposite bank of Howard Slough for 1.4 miles to Roaring River Slough. A hundred yards southeast of the levee crossing, the path leads to Steve's Ditch. Paths head east along both sides of the ditch.

To the north of the parking area, a grassy path leads 60 yards to a berm overlooking Pond 11. The elevated levee offers opportunities for spotting raptors and tule elk along the horizon.

LOT 4A. This path forms a 0.6-mile loop around a deep pond. Walk 20 yards north to a fork. Begin the loop in either direction. The area is teeming with waterfowl.

LOT 5. Heading south, cross a wooden footbridge over Grizzly Ditch. The brush-lined footpath leads to ponds along Steve's Ditch. Paths parallel the ditch along both sides, connecting to parking area 4.

To the north, the path crosses the upland fields where tule elk may be observed.

LOT 6. Bear left on the gated road. Follow the dirt road between a large pond on the left and Montezuma Slough on the right. Pass Dutton's Pond at 0.4 miles, a haven for river otters. At 0.7 miles is Poleline Road, which heads west along a water ditch. The Montezuma Slough Road follows the contours of the slough along the eastern edge of Grizzly Island.

Vehicle access ends at Lot 6. The trail (the old road) continues past old Lot 7. ■

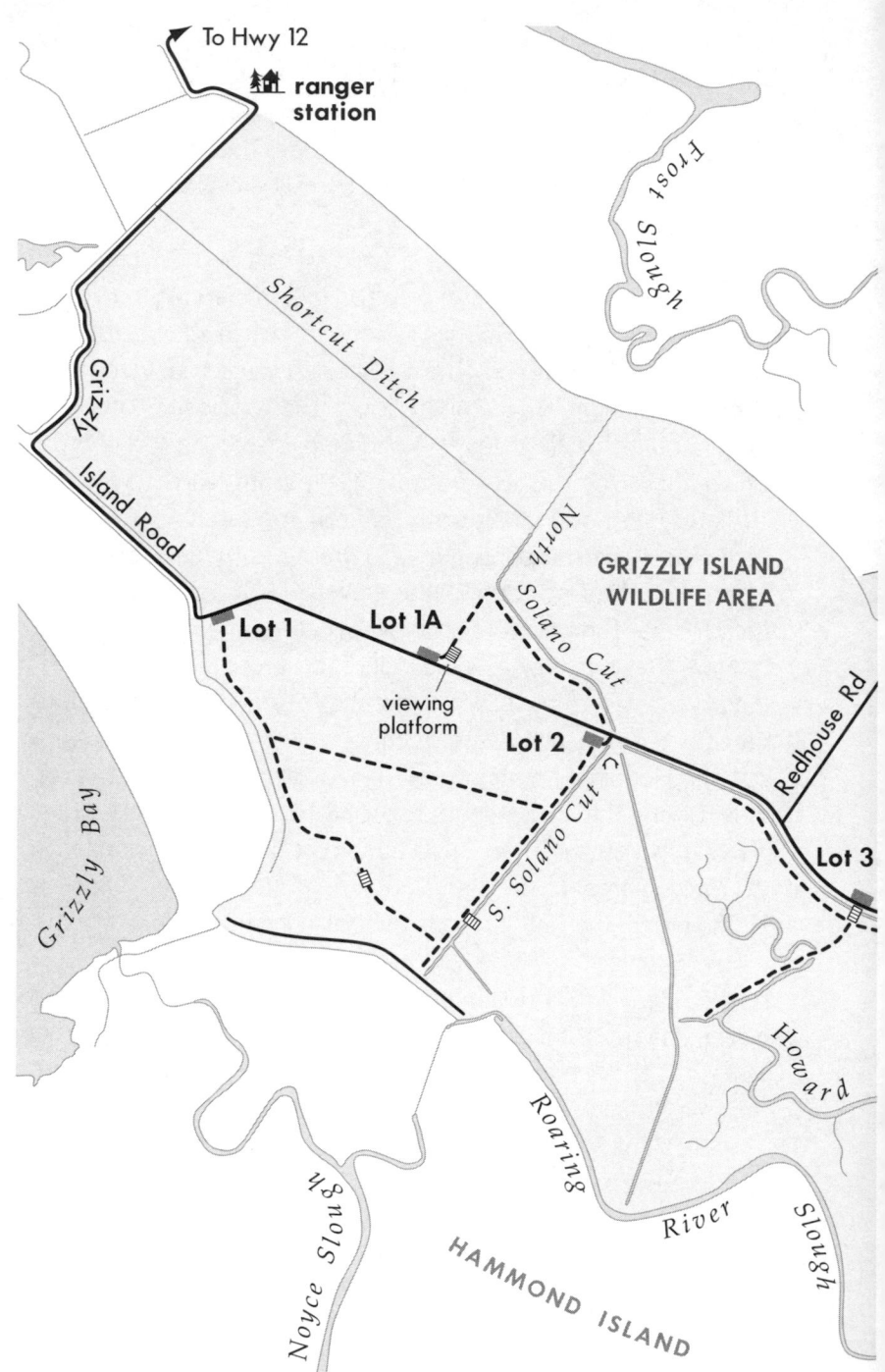

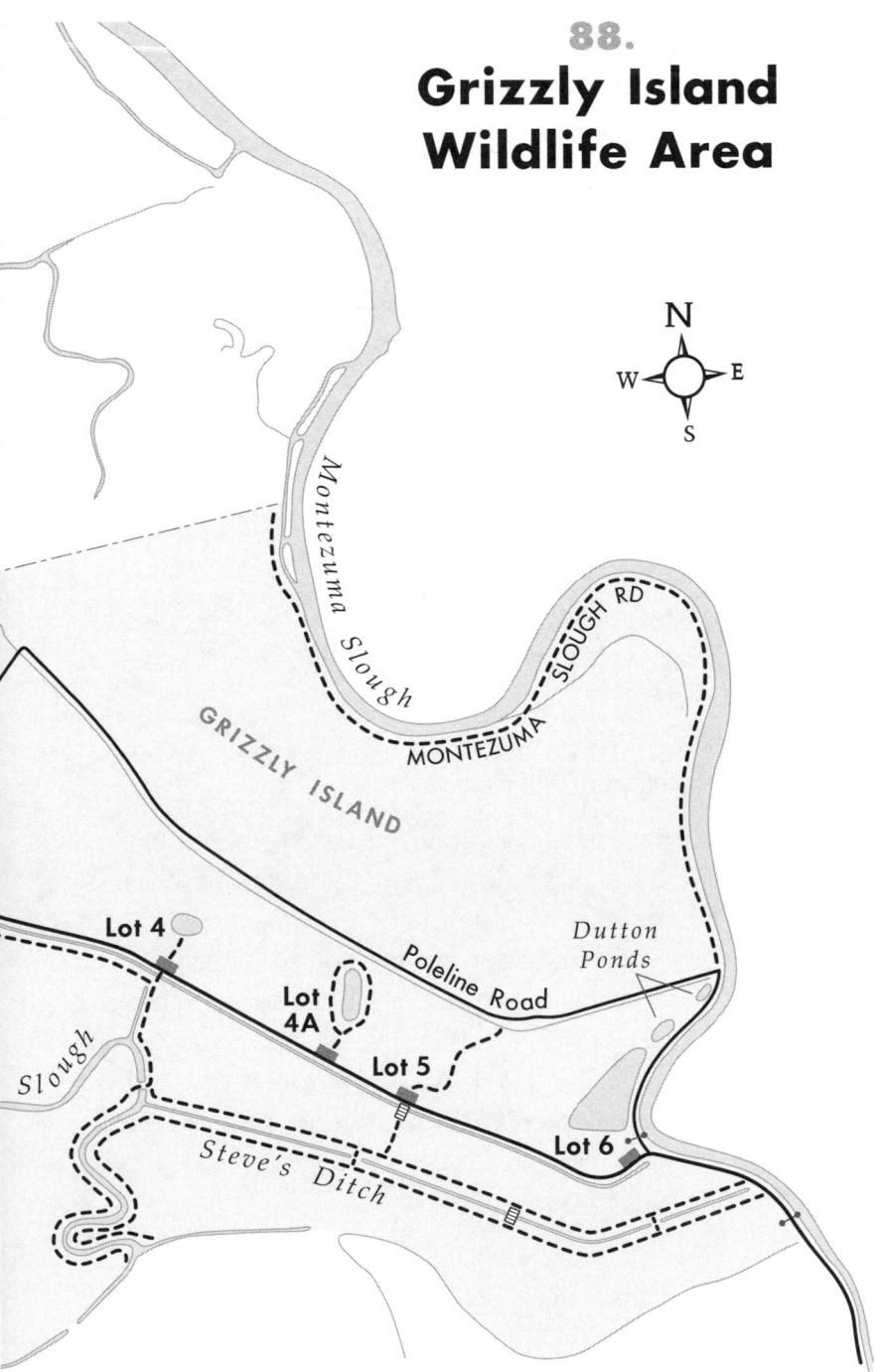

88.
Grizzly Island Wildlife Area

N
W E
S

Montezuma Slough

MONTEZUMA SLOUGH RD

GRIZZLY ISLAND

Dutton Ponds

Lot 4

Lot 4A

Poleline Road

Lot 5

Slough

Steve's Ditch

Lot 6

Napa Valley Accommodations
Author Recommendations

The following accommodations are places I stayed while hiking, writing about, and enjoying Napa County. All of the six lodgings are clean and comfortable with friendly, helpful staff. Their locations offer easy access to the surrounding area. I look forward to returning to all of these hotels, bed and breakfasts, or resorts. My wife, Linda, and I nearly always travel and hike with Kofax, our yellow labrador. All of these lodgings welcome dogs.

Calistoga

Brannan Cottage Inn

(707) 942-4200
109 Wapoo Avenue
Calistoga, CA 94515
www.brannancottageinn.com
innkeeper@brannancottageinn.com

The Brannan Cottage Inn is a six-room bed and breakfast located within walking distance to downtown Calistoga. The charming Greek revival Victorian inn dates back to 1860 and is on the National Register of Historical Places. It is one of Calistoga's three remaining original cottages from the 1860s that is still in use and the only one in its original location. The inn has a wrap-around porch and a private courtyard. All of the rooms have private entrances and refrigerators. The owners prepare wonderful breakfasts each morning and have nightly wine tastings with appetizers in the garden patio.

Chelsea Garden Inn

(800) 942-1515 · (707) 942-0948

1443 Second Street

Calistoga, CA 94515

www.chelseagardeninn.com · info@chelseagardeninn.com

The Chelsea Garden Inn is a five-room bed and breakfast located in the heart of Calistoga. Every unit is a private, romantic suite with its own bathroom, a fireplace, refrigerator, television and WiFi. There are lush gardens, a latticed courtyard with tropical plants, and a secluded swimming pool. They serve gourmet breakfasts and offer nightly wine tastings with cheese and hors d'oeuvres.

Meadowlark Inn

(800) 942-5651 · (707) 942-5651

601 Petrified Forest Road

Calistoga, CA 94515

www.meadowlarkinn.com · info@meadowlarkinn.com

The Meadowlark Inn is an exceptional bed and breakfast. It is located about a mile from Calistoga and sits on 20 gorgeous and secluded acres. The land has oak and fir groves, pastures with horses, gardens, and magnificent views of The Palisades (cover photo). All the rooms have private decks and marble-tiled bathrooms with whirlpool tubs for two. The resort also has a clothing optional area with a mineral pool, hot tub, sauna, and a sundeck. One of the real joys of staying here is having breakfast with the owners, Kurt Stevens and Richard Flynn. They have breakfast with the guests, sharing stories about themselves, the local history, wineries, and more. They are great storytellers and gracious hosts. On a couple of mornings, when I needed to get an early start on the trails, we visited until 11:00. It was hard to leave and go to work after such an enjoyable morning.

Healdsburg (Sonoma County)

Camellia Inn
(800) 727-8182 · (707) 433-8182
211 North Street
Healdsburg, CA 95448
www.camelliainn.com

The Camellia Inn is a historic 1869 Italianate Victorian inn with nine charming rooms, all with private baths. The bed and breakfast is located on a quiet residential street only two short blocks from the historic Healdsburg Plaza. The landscaped grounds include a swimming pool and more than fifty varieties of camellias. A delicious breakfast awaits each morning, and in the evenings are wine tastings with appetizers in the double parlor.

Kenwood (Sonoma County)

Kenwood Oaks Guesthouse
(707) 833-1221
Warm Springs Road
Kenwood, CA 95452
joan@kenwoodoaksguesthouse.com
www.kenwoodoaksguesthouse.com

The Kenwood Oaks Guesthouse is a two-acre horse ranch in a gorgeous pastoral setting. The small ranch has one guesthouse adjacent to a horse barn. The house overlooks a pasture backed by a wooded hillside that is covered with 300-year-old valley oaks. This charming house has a full kitchen and is very secluded.

I could easily live there full time. We have returned to this great guesthouse many times since discovering it and look forward to returning again.

Joan, the proprietor, welcomes dogs and offers boarding facilities for your horses. Sonoma Valley is filled with equestrian trails, and many are just a short distance from the house, including Annadel State Park, Hood Mountain Regional Park, Sugarloaf Ridge State Park, Jack London State Historic Park, and Sonoma Valley Regional Park (Hikes 41 through 64).

Lake Berryessa Area

RustRidge Ranch & Winery

(800) 788-0263 · (707) 965-9353
2910 Lower Chiles Valley Road
St Helena, CA 94574
www.rustridge.com · rustridge@rustridge.com ·
info@rustridge.com

RustRidge Ranch and Winery is a 450-acre working ranch with a bed and breakfast. The ranch is tucked into picturesque Chiles Valley in the mountains of eastern Napa County, between Lake Berryessa and Lake Hennessey. The ranch has fifty acres of vineyards and a winery. They breed and train thoroughbred racehorses. During your stay, you can walk through the vineyards, hike on their private hillside trails among ancient oak trees, visit the horses, and sip wine at the tasting room. The rustic bed and breakfast has four guest rooms in a one-story, southwestern-style ranch house. The rooms have private baths, fireplaces, open-beamed ceilings, and great mountain views. There is a swimming pool, eucalyptus sauna, and tennis court. They have delicious breakfasts and during the evening serve RustRidge wines with hors d'ouevres.

DAY HIKE BOOKS

Day Hikes On the California Central Coast ....978-1-57342-031-0 .....$14.95

Day Hikes On the California Southern Coast ....978-1-57342-045-7 ....14.95

Day Hikes Around Sonoma County ....978-1-57342-053-2 ....16.95

Day Hikes Around Napa Valley ....978-1-57342-057-0 ....16.95

Day Hikes Around Monterey and Carmel ....978-1-57342-036-5 ....14.95

Day Hikes Around Big Sur ....978-1-57342-041-9 ....14.95

Day Hikes Around San Luis Obispo ....978-1-57342-051-8 ....16.95

Day Hikes Around Santa Barbara ....978-1-57342-042-6 ....14.95

Day Hikes Around Ventura County ....978-1-57342-043-3 ....14.95

Day Hikes Around Los Angeles ....978-1-57342-044-0 ....14.95

Day Hikes Around Orange County ....978-1-57342-047-1 ....15.95

Day Hikes In Yosemite National Park ....978-1-57342-037-2 ....11.95

Day Hikes In Sequoia and Kings Canyon N.P. ....978-1-57342-030-3 ....12.95

Day Hikes Around Sedona, Arizona ....978-1-57342-049-5 ....14.95

Day Hikes On Oahu ....978-1-57342-038-9 ....11.95

Day Hikes On Maui ....978-1-57342-039-6 ....11.95

Day Hikes On Kauai ....978-1-57342-040-2 ....11.95

Day Hikes In Hawaii ....978-1-57342-050-1 ....16.95

Day Hikes In Yellowstone National Park ....978-1-57342-048-8 ....12.95

Day Hikes In Grand Teton National Park ....978-1-57342-046-4 ....11.95

Day Hikes In the Beartooth Mountains
Billings to Red Lodge to Yellowstone N.P. ....978-1-57342-052-5 ....13.95

Day Hikes Around Bozeman, Montana ....978-1-57342-054-9 ....13.95

Day Hikes Around Missoula, Montana ....978-1-57342-032-7 ....13.95

These books may be purchased at your local bookstore or outdoor shop. Or, order them direct from the distributor:

The Globe Pequot Press

246 Goose Lane • P.O. Box 480 • Guilford, CT 06437-0480
on the web: www.globe-pequot.com

800-243-0495 DIRECT   800-820-2329 FAX

DAY HIKES ON THE
California
Central
Coast
71 GREAT HIKES
Robert Stone
DAY HIKES ON THE
California
Southern
Coast
100 GREAT HIKES
Robert Stone
DAY HIKES AROUND
Sonoma
County
95 GREAT HIKES
Robert Stone
DAY HIKES AROUND
Napa
Valley
88 GREAT HIKES
Robert Stone
DAY HIKES AROUND
Monterey
& Carmel
77 GREAT HIKES
Robert Stone

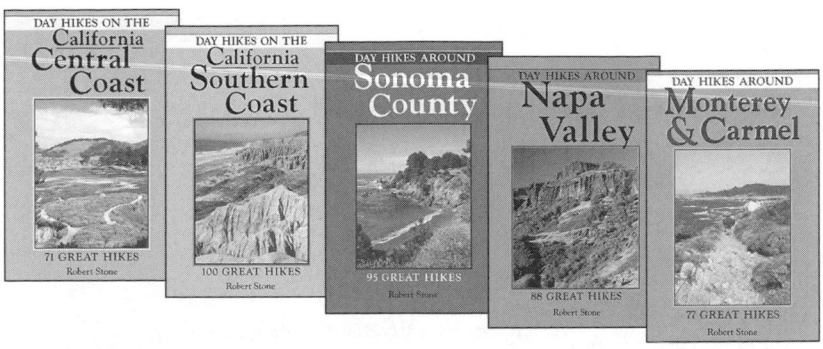

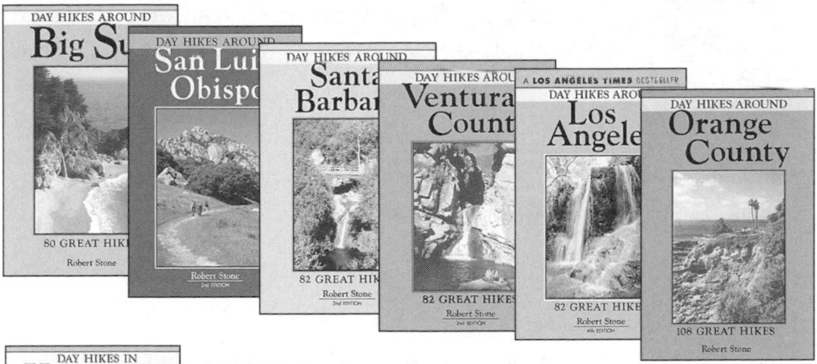
DAY HIKES AROUND
Big Su
80 GREAT HIK
Robert Stone
DAY HIKES AROUND
San Lui
Obispo
Robert Stone
DAY HIKES AROUND
Santa
Barbar
82 GREAT HIK
Robert Stone
DAY HIKES AROUN
Ventura
Count
82 GREAT HIKES
Robert Stone
A LOS ANGELES TIMES BESTSELLER
DAY HIKES AROUN
Los
Angele
82 GREAT HIKE
Robert Stone
DAY HIKES AROUND
Orange
County
108 GREAT HIKES
Robert Stone

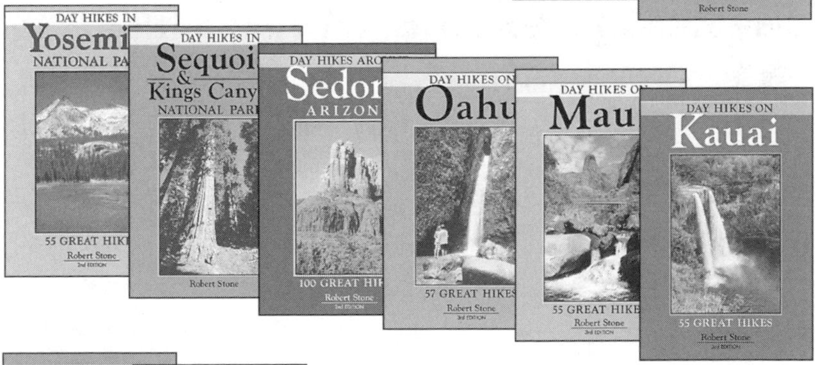
DAY HIKES IN
Yosemi
NATIONAL PA
55 GREAT HIK
Robert Stone
DAY HIKES IN
Sequoi
&
Kings Cany
NATIONAL PAR
Robert Stone
DAY HIKES AROU
Sedon
ARIZON
100 GREAT HI
Robert Stone
DAY HIKES ON
Oahu
57 GREAT HIKES
Robert Stone
DAY HIKES ON
Mau
55 GREAT HIKE
Robert Stone
DAY HIKES ON
Kauai
55 GREAT HIKES
Robert Stone

DAY HIKES
Hawa
90 Great Hikes on
KAUAI • MAUI • OA
Robert Stone
DAY HIKES IN
Yellowsto
NATIONAL PA
82 GREAT HIKE
Robert Stone
DAY HIKES IN
Grand
Teto
NATIONAL PA
72 GREAT HIKE
Robert Stone
DAY HIKES IN T
Beartoot
Mountai
Robert Stone
DAY HIKES ARO
Bozema
MONTANA
Robert Stone
DAY HIKES AROUND
Missoula
MONTANA
Robert Stone

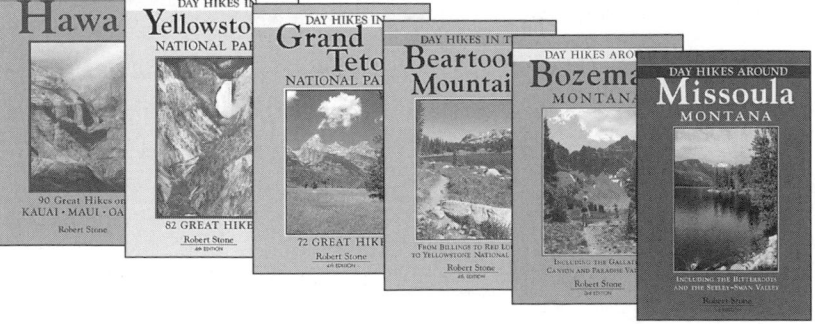

Day Hikes Around Sonoma County

California's Sonoma County is known for its wineries and a magnificent natural landscape — a picturesque mix of rugged coastline, steep cliffs, forested hillsides, and verdant agricultural valleys. The cities, towns, and villages are as diverse as the geography. Interspersed throughout the landscape are thousands of acres of undeveloped parklands, forests, and open spaces.

Day Hikes Around Sonoma County is a collection of 95 of the county's best day hikes, providing access to both well-known and out-of-the-way greenspace. A wide range of hikes accommodates amateur to avid hikers, from beachfront strolls to canyon treks.

272 pages • 95 hikes • 1st Edition 2007

Day Hikes In Yosemite National Park

Visitors to Yosemite National Park, one of the world's most loved parks, are continually awed by its grandeur. Yosemite is known for its huge granite monoliths; incredible waterfalls; and rolling, boulder-strewn meadows. Yosemite must be experienced on foot to absorb all its wonders! Outstanding scenery surrounds every trail.

Day Hikes In Yosemite National Park includes 55 day hikes in this extraordinary park. Hikes range from quiet paths through giant sequoia groves to strenuous climbs up chiseled gorges. Highlights include trails atop the park's famous rock formations, forest paths enshrouded by mist from ground-shaking waterfalls, spiritual groves of immense trees, and panoramic vistas from vertigo-inducing overlooks.

128 pages • 55 hikes • 2nd Edition 2002

INDEX

Notes

About the Author

Since 1991, Robert Stone has been writer, photographer, and publisher of *Day Hike Books*. He is a Los Angeles Times Best Selling Author, an award-winning author of Rocky Mountain Outdoor Writers and Photographers, and an award-winning author of the Outdoor Writers Association of California. He is also an active member of the Northwest Outdoor Writers Association.

Robert has hiked every trail in the *Day Hike Book* series. With 23 hiking guides in the series, many in their third and fourth editions, he has hiked thousands of miles of trails throughout the western United States and Hawaii. When Robert is not hiking, he researches, writes, and maps the hikes before returning to the trails. He spends summers in the Rocky Mountains of Montana and winters on the California Central Coast.